ZOLAR'S
ENCYCLOPEDIA
OF
OMENS,
SIGNS
&
SUPERSTITIONS

Other Books by *Zolar*

Zolar's Book of Dreams, Numbers, and Lucky Days
Zolar's Book of the Spirits
Zolar's Compendium of Occult Theories and Practices
Zolar's Encyclopedia of Ancient and Forbidden Knowledge
Zolar's Encyclopedia and Dictionary of Dreams

ZOLAR'S ENCYCLOPEDIA OF OMENS, SIGNS & SUPERSTITIONS

PRENTICE HALL PRESS
New York   London   Toronto   Sydney   Tokyo

A NOTE TO THE READER: The ideas, procedures, and suggestions contained in this book are not intended to replace the services of a trained health professional. All matters regarding your health require medical supervision. You should consult your physician before adopting the procedures in this book. Any applications of the treatments set forth in this book are at the reader's discretion.

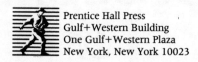
Prentice Hall Press
Gulf+Western Building
One Gulf+Western Plaza
New York, New York 10023

Copyright © 1989 by Zolar

PRENTICE HALL PRESS and colophon are registered
trademarks of Simon & Schuster Inc.

Library of Congress Cataloging-in-Publication Data

Zolar.
[Encyclopedia of omens, signs, and superstitions]
Zolar's encyclopedia of omens, signs, and superstitions.
p.   cm.
ISBN 0-13-984006-0 (pbk.) : $11.95 (est.)
1. Omens—Dictionaries.   2. Signs and symbols—Dictionaries.
3. Superstitions—Dictionaries.   4. Occultism—Dictionaries.
I. Title.   II. Title: Encyclopedia of omens, signs, and
superstitions.
BF1777.Z65   1989
133.3'34'03—dc19   88-13493
CIP

Designed by Irving Perkins Associates

Manufactured in the United States of America

10   9   8   7   6   5   4   3   2   1

First Edition

This work is dedicated to the five stars rising in my personal heaven: Timothy John, Lucienne Claire, Brent King, Tara Elizabeth, and Christopher Dowd.

ACKNOWLEDGMENT

I wish to extend my very special thanks to Karen Tufts, my able typist, without whose magical fingers this work would certainly not have manifested so easily.

INTRODUCTION

A Chat with Zolar

*Superstition may be defined as
constructive religion which has
grown incongruous with intelligence.*

—John Tyndall
SCIENCE AND MAN

Signs, Omens, and Superstitions . . . what do they mean for those of us living in the twentieth and soon the twenty-first century?

The word *superstition* itself comes from the Latin "super," meaning above, and "stare," meaning to stand. In Roman times, those lucky souls who survived in hand-to-hand combat were given the appellation "superstites." In short, they were fortunate enough to be standing above those who were killed in battle.

Viewed in this light, the word *superstition* is more than just a word used to describe those primitive beliefs that have survived scientific understanding and the development of civilization. In fact, it ironically may be said that superstitions are the survivors in the battle waged by reason.

Just as those who have survived war or accidents are later

possessed with a sense of guilt, so does modern man struggle between guilt in acting out a superstition and the fact that on an unconscious level he desperately wishes to believe!

Superstitions seem to strike a familiar cord in our unconscious minds, and that is why we find their continued existence.

I recently relocated from New York to Tarpon Springs, Florida, where I rented an old house in the Greek section of town. As I wandered throughout the house, opening closets and inspecting various cabinets, I discovered pennies placed auspiciously in all the corners. Although I have not yet met anyone who could tell me the origin of this particular practice among carpenters and home renovators, it did remind me of a superstition often followed by my maternal grandmother. Whenever she would give a gift of a woman's handbag or man's wallet she would always first place some pennies inside. It seems she believed that if the gift was received with money, money would never be absent. In the case of the closets and cabinets, however, the belief is extended to suggest that by placing pennies or coins therein, it will bring good luck to those who dwell within the house.

The true origin of superstition is no doubt found in primitive man's humble attempt to explain nature and his own existence. Given this origin, it is easy to understand how all superstitions may be explained in terms of three basic concepts: ignorance, fear, and custom.

First, ignorance. When one simply does not know how something works or where it comes from, one may assume causation to be of Divine rather than natural order. Throughout the ages, people have consulted various occult tests, oracles, and esoteric methods for discovering truth. For instance, in ancient China a nobleman might have consulted the *I Ching* or *Book of Changes*, which is said to enable one to foretell the future using various geometrical figures. And in ancient Rome, to get the same information, a noblewoman might have interpreted the shapes made by molten wax dropped into water. Today a Wall Street broker seeking to analyze and comprehend the current stock market might consult a modern psychic or astrologer.

In all three cases the desire is to know the future. In all three cases, too, an assumption is made that there is a connection between these various mirrors of reality and those events that will actually take place.

No doubt, were a primitive tribesman to have his picture taken with a modern Polaroid camera, seeing his own image appear out of the camera in a matter of minutes would suggest to him a Divine or supernatural origin for such a device.

Closely allied with ignorance is fear. One rainy evening, while emerging from a New York City subway station, I opened up my umbrella inside and it almost made contact with an empty light socket. Because of the dampness, an arc of electricity jumped from the socket to the umbrella, creating a mini Jacob's ladder effect. Ever since that happened, I must confess that I am much more aware of *where* I am when I open an umbrella. This, however, is rational fear and not the irrational fear that forms the basis of superstition.

In the world of our ancestors, earthquakes, thunder, lightning, and *even* the appearance of fire suggested the intervention of the supernatural. Certainly that which cannot be explained becomes fearful.

In ancient Greece, anyone who did not speak Greek and, therefore, could not be understood, was called a barbarian. Although the word originally meant "one who does not speak Greek," its meaning has changed over the centuries to mean someone of lowly character who is to be feared.

Last, custom. Nowadays, although most people are not unaware of the basic laws of science, it is possible that, through repetition, a particular superstition may find its way into our culture. I'm sure the person who placed pennies in the closets did so with little forethought. The same thing may be said for a person who is seen to throw salt over his shoulder after spilling it or who avoids walking under a ladder or crossing the path of a black cat.

One thing is for sure . . . and that is, that superstitions have always been contagious. It is for this reason that we are able to precisely catalog and define their usage.

Just as omens, signs, and superstitions are reflections of custom, fear, and the level of knowledge of a culture, so they are reflections of personal taste, social status, and education. For instance, in my research for this very work, I encountered a reference in a London periodical to the fact that John D. Rockefeller once admitted to a pet superstition. He revealed that he carried an eagle stone as a lucky charm—in his pocket. An eagle stone is a hollow stone whose concretions rattle when you shake it. It is of a brownish tint and is often carried by the eagle to its nest. Because these stones are rare, superstition has ascribed to them countless virtues, including their being a charm against disaster, shipwreck, and other calamities. Another belief is that, if a ribbon is passed through a tiny perforation in the stone, it will actually possess more power than the stone itself. It was said of Mr. Rockefeller that, when he wished to confer a special favor on someone, he would give that person a small piece of this ribbon.

The next time you feel compelled to knock on wood, throw salt over your shoulder, or place pennies in a gift handbag, remember Mr. Rockefeller!

—Zolar

ZOLAR'S
ENCYCLOPEDIA
OF
OMENS,
SIGNS
&
SUPERSTITIONS

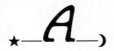

ABBOTSBURY: A city in England where, on the thirteenth of May every year, children carry large garlands and go from door to door seeking gifts. Once collected, the flowers are placed in boats and put out to sea to honor the ancient god Neptune. After some time has passed, they are brought back to shore and taken to church, where a regular Christian service is held.

Here we have an example of a mixture of ancient superstition with modern Christianity. The ancient idea was to honor the god and bring luck in fishing. Now, however, since the flowers are brought into the church, Christ has taken Neptune's place.

ABRACADABRA: Earliest mention of *abracadabra* is in a poem, "Precepta de Medicina," by Q. Serenus Scammonicus, a Gnostic physician of the second century A.D. Saying the word is recommended in this work as a cure for fevers and ague.

The word itself comes from the Syrian dialect and is said to be from *ab, ben, ruach, acadosch*—Hebrew for "Father," "Son," and "Holy Ghost." When engraved on a medal, it was believed to constitute a powerful charm against disease and misfortune. If a medal was unavailable, the word could be written or printed in the form of a triangle with each line containing one less letter. It was then to be folded in the form of a cross, worn as an amulet for nine days, and finally, before sunrise, thrown backward into a stream that flowed eastward. It was also believed that simply evoking the word *abracadabra* released great magical powers.

ABRAXAS: The Gnostic deity believed to be a combination of both good and evil. When written in the Greek text, the letters com-

1

puted numerically had a value of 365, which equaled the days of the year.

ACCIDENT: In Japan, if a sick person's medicine is accidentally spilled, it is an omen that the person shall recover shortly. No doubt this is based on the belief that if the medicine is unavailable, the person really did not need it.

In the East Midlands of England, there is a belief that accidents are most likely to occur when the locally grown broad bean is flowering. The superstition may have its origin in the fact that if someone was injured prior to the harvest, there would be no one available to bring it in.

ACHILLES' HEEL: A Greek legend by the poet Homer tells of a warrior who became invulnerable after being bathed by his mother in the river Styx. While bathing him, she held him by his heel—a fact that became known to Paris, who, guided by the god Apollo, shot Achilles with a poison arrow. Early physicians honored Homer by naming the muscle connecting the calf to the heel "the Achilles tendon." Hence, any vulnerable spot has come to be called our "Achilles' heel."

ACORN: A very ancient British superstition holds that a lady who carries an acorn in her pocket or bag will never grow old. No doubt this belief comes from the fact that the acorn itself falls from the oak tree, which was considered sacred by the ancient Druids. No ritual or rite of the Druids ever took place without the mistletoe or oak.

In the Vatican, too, one can find statues of the goddess Artemis (often depicted as a perpetual youth) wearing a necklace of acorns.

In Asia Minor, acorns were held sacred to the Goddess of Nature.

In Scandinavia, it was believed that the great god Thor (God of Thunder) himself protected the oak tree. It was further believed that one could prevent lightning from striking a home by placing an acorn on the windowsill. Hence, a dried acorn was often used as a window shade pull.

ACTOR: Of all professions, acting is perhaps the most fraught with superstitions. As the success of the player and the play is dependent on so very many unpredictable events, actors have, from the very beginning of time, taken for granted that to be successful they must court Lady Luck.

Different countries may generate different beliefs; following are some of those found in the English-speaking lands: It is bad luck for an actor to change a costume in which he found success. If the play has a long run, the same garment is often worn until it becomes threadbare.

The "Witches' Song" in *Macbeth* is believed to have the power of casting evil spells. Hence, seasoned actors seldom choose to play this part. To hum this same tune where it can be heard by a fellow actor will mean that you are likely to lose his or her friendship.

Actors will never repeat the last line of a play at a rehearsal, as it is considered an ill omen for the upcoming opening of the play.

Actors will not go on a stage where there is a picture of an ostrich or a peacock.

If the handle of a wrong door is turned while seeking entrance to the theater manager's or an agent's office, it is taken as an omen of failure. To correct this, the applicant must return home and start out fresh the next day.

Actors will not allow green or yellow to be worn on stage. Green is said to be unlucky for both the play and the performer while yellow is believed to create memory loss while learning a part.

Actors believe that wigs bring luck and will go out of their way to wear one even though the part does not call for it.

Should an actor's shoes squeak upon making an entrance, it is seen as a sign of audience approval and applause. Should an actor stumble over anything while making an entrance, he will forget his lines. Should a costume catch in the scenery as an actor is entering the stage, a new entrance must be made, or else bad luck will follow throughout the entire performance.

After the performance, should an actor kick off his shoes and have them alight on their soles, it is considered a good omen. Should they fall on their sides, however, it is a sign of bad luck.

For another to look in an actor's mirror while he is putting on his makeup is considered unlucky.

Should a cat run across the stage during the play, misfortune is sure to follow.

An actor must never look at the audience from the wrong side of a drop curtain. Finally, the peephole through which an actor looks out at the audience must be in the center. If it is placed to either side, it will bring bad luck.

ADDER: Many say it is an omen of good luck to see an adder, especially if the one you see is the first one seen in the spring and it is killed. Such will ensure success over one's enemies. Should this same reptile escape alive, however, one can expect disaster and bad luck.

An old English belief holds that an adder seen at the front door is an omen of death. Further beliefs are that the dried skin of an adder hung on the chimney will bring good luck and, if another skin is placed in the rafters of the hearth, the house will never catch fire.

Most superstitions associated with the adder have their origin in the British Isles, since it is the only venomous snake found there.

Many beliefs originated with the Gypsies, who said that the most effective cure for its bite was to rub its dead body over the wound. Many Gypsies also believe that a cast adder skin will draw out thorns. These same people hold that an adder fears the ash tree; hence, a blow from an ash stick will kill an adder immediately. If another wood is used, they believe the adder will not die until sundown.

In Devonshire, the part of a person bitten by an adder was stuck into a recently killed chicken's stomach. There it had to remain until the chicken was cold or assumed a dark color, at which time it was believed the poison was absorbed into the chicken.

In Wales, it was believed that a person could overcome the adder's bite by leaping across the nearest water before the reptile vanished. In Somerset, an adder's bite could be best cured by tying a circle of ash twigs around the neck of the patient.

Last, in other parts of the United Kingdom, a bitten person was wrapped in the reeking skin of a newly killed sheep.

ADDER STONE: Often called "serpent's eggs" and "snake eggs," they were held in high esteem among the Druids. It was believed they would cure all maladies of the eyes if carried in the pocket.

In Scotland, it was believed that whooping cough could be prevented by hanging an adder stone around the neck of a child. It was also believed that adder stones secure success in lawsuits by granting access to kings, rulers, and those in authority.

Legend has it that the stones are actually made by serpents. (However, they were never associated with the curing of a serpent's bite.)

Stones are found of various colors—green, pink, red, blue, and brown. Many are perforated and have been preserved in museums in the country. It was believed that the perforation is a result of the serpent sticking its tail through the stone before it was formed.

To test the genuineness of an adder stone, some say you simply have to throw it into a moving stream. If genuine, it will float against the current, and no weight attached to it can make it sink.

AGATE: Here we find the belief that evil can be transferred to stones. For example, a person bitten by a poisonous insect would press an agate on the spot to cure the bite. Likewise, if placed on the head of a person suffering from a fever, the fever would supposedly depart.

Agates were also thought to be especially sensitive to the approach of poison. Worn suspended from one's neck or set in a ring, they would lose their natural color and warn the wearer of oncoming danger.

Genuine agates were also known for their ability to cool boiling water.

When red-veined, it was believed they bore traces of the blood of the gods.

In Italy, the agate is especially known for its ability to ward off the evil eye and to promote eloquence.

It is also said to protect its owner from thirst and to sharpen the vision. Besides snakebites, it is predisposed to cure spider, viper, and scorpion poisons. It was believed useful against dropsy and all hemorrhages. When cut in the shape of a triangle, it was said to cure stomach ailments, while dark varieties of the stone would treat diarrhea.

Should a woman find herself barren, it was believed she should drink water into which the green agate had been dropped to again become fertile. Likewise, if an agate with tree-shaped veins was placed between the horns of an ox used for plowing, it would bring fertility to the earth and a great harvest.

When burned, it is believed the agate will drive away tempests as well as lightning. It is said to bring great success to a man who carries it, especially in courtship and in receiving favors from women.

If solid colored, the agate will make an athlete invincible, especially if he hangs it around the neck with a lion's hair. (But how does one get the hair from the lion!)

A green agate is believed to cure vision trouble and to bring happiness in life. A bloodstone, green and red in color, is said to protect one against infidelity.

Jasper, an opaque variety of agate, was believed to stop bleeding and to ease pain. Hence, it was often placed on the stomach of a woman about to give birth.

Jasper is also believed to cure epilepsy and to possess the ability to attract rain. Country folk believe that one can counter a drought by placing a vase of jasper on the windowsill.

AGE: In some country districts of Britain, it is believed to be unlucky for a woman to disclose her age. Most likely this idea came from the ancient belief that to number something makes it identifiable to evil spirits.

Should one wish to find out the truth about a lady's age, however, one can obtain a hair from her head, tie it to a small golden ring, hang this inside a glass tumbler, and wait for it to begin oscillating. According to tradition, the ring will strike the sides of the glass once for each year of her life.

AGNES: In Lincolnshire, England, the name *Agnes* was never given to native-born children in the belief that persons so named always went mad.

AGUE: Superstitions abound concerning the cure of ague, or fever, with either chills or sweating. Some of the different cures are as follows: If you wrap a spider in a raisin and swallow it, the ague will disappear. If you take a good dose of medicine and hang three spiders around your neck, the ague will be driven away. Visit the nearest crossroads five different evenings at midnight. While there, bury a newly laid egg. With the egg, you will bury the ague.

Other remedies: Break a salted cake of bran and give it to a nearby dog; the malady will be transferred to the animal. Go alone to a crossroads and wait for the clock to strike midnight. When you hear the striking, turn around three times. Then drive a large nail into the ground up to its head. Walk backwards from the nail before the clock has finished its twelfth stroke. If you do this, the ague will leave you, but will go to the next person to step over the nail.

In Devonshire, there is a belief that you can give away your ague by burying under your neighbor's threshold a bag containing the parings of a dead man's nails, together with the clippings of some of the hairs of his head.

In Somerset, a large spider would be shut in a box and left to die. As it died, it was believed the ague would too.

In Flanders, a spider is imprisoned between two halves of a walnut and worn around the sufferer's neck.

In Wales, one could cure ague by simply crossing water to reach a hollow willow tree. By breathing into this tree three times, then stopping up the hole and going home without looking around or speaking a word, you would be cured.

In Lincolnshire, ague was charmed away by nailing three horse-shoes to the foot of the sufferer's bed.

AIRPLANE: Air Force crews are said to believe that, when touching wood for luck, that wood should be a "living" tree—not a wooden table or chair, which is considered "dead."

Pilots often carry small charms and dislike it when people take flowers on board, especially red and white ones.

Pilots are also said to be able to enhance their luck by emptying the contents of their pockets on the ground after landing. (When the Pope visited the United States in 1987, he kissed the ground after emerging from the airplane.)

World War II pilots were said to cross unused seatbelts before taking off, so as not to irritate the spirits of the unseen.

Last, flight crews deliberately avoid using the word *crash* before taking off. They also hold the belief that an accident will be followed by two more.

ALBATROSS: Most sailors believe that to kill an albatross is to bring bad luck to the ship and everyone on it. Albatrosses that follow a ship are supposed to carry the souls of drowned sailors who want to be near their former crew.

Some believe that an albatross actually sleeps while it flies, because its flight seems to be without motion.

During the days of the schooner, an albatross flying around the ship was believed to herald stormy weather.

The albatross was best immortalized by Samuel Taylor Coleridge in his great poem about "the ancient mariner."

ALL SAINTS' DAY: (See *Halloween*.)

ALMOND: The Greek historian, Pliny, advised that eating five almonds would prevent drunkenness.

To the ancient Greeks, the almond tree and its blossoms were associated with a legend about Demophon and Phyllis. They had arranged to be married, but before the ceremony could take place, Demophon was recalled to Athens for the funeral of his father. He promised to return, but he miscalculated and arrived three months later to find that Phyllis had hanged herself. As is often the case in Greek myths, the gods were so moved by her love, that they transformed her into an almond tree. Demophon sacrificed to the almond tree, and in response, the tree blossomed.

Many believe that, if foxes eat almonds with water, they will die.

In Victorian times, the almond was held as a symbol of indiscretion and youthful impetuousness.

In modern times, the American Seer and Sleeping Prophet, Edgar Cayce, advocated eating a few almonds each day to prevent cancer.

AMEN: This word is a derivative of the word *aum*, which came from the Indian word *om*, said to be the sound most like that of Brahma. In the Bible is the statement, "all the people shall answer and say Amen." (Deuteronomy 27:15.) Hence, saying "amen" before and after prayers is a sign of affirmation.

Amen, or Amen-Ra, was the local god of the city of Thebes in ancient Egypt. This god assumed national significance when the kingship passed to a family of Theban nobles during the Middle Kingdom (2000 B.C.). After the Hyksos invaders were expelled (1550 B.C.), the Egyptians ascribed all victories to Amen and exalted him above all the other gods.

Amen-Ra is usually represented in human form wearing a flat crown surmounted by two tall wide plumes. The name Amen also appears in the word *amentet*, or *amenti*, which were names for the afterworld in ancient Egypt.

AMETHYST: From the Greek *ametusios*, this wine-colored stone is believed to prevent the wearer from becoming drunk. Hence, drinking cups were crafted from amethyst to prevent intoxication.

Supposedly, if a drunkard wears an amethyst that is presented to him in February, he will become disgusted with his vice and give up the habit.

The connection with drinking and intoxication comes from a Greek legend about Bacchus, God of Wine and Revelry. Supposedly, angry with the goddess Diana, Bacchus swore vengeance upon the first mortal he saw. This happened to be a young maiden, named Amethyst, who was worshipping at Diana's altar. When Bacchus's tigers were about to pounce on her, she called Diana for help and Diana changed her into a statue to protect her. Bacchus, feeling somewhat contrite, poured wine over the statue, making Amethyst a beautiful grape color, which granted her immunity against the effects of the beverage.

During the Middle Ages, the gem became known as the "bishop's stone," since it was worn on the third finger of the priest's right hand to indicate marriage to the church. This was done in the belief that the stone generated sobriety, temperance, wisdom, and humility.

To the Hebrews, the amethyst was the stone of Daniel—one of the twelve tribes of Israel—and stood for judgment, justice, and courage.

The Romans believed should the moon or sun be engraved on an amethyst, protection is assured against storms. Other engravings are thought to protect against thievery, to ensure pleasant dreams, or even to keep a spouse faithful.

In addition, it has been alleged that amethysts help against toothaches, gout, and headaches.

Certain inscriptions and figures were said to enable the amethyst to become an antidote for plagues, hail, and locusts.

Last, it is said to be a lucky stone for hunters, most likely due to its association with Diana, the Goddess of the Hunt.

AMULET: The word *amulet* comes from an Arab word *hamala*, meaning "to carry." Hence, anything that is hung around the neck, worn like a bracelet on the wrist, or otherwise attached to a person, as an imagined protection against sickness or other evils, is an amulet. (A charm is, essentially, the same thing.)

Generally speaking, an amulet must be a natural item and not one made by man. It is anything the owner believes has special powers. A ring, a stone, a book, a horseshoe, a part of an animal—anything of this sort can become an amulet.

Perhaps the most popular amulet is the rabbit's foot. Other animal parts are also very popular. Examples are fox tails, which children attach to their bikes to increase speed; animal teeth, which are worn for courage; even Davy Crockett's raccoon-skin cap, worn for cunning and wisdom.

In Italy, red pepper is a popular amulet believed to drive the Devil away. Strangely enough, when the red pepper dries, it resembles the Devil's horn. In modern times, manufacturers have produced plastic red peppers.

Other popular amulets include coral, four-leaf clovers, human hair, teeth, sculptures of the human hand, and even medals of the saints.

Amulets are differentiated from talismans inasmuch as they need only to be worn to be effective. A talisman, however, requires a ritual to make it active. Wearing the appropriate birthstone for one's birth month may be considered as use of an amulet.

ANGEL: The word *angel* is derived from the Greek *angelos,* or the Hebrew *malak,* which means a "person sent" or a "messenger." Hence, it signifies an office and, in a lesser sense, a spiritual being.

To the Jews, the angel of the congregation was the chief of the synagogue. The term *angel* first appears in the Old Testament in the phrase, "angel of the Lord," the title given to the divine message bringer who told Hagar she would give birth to Ishmael. (Genesis 16:7.) It is suggested by this text that, when God wishes to make His will known to mankind, He can assume a visible, human form and come as a messenger or angel. In Genesis the angel of the Lord calls from heaven to restrain Abraham from killing Isaac. (Genesis 22:12–15.) In Exodus, the angel of the Lord appears to Moses in the midst of the burning bush. (Exodus 3:2.) Hence, angels seem to fill the need by theologians for human forms and voices to convey the will and presence of an unseen God. Generally speaking, in the Old Testament, angels worship God and attend to Him, always ready to do His will, and announce prosperity or destruction. They invariably manifest no personality of their own apart from God, whose message they convey. They are never summoned; they arrive with their message and quickly vanish.

After the Old Testament, angels were given more individual prominence and personal names; they were organized into various ranks and were assumed to actually intercede for men and the affairs of various nations. In Matthew, an angel of the Lord appears to Joseph and tells him of the conception of Jesus. (Matthew 1:20.) Likewise, an angel of the Lord announces the birth of Jesus to the shepherds. When an angel appears to Zechariah to announce the conception of John the Baptist, he is given a name—Gabriel—suggesting a personification of angel energy into a particular form.

While some scholars believe angels derived from Babylonian and Persian influence, such angels were essentially abstract principles and not the messengers of the Old Testament.

Since the number *seven* recurs in Jewish and Christian lore about angels, some authorities assume that angels evolved from the Assyrian belief in seven planetary gods. In time, specific angels, such as the Angel of Repentance or the Angel of Death, emerged.

Following Saint Paul, beliefs arose in various heavens that were inhabited with different grades of angels. The lower heavens were said to be occupied by those angels in charge of human affairs, whereas the higher heavens were under the guidance of the Angels of the Presence.

Heading the seven heavens were seven archangels. These were said to be God's first creation and to have been formed from fire. Often described as being of enormous height and wing measurement, throughout the Middle Ages speculation about them reached the point of debating how many angels could dance on the point of a pin.

To modern theologians, angels may best be described as "pure spirits without physical bodies" or "mirrors of God's mind and will."

ANIMAL: An old English superstition states that, if fruit trees are planted without a dead animal being buried under their roots, they will not bear crops. Whether this tradition stems from the scientific fact that the carcass provides good fertilizer for the soil, or whether there is a magical meaning, is not known. Certainly, based on the belief in their ability to foretell the future, throughout history animals have been ascribed certain magical qualities.

Horses, in particular, have been seen to tremble when they come near a dead human body, even though the body might be invisible to them. Likewise, the howling of a dog is said to be prophetic of the illness or death of its master.

We often find ignorance the probable cause of superstition. Researchers tell us that some animals have the ability to sense, smell, and hear persons or events beyond the range of human experience. Rather than supernatural, this is a natural occurence.

In any event, animals, in general, may be said to take on the essence of their masters, thereby becoming an extension of those who possess them. (See **cat, dog, horse**.)

ANKH: The ankh is a circle, which symbolizes eternity and life, placed above a cross, which symbolizes matter. Called the "crux ansata," its origin lies in ancient Egypt, where it appears frequently in various forms of Egyptian art.

Usually, the ankh is held in the hand of a god, or applied to the nose of a dead man, to give him life in the afterworld. Egyptians wore it as a necklace or as a charm to prolong and ensure life after death. In some ways, the ankh looks like a key, which may account for its symbolism as an instrument to unlock the Gates of Death.

Due to the influence of the Coptic Christians, the ankh appears in some early Christian tombs. Generally speaking, the ankh is no longer thought to have any special mystical powers.

ANT: In the British Isles, it is considered unlucky to destroy a colony of ants.

Among country folk, when clusters of ants are unusually active, bad weather is thought to be at hand.

Among Cornish peasants there is a belief that, during a certain stage of the moon, a piece of tin placed in an ant nest will be turned to silver.

In other lands, stepping on ants is thought to bring rain.

Another curious belief is that ants never sleep and, if you eat their eggs with honey, it will act as an antidote for lovesickness.

Last, the unexpected appearance of ants in the house is said to portend illness for the master, and should ants build a nest near your door, you can expect security and riches.

APOSTLE SPOON: Being "born with a silver spoon" in one's mouth is a saying known to most. A fifteenth- to sixteenth-century custom of presenting spoons (usually engraved with figures of the apostles) to godchildren at a christening may be the origin of this reference.

APPLE: If ever there was a piece of fruit that got bad press, it was certainly the apple, for it was this that Eve gave Adam to eat. Hence, one of the earliest superstitions was to only eat an apple that had been rubbed clean; otherwise the "evil one," Satan himself, would appear.

Ever since the Roman occupation of Europe, the apple has been held as a sacred tree. In fact, a seventh-century poem states that a man who cuts down an apple tree must pay a fine of one cow. An early Irish poem calls for the sacrifice of a living creature in payment for felling an apple tree.

In essence, the apple stands for immortality, eternal youth, and happiness. Arabs believed that the apple had curative powers, as well, and in Scandinavian mythology, the gods keep themselves young by eating the golden apples of Idun, Goddess of Youth and Springtime.

Among Welsh legends, after death, kings and heroes live in a paradise of apple trees called Avalon, possibly derived from the Welsh word for *apple*, "afal."

An American superstition holds that, if the sun shines through the boughs of an apple tree on Christmas Day, the fruit will be abundant the next year.

Gamblers are said to count an apple's seeds to find a lucky number to bet on.

Everyone has heard the saying, "An apple a day keeps the doctor away." Another old English proverb says, "A bad woman can't make good applesauce."

To find a future husband, a young girl could twist the stem of an apple for each letter of the alphabet. When the stem finally broke, the last letter spoken was thought to be the first initial of her true love's name. Maidens had other methods of divining the future, as well. For example, if one stood in front of a mirror with an apple, sliced it into nine pieces, stuck each piece on the point of a knife, and held it over her left shoulder, she would see in the mirror the image of her future husband. A variation was to let a girl pare an apple and fling the skin over her left shoulder. In the twists of the skin would be found the initials of her future husband's name. Both practices should be done on Halloween.

In the United States, the most famous story connected with apples is that of Johnny Appleseed, the name given to John Chapman, an eccentric who roamed the frontier planting apple trees wherever he went. Often called the American Saint Francis, Chapman spent forty-eight years of his life roaming around the frontier barefoot and dressed in rags, with a sack of apple seeds over his shoulder.

An Austrian custom holds that an apple cut on Saint Thomas's Night can foretell the future. If there is an even number of seeds, a marriage is promised. Should one of the seeds be cut through, it means trouble. If two seeds are cut, death or widowhood is promised.

In some countries it is customary to place an apple in the hands of a dead child, presumably to symbolize innocence.

Finally, one must remember that it was an apple that fell on the head of Isaac Newton, inspiring his discovery of the law of gravity.

APRIL FOOLS' DAY: The origin of April Fools' Day has, unfortunately, been lost to antiquity. *Poor Robins Almanac* (1760) makes note of this fact with the following verse:

> *The first of April, some do say,*
> *Is set apart for All Fools' Day;*
> *But why the people call it so*
> *Nor I, nor they themselves, do know.*

In Scotland, an April Fools' Day custom was to send a young youth out to deliver a sealed envelope to a particular person. The recipient opened the letter, read the joke, and rewrote it or merely dispatched it in a fresh envelope to another address. So it was, ad infinitum, until the youth realized he had been tricked.

In England, other foolings included sending a young person to the store for some pigeon's milk, a history of Eve's mother, a left-handed knife, or a sky-hook to lift boats out of the ocean.

In actuality, the practice appears to have come to England from France in about 1564, at which time the New Year was moved from the twenty-fifth of March to the first of January and the Gregorian calendar was adopted. As the twenty-fifth of March so often fell during holy week, the church postponed the celebration until the octave, or the first of April. Therefore, when New Year's Day was moved to the first of January, French peasants often paid mock visits to their friends on the first of April, with the object of fooling them into the belief that this date was still the first day of the New Year.

An older Hindu tradition, called the Huli Festival, held at the same time of year, had a practice of sending people on errands that were bound to end in disappointments.

Tradition holds that, if you are fooled by a pretty girl, you will marry her or at least become a friend (if she is already married).

Should you lose your temper when sent on an April Fools' errand, you will encounter bad luck.

Should you have the misfortune of getting married on April Fools' Day, it is said the lady of the house will wear the breeches.

Children born on this day are said to be fortunate in everyday affairs, but especially unlucky in gambling and speculation of any kind.

Last, mention must be made of the rape of the Sabine women by the ancient Romans, which also occurred around this same time. The Romans announced that certain games were to be performed in honor of Neptune. Upon receiving notice of the games, the bordering inhabitants flocked to Rome to see the celebrations, allowing the Romans to go out into the countryside and seize a number of Sabine virgins.

APRON: An old English superstition holds that, should a fisherman meet a woman wearing a white apron on the way to his ship, bad luck will be had during the voyage. If, however, the fisherman returns home and waits for the next tide, this ill luck can be averted.

Among country folk, it is considered lucky if, by accident, one puts an apron on inside out. Should the day bring a number of small accidents, however, one would be well advised to reverse the apron.

Generally, in the British Isles, it is said to be a sign of bad luck for an apron to suddenly fall off. Some folk hold that this is an omen that the wearer can expect a baby within the year. Should a young single girl lose her apron, it is a sign that her lover is thinking of her at that moment. Among German peasants, a belief exists that, if a man wipes his hands on a girl's apron, he will fall desperately in love with her. Once this same girl is engaged, though, she is advised not to let her fiancé use her apron in this same manner, for it will lead to quarrels.

Aprons are also used in the ritualistic ceremonies of the Freemasons and Rosicrucians. Both these groups believe that the apron was first used by Solomon when building his temple.

ARCH: The use of arches or other special passageways is universal. Some Englishmen believe that whooping cough, blackheads, boils, rheumatism, and other diseases can be cured by passing under an arch of brambles.

Among country folks, passing a child with rickets through a split trunk of an elder or ash tree, held open by a wedge, was said to cure this disease. Most likely the origin of such traditions is the belief that illness is caused by an evil spirit which cannot pass through an arch that has been specially blessed.

The British have long believed that one can cure a disease by passing the sufferers through some kind of hole, ring, or hoop.

Mention has been made throughout this work of passing someone under the natural arch formation of a bramble bush in order to cure various illnesses. The belief here is the illness will become stuck or attached to the hole.

On the other hand, there is the belief that should the bush or rock formation itself be damaged at some later time, the cured patient would feel the damage in his own body. For instance, should a tree wither and die under which a child had been passed, it is said that the child itself would suffer a similar end.

ASCENSION DAY: Ascension, the day that Christ is said to have risen to heaven, is the Thursday that follows the fifth Sunday after Easter. Hence, it falls between April 30 and June 3. In Wales, tradition holds that it is inadvisable to work on this day.

A generally held weather superstition is that, if it rains on Ascension Day, a scarcity of crops, together with illness (especially of cattle), is likely during the coming year.

Old Devonshire superstitions hold that the figure of a lamb, symbolic of Christ, will appear in the sky in the east on this day. Eggs laid on Ascension Day are believed to never rot, and, if placed in the roof of one's house, will preserve the house from all harm.

In Sicily, it is believed that this day holds special healing vibrations.

One tradition held that those suffering with goiter should gather at midnight on Ascension Day to bite the bark from the trunk of a peach tree. This biting must be done when the clock strikes midnight. The illness would then pass into the sap of the tree, whereby its leaves would wither as the patient recovered.

In Switzerland, young girls were said to climb the towers of their churches to ring all the bells, ensuring a prosperous harvest of flax.

Tradition holds that alms given to the blind or lame on this day will come back a hundredfold. Coins given away on this day, no matter how small the amount, are said to bring an unexpected fortune within the year.

ASH: The use of ashes as a fertility charm is universal. Very often the ashes of sacred fires, burned on Halloween or Midsummer's Day Eve, were scattered on fields after seeds had been planted to ensure a sound harvest.

In Wales, it is believed that, if one takes ashes from the Beltane fires (lit in May) and places them in one's shoes, they will protect the wearer from great sorrow.

If, before going to bed on New Year's Eve, one spread the ashes of a raked-out fire over the floor, footprints found the next day were said to portend the future. If they pointed to the door, a member of the household would die during the year. If they pointed away from the door, there would be an addition to the family.

In France, it is believed that, if ashes are scattered over one's house, this will prevent damage by thunder and lightning.

ASH TREE: To many, the ash tree is as significant as, or, perhaps, even superior to, the oak. Various Nordic myths hold that man, himself, was created from the wood of the ash by the god Odin. The word *ash* is derived from the Norse *aska*, meaning "man."

In a collection of old myths and legends, entitled *Edda*, the ash becomes the Yggdrasill, or world tree. It is believed that its branches enshadow the world and reach up to the heavens, while its roots penetrate the abyss known as "hel," from which our modern word *Hell* has been derived.

For the Kabyles, the Berber tribespeople of Tunisia or Algeria, the ash is believed to be the first tree to have appeared at creation. Hence, it is believed to be feminine in nature, which means no man can plant it. If a man breaks this taboo and plants the ash tree, a male member of his family is soon to die.

Further traditions have associated the ash with snakes. Pliny, in the first century A.D., commented on the ash's magical ability against snakes, and that a snake would rather be destroyed by fire than crawl over an ash twig.

American folklore holds that, should one carry an ash twig or wear ash leaves in one's hat, protection against snakebites is assured. Should one be bitten, nevertheless, drinking ash sap was believed to cure the bite.

In Great Britain, there is a tradition of burying the first parings of a child's nails under an ash tree; the child will then be blessed as a fine singer.

A general belief also holds that passing a child with rickets or a rupture through the cleft of an ash tree is certain to cure him. A more sinister side to this belief, however, holds that, should the tree die at any time during the life of the child, the rupture would return and the child would die, even though he may have by now grown to adulthood.

Young English girls believe that an ash leaf placed in their left shoe would cause them to marry the first man they encountered.

When ash trees fail to produce fruit, it is said to be an omen of the death of a king or important world figure.

A forked ash stick used in the hands of a skillful dowser is said to indicate where underground copper mines may be found.

The following weather superstition connected with the ash and oak is found in many countries with some variation of the wording:

> If the ash is before the oak,
> Then there will be a very great soak.
> But if the oak before the ash,
> Then expect a very small splash.

ASPEN TREE: Tradition has it that the aspen was used to make Christ's cross. From that time on, the boughs of the aspen trees have been filled with horror and trembled ceaselessly.

Because of this superstition, the aspen tree was said to have the ability to cure a fever. If parings of a patient's nail were inserted into the aspen tree, which was then plastered up to prevent the fever from escaping, the patient would be cured.

Since a person stricken with fever often trembles and the leaves of the aspen itself tremble, these two beliefs were united. In actuality, though, the construction of the foliage of the aspen, with its broad leaves on a long flexible stalk, make it particularly sensitive to even the lightest of breezes.

In Cheshire, the aspen tree was used for the curing of warts. Warts first had to be rubbed with a piece of bacon, which was then put into a slit of the bark of the aspen tree. The warts would supposedly disappear from one's hands and reappear as rough knobs on the bark of the tree. It was probably the salt and brine of the bacon that destroyed the virus which had caused the warts.

Ass: Three hairs taken from the black cross on the shoulders of an ass were believed to cure whooping cough. To work, they had to be placed in a muslin bag and hung around the neck of the sufferer. The animal from whom they were taken was declared useless afterwards. A further requirement was that the sex of the animal should be opposite that of the sufferer. It is suggested that the origin of this superstition lies in the fact that the ass is a sacred animal in that it bore Christ on its back.

Yet another tradition holds that the ass is deaf to music.

Greek mythology told that Apollo gave the ears of an ass to Midas because he preferred Pan's pipe to the music of Apollo's lute.

Another tradition explains that the ass earned its reputation for stupidity because, when asked its name by God, it could not remember.

Rain is said to be on the way when the ass brays and twitches its ears.

Other beliefs hold that an ass knows when it is about to die and will hide itself away. Hence, it is said that "one never sees a dead ass." The Devil can never take the disguise of an ass, since it wears a cross drawn on its back.

If an ill child is set on the cross and the ass makes nine circles, the child's recovery is assured. Likewise, covering a child with the skin of an ass keeps him or her from fear. Early medical beliefs were that the lung of an ass cured snake and scorpion bites, if placed on the wound.

Asthma: In Cornwall, it is believed that one can cure asthma by collecting spider webs, rolling them into a ball in the palm of the hands, and swallowing them.

During the sixteenth century, a widespread belief was that

asthma could be cured by eating raw cat's meat. Yet another variation is to eat the foam from a mule's mouth, and still another was that, if a sufferer ate boiled carrots exclusively for a fortnight, his asthma would be gone. No doubt, this superstition is based on the fact that carrots contain a high level of Vitamin A, which, evidently, has a healing effect on the mucous membranes of the lungs.

Axe: As the axe was one of the first tools invented by primitive man, it no doubt has always been thought to contain magical power. Often made of stone, sparks would fly from it, reminding one of lightning of the storm gods. As the iron first used by man came from meteors, its conversion into an iron axe continued this magical tradition.

The symbol of the double axe, called the "labrys" by the Celts, has been found carved on the pillars of Stonehenge.

In Europe, there is a belief that, if cattle are made to step over an axe on the way to pasture, especially in the spring, no evil magic or spells will affect them. Likewise, according to American superstition, should one inadvertently carry an axe into a house, a death in the family will be brought about.

In Scotland, a spade (which is a derivation of the axe) was thought to cause bad luck, if taken indoors, since it symbolized death and was often used by grave diggers.

To dream of an axe is said to be unlucky and an omen of danger.

According to one superstition, you can find buried treasure by putting a round agate on the red-hot edge of an axe standing upright on the ground. Should the agate adhere to the axe, look elsewhere for the treasure. Should the agate fall and roll three times in the same direction (this seems highly unlikely), such would point to where the treasure is buried.

An ancient method of detecting thievery was to have those thought guilty dance in a circle around an axe that was standing head downward on the ground. When the axe tottered and fell, the direction in which the handle pointed indicated the possible thief.

During the witchcraft era in Europe, it was believed that witches could strike an axe into an upright post and "milk" the handle. This would magically milk the cows in the neighborhood dry.

BABY: Everyone loves babies so it is not surprising that there are countless numbers of superstitions regarding their proper treatment.

In Scotland, upon the birth of a baby, a tradition calls for a knife to be placed under the door sill of the house to protect the baby from the evil eye.

One superstition warns against rocking a cradle if the baby is not inside it; yet another says that, if a cradle is rocked while empty, the baby will have plenty.

In Ireland, spitting upon a newborn baby is said to bring good luck.

Children born "feet first" will be lamed from an accident before they reach adulthood, unless bay leaves are rubbed on their legs within a few hours of birth, say some. However, this same child who has become crippled is said to possess healing powers for those who have muscular problems.

Superstitions of all kinds abound: Babies should not be allowed to look at themselves in mirrors; they will either develop rickets or die before the year is over. A baby's nails should not be cut before it is a year old or the child will grow up to be a thief. It is okay, though, to bite the nails off, which is said to bring good luck.

Babies born at the midnight hour have the ability to see ghosts. Those born at three, six, nine, or twelve o'clock can see things that are hidden from others.

If a mother pulls on the baby's clothes over its feet, it will not

21

grow up to be healthy. This is because the feet are inferior to the head.

Visitors should kiss a newborn baby boy to bring themselves good luck.

Should someone step over a crawling infant, the baby's growth will be stunted. Likewise, a child who is passed through the spokes of a wheel or under a car will not grow.

When brought home from the hospital, the baby should be carried through the downstairs to the top of the house before it is brought downstairs for the first time.

More advice: If the baby's first bath water is thrown out under a tree, especially a tree in bloom, the baby will become a handsome adult.

Children born with teeth are said to be selfish. If born with hands open, the child will prove to be generous.

If the child first clasps an object with the left hand, rather than the right, it will not be lucky in life. (Another superstition holds that the child's right hand should not be washed for at least one month after birth.) Should the child be allowed to sleep upon bones (for example the mother's lap), the child's growth would be impeded.

Newborn children should not be weighed, according to one superstition, although this is commonly done in the hospitals.

A child's first journey must be upwards or it will never do any good in this world.

A baby should not be named after a dead brother or sister or the baby will die.

A baby born at or near the new moon will never do any good in the world. Boy and girl babies should never be christened at the same time, for they will become rivals for the favor of the spirit world.

Should a mother give away all of her baby's clothes, she will find that she soon needs them for a new child.

Jewish traditions hold that a sleeping child should never be washed, for this is a practice reserved for the dead. Likewise, Satan will threaten your child if he is called handsome or charming. This can be altered, however, by saying three times in Yiddish, "Whoever gave you the evil eye, may it fall on them."

American country folk believe that an old diaper should never be placed on a baby, or he will grow up to be a thief. When first cursed, he should be carried on the left side, or he will become left-handed. A child weaned in the early spring will become pre-maturely gray-haired.

American superstitions say that a baby thrown in the air will grow up to be dim-witted, and that a bald child will grow up to be a brilliant scholar.

An old Cajun superstition holds that you can predict a child's future by placing a Bible, a deck of cards, and some coins within his reach. If the Bible is chosen, the child will be happy; if the cards, he will be a gambler; if coins are grabbed, he will be successful in business.

An East Yorkshire tradition calls for the baby to be presented with some objects—namely, a box of matches, an egg, some salt in a piece of paper, and a piece of money—when first visiting any house. Through this, it is guaranteed that the infant will have light, food, friendship, and money throughout its life. Another tradition holds that an egg promises immortality; salt, salubrity of mind and body; bread, all material things needed throughout life; and matches, a light to heaven. According to another Yorkshire custom, every new article of clothing presented to the child should contain a small sum of money within one of the pockets.

In Plymouth, if you tickle a baby's feet, the child will stammer in later years. Likewise, two children should not kiss before knowing how to talk, or they will become mute, and to ensure strength and health, a child should be swung nine times over the first Saint John's fire that follows birth.

In Japan, it is believed that, if a child covers his head with a basket, he will not grow.

An English superstition holds a newborn allowed to urinate in the fireplace will quickly grow up to be well-behaved. It was thought unlucky to dress a baby in black, as such would destine the child to have a short life. One is also warned never to measure a baby with a string or tape measure, as it will stop the child's growth; handing a child through an open window will have the same effect. Crying children are sure to have good luck, but children should never walk backwards when going on an errand.

A Scottish tradition holds that, when young babies are taken out for the first time, the mother or nurse should give food to the first person she greets. This is said to ensure the baby's good luck. A child visiting a neighbor's house for the first time should be carried by only the mother in order to ensure its future.

Children who creep will have better luck than those who do not, and to protect a child from all illnesses, place two crossed sickles at the foot of the bed.

Brushing a baby's feet with a rabbit's foot, placing a coral necklace around its neck, and making certain that it sneezes to rid itself of evil spirits are thought to be essential.

Finally, remember that a young baby smiling in its sleep is said to be conversing with the angels. (For additional superstitions see **birth, conception,** and **teeth**.)

BACHELOR'S BUTTON: This little blue flower (cornflower) has long been associated with marriage. In the Orient, the flower is used to predict a happy marriage. The young man picks it early in the morning and carries it in his pocket for twenty-four hours. If the plant remains fresh, the young man and his beloved will have a good marriage. If the flower withers, the young man will soon seek another sweetheart. Young women carried bachelor's buttons under their aprons. Supposedly, if they did this for forty weeks, they would receive a favor.

BACON: Stolen bacon is said to be especially powerful for the cure of fever and constipation.

BADGER: Keep one of its teeth on your person and you will be sure to win at cards and to generally have good luck.

BAKER'S DOZEN: A baker's dozen has always meant thirteen instead of twelve in many diverse cultures.

In ancient Egypt heavy fines were levied for those who made light the scale. To avoid shortages and a possible penalty due to shrinkage, an extra loaf was included. Another tradition holds that, when bakers brought their loaves of bread for resale, they received an extra loaf free as commission. A yet older legend says "twelve for the baker and one for the Devil."

BAKING: In olden times, ovens were heated by burning a large fagot of sticks fastened by a twisted branch called the "withe." A superstition from Sussex said that if the withe is placed in the oven by mistake, the oven will not heat and the bread will not bake.

Another superstition surrounds the practice of using up scraps of pastry left over from baking. Small cookies were made for children in the belief that the entire cake would be spoiled if this was not done. Should such scraps be thrown away, bad fortune would ensue.

More superstitions: One should never count the number of loaves or cookies taken from an oven or they will quickly go stale. Should a loaf emerge from an oven cracked open, as sometimes happens, expect a stranger to come to the door to share it with you.

BALDNESS: Here's a recipe that many men will not wish to follow. It may be a "peasant" one, but it is certainly not a pleasant one. It requires that large amounts of goose dung be rubbed into the bald patches. Perhaps it is better to avoid baldness altogether by never cutting the hair when the moon is waning.

BALL: If you want to have a bad round of golf, take a new still-wrapped golf ball out on the green. For a bad tennis game hold three balls in the hand while serving.

BANANA: Superstition in the Caribbean Islands holds that bananas may be wish bringers. Simply cut a slice from the stalk end of the banana while making a wish. If a Y-shaped mark is found, your wish will come true.

BANSHEE: According to an old Gaelic tradition, a banshee is a household spirit, most likely feminine, who takes particular interest in the family. When death is near, she lets out a wail that can be heard everywhere. The word itself means "fairy woman."

Highland tradition holds that the banshee attaches itself to a particular family or clan much like an ancestral ghost.

BAPTISM: Here we find almost as many superstitions as there are involving babies. To begin with, English superstition holds that children never thrive until they are baptized.

If a child does not cry at its baptism, it may be "too good to live."

Should a boy and girl be brought to the font at the same time, but the girl is christened first, the boy will be condemned to a life of beardlessness and the girl will have hair on her face.

There is a North Country superstition that when a child cries during baptism, its voice is that of an evil spirit being driven out by the holy water.

A Sunday christening is considered best of all.

Children to be baptized should always be dressed in white, and red ribbons should be avoided.

Baptism in a church brings better luck than baptism in a private dwelling.

Should a stranger enter a house in which an unbaptized child lives, unless the person eats or drinks, the child may be deprived of its beauty. Actually, according to a Scottish belief, a mother should not even enter a neighbor's house before her child is "kirked" (christened); nor should she take the child to the house of a friend, until it has been baptized.

A child not yet baptized can be protected against the Devil, if covered by an article of clothing worn by the father. Another way is to hang herbs, bread, salt, or a piece of metal over the cradle.

A candle lit at the time of birth and extinguished only upon returning home after the baptism will ensure the child's safety.

Some believe that a child's given name should never be revealed until baptism. So, too, the child's initials should not themselves form a word, for such is an omen of evil, and children should never be named after a dead brother or sister.

While going to the church for the baptism ceremony, whoever carries the child must take the shortest path and not turn back should someone call their name. So, too, the church bells must ring a full peal or the child will be deaf and will sing off-key.

Two children should never be baptized with the same water, because the first will take all the fluid and leave its sin for the second. Likewise, a baby's face must never be wiped dry; rather, it should be left to dry on its own. Should the baby not cry, this indicates that an evil spirit was not exorcised and that the child is likely to grow being disobedient. Should the baptismal water be given to the child to drink at a later date, the child will develop an excellent singing voice.

In Northern England, it is said that a child should never be the first one baptized in the new church, due to the custom of burying a child or man under the foundation. Baptisms should not take place after burials, but rather after weddings to assure a happy life, and should the child arrive at the font before the priest, they say the child will be endowed with second sight. Should the priest make a mistake in the ritual, the child will surely stutter, and if he or she is to grow quickly, he must be held high above the baptismal font.

The christening cap should be kept on for at least the following twelve weeks. In the border counties of England, it was held that anyone who stepped on the grave of an unbaptized child would suffer the same fatal disease that took the child's life.

In ancient times, the Greeks would never leave a child unattended during the first eight days of its life; nor would the Greek Church baptize a child until eight days had passed.

An old Scottish tradition says that spit should be used by the parson to christen the child, and in ancient Scotland, a child was taken home after the baptism to be "sained" by fire. (See **saining**.) One method was for the child to be placed in a basket with a cloth; bread and cheese covered it. This was then moved three times around the iron crook hanging over the fire. The mother or midwife would perform the saining with the following words, "Let the fire consume thee now, if ever." Such was said to counteract witchcraft and other evil. The word "sain" comes from an old Saxon word meaning "to make the sign of the cross."

Another Scottish belief was that children who died unchristened would haunt woods. A Cheshire superstition held that unbaptized children *could* not die.

Last, to seal the child's luck, it was suggested that a feast be held after the baptism. The more lavish the feast and abundant the drink, the better. The popular saying "Wetting the baby's head" no doubt comes from the orgies that accompanied many such christenings.

Barnacle: According to an English seamen's legend, a barnacle broken from a ship's bottom will turn into a solan goose—a large marine bird that nests in the British Isles.

Baseball: Should a player see a cross-eyed man in the stands, he will have good luck. If he sees a cross-eyed woman, however, no runs will be made, unless he spits through his fingers without her seeing it. Cross-eyed umpires are especially considered bad luck, while left-handed pitchers are said to bring good luck to the team. Should a redheaded woman be seen, luck is assured, especially if she will give the player a hairpin.

Players' gloves are said to be lucky if, when the player goes to bat, the fingers are left on the ground pointing to one's own dugout.

Baseball bats should not be loaned to teammates, and bats that are split, even if the damage is insignificant, should never be used.

Should a dog walk across the playing field, it omens bad luck to the team at bat. Should part of a player's uniform be missing or damaged, expect bad luck for the team.

If, on the way to the game, any player encounters a name suggesting the name of his team, his team will be successful. Should a player have the misfortune of bumping into a clergyman before the game, bad luck will ensue; the antidote was for him to cross his fingers until a dog can be seen outside the stadium.

It is said that the team losing the first few innings is likely to win the game at the end.

Last, no season should ever begin on a Friday.

BAT: Should bats emerge from their holes directly after sunset, it is an omen that there will be fair and calm weather.

To the Chinese and the Polish bats in general are a good omen. (The Chinese regard the bat as a symbol of long life and happiness.) In Ireland, however, the bat is a symbol of death.

Other bat superstitions include these: Should bats move into a house, the occupants will shortly leave. Should the heart of a bat be dried, powdered, and carried in someone's front pocket, it will deflect a bullet or stop him from bleeding to death. Should one wash his face in the blood of a bat, he will be able to see in the dark.

A Scottish superstition holds that, when a bat is observed rising and descending earthwards, such signifies the "hour of the witches."

Along the Gold Coast, the natives of Tendo maintain that flocks of bats, leaving the island and heading for the river, are the souls of the dead, who must present themselves each evening to Tano, the ruler of the river of that name.

In Australia, certain tribes believe that the life of a bat corresponds to that of a man. Hence, if a bat was killed, the life of a man would also be shortened.

Should a bat fly into a house, especially a room occupied by its owner, it is an indication of death or bad luck to come. Bats hitting a building signify rain. Carrying a bat's bones on one's person is said to be one of the luckiest talismans around; carrying the right eye of a bat in the waistcoat pocket is said to make a man invisible.

A common country belief is that a bat flying into a woman's hair will become so entangled, that it can only be released by cutting her hair. Still another superstition holds that if a bat lands on your head, it will not leave until an approaching rainstorm or the sound of thunder is heard.

An Orthodox Jewish superstition says that a bat killed with a gold coin will bring good luck.

Should a bat fly close by, it is a warning that someone is trying to betray or bewitch you. Should a bat hit the windowpane of an ill person's room, it was believed the person would die. To keep witches away, one was instructed to nail a bat to the barn or shed door.

Aesop said that the nocturnal habits of bats were simply an attempt to evade creditors. (Scientific studies of bats have shown that their ability to fly in complete darkness is due to a supersonic detection device similar to modern radar.)

Sicilian peasants believed that the Devil can assume the shape of a bat. Bats' blood was believed to be an ingredient of the witches' "flying ointment"; supposedly it would give them the ability to fly at night.

The Hessians believed that the heart of a bat could be attached to a gambler's arm by a red thread to make him successful at cards.

In Central Europe it is said that girls enticed their reticent lovers by adding a few drops of bats' blood into their lover's beer.

The supreme deity of some American Pacific Coast Indians was Chamalkan, the bat.

According to an old European legend, a bat decided to join the war between animals and birds. Uncertain as to which group to join, he fought on both sides.

Bats were also believed responsible for stealing bacon from farmhouse chimneys.

A rhyme still heard among English country folk is the following: "Bat, bat, get under my hat and I'll give you a slice of bacon."

As recently as 1962, an edict passed by the New York City Council prohibited the sale of voodoo drugs: bat's blood was included on the list.

BAY TREE: Shakespeare in *Richard II* echoed a superstition that a withering bay tree is an omen of death in the family: "Tis thought the King is dead; we will not stay. The bay trees in our country are all withered."

Pliny held that bay trees are never struck by lightning, and the Roman Emperor Tiberius crowned himself with bay leaves during every thunderstorm.

In ancient British funerals, bay leaves were used as a symbol of the Resurrection, since the bay would revive from roots alone when seemingly dead. Too, the bay tree was said to protect one against devils and storms; hence, it was often planted nearby country homes.

Should bay leaves be thrown into a fire and crack loudly, such indicates good fortune. Should they burn without noise, bad luck is foretold.

BEAM: In Scotland and in parts of northern England, a dying person's position was moved if he was lying under a cross beam of a house, because it was believed that no one could die comfortably that way. Likewise, a dying person's bed would be set across the length of the floor boards. The origin of this superstition is, unfortunately, lost to time.

BEAN: In England, should one bean in a row be white instead of green it was said that a death in the family would occur within the year. Furthermore, unless planted on the third of May, it was believed that kidney beans would not grow.

In the Midlands, people believed that accidents would occur more frequently when the broad bean was in flower. Likewise, it was believed that broad bean flowers contained the souls of the dead.

In the Far East, beans are often scattered about one's house to keep demons away.

One should never sleep when the blossom of broad beans can be smelled or you will have nightmares. On Midsummer's Eve, a tradition was to hide three broad beans and have someone search for them. One bean was left in its skin; another was half peeled, and the third was completely peeled. The future of the searcher's life was determined by which bean he discovered. The one left in its skin indicated riches; the half-peeled one, a comfortable life; the peeled one, poverty. In Italy, a variation of this ritual was the drawing of beans by unmarried girls anxious to foresee details about their future husbands. A rich one was promised if a whole bean was drawn; one penniless, if the skinless bean; and a possible invalid from the "blind" one.

It is thought that ancient superstitions about the bean proliferated because of its resemblance to the kidneys or possibly the testicles. In astrology, the bean falls under the rulership of the planet Venus; hence its connection with sexuality.

The Egyptians held the bean sacred and would not eat it.

Pythagoras believed that beans contained blood and he would not consume them. Legend has it that he met his death because he was chased into a field of such beans, which he refused to step on because he believed the plants carried the souls of the dead.

Ancient Romans believed ghosts of the dead, called "lemures," threw beans at houses during the night; hence, there were various ceremonies to placate these spirits, consisting of throwing beans on graves or burning them.

The Iroquois Indians in North America held a bean festival in August. Various dances and rituals gave thanks to the beans, which were believed to be a special gift from the gods.

The Hopi Indian springtime rites involved puberty and a means to ensure the sprouting of beans.

An ancient method of determining guilt would be for a person to draw a bean from a bag. Should a black bean be chosen, the person was considered guilty; the white one meant innocence.

A Twelfth Night custom surrounded baking a cake with a bean hidden in it. The person whose slice held the bean was considered "the bean king" and "master of the revelry."

BEAR: Superstitions about bears abound.

Foremost is the idea that bear cubs are born shapeless and that their mothers lick them into a shape. Hence, unless they have been badly licked, bears are known for gluttony and courage. The painter, Titian, was said to use as his personal signature a female bear shaping her young.

In the sixteenth century, bear grease was considered a cure for baldness. It was also believed to work against garden blight, if rubbed on garden tools.

Should a child ride on a bear's back, some say it will never contract whooping cough. A similar belief holds that riding on the back of a bear will cure a young child of fever forever, but an infant of hay fever only. The fur of a bear was considered an excellent talisman against blindness.

Country folk in the United States held a belief that bears bred only once every seven years. When they did, cattle about to calve would lose their young.

A bear's tooth was used as a teething implement for babies in rural America, and sleeping on a bear skin has been said to cure backache. Legends of bear ghosts appear in the American South and in some parts of Great Britain.

For the North American Indian, the bear was his greatest competitor. Various Indian tribes ceremoniously apologized to the dead bear, who was thought to possess great supernatural powers. Often its head and hide would be used in the ceremonies. In the mythology of the Sioux, the Chippewa, and the Pueblos, the bear is often depicted as a healer. The shaman or medicine man often dressed as a bear. Tribal legends abound concerning a marriage of a strange woman who is later found out to be a bear in human form. Then, too, it was thought that a woman and a male bear could unite to produce a divine infant.

The name of the English hero, Beowulf, was derived from "bee-wolf," or honey eater, in reference to the bear.

In Finland, before one kills a bear, one must ask forgiveness.

Archaeologists have excavated skulls of bears placed by Neanderthal men on primitive altars. The ancient Greeks believed that a bear goddess named Callisto had been transformed by Zeus into the constellation that came to be called the Great Bear.

In southern France, an annual spring celebration would be held in which a man dressed as a bear. He emerged from a symbolic cave, frightened the townsfolk, and performed a mock abduction of a woman. In western European and some Slavic countries similar ceremonies still exist. The bear's habit of hibernation has been likened to the phenomena of rebirth, since he seemingly "dies" and is "reborn."

Last, a tradition from the American Ozarks holds that, when you go bear hunting, you should injure the bear, but not cripple it. He will be so angry that he will chase you all the way home, thus saving you the trouble of packing the meat home yourself!

BEARD: Generally speaking, a beard has been revered as a symbol of royalty for centuries.

Since it continued to grow even after being shaved away, the beard was thought to be of divine origin. Hence, it was unlucky to cut one's beard for fear that the devil or an enemy would get hold of the clippings.

Moslems take their oath by the beard of the prophet Mohammad.

The Greek word *pogonotrophos* means "man with a beard," which became synonymous with the word for "philosopher."

King Tutankhamen was depicted in Egyptian hieroglyphics as having a black beard attached to his chin.

Beards were often perfumed or powdered for various festivals, and Persian kings were said to intertwine their beards with gold.

During Elizabethan England, clean-shaven faces suddenly became popular when the Queen decided to tax Englishmen who wore beards.

In Mesopotamia, curled beards were attached to the image of their Bull God. Such was considered a sign of strength and masculinity. Consequently, only Sumerian kings were allowed to grow long beards.

In the eleventh century, following the injunction of Saint Paul—"If a man have long hair, it is a shame unto him" (I Corinthians 11:14.)—Saint Wulfstan, Bishop of Worcester, was known for his sudden attacks upon unsuspecting passersby whose beards he proceeded to hack off with his knife. This he followed with the command that they shave off the remainder or go to hell.

Not to seem out of place when Francis I of France grew a beard to conceal a scar on his chin, the entire male population was ordered to do the same.

Czar Peter the Great of Russia ordered that any beard seen in public, without an accompanying tax receipt, could be cut off on the spot. Members of the Sikh faith are forbidden to shave or cut any part of the body hair and, hence, they all have beards.

A German proverb holds that a red-bearded man is never any good. A Basque proverb says that one should beware of women with beards and men without them. Beware of a man whose hair is one color and beard another, says yet another proverb.

A more practical approach was taken by Alexander the Great,

who ordered his troops to shave their beards so that they could not be grabbed by them and to make it harder for the enemy to decapitate them.

Saint Uncumber, whose hand was sought in marriage by a king of Sicily, asked God to disfigure her so she could escape the marriage. Her prayers were answered, and she grew such an abundant beard that she was rejected in disgust by her suitor. This fact, together with her public devotion to Christianity, so outraged her pagan father, that he took her out and crucified her.

BEAUTY: For those who desire this trait, simply collect dew on the first day of May and bathe in it. A German superstition recommends using cold coffee instead of dew, while the Hungarians (no doubt due to the influence of Count Dracula) suggest that human blood will work just as well.

BED: Since life is conceived in a bed, begins in a bed, and often ends in a bed, it is no wonder that superstitions and legends abound about this particular household item.

Foremost is the idea that, if one gets out of bed on the wrong side, he will have a bad day. In fact, it is said that bad luck is sure to be yours should you get out of the bed by the side opposite to the one you got in. Upon leaving bed, always put your right foot down first.

The bed itself should be placed in an east-to-west direction like the movement of the sun across the sky. The person sleeping should not be touched by moonlight, nor should his bed form a cross with the ceiling beams.

One can ward off bed sores by placing two buckets of fresh spring water under the bed each day.

To sweep a bedroom before the guest has been gone for at least one hour will bring bad luck to a friend of the family.

A bed should be made by one person all at once or delays will be encountered all throughout the day. Furthermore, if three people take part in making up a bed, a death in the house within a year is certain, according to an Oxfordshire tradition. Some say beds should never be left turned down during the day, to do so would invite the presence of demons. If one turns a mattress over on a Friday, those occupying the bed will dream about the witches' sabbath.

Straws tied in a cross and placed at the four corners of the bed were said to ward off nightmares. Finally, one should never put a hat on a bed at any time.

BEE: Due to the common habit among country folk of keeping bees for their honey, a number of superstitions are found about bees.

One must tell the bees if a member of the family dies or marries, or the bees will leave their hives and not return. Should the head of the house die, the hives should be turned around at the moment the corpse is taken for the funeral.

Bees that are stolen will never thrive, but will themselves pine away and die.

It is unlucky for a stray swarm of bees to alight in your premises. Likewise, should the bees swarm on a dead hedge or tree, a death will most surely happen in the family.

Before moving the hive, bees should be told by the owner, or they will sting him, and bees should never be removed on Good Friday or they will die.

When many bees enter the hive and none leave, rain will soon come.

Legend holds that bees first appeared in the Garden of Eden, and thus are called by some "the little servants of God."

Bees should never be sold, but rather, bartered or traded. Giving a hive to someone provides them with honey and also good luck.

Should a bee fly into your house, expect a visitor to arrive soon.

Bees seen flying around a sleeping child indicate a happy life for the child, but should a bee die in your house, expect bad luck, and killing a bee will always bring several years of it. A bee landing on your hand indicates money to come, and if it settles on your head, expect future fame.

Any girl who is a virgin can pass safely through a swarm of bees without being stung.

For Christianity, the bee became a symbol of virtue and chastity. Indeed bees are alleged to make a loud humming noise in their hives at midnight on Christmas Eve in celebration of the Christ Child, and legend has it that bees sprang from the tears shed by Christ on the cross.

Bees remaining strangely idle for a long period of time are said to indicate that war is coming.

Mississippi blacks believe that, should one dream of a swarm of bees alighting a building, misfortune is certain to come.

Dead bees burned to ashes and sprinkled in the shoes are said to cure flat feet. One belief (not to be counted on, however) is that holding your breath or clenching your fist (or producing some other tension) will keep the bees from stinging.

The belief that the sting of a bee is a cure for rheumatism exists in many cultures.

In ancient days in Britain, bees were known as "birds of God." In Germany they were known as "Mars birds." The Greeks consecrated bees to the moon. Plato's "Doctrine of Transmigration of Souls" held that the souls of sober, quiet people, who are unexposed to philosophy, come to life as bees.

Paramount is the belief that the bee is the soul of one departed.

During the Inquisition, it was believed that a sorceress could eat a queen bee before being captured, and would then be able to sustain torture without confessing.

BEET: According to legend, the Greeks served beets on a silver platter to the god Apollo at his temple at Delphi. Like almonds, some believe eating a raw beet each day will keep cancer from developing.

The English herbalist, Culpeper, believed that beets were good for headaches, colds, and for cleansing the liver and spleen.

BEETLE: The ancient Egyptians regarded the beetle, or scarab, as symbolic of the sun and of eternal return. Hence, one finds its form on rings, amulets, and talismans.

The beetle is said to be a sign of death should it walk on your shoe or emerge from a shoe placed near a door.

Should a beetle enter a room in your home where the family is seated, misfortune is yours, according to a Scottish superstition. Should the beetle be killed, the greater the misfortune.

Throughout Europe there is a general belief that beetles attract storms. It is most likely beetles were considered unlucky there due to their tendency to devour the bean crop.

Should certain beetles produce a clicking noise while calling their mates, such was regarded as an omen of death to follow soon after.

Aristotle believed that beetles arose from putrifying flesh and from dung, near which they were often seen to gather.

In Germany, the stag beetle was symbolic of thunder, since it was often found on the oak tree, which is the tree most often struck during a storm. According to a legend in the Hebrides, the burrowing beetle betrayed Christ by describing the path of his flight into Egypt to his pursuers. The dung beetle, however, contradicted this, leading the pursuers astray. Hence, young boys would kill the burrowing beetle, but simply leave the dung beetle on its back, since its lie was for a good cause.

In Ireland, the devil's coach-horse beetle is said to place a curse on you when it raises its tail.

In Africa, women of the Baronga tribe throw beetles into a lake as part of a rain-making ceremony.

Among Arab magicians there exists a practice of tying a beetle of the sex of a runaway slave to a nail. They believe that, as it crawls around and around, ensnarling itself, the slave will be drawn back to its master.

During the nineteenth century, in East Anglia, whooping cough was said to be cured by suspending a beetle around a child's neck.

BELL: In North America there is a general belief that bells will drive away evil spirits, especially on Midsummer's Day Eve. Should two bells ring at the same time in one house, it was said to be indicative of a parting. Still another belief involves two bells ringing during a storm; bad weather is said to cease.

Bells were believed to have the ability to cure fevers and illnesses, and to chase away mice and snakes. Likewise, it was believed that a witch in flight hearing the sound of the bell would fall to earth.

Should a bell sound without being rung, it was always considered to be an evil omen. For many, this indicated that a soul had ended its time in purgatory and was seeking entrance into heaven.

Should one hear the sound of bells while at sea, far from the shoreline, it was believed that the bells belonged to the mythical city of Is. It is believed that the first person to see a bell surface or hear its ringing is witnessing the rebirth of Is and will become king of the country.

To call the dead, one was instructed to make a hand bell of seven metals—mercury, lead, silver, gold, tin, copper, and iron. On the outside one should engrave the sacred word, *tetragrammaton*, as well as the names of the spirits that govern the seven planets. At the top of the bell one should inscribe the word *adonai,* and, on the ring, the name *Jesus.* Such must be kept wrapped in green taffeta at the bottom of a freshly dug grave for seven days before being used ritualistically.

The expression "bell, book, and candle" comes from a solemn form of excommunication used by the Roman Catholic Church. When the officiating cleric closed the book from which he had read the curse, a bell was tolled, as for a dead man, and the candles were extinguished as a sign that the soul of the offender had been removed from the sight of God. In time, this expression came to indicate that someone was a witch, since, not being a member of the church and being a witch were said to be one and the same.

The expression "bell don't make bump" is often heard among the Pennsylvania Dutch to indicate that a bell did not ring.

Last, the expression "to be there with bells on" refers to the use of bells on the backs of the horses that pulled huge Conestoga wagons. Should a driver of such a wagon find himself stuck in a mud hole and have to request help, the price he was forced to pay was a set of bells. Hence, to be there with bells on meant that one was successful in their journey.

BELT: A belt was said to protect one from sorcery, because it wrapped completely around the body. Hence, it should never be thrown away, as its possession by a witch would hold the person at her mercy. Wearing a belt that had been blessed by a priest, however, was said to make difficult childbirths easier.

BIBLE: As a major foundation of Christian theology, the Bible has been held sacred because of its content and its intrinsic power.

Often used by Christians as a "book of divination," one was advised to open the Bible at random, with eyes closed; placing a finger on a word or phrase would yield the answer to one's question. A variation of this was to "cut" the Bible with a silver knife. Whatever page was so indicated, and whichever phrase was first seen, would yield the answer.

On New Year's Day in Oxfordshire there is a custom of divining the upcoming year. Carried out before noon, one should open the Bible and notice which passage first caught one's eye. The tenure of that passage was said to be a prognosticator of coming events. (This particular tradition of opening a sacred book at random has its origin in ancient Greece. Here the poems of Homer and Virgil were used instead of the Bible.)

Yet another practice is to read from an open Bible, while another person supports a key on the tips of the fingers. That person calls out the names of those suspected of theft. The key will "turn" at the mention of the guilty person's name. ("Turning" meant that the key would fall to the ground from the fingertips.)

On the Scottish Isle of Collonsay, a belief exists that you may cure a patient of illness by fanning him with the leaves of the Bible.

An American folk belief is that the Book of Proverbs can be utilized by a young man to determine the character of his future wife. He must first find out her age and then seek the appropriate corresponding verse from the first chapter of Proverbs. The verse indicated will provide a clue to her temperament, assuming that she has given her correct age! For young girls, a similar answer can be found by placing her door key in the "Song of Solomon" section, leaving the key ring protruding. The Good Book must be tightly bound with her garter or stocking. Two other people must hold it by placing a finger under the key ring. The following verse must be repeated:

> Many waters cannot quench love, neither can the floods drown it. Love is as strong as death, but jealousy is as cruel as the grave, and burneth with the most vehement flame. If a man should give all the substance of his house for love, it would be utterly consumed.

Should the book turn or fall when these words are spoken, the girl will assuredly marry. Should nothing occur, she will most likely become a spinster.

Placing an open Bible in a baby's cradle will keep the baby from harm. Putting one under one's pillow at night will protect the sleeper and is alleged to help children learn to read. Placing a leaf from a Bible under one's doorstep will cause a thief to stumble and wake the house.

BIRD: As birds are aerial, they are said to be in closer contact with the heavens and with spirits than are other creatures. Some believe that they are the returned souls of dead people.

Should a bird fly in and out of a room through an open window, some see it as an omen that death will occur to the owner of the house. Likewise, should birds hover around a house, rest on a windowsill, or tap against the pane of glass, it indicates death for the residents. Should a sick person be lying within a room and a robin taps on the window, death is certain.

Superstitions about birds abound: Should a child die before being baptized, it will be transformed into a bird, until baptized by John the Baptist. Should birds fly from right to left in even numbers, good luck will ensue, if from left to right in odd numbers, expect bad luck. Seeing a magpie is a sign of death to come. Should jays or crows forsake a forest in large flocks, expect great famine or mortality.

Foul weather can be predicted when ravens or crows make a hoarse or hollow noise, and when peacocks clamor harshly, expect rain. Should one kill or disturb the nest of a tom tit or wren, expect to break a bone during the coming year. It is always bad luck to kill a swallow.

If you should see a flock of birds at the onset of your journey, it is believed that the direction of their flight indicates success or failure for you. Should they fly to the right, all will be well; should they fly to the left, you are advised to stay home.

It is unlucky to have wallpaper with a pattern of birds. White birds are said to indicate death, blue jays are said to spend every Friday with the Devil, discussing with him those things that we have done.

Should you hear a bird call, you must note the direction from which it came. Should it come from the north, expect tragedy, from the south, a good harvest, from the west, good luck, and from the east, good loving. If a crow should fly over a house and croak three times, someone in the family will soon die. Should you hear the sound of night birds, you should throw salt into a fire to ward off evil.

In Brittany, birds were believed to answer questions with their song. Should the sound of the night jar be heard by a householder, death is likely, says a Pembrokeshire legend.

According to the Scots, should a caged bird die on the wedding morning of a family member, the marriage will be unhappy and the couple will eventually separate.

British traditions hold that should a bird drop on you, it is considered bad luck. According to the Irish, if black and gray birds are seen flying around trees in the dark never settling, these are souls accomplishing penance.

Moslems believe that no bird can be trusted, since birds opened the "Gates of Paradise," thereby letting Satan enter.

In the faroes of Denmark, a girl tries to foretell from where her future husband will come by throwing stones at a crow and watching in which direction it flies.

Generally speaking, the beliefs associated with many birds are determined or influenced by their colors. For instance, the cock crossbill's red crown and twisted bill gave rise to the tradition that the bird acquired these characteristics through efforts to remove the nails from Christ's cross. The American robin redbreast was said to receive its coloration from Christ's blood when it pulled the thorns from his crown.

It was believed one could cure himself of jaundice by fixing his gaze on the yellow eye of the stone curlew. This would cause the disease to be transferred to the bird. Blackbirds and crows were long thought to be connected with the devil and witchcraft. Tribespeople of many lands believe souls of the dead are conveyed to the next world by birds. Some West African tribes, for instance, used to bind birds to the body of persons to be sacrificed; South Sea Islanders would bury their dead in a coffin shaped like a bird; Borneo natives represent tempon-talon's ship of the dead in the form of a bird. Indian tribes in the American northwest had rattles shaped like ravens, since the raven was thought to carry the soul of the deceased to the home of the sun. (For additional information on birds and superstitions see listings for specific birds.)

BIRTH: Although a number of birth superstitions have already been discussed (see **baby**), there are many general beliefs of great interest.

Traditions surrounding birth abound in the British Isles. For instance, in Yorkshire children born during the hour of midnight will have throughout their entire life the power to see the spirits of the departed. Also in Yorkshire, to ensure sexuality, some of the father's clothes are placed over a female child at birth; the mother's apron or petticoat is placed over a male. To ensure good luck, babies should be rubbed with lard immediately after birth and especially before they are washed.

For purity, a newborn child should be given to the arms of a maiden before being held by its mother, and to prevent accidents, an infant should be brushed with the foot of a rabbit.

In Scotland, it is believed that a child born on a Sunday is especially favored. Those attending the birth of a baby in Scotland were served cake, new cheese, and tea seasoned with brandy or whiskey. It was considered unlucky for anyone to fail to participate in this affair.

In the north of England, once the mother delivered, the doctor was favored to cut both the cake and cheese. It was believed that, should he fail to do this, the child would grow up ugly and without charm. In Durham, however, the nurse or midwife would present the cake and cheese to the first person of the sex opposite the child's that she encountered. More specifically, in Oxford, the cake was cut in the middle and shaped in the form of a ring. The child was passed through the ring cake on its Christening Day for further luck. In many rural areas of Europe, custom has it that all doors and locks—even knots on any items of clothing the would-be mother is wearing—should be opened to ease the actual birth process.

In Kent there was an old practice of the midwife preparing two nightshirts before the birth—a boy's and a girl's. Should a girl be born, it was placed on the boy's nightshirt; should a boy be born, it was placed on the girl's. This was done in the belief that the boys would then fascinate all women; and the girls, all men.

The eight days following a child's birth were considered unusually inauspicious. The child was in danger of being seized by the fairies. To prevent this calamity, salt was placed in the cradle or iron was sewn into the child's clothes. (Iron was believed to bar the way to fairies and witches.) In Scotland, it was said that an article of clothing worn by the child's father would protect him in a similar manner.

The day of birth is believed to itself carry great significance. Sunday is perhaps the most favorable day, since it marked the day of the sun and also the day of Christ's resurrection. Friday, the day of Christ's death, was considered by many to be most inauspicious. However, in Anglo-Saxon times, children born on this day were believed to be loving and generous, given Friday's rulership by the planet Venus. Children born on Wednesday were said to be melancholy; those on Thursday, sure of fame; those on Monday or Tuesday, remarkably physically attractive. Being born during a full moon was said to bring luck in life. When a child is born under a waxy moon, it is said the next baby will be of the same sex.

Children born with a blue vein in their forehead would not live to be old. If a pregnant woman was frightened, or if she had a great many dreams, or was dissatisfied, it was believed that the child would be born with strawberry marks. These marks could be removed with the mother's saliva if she licked them several days in a row.

A German superstition holds that one should look up at the clouds at the time of a child's birth. Should the clouds take the form of sheep or lambs, it is an indication that the child will enjoy good fortune throughout its life.

In Maine, a popular superstition is found in the following lines: "First a daughter, then a son, the world is well begun. First a son, then a daughter come, trouble follows after."

In Herefordshire, legend has it that the father of a child suffers the pain of birth as much as the mother. Hence, if a woman gives birth to an illegitimate child and refuses to disclose the name of the father, it can be found by finding out which of the possible men were ill at the time of birth.

Tradition holds that the mother should soak her wedding ring in a glass of wine and give the child a few drops to drink when born. This was said to protect the child against the evil eye. Also, one could prevent and distract evil spirits from noticing the birth of the child by throwing coins out of the window.

The custom of planting a tree when a child is born is an ancient one. Hebrews chose cedars for boys and pines for girls.

More traditions: To gain a ruddy complexion and generally good health, one should wash the child's face with his first wet diaper. The diaper then must immediately be given to a young girl.

One should never compliment a baby on its beauty. If done in error, one should either spit on the baby or verbally retract the compliments.

Should a child refuse the breast, it was said to be bewitched. Should a baby boy urinate over his shoulder, a happy life would be ensured.

Should the baby's navel fail to heal, a plowshare should be buried while five Our Fathers are recited.

Children should not be left alone on foggy days, until they have their first tooth.

A mother's placenta should never be exposed to the sun or moonlight, or to a dog or a cat. Tradition holds that it is best to bury it under the cellar stairway.

The first words of a child are equally significant. Should the child say "papa" first, the nextborn child will be a boy. Should the child say "mama," expect a girl. Children born with the caul (a fetal membrane) were held to be especially blessed. (Cauls were valued by sailors as protection against drowning and believed to confer powers of second sight on their owners. See **caul**.) Last, should the child be the seventh born to one who was a "seventh" born, the child would have great healing powers and access to the spirit world.

BIRTHMARK: For some, this is called the mark of the Devil; for others, the mark of God. Primitives believed that birthmarks appeared because the mother experienced something unpleasant or had been touched by some spirit power during her pregnancy.

A midwest superstition says that a baby born with a double crown birthmark on its head would travel a great deal during its lifetime. Often considered to be good omens, one tradition went so far as to recommend throwing black pepper on the expectant mother to ensure that her child would be born with birthmarks. (See **moles**.)

BLACKBERRY: In France, some persons will never eat blackberries, believing that the color comes from the spit of the Devil. In England, picking blackberries after October 11 will create bad fortune. Tradition has it that the Devil fell into a blackberry thicket on October 11, cursing the thorns that injured him. Michaelmas Day originally fell on September 29 and was moved to October 10. This served as the basis for the legend that, when Saint Michael cast Satan from heaven, he landed in a bramble bush; hence, the taboo. Another explanation to this tradition may be that blackberries ferment or mildew early in October.

In the Highlands, the blackberry is called the "blessed bramble" and the belief is widespread that evil spirits can be kept away by a wreath of bramble, rowan, and ivy.

BLACKBIRD: Tradition holds that a blackbird nested in the hand of Saint Kevin as he held it forth from his hermitage. Blackbirds are generally considered to be beneficial, although some believed that blackbirds and crows were used by witches as familiars.

Blackbirds seen sitting together is said to be a good omen. In Wales, however, this same occurence is believed to be an omen that someone in the household will die.

Should the heart of a blackbird be placed under the head of a sleeping person, it is believed he will reveal all his secrets.

Should one have an uninhabited house and seek to prevent intruders from sleeping there, one could simply hang the feathers of a blackbird's right wing by a red thread.

The term "blackbirding" was used to describe the practice of clandestinely kidnapping African tribesmen and bringing them to the American South to be sold as slaves.

BLACK CAT: Due to its long association with witchcraft, the black cat is often symbolic of Halloween. Many thought black cats to be witches in disguise. Such creatures were said to perch on sleeping babies and the elderly to suck the breath out of them.

Superstitions and traditions about black cats abound: If an unknown black cat comes to visit, for example, good luck will follow. In England, a black cat coming towards you is also good luck. In America, however, a black cat crossing your path is considered bad luck.

In general it is said that a black cat without a single white hair is a lucky sign, if it comes to you unsolicited. Should you try to coax a black cat toward you and he runs away, however, expect disappointment in your affairs. Should a black cat be killed inadvertently, expect misfortune for an entire year, and a black cat meowing at midnight is an omen of death to come.

Among the ancient Egyptians, cats were regarded as expressions of the deity, Bast, and were mummified and buried with their human owners. According to a Norse legend, the goddess Freya's chariot was pulled by black cats.

The brain of a black cat often appeared in the Middle Ages as an important ingredient in witches' potions. In France, it was believed that one could chase away evil spirits by burning a black cat on the first week of Lent or in a Saint John fire. In fact, Charles I was alleged to own a favorite black cat. When it fell ill and died, he said, "My luck is gone." The next day, Charles was arrested.

In the thirteenth century, Pope Gregory IX issued a papal statement in which he accused the Stadinghi, a heretical sect, with the expressed crime of keeping black cats, thereby accusing them of being witches.

In Brittany, an interesting superstition says that, if you go to the intersection of five roads and call the name of the Devil, a black cat will appear. Black cats were said to hide the Devil's hair in their tails as well as to possess a single white hair, which offered great power whenever found.

The left paw of a black cat surreptitiously placed in a hunter's left pocket was believed to prevent him from success in hunting.

The disease "Saint Anthony's Fire" could be cured by drawing blood from a black cat's ears and rubbing it upon the part affected. Likewise, shingles could be cured by taking the blood drawn from a black cat's tail and smearing it over the affected part.

In Sumatra, when rain is needed to overcome a drought, a black cat is thrown into a river and made to swim about. He is allowed to escape to the bank, only to be pursued by scantily clad village women, who splash the animal and themselves with water.

In Yorkshire, the presence of a black cat in a fisherman's house was said to ensure his safety at sea. "Black cat" is also a term used by sailors and fishermen on Lake Superior to describe a boat upon which a "spell" has been cast. Such a boat is never to acquire a full crew.

In Slavonia, tradition has it that women can compel a man to fall in love with them if they can secretly cause their lover to eat the heart of a black cat killed at the new moon. What better way to end this section than with the anonymous poem, "If the cat in your house is black, of lovers you will have no lack." (See **cat**.)

BLACKHEAD: There appears to be only one superstition in regard to blackheads, and that is this: They will disappear if you creep on your hands and knees through a bramble three times, with the sun from east to west. Here the cure seems far worse than the disease!

BLACK SHEEP: Despite the fact that someone unpopular in one's family is often called a "black sheep," black sheep foretell good luck, according to a Kent tradition.

In Sussex, it was thought equally lucky for a shepherd to have at least one black lamb or sheep in his flock. In Shropshire, however, bad luck was said to be in store for the flock into which a black lamb was born.

In Scotland, one was believed able to divine the future by scraping the shoulder blade of a black sheep, avoiding the use of iron. The seer then held it lengthwise over his left shoulder, while another inspected the broad end, interpreting the lines and shades.

BLACKSMITH: Here only one tradition is found, from western Ireland: no harm or ill ever came to one whose profession was that of a smithy.

BLOOD: Want a woman to fall madly, passionately in love with you? British countryfolk say to take a drop of blood from the little finger of your left hand and secretly place it in a woman's drink.

In Devonshire, if one wished to stop bleeding, he would repeat the following:

> Our Saviour Christ was born in Bethlehem, and was baptized in the river of Jordan. The waters were mild of mood. The child was meek, gentle and good, he staggered with a rod and still it stood. And so shall thy blood stayeth. In the name of the Father, the Son, and the Holy Ghost.

When this was repeated three times, followed by the Lord's Prayer, all bleeding, it was said, would cease.

A general Anglo-Saxon belief was that no one who bled on Halloween would live. Generally, bleeding is held as an evil omen, as blood is considered a vehicle of the soul. If one is bleeding and the previous instructions have not worked, then try one of the following remedies: Tie a key around the bleeder's neck or slip a wrought-iron key in back of him; place ashes, spiderwebs, or snakeskins on the wound; cut a blade of grass in two and form the sign of a cross on the wound, being sure to spit on it; urinate on the wound and rub it with dung or earthworms; place a snail on the wound and then a stone, and then after some time return the stone to where it was found; sprinkle some holy water on the wound. To stop a bleeding nose, specifically, eighteenth-century pundits suggested soaking a linen rag in vinegar, burning it, and then blowing the ashes up the nose through a quill. Should this not work, they suggested mixing three drops of blood with some water in a cup and drinking it (no doubt quickly). Two sticks of straw crossed behind the person's back, without his awareness, will also stop a nose bleed.

Should one suffer from bad circulation, walnut leaves gathered on the twenty-fourth of June, before sunrise, should be consumed.

In Borneo, the Kayans smeared themselves with the blood of fowls to protect themselves from the souls of the panthers they had killed.

Witches were said to sign their pact with Satan in blood. With the same blood, they suckled their familiars. Blood, hair, nail parings, and urine of a bewitched person were used in the "witch bottle," a medieval device for breaking the spell of a witch.

A strange phenomenon occurs each year in Maine. A pinch of moss turns blood red at the scene of an Indian massacre. Also in America, among Indian tribes, there was a widespread practice of becoming "blood brothers," which consisted of cutting each other and touching the wounds together.

BLOSSOM: There are several superstitions regarding trees and shrubs blossoming out of their season.

Geraniums, which flower in the house in winter instead of summer, are said to be unlucky. Christmas roses flowering late in the spring, or primroses in June, or summer roses in December are all regarded as omens of bad luck, according to Welsh country folk. Should a fruit tree flower out of season, it is an omen of sickness or death in the neighborhood, and hard winters are predicted when an entire district breaks out in blossoms out of season. A Welsh proverb says, "untimely fruit, untimely news."

BLOWING OUT CANDLES: It is said the tradition of blowing out candles originated with the Greeks. Candles were said to symbolize life; hence, the number displayed represented the years gone by.

Should you blow out all the candles on a cake with a single breath after making a wish, the wish will surely come true. You must be sure to tell no one what you have wished for, though.

BOIL: Crawling under a bramble that has grown into the soil at both ends, thereby forming an arch, is said to cure boils. If one wished to cure boils for a friend, he simply had to go into a churchyard on a dark night, walk six times around the grave of a person who had been interred the previous day, and crawl across it three times. Should the sufferer be a man, the ceremony had to be performed by a female friend; and vice versa for a female. The charm was said to work only if the night was completely dark.

BOLT: Should locks and bolts of a house be fastened, it was believed that the soul of a dying person would be hindered in its departure. In rural areas of Britain, doors and windows are opened so that the struggle between life and death can be an easier one. In Scotland, keeping a door to one's apartment shut is believed to prolong one's passing. The Chinese are said to make a hole in the roof of their homes in order for the soul to have an easy passage.

BONE: Many of us participate in the practice of breaking a fowl's "wishbone" for luck, especially on Thanksgiving, and bones are used in a variety of rituals and practices around the world.

Human skulls pounded into powder were recommended for the cure of epilepsy, and dysentery was said to be cured by powdering human bones and mixing them with red wine. An amulet made from a fragment of a human bone is said to cure stomach disorders, and should one recover a femur or other long bone from a cemetery, touching it is said to cure fever.

Arabians say that two bodies should never be buried in the same coffin; on Judgment Day their bones might be intermixed.

Musical instruments made from human bones are said to keep away evil spirits.

In the Pacific Islands, a pointy bone is used as a magic wand, and American folk medicine holds that carrying a bone cures backache, toothache, cramps, and fits.

Bushmen witch doctors foretell the future by means of bones marked with special signs. These are consulted on every important occasion and read according to laws governing their position. In the Congo, witch doctors, called "mganga" or "mufumu," use for divination the highly polished leg bones of goats, which are shaped to resemble the heads of various animals. While in a self-induced trance, the witch doctor casts these and interprets them accordingly. Bones signifying crocodiles or lions standing erect predict danger. Those representing friendly animals predict successful journeys.

Last, mention must be made of Ezekiel in the Old Testament, witnessing dry bones being clothed with flesh and skin and coming to life again—a symbol of Israel's future regeneration.

BOOT: In jolly old England it was believed that, if you placed a person's boots on a table or a chair, the owner would be hanged. A less grim belief was that putting a pair of boots on a table was an omen that a quarrel between the inhabitants of the house would occur.

BORROWING: An old Yorkshire belief is that, if one borrows a knife to cut an apple or any other fruit it must be sent back "laughing," or else bad luck will attend its owner. In other words, part of the fruit had to be returned with the borrowed knife.

The first three days in February and the last three days in March were said to be unlucky for borrowing. In Scotland, one was advised not to seek loans on these days and also to refrain from planting any seeds.

BOXER: Boxers, like other sportsmen, have a number of traditions that they believe bring them good luck in the ring. For some it can be carrying a ten dollar bill; for others, a rabbit's foot.

Should a fighter see a hat lying on a couch or bed before a fight, it is considered unlucky. No fighter likes to be the first one in the ring. A challenger should duck under the ropes before his opponent. One should never wear new shoes in an important match. Last, a fighter is often seen to spit on his gloves before confronting his opponent.

BRAMBLE BUSH: It is said that numerous ailments—whooping cough, boils, rheumatism, and even blackheads—can be cured if the sufferer passes under the natural arch formed by a bramble bush that has roots at both ends.

BRASS: This metal was held sacred by the Hebrews, the Greeks, and the Romans. Since it is highly resistant to wear, it was believed to contain the characteristics or immortality and incorruptibility. It was often used for the making of bells and frequently replaced by a similar alloy, bronze.

In rural England, it is believed that one must always have polished brass on horses' harnesses in order to keep away the Devil.

To the ancient Chinese, the sound of brass instruments was thought to terrify devils, and in Tibet, brass trumpets are still used in rites of exorcism today.

Among the Japanese, a custom required an undertaker to receive from the husband, wife, or parent of the dead a brass ring. This was worn on his right arm until the corpse was interred in the ground.

In certain regions of France, milking a cow for the first time requires that the milk be collected in a brass container.

BREAD: Since there are so many superstitions with regard to bread, you might say it is a wonder that it is ever eaten at all. The following represent some of the many beliefs.

When one is baking the sign of the cross should be made over the dough while left to rise; this will protect it from Satan's influence.

Only one person should put the bread in the oven. Should two people do it, there will be an argument.

While it is baking (regarded by some as a sacred ceremony), no other bread in the house should be cut with a knife, or else the new loaf will be spoiled. Should bread be required during this time, it must be broken by hand.

The bread must never be stuck with a fork or knife during the baking process, and some believe it must never be broken with the hands over a bare table. During the baking process, should the bread overflow or burst, it is an omen of death or illness in the family. Certainly, bread should never be burned.

Should bread form a hole in the middle while baking, or should the soft part be pulled out, death for a new relative would ensue. If baked on Christmas Eve, it was believed the bread would never dry out or would become moldy. Likewise, bread baked on a Good Friday would stay fresh all year long. If baked on New Year's Day, its crust would be thrown into a well to keep the well from drying up. Again, the sign of the cross should be made over it before first breaking. Bread should never be cut or made with a pointed object that was said to cause a wound to wandering souls in search of nourishment.

A round loaf of bread should never be turned over, or else misfortune will be brought to the house. Others believe that this would make the Blessed Virgin cry, thus causing rain.

During the Middle Ages, bread reserved for the hangman was deliberately placed aside and turned over so that the evil spirit of death would enter the bread. It is also said that a woman who sets a round loaf upside down most likely earns her living by lying on her back and engaging in the world's oldest profession.

Leftovers must be given to the birds. Should bread crumble when cut, there will be arguments in the family.

On Maundy Thursday, hanging a loaf of bread from the ceiling was thought a good way to keep illness away from the family.

So magical was bread that, if placed in a newborn's cradle, it would facilitate growth. Likewise, placing it near the body of one who recently died would allow the soul to continue to sustain itself. A small piece of bread was often placed near a baby about to be baptized.

It was considered unlucky to cut bread at both ends, or for it to be held by one person, when another person was cutting it. It was also said to be unlucky to take the very last piece of bread, unless it was offered. If offered, however, and one refused it, it would bring bad luck.

Bread should never be passed around on a knife or fork; nor should a knife be stuck in a loaf and left. If one toasts bread on a knife, it is said that he will be poor all his life.

Should two people inadvertently reach for the same piece of bread, such foretold the coming of company.

The heel of the loaf should always be saved for a family member, since it is an omen of the best luck of all. Should a loaf of bread turn upside down, such portends death or difficulty for a sailing ship.

According to an old English tradition, a loaf weighted down with quicksilver, set on a river, will travel toward the spot at which a drowned body is lying on the bottom. Should a round loaf of bread be topped with a candle from a church and set afloat, it would stop over a drowned body.

Should one be afraid of losing a knife he has just purchased, he should cut a piece of bread with it and give the bread to his dog. Should a person eat from a slice of bread that another person has already bitten into, he will make enemies or catch rabies.

Should a piece of bread be held under the armpit and then fed to a dog, it will kill him.

Bread fed to a goose will cause its feathers to fall off; fed to a donkey, it will increase his desire to mate.

One last word: should one suffer from diarrhea, bread crumbs grated from a loaf that has become dry and hard, and mixed with hot water is said to cure this particular curse with great haste!

BREAD AND BUTTER: In many lands it is common to say "bread and butter" and cross your fingers should an object or another person come between you and a friend. Just as bread and butter go together, so this tradition is said to prevent friendships from breaking up.

A slice of buttered bread can also be used for divination. Should the slice fall on the buttered side, it was held as bad luck; should it fall on the unbuttered side, a visitor would soon arrive. An unmarried girl who eats the very last piece of bread and butter at tea time would be the recipient of a proposal from a handsome gentleman with a large income.

BREAKFAST: Some believe that, if you sing before breakfast, you will cry before nighttime.

BREAST: In Devonshire, there is a belief that women with sore breasts may cure them by proceeding to the church at midnight and taking some lead from one of the stained glass windows. This is to be shaped into a heart and worn around the woman's neck.

BREEZE: European tradition holds that a breeze can be created by sailors on stalled ships if they scratch a fingernail on the foremast.

BRIDE: Here we find sexism at its most obvious. Traditions surrounding brides are manifold, but there is not a single mention in any of the classic works on superstitions regarding the groom. Indicators of a good or bad future for the bride seem to come in every size and shape. The following are some good and bad luck signs.

It is unlucky for a bride to see the bridegroom on the morning before the marriage. So, too, a bride should not try on her completed wedding dress before the wedding day. Once fully dressed, she should never look at herself in the mirror. For additional good luck, a stitch should be added to the bride's gown just before she leaves for the church.

Should a cat sneeze on the day before the wedding, a lucky marriage is portended. Should the bride leap over a rope or stool at the church gate, it is said that she will leave all her pets and humors behind her. Likewise, a bride who married in old shoes was considered lucky.

It was considered bad luck for a bride to step over the doorstep when entering her new home. Rather, she should be carried over by her husband. Should the bride fall asleep first on the marriage night, it was said that she is certain to die first as well.

In some parts of the continent, brides are asked to carry bread, which they break and scatter on the way to the church. Should birds come and pick up these crumbs, it indicates future happiness.

Among the Japanese, the bride's room is not swept for a few days after she leaves for the marriage ceremony for fear that her luck would be swept out as well.

Neither bride nor groom should ever wear purple in the belief that this would cause the marriage to soon be dissolved. Likewise, a bride is considered unlucky if she marries in green.

Those who follow the old adage, "something old, something new, something borrowed, something blue" are said to have the best luck of all. The something "old" can be a bride's garter, her slippers, or a handkerchief. The "blue," which is the only color a bride can wear besides white, must, of course, be heaven's blue. The something "borrowed" is often varied to something "golden" or something "stolen."

Bulgarian tradition is for the whole person to be completely washed only once in a lifetime—the evening before the marriage. Two bridesmaids were expected to attend this washing ceremony. Although naked too, they were not allowed to bathe.

In Devonshire, an ancient custom requires an old woman to present the bride with a small bag containing hazelnuts. As in Germany, to go "a nutting" was a euphemism for lovemaking. This tradition, no doubt, signifies fruitfulness for the couple. Throwing rice at the marriage ceremony has a similar significance.

In Cheshire, it is held that, should a bridal couple happen to pass under the lych gate of a churchyard, one will die within a year or the marriage will be an unhappy one. (*Lych* is an Anglo-Saxon word for corpse.)

In Nottingham lacemakers often embroidered a long hair from a fair-haired girl through the bridal veil along with the silk. If the hair went through without breaking, such foretold a long and happy marriage. If it broke at the beginning, the wife would die early; if at the end, the husband.

In northern England, after the bride entered her husband's house, which was soon to be her own, she was handed a poker, shovel, and tongs. This was in recognition of her authority as housewife. When poked, should the sparks of the fire fall on the upper portion of her apron, such would indicate that she would indeed have children.

An old tradition in Britain requires that a bride, after the wedding ceremony, leap over the burnt ashes of wood, a tree, or a bush. This would bless the woman with offspring from the tree spirits.

The bouquet carried by the bride is said to symbolize sex and fertility, as well as to ensure her marital happiness. Ribbons tied around the flowers are said to convey good luck, as well as best wishes for health and happiness from the bride's friends.

After leaving the ceremony, it was considered a bad omen for a bride to meet a pig or a funeral party. However, should her path be crossed by a chimney sweep, an elephant, or a black cat, this was considered fortunate. (See **marriage** or **wedding**.)

BRIDESMAID: The tradition of bridesmaids seems to date back to Anglo-Saxon times. The bride was then led by a matron, called the "brideswoman," followed by a company of unmarried maidens, who came to be called the "bridesmaids." In time, a tradition arose whereby the bridesmaids led the bridegroom to the church and the bridegroom's men led the bride. No doubt the tradition of guarding the bride with the bridegroom's men was one of protection against a rival who might carry her off. Hence, a "best man" was one who had the best interest of the groom at heart.

In Sweden, traditional weddings took place under cover of darkness for this same reason.

One authority maintains that the custom of having bridesmaids and best men originated with an old Roman law that required ten witnesses to a marriage. This was needed in order to outwit evil spirits, who were thought to attend happy functions. According to this tradition, the bridesmaids dressed like the bride and the ushers dressed like the groom therefore Satan would not know who was actually being married.

There are a number of traditions and beliefs concerning bridesmaids, many of which are still in practice. For example, bridesmaids traditionally hoped to catch the bride's bouquet when it was thrown to ensure a wedding for themselves. It was considered unlucky for a bridesmaid to stumble on her way to the altar, or else she, herself, would become an old maid. Likewise, it was said to be unlucky to be a bridesmaid three times. If one had this misfortune, she would have to pursue the same course for at least four more times or she would never marry. Should a bride have a matron of honor (a bridesmaid who is a married woman herself) attend her wedding, it was said to be particularly lucky for the bride.

Should a bridesmaid throw away a pin on the wedding day, it indicated good fortune. Should she be stuck by one, however, it was a bad omen. In Brittany, if a girl obtained the pins used to fasten the bride's dress, it indicated an early marriage.

In Sussex, it was required that bridesmaids steal these pins from the bride's gown, while she was changing for her departure.

It is said that a bridesmaid's dress should preferably be blue, pink, or yellow. It is also said that a bridesmaid, or any other young, unmarried girl at the wedding, can place a piece of wedding cake under her pillow, and dream about her future husband.

BRIDGE: Most common is the belief that, if you part from a friend beside a bridge, you will part forever. Other beliefs include one that warns against being the first person to cross over a new bridge.

Some additional warnings about bridges include: Never talk when standing or walking under a bridge. Never pass under a railroad bridge while a train is passing overhead, and never stand on a road over a railway while a train is passing below. Never follow a coffin across a bridge. Take a detour or the bridge will collapse.

Often a few drops of wine were placed in the mortar that held the key stone for the bridge in order to protect it against the evil eye. Sometimes a coin or iron object was mixed into the masonry for the same reason.

BROOM: Certainly, the most common superstition connected with brooms is that they were used by witches to fly on.

It was in the fourteenth century that brooms were first regarded as a vehicle for witches' transportation. This tradition may stem from the fact that, in many of their ceremonies, witches did dance with a stick between their legs, jumping high in the air. Toward the end of the eighteenth century, the question of witches flying was settled once and for all in an English law court. Lord Mansfield declared that he knew of no law that prohibited flying and, therefore, anyone so inclined was perfectly free to do so. Shortly thereafter, reports of witches flying on broomsticks ceased (except for isolated reports of East Anglian witches skimming across church spires).

There are many beliefs that have to do with when you may use a broom. For example, it is said that a new broom should sweep dirt out of a house only after it has swept something in. "Buy a broom in May, and you will sweep your friends away," says an English superstition. Another belief is that one should never sweep after sunset since so doing will chase away happiness or hurt a wandering soul. Likewise, one should avoid sweeping on Good Friday or New Year's Day.

According to a Yorkshire belief, should a young girl inadvertently step over a broom handle she will become a mother before a wife.

Among the Dyak people of Indonesia brooms made out of the leaves of a certain plant are sprinkled with rice water and blood. These are used to sweep one's house, and the sweepings are placed into a toy house made of bamboo. The toy house is then set adrift on a river. It is believed that bad luck will be carried out to sea with it.

In Africa, should a man be struck by a broom, he will grab hold of it and hit the broomstick seven times, or he will become impotent.

In many parts of England, a woman would prop a broom up outside her door when absent or push the broom up the chimney to indicate that she was not home.

In Sicily, on Midsummer's Day Eve, people often put a broom outside their homes to protect them against witchcraft. In Ireland, tradition has it that one should lay in a stock of brooms before the first of May, since the making, selling, and buying of brooms is believed inauspicious during the month of May. (One explanation of the tradition regarding the month of May being unlucky to make a broom is that this month was thought infertile and unsuitable for weddings.) In fact, an old English saying goes like this: "If you sweep the house with broom in May, you'll sweep the head of the house away."

In India, a sweeper's broom is often tied to the masts of ships, supposedly to sweep storms away.

In Wales, especially among Gypsies, an old custom of the broomstick wedding persisted for some time. The couple solemnized their rites before witnesses by leaping over a broom placed in a doorway, without dislodging the broom. Should they wish to dissolve the marriage, they simply had to reverse the process, jumping backwards out of the house, over the broom, before the same witnesses.

American country superstitions see no luck in taking a broom across water, leaning a broom against the bed, or burning one. Good luck can be had, say these country folk, by sending a new broom and a loaf of bread into a new house before entering it. Likewise, brooms laid across doorways are believed to keep ghosts away.

Traditional rules about brooms include these as well: Never use a broom when there is a dead person in the house. Never use a broom to sweep outside the house, unless the inside of the house has been cleaned first. Never walk on a broom. (Most likely this is because of its connection with witchcraft.) Never sweep upstairs rooms in the afternoon. Never sweep the room of a departing guest until he has been gone for some time, or else your sweeping will bring him back. Never borrow, lend, cut brooms into pieces or burn them. Never bring old brooms into new houses.

Should one suspect another of witchcraft, simply place a broom across the doorway. A witch will never step over such a broom in fear that it will come alive and fly her to the sabbath. Never leave brooms outside on Saturday, because they will join other brooms at the sabbath.

Should a child take up a broom and begin to sweep the floor, it is said to announce unexpected visitors. Newborns can be protected by turning brooms upside down and placing them on each side of the bedroom door or the door to the house, after placing three grains of salt on each one, and new brooms, some bread and salt insure domestic happiness.

Finally, should dust balls be swept into the middle of a room, they will protect against bad luck.

BUBBLE: Many believe that bubbles seen floating on the surface of a cup of tea or coffee are an omen that the drinker will soon come into money.

BUILDING: Nothing is as bad an omen as an accident in which someone is killed during the construction of a new building. The building will be unlucky, and many other deaths will occur there.

BUMBLE BEE: Some believe that, if a bumble bee enters your house, you will have a visitor.

BUNION: Want to get rid of this problem? Some say to make a poultice of fresh cow dung, mix it with some fish oil, put it on the bunion, and let it stay all night.

BURIAL: A Highlands tradition holds that the spirit of the last corpse to enter a churchyard or cemetery will guard the graves until the next corpse takes its place.

A Brittany legend holds that the last person buried each year is called the "ankon," who is in fact Death itself. He is said to ride through the village in a chariot, appearing in the form of a skeleton and warning others who are about to die.

Widespread is the belief that the coffin should always be carried to the grave in the same direction that the sun travels; that is, east to west.

A Yorkshire custom holds that, before the coffin lid is affixed, the dead person's Sunday School class ticket, his hymn book, and Bible must be placed therein. Bearers of similar age to the dead were also required to carry the body to the gravesite.

At the funeral of a maiden, a pair of white gloves were carried at the head of the possession by a girl of the same age. Afterwards, these gloves were hung up in the church near the seat usually occupied by the departed. The gloves bore the maiden's name, age, and date of her death. The bearers were also usually dressed in white. (See **corpse, death, funeral.**)

BURN: To cure a burn, a Shropshire suggestion is to apply a mixture of goose dung and the middle bark of an elder tree, which have been fried in May butter. For Cheshire residents, church linen was said to do the same thing.

An Irish belief holds that one should simply lay his right hand over the burn, very softly, and while gently blowing on the burn he should repeat three times: "Old clod beneath the clay. Burn away. Burn away. In the name of God be thou healed." After this, it is said that the pain will disappear and the patient will fall into a deep sleep.

BUSH: Here's one that American Midwest farmers can use. To prevent mildew or smuts from affecting your wheat, cut a large thornbush, make a fire in the wheat field, and burn a portion of the thorn. Afterwards, hang up the remainder of the thorn in the farmhouse. the origin of this tradition lies in the belief that thorn shrubs were a curse to witches and other evil spirits.

BUTTER: Perhaps the origin of various superstitions regarding butter has to do with the Celtic tradition of using butter, honey, and wax to bribe the evil forces. In any event, there are a great many beliefs surrounding butter.

In England, for example, it is claimed that the milk will refuse to curdle when the tide is going out. In France, on the contrary, the right moment for churning is at slack tide. The churn itself must be made of hazelwood, since this wood frightens evil forces.

In northern Scotland, the churn is disassembled when an unknown person approaches. Nine pinches of salt must be thrown into the churn, and nine into the fire, or butter will not come, says a Lincolnshire tradition.

In Alsace, it was believed that witches would cast spells on the cows so that their milk would be undrinkable. To keep witches away, thorns were placed in the churn or the milk was boiled with a sickle in it. It was believed that this would cause the witch to rub her skin on it or get caught stealing the milk or butter. To increase butter production, it was suggested that the bottom of the churn be rubbed with cat fat.

A Scottish charm used when butter would not form in the churn, is as follows: "Come, butter come. Peter stands at the gate, waiting for a buttered cake, come, butter come."

In the Highlands, it was recommended that the peg of the cow's shackle and the handle of the cross of the churn staff be made of rowan wood (mountain ash) to guard against the interference of witches.

It is believed that, on Saint John's Eve, the Estonians light bonfires to ensure that the butter will be as yellow and as gold as the sun of the fire throughout the entire year.

A New England superstition holds that a heated horseshoe dropped into the cream will drive out the influence of a witch who is preventing butter-making.

BUTTERCUP: As a child I picked buttercups and held them under the chins of friends to see if they liked butter, too. If they did, a yellow glow was reflected, but only when the sun was shining! This flower may have gotten its name because the cows that fed on it gave milk that was more yellow in color.

Some believe an ointment made from buttercups will draw a blister to a head.

Lunatics are said to be cured if you hang a bag containing buttercups around their neck.

Butterfly: Widespread is the belief that the soul takes the form of a butterfly. Medieval angels were sometimes depicted with butterfly's wings. Likewise, fairies are often shown with them.

In Northern Europe, to see a butterfly flying at night was considered to be an omen of death. In Great Britain, should one wish a favorable year, you must kill the first butterfly you see. According to a Gloucestershire belief, however, should the first butterfly you see in the year be a white one, you will have bad luck.

In Ireland, seeing a butterfly nearby a corpse was an omen for eternal well-being for the deceased. In Scotland, too, it is considered fortunate indeed for a golden butterfly to be seen near a dying person.

To see three butterflies together is as lucky as seeing three magpies, says a Nottinghamshire superstition.

Pink butterflies are said to promise lifelong happiness.

If on a given day the first butterfly you see is yellow, this foretold an illness; should it be white, good luck. To see three butterflies together on a flower was said to bring misfortune.

Among the Blackfoot Indians, there is a belief that dreams are brought to us by butterflies. Hence, a mother would often embroider the sign of a butterfly on a piece of buckskin, which she would tie to her baby's head when she wished him to sleep. The Zunis of New Mexico believe that, when white butterflies are seen, warm weather may be expected. Should they fly from the southwest, however, rain is on the way.

In parts of the United States, a butterfly in the house is a sign of a wedding to be. In Maryland, should a white butterfly come into the house and fly around you, it is said you will die. In Louisiana, however, such is taken as an omen of good luck.

Some country folk believe that, if a butterfly flies in one's face, it indicates cold weather. Others say a yellow butterfly will bring weather that will turn leaves yellow in a single week.

Button: Should a button or hook be placed into a wrong hole when dressing, a widespread belief is that misfortune will occur during the day. Disaster can be warded off, however, by taking off the garment and starting over again.

Should a young girl wish to know her future husband's profession, she can count the buttons on her blouse from the top to bottom saying, "Doctor, lawyer, businessman, statesman, rich man, poor man, beggar man, thief." Through repetition (or by buying blouses with only six buttons), one can divine the future.

Should one find a button, it is said that a new friend will soon appear. Tradition also has it that one should only button an odd number of buttons. Hence, if you have only one button it can always be done. Should you have two buttons, however, only the top one should be closed or the garment should be worn open. Should the garment have three buttons, all three must be closed or only the middle one. (The fact is that, until the thirteenth century, when buttonholes were invented, buttons were worn strictly as ornaments and not for their function.)

When given as a gift, buttons are said to bring good luck.

If someone believes his illness is caused by an evil spell, he should leave a black button where another person can find it, thereby passing on the illness.

CABBAGE: If found growing double (two shoots from a single root), it is said to be an omen of good luck.

CAESAREAN SECTION: According to a Cornwall tradition, a child delivered by Caesarean section has unusual strength, the ability to see spirits, and may discover hidden treasure.

CAKE: Should one cut the first cake from the oven, the rest will be heavy, according to a Durham tradition. The answer? Break the cake; do not cut it.

Among Southern blacks, a cake was awarded to the person who had the most erect walk. The expression "cake walk," a high prance that came into vogue around 1910 had its origins in this practice.

CALF: Here we find a great many traditions, especially from Great Britain. For example, to secure luck for the rest of one's herd of cattle, an Isle of Man tradition held that a calf should be burned. In order to stop the murrain, a common cattle disease, some believed that a calf should be killed. Generally speaking, it was advised that a sacrificial calf be burned alive in the belief that a live calf appeased the wrath of God, which had been the cause of the illness of the herd in the first place. In Durham, a less dramatic belief held that a leg and a thigh of a calf that had died should be hung in the chimney of the farmhouse by a rope in order to stop disease among the herd.

In some parts of England, it was thought unlucky for a cow to have twins. Should either twin have a white streak on its back, it was considered a double misfortune. Likewise, it was held unlucky to step over a calf when it was lying on the ground.

In Wales, calves weaned with the waning moon are said to never grow fat. The tip of a calf's tongue carried in one's pocket will protect one from danger and the pocket will never be without money.

A Worcestershire belief holds that a Christmas mistletoe bough must be given to the cow who is first to calf in the New Year, or else bad luck will attend the rest of the herd.

CAMPHOR: A common belief is that carrying camphor on one's person will ward off any infections. Furthermore, should unmarried maidens carry camphor on themselves, it will preserve their chastity. This is no doubt due to the Greek story of Daphne, who kept her virginity by turning herself into a laurel tree.

In Malaya, those hunting camphor speak a special language and make offerings to the camphor spirit.

CANCER: A common belief is that cancer is caused by sorcery and, therefore, must be exorcised. The disease was personalized in the form of a crab or worm, which each day claimed its food. The crabs or tumors then had to be fed in order to keep the patient from growing weak. Some traditions held that at regular intervals raw meat should be placed by the ill person's bed or on the sore itself. A toad that has been soaked in olive oil or a black hen cut in two, while still alive, was said to work equally well.

A rural eighteenth-century belief was that toads have the power to suck out the cancer poison from the system. According to a Scandinavian tradition, in order to be cured, a sick person must swallow a frog or small toad. In Mediterranean countries, a raw lizard is said to do the same thing.

A spider passing in front of a sleeping person's face is said to bring cancer.

In Brittany, when a person died of this illness, a pat of butter was placed by the corpse. It would be thrown out after the burial, in the belief that it had assumed those evil forces that could attack other family members.

CANDLE: Since time immemorial, candles have been used for various sacred rites as well as for divination.

In Catholic countries, candles are brought to church in honor of one's favorite saint or of the Madonna. For example, candles offered to Saint Blase on the third of February, specifically, were claimed to cure toothaches and diseased cattle. In the case of

OMENS, SIGNS & SUPERSTITIONS

serious illness, candles will be lit in honor of all the healing saints. The candle that goes out first will designate the saint to be called upon. Many saints are said to have their own peculiar preference as to the color of their particular candle.

Tradition holds that three candles should be lit, one after another, and put by a sick person's bedside. If the third candle goes out first, the person will expire. Should it be the second, the illness will be long. Should it be the first, a quick recovery is portended. This method can also be used for knowing the future of one's projects.

Should a candle refuse to light, rain is on the way. Should a flame flutter, bad weather is predicted. Should it burn blue, expect a death in the family. Windy weather is expected when the flame gutters and sways.

Should wax running down from a candle spread out into folds that form a "winding sheet," it is an omen of death for the person sitting opposite the candle or for someone else in the family. Should the wick spark, such foretells the arrival of strangers; the direction in which it leans tells the direction from which the strangers shall come.

A bright spark in a candle indicates that the person sitting opposite will soon receive a letter.

Among French and Germans, it is believed that a candle can test virginity; one who is "pure" can make a wick burn that is sputtering and dying.

To kill a moth that is hovering above a candle is said to bring good luck. However, should the wax of a candle form a loop resembling a handle (called a "coffin handle"), this portends illness.

Should a candle be snuffed out accidentally, a wedding is on the way.

A blessed candle from a Candlemas service can be used for conjuring, especially storms.

Candles should be lit at the birth of a child in order to keep evil spirits away. Likewise, they should be lit at death, so that demons will not seize the soul of the dying.

A birthday cake should have as many candles on it as there are years in the person's age. Often, one additional candle is added "to grow on."

Following are some traditional rules about candles: Never light a candle from another candle. Never light a candle from the fire in the hearth or you will certainly die poor. Never allow candles to sputter out; rather, blow them out or snuff them out with your fingers, otherwise misfortune is predicted. Never light three candles with a single match; nor should you allow three candles to burn together in the same room.

In northern England, candles are used as a love charm. One sticks two pins through a candle in the belief that, by the time it burns down to the pins, the sought-after lover will arrive. While inserting the pins, the young maiden recites the following, "It's not the candle alone I stick but [the "name" of the man's (or woman's)] heart I mean to prick; whether he (she) be asleep or awake, I'll have him (her) come to me and speak."

In Brittany and Alsace, during wedding ceremonies, candles are lit in front of the bride and the bridegroom. Whichever candle goes out first indicates which of the two will die first.

In the sixteenth and seventeenth centuries, it was believed that, if a thief had a candle made from the fat of an evildoer who had died on the gallows, or from the fat of a newborn or unborn child, it would protect him from being arrested. This candle, if placed in the dismembered hand of a man who had been hanged, was called the "hand of glory." When lit, it would render motionless anyone in the house, thus allowing the robbery to take place.

In Ireland, twelve candles are placed in a circle around a dead body as protection against evil.

In medieval Europe, a Jewish tradition required one to put a lit candle in a spot that had no draft during the ten days before Yom Kippur, the Day of Atonement. This was believed to be the time during which each man's fate for the coming year was settled in Heaven. Should the candle go out, the person it represented would not live till the next Day of Atonement. Should it burn down to the end, he could expect another year of life. In another Jewish tradition, during the Festival of Lights (Hanukkah), a candle is to be lit on the first evening, two on the second, and so on throughout the eight days of the festival.

A quartz candle, or fetch candle, is a mysterious light that hovers in the air and moves away from you if you follow it. It is considered to be an omen of death. This name was given to flames seen in a marshy ground or churchyard, or over a grave. In parts of Britain these were known as "will-o-the-wisps."

CANDLEMAS: The Christian Festival of Candlemas on the second of February commemorates the purification of the Virgin Mother that took place when she took the infant Jesus to the temple and was told he would grow up to be the light of the world. By the fifth century, candles were associated with this holiday and a procession with lighted candles became part of the Roman Catholic ritual.

The origin of the holiday may be traced back to Roman times. It was associated with Mars, the God of War. Mars's mother was called Februa, after which the month of February was named. Traditionally, Romans carried torches and candles around the city in worship of Februa in the hope of gaining help from her son, Mars. Seeing that many Christian converts still celebrated this festival, Pope Sergius transformed it into worship of God and the Virgin Mother.

This date also marks one of four witches' Sabbaths. The other three are held on April 30, Roodmas; August 1, Lammas; and October 31, Halloween. Coming as it does after the beginning of the New Year, Candlemas stands between the old and the new season. Medieval calendars, based on the seasons, had spring beginning on Candlemas, rather than on March 21, the vernal equinox.

In the Alsace region candles from this day are saved and used to ward off evil spirits, should a grave illness or a storm arise. In France, if one can keep a candle from this festival lit in his home, it is believed that he will not die during the year. This holy candle from Candlemas will protect a home and its inhabitants.

In Scotland, there is a saying that if the weather on Candlemas Day is fair and clear, there will be foul winters ahead. Likewise, in East Norfolk, should the sun shine on Candlemas, bad times are ahead.

If Christmas decorations have not been removed from the church before Candlemas Day, a death will occur, during the year, to the family occupying a pew where a leaf or berry was left behind.

In Cornwall, at the manor house of Godolphin, there exists an unusual custom. The steward of the manor of Lamburne comes on Candlemas Day to collect a rent and there is a time-honored ceremony. In the presence of neighbors and sightseers, he knocks three times upon the open door and says,

I come to demand my Lord's just dues—eight groats and a penny, a loaf, a cheese, a collar of brawn, and a jack of the best beer in the house. God save the King and the Lord of the Manor.

After this ceremony, the steward and guests are entertained by breakfast.

Originally, Candlemas preceded Lent, to which the celebration of Mardi Gras has been ascribed. The French tradition of eating crepes, therefore, now corresponds to the end of the festivities that precede fasting. On Candlemas Day, should a crepe be flipped onto the top of a buffet, it is said that the year will be a happy one. Should crepes be eaten after 8:00 P.M., however, bad luck is predicted. To ensure wealth, one should either hold the pan handle and a piece of silver or gold in the same hand, or toss seven crepes in a row up into the air. Also, should a crepe be rubbed on one's face before eating it, he will not be stung by a wasp for the entire year. If the crepes are given to the hens, it is said their production of eggs will increase for the year.

In the Yonne region of France, crosses of twigs are planted in the fields on this day to ensure a good harvest. Bears are said to come out of their dens on Candlemas Day to test the weather. Should the weather be freezing or snowy, they will remain outside and wait for good weather to arrive. Should the weather be fair, they will go into their dens, knowing the sun will not last. Wolves also come out of their lairs on Candlemas Day. If they go back in, winter will last another forty days.

Should a lark ascend singing on Candlemas Day, it will take six weeks for it to return with the spring. Hence, winter dies or comes alive on Candlemas. (In the United States, Groundhog Day corresponds to Candlemas. If the groundhog sees its shadow, which means that the sun is out, there will be six more weeks of winter. If there is no shadow, spring is on its way.)

CANE: Before caning was banned in English schools as a form of corporal punishment, many students believed that a strand of horsehair picked from a living horse and stretched across the palm of the hand would cause the caning master's cane to split and fall apart.

CARROT: Eating carrots in large quantities at every meal is said to be a cure for asthma. Similarly, during World War II many British airmen ate a diet of raw carrots, thinking that it would enable them to see in the dark. (No doubt due to the large quantity of Vitamin A they contain.)

CAT: Although most traditions regarding black cats have already been discussed (see **black cat**), cats in general have their own mystique.

Cats were objects of worship in Egypt about 3000 B.C. The Egyptians worshipped the cat-headed goddess, Bast. Bast was said to protect pregnant women and to enjoy music, dancing, and the good life. Should a cat be killed, even accidentally, such was considered a capital offense in Egypt. Similarly, should a household cat die, members of the family had to shave their eyebrows and mourn.

In Burma and Siam, the belief existed that, when a holy man died, his spirit entered a cat. When the cat died, it was said that his spirit had gone to Heaven.

The prophet Mohammed is said to have rewarded a cat for its respect by stroking it three times on its back, thereby granting the cat its ability to land on its feet.

The following represent some common beliefs about cats: Illness in a family can be cured by washing the patient and throwing the water over a cat. When the cat is driven out-of-doors, it will take the illness with it. A sailor's superstition holds that, should a cat be frolicsome on board a ship, such presages wind, gales, and rain; should a cat be thrown overboard, a storm will arise at sea. Yet another seamen's practice was to place a cat under a pot on the deck should a ship need wind to rise.

It is generally thought unlucky to let a cat die in one's house. Should a cat sneeze, rain is on the way. Should a cat sneeze three times, colds will run through the family. Should a cat scratch the leg of a table, a change in the weather is predicted. A cat sitting with its back to the fire is a sign that a storm is on its way, and a great deal of rain is predicted when a cat washes her face over her ears.

A cat in the presence of a bride indicates good luck for her in matrimonial affairs, but should a cat pass over a coffin, it indicates disaster, unless the cat is caught and killed.

Cats that are purchased are said to be useless for catching mice.

In Devon and Wilshire it is believed that cats born in the month of May never catch rats or mice, but rather snakes and glowworms.

Never drown cats for this tempts Satan to take your soul. Never kick a cat or you will get rheumatism.

In New England, tradition holds that one can tell time and the tides by looking into the pupils of a cat's eyes. Should a cat meow on board a ship, a dangerous voyage is portended according to a Welsh tradition. In Wisconsin, if a cat washed itself while seated in a doorway, it was believed that a clergyman would soon visit the house. In Ireland, it is considered bad luck to take a cat when one moves from one house to another.

Some West Africans believe that the human soul passes into the body of a cat at death. An Italian legend told of a cat that gave birth to kittens beneath the manger in which Christ was born.

In some parts of Europe, a cat was often personified with the spirit of the harvest of corn. At Briancon, France, for instance, a cat is ceremonially dressed in ribbons, flowers, and corn ears, and in Amiens, a cat was ritually killed when the last sheaves of corn were cut.

On Shrove Tuesday and on Easter, in some European communities, cats were roasted alive in the belief that this would drive away evil spirits. One tradition held that sacrificing a cat would protect a building against fire.

The belief that cats are able to see in the dark is widespread. Likewise, common is the belief that a cat has nine lives. Popular, too, is the myth that cats should never be left alone in a house with a baby; some country folk believe it will jump up on the infant and suck out his breath.

Legend has it that drawing the tail of a cat downwards over one's eye will cure a sty. Likewise, the "tail cure" was said to be effective in the treatment of warts, whitlows, and general itching. Toothaches could be relieved by applying properly dried cat skin to one's face. At one time, a whole cat boiled in olive oil was thought to make an excellent dressing for wounds.

CATERPILLAR: In East Yorkshire there is a superstition that, if you find a hairy caterpillar, you should throw it over your left shoulder for good luck. Should you wish to attract a caterpillar, walk around his garden three times and say, "Caterpillars and baby caterpillars,

I am going, follow me." Also in England, there is a belief that carrying a caterpillar about with you will ward off fevers.

Caterpillars were believed to die if it rained during the singing of the Corpus Christi Mass. Another alleged cause of concern for caterpillars: women menstruating.

American folklore holds that caterpillars were made with the Devil's help; those of German descent believed that they are the Devil's cats.

A species of caterpillars called "woolly bears" (which are black at both ends with a reddish brown midband) are said to predict the severity of the winter, according to American folklore. Should the width of the center strip widen, a severe winter is expected. Among those living in the Ozark Mountains, there is a tradition that these particular caterpillars can grow so large that their fur can be stretched on walls or tanned for lap robes!

CAUL: A caul is a part of the amnion, or thin membrane that covers the head of some newly born children. If a child is born with a caul, it is said to be an omen of good fortune and carries with it powerful magic. Children born with a caul were believed to receive second sight in later life.

According to one tradition, a caul must be of reddish color to bring good fortune. Should it be black, it is an omen of ill fortune.

Cauls were often kept locked up in a box by their owner and used regularly for divination. Should the caul shrivel up, danger was threatened. Should sickness be foretold, it was said to become damp. When good fortune was near, the caul laid itself out smoothly. When others at a distance were talking about its owner, it was said to rustle in its paper.

Should one acquire a caul by purchase, he will be fortunate and will escape dangers. No one possessing a caul could ever drown. Should a lawyer purchase a caul, he was believed to acquire eloquence.

An ancient tradition held that, should the rice stalks turn black or the ears refuse to set, a man should take a caul in its preserving box and run around the field, thereby casting a fortunate influence over the harvest.

Still another belief held that the caul should be buried with the person who was born with it or, after death, his spirit will walk searching for it. In the "Horn Castle" area, the caul is referred to as "a silly hood."

CHAIN LETTER: Supposedly, the earliest chain letters arose during the Middle Ages. Often sold by fortune tellers, they carried details of simple cures and prayers. In modern times, however, these have become "begging" letters that contain instructions to send money to the names listed, with further instructions to copy the letter and send it to a dozen or more persons, who will, in turn, send you money. Like multiple-level marketing schemes, there is little likelihood that anyone following these instructions will obtain good fortune. To ensure that you do follow the instructions, however, letters often contain the suggestion that, should you break the chain, bad fortune will follow.

CHAIR: Like other household effects, chairs have taken on special meaning for those who are generally superstitious.

It is said that tipping over a chair will bring misfortune. Should this happen, you must cross yourself at least five times. The following are some general superstitions about chairs: Should a chair be spun around, the owner will soon have a disagreement with relatives or be brought to trial. Always place as many chairs around a table as there will be guests. Should you forget one, it is an omen of approaching death. When one leaves the house of another and places his chair back against the wall, tradition holds that he will never return to that house. Should three chairs be placed side by side in a row, a death in the family will occur. Should you inadvertently tip over a chair in getting up from a meal, it is a sign that you are a liar.

Before sitting down to play cards, gamblers spit under their chairs, or else walk around them three times, in order to attract good luck. Should chairs be knocked over in a hospital by a nurse, she can expect a new patient in the ward, and should the cushion on a praying stool be turned over when you sit down, you will have twenty bad Sundays.

CHEEK: The nature of a person's cheeks can indicate his disposition, according to many popular beliefs. Plump cheeks, for instance, indicate sensual appetites; gaunt cheeks, a reserved and rigid temperament. Jowls indicate mediocre intelligence; full, round cheeks, a wise person full of spirit. Hollow cheeks indicate meanness and jealousy, while men with prominent cheekbones are said to be sensitive and gentle.

Wrinkles on the cheeks indicate insanity. Generally, dimples are considered lucky, although some hold that they are fingerprints of angels or of God himself. Others believe that dimples are the heel mark of the Devil's shoe.

Should your cheeks feel as though they are burning, someone is talking about you.

CHERRY: A Kent superstition holds that, should you visit a cherry orchard and not have your shoes rubbed with the leaves of a cherry tree, you will die from cherrystone suffocation!

Young maidens are supposedly able to predict when they will marry by counting the cherrystones in their plate after a meal, while, at the same time reciting, "This year, next year, sometime, never." The last stone counted is said to give the answer.

In Switzerland, tradition holds that a cherry tree will bear fruit abundantly if its first fruit is eaten by a woman who has recently given birth.

Should one shoot a cherry pit from between his thumb and index finger and, on the first try, it hits the ceiling of the room in which the cherries were eaten, he will be married soon.

Should one desire a vineyard to produce good wine, a cherry tree must be planted in the middle of it.

CHESTNUT: The horse chestnut is believed to have magical powers to cure backaches, rheumatism, and arthritis. It is considered lucky, therefore, to carry one or two chestnuts in your pocket, which will guard against rheumatism and circulatory problems. Also, if boiled together with honey and glycerine, chestnuts are alleged to cure asthma.

At funerals, chestnuts should be left behind as offerings for the deceased and on Halloween, chestnuts are left on the table for those souls of the dead who roam about on that night.

The fruit of the chestnut tree is said to serve as food for the poor.

CHICKEN: In ancient times, chickens were used for divination. The most favorable sign was when the birds ate gluttonously and food fell from their beaks. Over time, a great many beliefs have evolved.

In the British Isles, if you set a hen on an even number of eggs, no chickens will hatch. Should all the eggs of one laying turn out to be cockerels, good luck will come to the owner and his family.

In Upper Burma, chicken bones are used to determine which tree in the village shall be felled for the maypole and to decide which of the days in May is the luckiest for the celebration to take place.

In Devonshire, should one be bitten by a snake, a chicken would be killed and the wounded part immediately thrust into the stomach of the bird. When the flesh of the chicken assumed a dark color, the cure was alleged to be complete.

In the Midlands, there is a belief that chickens will roost at midday, rather than their usual time, right before the death of the farmer.

Eggs laid on Good Friday should be preserved intact to ensure the strength and fertility of all the hens, and should a cock crow outside the back door, the woman of the house will soon receive a stranger.

CHICORY: Carry this plant and you will become invisible. Other traditions hold that chicory has the power to open locks or remove obstacles.

CHILBLAINS: Over the years, a variety of measures were believed to be cures for chilblains. Following is a sampling: To protect yourself and your family against chilblains and chapping, place a half-eaten Christmas cake under the bed. You can also prevent chilblains by melting the first snow and passing it over ears or hands. Strawberry juice and human urine are said to do the same thing. Shoes and gloves of wolf skin also offer excellent protection.

If you keep feet or legs crossed while thrashing the chilblains with holly, the chilblains will disappear. Placing the Yule log on the fire for a short time each day, from Christmas until Twelfth Night, and then keeping it under the bed was said to protect the entire household from chilblains for a year. (Damage from thunder and fire and other maladies was also believed assuaged by this practice.)

If on the morning of May 1, you place your hands in manure, then beat them three times in a row using a lid to a bread box, chapping will be prevented. On other dates, walk around a mare three times, while holding your shirt between your teeth.

To mitigate the pain, place walnut oil on chilblains and then lick it off, holding it in your mouth for a while. Lighting a candle and dripping wax on the affected area is said to work miracles, too. If possible, soaking the area in water into which slaughtered pigs have been dipped is also recommended. Shoemaker's wax base, turnip pulp, hot ashes, or carpenter's glue are also said to work as ointments. A mixture of soot and vinegar was believed especially effective.

CHIMNEY: As fireplaces and their accompanying chimneys were once the only means of heating one's home, a number of superstitions surround their use. The hearth is said to be a magical place with its own powers, since, once fire is lit there, smoke connects earth and sky. Chimneys must, therefore, be protected, since evil forces can enter the house by this means.

During births or deaths, salt or holy water were thrown into the fire and the sign of the cross made again. Brooms and fire tongs were always placed to the right of the hearth and turned upside down on special occasions to ward off witches. A fireplace was never to be spit into nor pointed at with a finger. A stranger would never be allowed to poke one's fire. Logs to be burned would be spit on and placed into the fireplace, small end first.

Chimneys were never to be used for the very first time on a Friday, the day of Christ's death and of the witches' sabbath, or on the feast day of Joan of Arc or Saint Lawrence. Before lighting a fire, Solomon's seal or three signs of the cross in the air would be made. Three grains of salt would also be thrown into the fireplace. Once lit, should the fire on the hearth go out, it was certain to bring about ill luck, according to Highlands and Gaelic traditions.

Some additional beliefs about chimneys: Should one hold a log by the small end, seven years of poverty will be forthcoming. One should never repair damaged bellows, or the master of the house will die from suffocation. Should a snake or clump of soot fall into the house from the chimney, such presages bad fortune. Should a fire roar up a chimney, there will be a disagreement in the house.

Because of the sacredness of the chimney itself, chimney sweeps were said to bring good luck to any bride one met coming from church. To ensure her fortune, however, the bride must kiss his grimey face! Should a gambler meet a sweep while on his way to place a bet, his success is assured.

Tradition holds that a sweep once saved the life of an English king who, to show his gratitude, bowed low to his rescuer. Because of his grimey face, his countenance could not be recognized. Since then, all sweeps are considered lucky and held in great respect.

Still another tradition holds that, should soot fall from the chimney while the wedding feast is in progress, ill luck will surround the couple.

CHINA ORNAMENT: Small ornaments, especially those of animals, should always face into a room and never toward the door; otherwise, the luck of the owner will run out of the house.

CHOLERA: Tradition holds that cholera can be detected by throwing a piece of raw meat up into the air. If the disease is present, the meat will turn black.

In Australia, those affected with cholera were advised to go and sleep in the churchyard.

CHOPSTICK: To break one's chopsticks while dining is said to be a bad omen.

CHRISTMAS CARD: Sending Christmas cards is a relatively modern practice that began in 1843. The very first card, designed in London by J. C. Horsley, depicts a party of grown-ups and children with glasses of wine raised in greeting, over the words, "A Merry Christmas and a Happy New Year to You." It is dated December 23, 1843, and was said to still be extant in 1947.

CHRISTMAS DAY: In the north country of England superstitions hold that the first to enter a house on Christmas morning should be a dark-haired man. A Yorkshire belief is that it is unlucky for anyone to leave the house until the threshold has been consecrated by the entrance of a male. Should a female be the first to enter on Christmas Day, such would presage disaster.

The tradition of a man being the first to enter was called "first-footing." In Yorkshire, the first-footer was designated as the "lucky bird." The first-footer, however, must never be a redhead, because this color hair was associated with Judas Iscariot. Often the first-footer's entrance into the house was accompanied by a sprig of evergreen. Tradition had it that he should enter at the front door, go out the back, and be given sixpence for his "footing." After his departure, all members of the household, including any guests, went out of the house unwashed (even their hands). Together they carried a sprig of evergreen or a bough and brought it into the living room.

In other traditions the "lucky bird" was given bread, salt, and a groat (a British silver four-pence piece).

Some families, wishing to make certain that no ill luck befell them (meaning no female, by chance, would visit first) arranged with a dark man to visit their house immediately after midnight. Female servants and other household help had to sleep in the house on Christmas Eve so that they would still be available for morning chores.

Yet another Christmas Day superstition required choirboys to carry large baskets of apples, each adorned with a sprig of rosemary, and present them to members of the congregation in exchange for small sums of money.

Yet another tradition is that of wassailing the apple trees. Parishioners walked in procession, visiting the principal orchards in the parish. They would single out one tree, over which cider was thrown and the wassail chanted. In some places cakes soaked in cider were placed in the oxforks of the principal trees.

The wassail bowl was said to hold as much as two gallons and was made of beechwood. In time, the wassail bowl gave rise to the wassail cup, and, later, a box containing two wax dolls representing the Virgin Mary and the Baby Jesus. This was covered with a white cloth, which was removed at the request of anyone desiring to see the wassail. Should anyone send away a wassailer without a donation the worst possible luck would come to the household.

CHRISTMAS DECORATIONS: Of all Christmas decorations, the use of the mistletoe (a plant parasite well known to the ancient Greeks and Romans) is perhaps the best known. (See **mistletoe**.)

Mistletoe was held in high esteem by the Druids and used in their incantations. Usually hung from chandeliers, the tradition arose that a girl standing under mistletoe could be kissed by any man who found her there. Should she refuse the kiss, she was said to court bad luck. Should she be kissed seven times in one day, it was said that she would marry one of the seven lucky fellows within a year.

In Wales and Scotland, it was thought bad luck to hang mistletoe in the house before Christmas Eve.

Another tradition holds that all evergreen decorations should be taken down on the old Christmas Day (January 6) or else bad luck will follow. These same greens must never be burned, but, rather, carefully thrown away. Should they be thrown out of doors, it was said that a death would occur in the house before next Christmas. A Shropshire tradition required that they be burned on Candlemas Eve.

Taking holly into the house before Christmas Eve was said to invite bad luck. Both holly and ivy should never be burned. Rather, they should be kept until next year to protect the house from lightning.

CHRISTMAS EVE: Up until the year 340, at which time Pope Julius I fixed the date of Christmas as December 25, various dates for the celebration of Christ's birth were already in practice. For some, it was the sixth of January, for others March 29 and for others December 25.

Festivals corresponding to Christmas were held in Rome in honor of Bacchus. The Yule Feast of the Norsemen and the Roman Saturnalia generally extended from the thirtieth of November to February 2. A characteristic of the Saturnalia was that gifts were made by the wealthy and distributed to the poor in honor of the god Saturn. During this time, slaves were allowed to change places with their masters, and even elected one of their own as a mock king who ruled throughout the festival.

When in A.D. 597 Pope Gregory ordered Saint Augustine to convert Saxon England to Christianity, he was told to accommodate as many of the heathen ceremonies and festivals as possible.

Both pagan and Christian celebrations existed side by side on the continent for many centuries. Even the Reformation, at first, had little effect upon changing the pagan content of the holiday. When the Puritans came to power in 1644, they sought to do away with many of the old heathen traditions and beliefs that accompanied this night. Some of these are as follows: It was unlucky to give out fire or light from a house on Christmas Eve. Rosemary would burst into flower at midnight on Christmas Eve. Fairies would meet at the bottom of mines and perform a mass in celebration of Christ's birth. Should a girl wish to see an image of her future husband, she need only walk backwards to a pear tree, walk around the tree three times, and she would see his image. All the doors should be open to let out evil spirits when the clock struck midnight.

Straw or hay bands would be tied around fruit trees on this night. This would cause them to yield plentifully during the next year.

Should a maiden go to the hen house and tap sharply, she could determine if she would wed before the end of the year. If a hen cackled, she would not wed; if a cock crowed, she would. Should the same maiden go into the garden at midnight and pluck twelve sage leaves, she would see the shadowy form of her husband-to-be.

Becoming engaged on Christmas Eve was a sure sign of a happy married life to come.

Other marriage divinations connected with this evening are as follows: Each unmarried member of the family would select one of the bands around the fagot of the Yule log as her own. The first one burned through would indicate the first to be wed.

Burning the Yule log, a practice linked to ancient tree worship was a common tradition. A log for each inhabitant of the house was placed in the hearth. The fire was never allowed to go out and had to be tended only with one's fingers. Should this fire yield a number of sparks, it was believed that the harvest would be plentiful the following summer. Should headless shadows be projected on the walls, it was believed that some members of the family would die during the year. The ashes of the burned yule were saved as protection against storms, for curing illnesses, and for fertilization. Should one inadvertently sit on a log reserved for Christmas Eve, it was believed that person would get boils.

An Oxfordshire superstition held that a maiden should make a dough cake in silence and, after pricking her initials on the dough, place it on the hearth. At midnight, her future husband, or his spirit, would come in and prick his initials beside hers.

Yet another tradition held that, at midnight, the cattle and other animals kneeled and acquired the gift of human speech in order to converse with one another. It is also said that a hole dug in the cemetery at midnight would yield gold.

Should one leave the church during the consecration at midnight mass, it was said that the procession of the dead souls could be seen moving through town. Should one fast on Christmas Eve, enter the church backward, and take holy water with his left hand, he would learn all those who would die within the year.

CHRISTMAS PUDDING: Stirring the Christmas pudding while it was being made was considered lucky for all those participating. It was required that the pudding be stirred sunwise, that is east to west, in honor of the Sun God, whose birth was celebrated by pagans on December 25. Into the pudding one placed a silver coin (said to bring fortune to the finder), a ring (to bring a wedding), and a thimble (to bring a life of single blessedness).

CHRISTMAS STOCKING: According to tradition, Saint Nicholas heard that three lovely sisters were so destitute that they could continue living only if they pursued a life of shame. Through a smoke hole in the roof, he tossed three pieces of gold, which fell into the stockings that were hung over the fire to dry. The tradition of hanging Christmas stockings on the chimney or over the hearth evolved from this.

CHRISTMAS TRADITIONS: The giving of gifts no doubt started with the gifts of the Magi, although, as already noted (see **Christmas Eve**), the Roman holiday Saturnalia also included this tradition.

Santa Claus was introduced by Thomas Nast in a series of Christmas cartoons that ran in *Harpers Weekly* from 1863 to 1866. Nast's character was based on Saint Nicholas, traced to Asia Minor from approximately 350 A.D. Saint Nicholas Day was celebrated on December 6 with the exchange of gifts. In time, the Saint Nicholas character combined with Kris Kringle, a nineteenth-century German creation.

The singing of Christmas carols began during the 1800s. The word *carol* itself is an old English one meaning "to sing joyously."

The use of poinsettia plants was introduced by Dr. Joel Poinsett, an American minister living in Mexico, who brought back the plant in 1828. According to tradition, a little Mexican boy, who was too poor to put a gift in the poor box on Christmas Eve, prayed outside his church. Where he knelt, a beautiful plant bloomed. The child gave this plant to the statue of the Christ Child. In Mexico, the poinsettia is known as "flor de la noche buene" or "flower of the holy night."

CHRISTMAS TREE: Various accounts explain the evolution of the Christmas tree. Some authorities hold that the most likely beginning for this Christmas tradition was the Egyptian practice of using a palm tree, known to send forth a shoot every month at the time of the winter solstice (December 25), as a symbol of the year completed.

Some say it is a survivor of Norse mythology and was first made popular in Scandinavian countries when they adopted Christianity. It supposedly symbolizes the evergreen and abiding power of salvation.

Others trace the tree custom back to Saint Boniface, a missionary working among the German Druids from A.D. 675–755, who found a little evergreen tree hidden behind an oak that was being cut down. Actually, it was the Druids in Britain who were accustomed to decorating at Christmastime with all kinds of green plants, including the evergreen. Evergreen leaves and boughs were believed to bring cheer and luck.

Other traditions hold that Martin Luther used an evergreen tree to illustrate the wonder of the winter night sky to his wife and children. Supposedly, he put candles on the tree to indicate the stars.

In actuality, the fir or pine tree has long been held as a symbol of immortality and fertility. The Romans believed that unopened pine cones represented virginity. Hence, virgins would wear pine garlands at various ceremonies.

In an ancient German ritual, girls danced around a fir tree in the belief that an imprisoned imp held in the tree would give them whatever they wished for. This imp was later associated with Saint Nicholas or Santa Claus. As the tree was often decorated with eggs and other objects, it seems that this fertility ritual might very well have been the origin of our modern Christmas tree.

The first actual "Christmas tree" was erected in England, at Windsor Castle, by Queen Victoria and Prince Albert in 1844.

CHURCH: Throughout history, the church has been the center for all Christian activities, including baptism, wedding, and burial. It is no wonder that a great many superstitions surround it.

The building itself is said to be most blessed if constructed in the form of a cross. Should you be the one to pull the first stone out of an old church, even if it is for the purpose of constructing a new one, a Scottish tradition says you will come to a violent end. Also, should a church door rattle without any reason, it is a sign that it will shortly admit a coffin.

Some beliefs surrounding the church are as follows: A bird perching on a weather vane of a church is said to indicate that a death will occur in the parish within a week. It is also believed that metal rooster weather vanes, often placed on the steeples of churches, will come alive and crow on Judgment Day.

Should you turn a hassock over in a pew, even though it may already be upside down, it is said that you will have a sequence of twenty unlucky Sundays.

Among the Anglo-Saxons there is the belief that one can see all those who will die entering the church on Halloween. Likewise, whoever watches from the porch of a church at midnight on Saint Mark's Eve will see the shadows of those who are to die within the next twelve months.

If you bring church dust to the bedside of a dying person, you can shorten and ease the pain of passing.

Should a robin fly into a church and begin to sing, a death would occur among the parishioners. However, if any other bird flies into the church, especially during the service, good luck will come to all those in attendance.

Widespread is the belief that the first living thing to enter a newly constructed church becomes the property of Satan. Hence, there is a German tradition of driving a dog into the church, so that it would be first. Likewise, the first child to be christened in a new church was said to be claimed by the Devil and, hence, certain to die.

Another practice (of unknown origin) is that of the entire congregation cracking nuts in their pews on Michaelmas Eve (September 28).

In Scotland, there is a belief that if one sits on a three-legged stool at three crossroads on Halloween night, while the church clock is striking midnight, the names of those parishers who will die during the year will be called out one by one. The brave soul could save each parisher's life by throwing away an item of wearing apparel, one by one.

CIDER: In Devon and Hereford, the tradition exists that cider should be made only when the moon is on the wane. Otherwise the apples will "shrump-up" when gathered and the cider turn sour.

CIGARETTE: In Britain, there is a general superstition that dates back to the Boer War and was carried over to the Americas regarding cigarettes. Namely, one should never light three cigarettes from a single match. One explanation of this is that the Kruger's men were perfect snipers and could "ready, aim, fire" after seeing the lighted match in the same position. During the Crimean War, however, Russian prisoners followed this same tradition, citing a ruling by the Russian Orthodox Church that allowed only a priest to light three candles on an altar with a single taper.

For those who suffer from insomnia, smoking a cigarette made from the bones of a toad was said to guarantee twenty-four hours of rest.

Tobacco itself was often placed in the foundation of a house to appease the gods. It was also said to ward off snakes and to keep a baby's cradle from evil.

CIGAR: According to one authority, girls in Salem, Massachusetts, believed that accidentally stepping on a cigar end would result in their marrying the first man they met.

Another tradition holds that a young woman who takes the last puff of a cigar will marry the first man she meets immediately afterward.

CINDER: Cinders shooting out of a fire were said to be of two kinds, and each indicated something different: An oblong one, called a "coffin," meant a death in the family; an oval one, called a "cradle," announced an upcoming baby's birth. Should either cinder give a clinking noise as it shot out, however, good fortune would follow.

CIRCLE: A circle is said to be a symbol "of all things"; it can be imagined as a line drawn around everything. At the same time, it is a symbol of "one thing," because it is a single figure. Hence, one may say that a circle is symbolic of "all as one."

For the alchemist, a circle formed by a snake or a dragon swallowing its own tail (called the "ourobouros") was often followed by a recitation of the Greek phrase *en to pan*, "all is one."

Throughout time, priests, sorcerers, witches, and magicians have sought to contain magical power within or outside of a circle. Thus, there is the tradition among Moslems that, once in their lifetime, they must walk around the *kaaba*, a cube inscribed in a circle; and there is a tradition that one must go around a Saint John's fire three times, and cross oneself, in order to be protected from headaches and kidney ailments for one year.

Since a circle with a single dot in its center is said to be symbolic of the sun, and is so used by astrologers, it was believed that evil forces could not enter such a circle.

One authority even suggests that the habit of using lipstick might very well come from sun worship. The mouth is an entrance to the body; a red circle drawn around it would keep the soul within and the Devil without.

Mention must be made as well of the traditions of kings wearing crowns and the wearing of rings on fingers. Crowns and rings are, in essence, circles. Certainly, the tradition of wedding bands is one not likely to be forgotten. Likewise, the Christian use of the consecrated wafer, itself round and white, which replaced bread as the representation of Christ's body, somehow links together the old and the new.

The tradition of dancing around in a circle appears in a great many ancient and modern rituals. In order to honor the cycle of the sun, people were instructed to do things sunwise (east to west).

American Indians performed major ceremonies in a sunwise circle and the Jicarilla Apache traditionally circled an enemy's camp sunwise before an attack was begun. Last, housewives are instructed to beat batter sunwise to improve baking.

CLOCK: Since there is rarely a home without a clock, it is not surprising that here, too, a number of traditions are found. For example, it is said that a person's favorite clock or watch will stop when he dies. Also, should someone die in the house, many believe that all the clocks in the house should be stopped immediately, not to be wound again until after the burial. This is to indicate that the soul has entered eternity.

Should an alarm clock sound or should a clock strike the hour at the same time that church bells are pealed, it is said to be a bad omen.

In Wales, should a town clock strike while the church bells are ringing, a fire will break out in the parish. In Somerset, should a clock strike in the church while the text is being read, a death may soon be expected.

Yet another tradition holds that, if a clock that has not been running suddenly strikes the hour or a number of chimes, a death will certainly follow in the family. Should a clock chime during a wedding ceremony or during a funeral, another similar ceremony will soon follow.

Finally, if one can make a clock sound thirteen times it was said it would summon the Devil.

CLOTHES: Should you inadvertently put an article of clothing on inside out, it is said to indicate good luck, but, unless you discover this in time and change it, accidents may occur during the day.

It is thought of as a good sign if your vest or shirt are buttoned so that the buttons and holes come out uneven. Furthermore, if you break a button off while dressing, it is said to be a bad sign that must be corrected at once before leaving home.

According to one European superstition, when a new article of clothing is purchased, some money should be placed in the right-hand pocket, or your income will be limited as long as you wear it.

There is a general superstition to the effect that if you mend or sew the clothing you wear on your back, your fortune will take a turn for the worse. However, if a woman sticks herself or breaks a needle while mending a garment, she will receive a kiss on the day it is worn. It is said that good luck can be had by placing the sock or stocking of the right foot on first and then the shoe of the left. Should you find a hole in your sock or stocking, it is good luck for that day. Should the same sock or stocking be worn a second day, however, such will bring you bad luck.

A woman who dresses herself with three new articles of clothing on Easter Day is said to ensure happiness for the coming season.

Should you rip a garment the first time it is put on, it is considered bad luck. However, should you meet a person wearing new clothes, he should be pinched for good luck.

Should you burn your clothing, someone is telling a lie about you.

One tradition holds that you should never give your old clothes to the elderly or sick. When they die, the same fate may be transmitted to you.

In Prussia, tradition holds that if a robber enters your house and leaves some article of clothing in his hasty departure, hit it with a stick three times, in the name of the Father, the Son, and the Holy Ghost. He will fall ill and reveal the crime. (The stick itself had to be cut from a one-year-old hazel sapling.)

Some country folk believe that, when a person is dying in the house, all buttons on clothing should be undone. This is said to enable the soul to leave the body easily. Still another tradition holds that one can outwit the Angel of Death by wearing their clothing inside out. (Also curious is the belief that, when searching for snails, one's jacket should be worn inside out.)

The time you choose to wear a new suit of clothing for the first time will determine your luck. Wearing it on Monday means it will soon tear; on Tuesday, be careful of fire and avoid speculation; on Wednesday, things will go well and you will succeed at gaming; on Thursday, you will appear neat and well dressed, always make a good impression, and get what you are seeking; on Friday, you will be successful only as long as the clothes themselves last; on Saturday, you are advised to be careful of catching cold. This is considered a bad day for a new suit. Sunday, however, is the day best suited for happiness and good luck.

CLOVER: Tradition holds that Eve stole a four-leaf clover from the Garden of Eden before leaving. Certainly, the four-leaf clover might be called the best-known talisman in the West. It is said to bring luck to anyone who discovers it, especially if it is immediately given to another. Whoever finds this special talisman is said to meet with love the very same day. If a man finds it, he will escape military duty.

In the United Kingdom during World War II, tradition held that a man who found and wore a four-leaf clover in his buttonhole would not be drafted. Should the discovery of a four-leaf clover fall on the evening of Saint John, it is said to confer supernatural powers as well.

Since the clover is three-leafed, it is said to be a symbol of the Trinity, and thus to provide protection against evil and witchcraft. In folk medicine, clover infusions are said to cure various skin diseases.

Tradition holds that the Druids were the first to believe in the power of the four-leaf clover, and to believe that one possessing such a lucky piece could see evil spirits and witches, thereby easily avoiding them.

When it comes to five-leafed clovers, traditions are varied. According to some, finding a five-leaf clover means you will become very wealthy. To others, this is considered an unlucky omen, causing sickness for the finder, unless he immediately gives it away.

CLUB MOSS: If properly gathered on the third day of the new moon, when the crescent is seen for the first time, club moss is said by the Cornish to cure all diseases of the eyes.

COAL: An ancient belief is that carrying a small piece of coal in one's pocket or handbag will bring good luck. A definite way to ensure someone's luck in the future is to give coal as a Christmas present. It is then placed on the fire and a wish is made. Furthermore, should you be out walking and find a piece of coal, it is said to bring good luck, but only if you throw it over your left shoulder after you spit on it. Should a piece of coal be washed upon a shore and given to a sailor, some believe it will protect him from drowning.

On New Year's morning, coal should be brought to you by the "first foot that enters your house." In general, coal must be brought in through the front door and not fetched from the basement or inside the house.

According to a Scottish tradition, should a burglar carry coal in his pocket, he will escape arrest. In England, it was thought unlucky to give a neighbor a live coal to rekindle his fire on Christmas morning.

In Kentucky, there is a belief that if a woman's petticoat shows, she will soon have to shovel coal.

COBWEB: Here, two common and widespread beliefs are found: first, that it is unlucky to destroy a cobweb; and, second, that a bleeding wound can be stopped instantly by laying a cobweb over it.

Tradition holds that the infant Jesus was hidden from the messengers of Herod by a cobweb.

COCK: No doubt the sexual ardor of the cock, combined with its striking appearance and loud crowing, are some of the reasons for the many folk customs and traditions that surround this particular bird. A cock was depicted on a Sicilian coin early in the fifth century. In Persia, the bird was considered sacred and to kill one was regarded as a serious offense.

In mythology, the crowing of the cock, which naturally occurs at about dawn, was linked to a Greek story about a love affair between Mars and Venus. Mars supposedly commissioned Alektraon (the Greek word for "cock") to keep watch. When Alektraon fell asleep, however, Mars was surprised by Venus's returning husband, Vulcan. To punish Alektraon, Mars turned him into a cock and, he, as such, has performed his duty at dawn ever since.

The Greeks believed that the cock was sacred to Apollo, God of the Sun. In the Platonic dialogue, *Phaedo,* Socrates requests that a cock be offered to the healing god, Asclepius, on his behalf, before drinking the hemlock.

The Persians believed that the cock's crow actually awakened the dawn. So powerful was the cock's crowing, that travelers in Libya carried one with them to frighten away lions and basilisks.

In Mexico, cocks were sacrificed to the sun, and in Ceylon, a red cock was dedicated to a sick person and sacrificed in the belief that he would recover. In Scotland, the blood of a red cock was mixed into a flour cake and fed to an invalid, while in Germany tradition holds that illness and bad luck can be avoided by hiding the head, heart, and right foot of a cock in one's house. In Germany and Ireland, cocks were traditionally sacrificed on Saint Martin's Day or Eve, November 11.

The cock symbolism is quite important in Christian tradition. A cock was said to crow when Saint Peter repudiated Christ (Matt. 26:74.). Hence, it has become symbolic of a Christian's duty to remain alert against temptation by the Devil. For this reason, a weather cock is often placed on church towers and steeples.

A fourth-century tradition held that a cock announced the birth of Jesus, and a medieval belief held that, on Judgment Day, all cocks will sing and wake up both the living and the dead, even those appearing on belfries. Supposedly, the weather cock appearing on belfries is a survival of ritual sacrifices of such animals which accompanied the ground breaking of a house or church in ancient times.

The following are some popular beliefs about the cock: If a cock crows near your door with his face toward you, a stranger will arrive, according to a Yorkshire belief. If a cock crows at midnight, spirits are driven to their proper places. Yet, in Cornwall, a cock crowing at midnight means the Angel of Death is passing nearby. Should a cock stay on its perch longer than usual in the morning, expect rain.

If a cock crows on going to bed a rainstorm will arrive before morning. In Midlands: The following verses were recited.

> *If the cock moults before the hen, we shall have the weather thick and thin. If the hen molts before the cock, we shall have the weather as hard as a block.*

In Lorraine (France), it is said that a cock born on Good Friday will crow before all others. In Norway a cock will crow when approaching a body of a drowned person.

White cocks were said to be unusually lucky whereas the black variety were held by some to be consorts of the Devil. Some say a black cock will chase away rats in a poultry yard.

A popular "ready cure" was to rub a cock on one's body and either cast the cock out to sea or bring it to another district. The cock was said to take the illness with it. Others believed that, for medicine to be effective, it should be given at cock crow in the morning.

Some other beliefs: to cure epilepsy bury a black cock alive, together with a lock of the patient's hair and nail parings, and never eat a cock on Thursday.

Cockfighting continues to be a popular amusement in some eastern countries in Central and South America and in certain areas of Europe and the United States. It is generally considered illegal in the United States, and the third-century Christian writer, Lactantius, declared it an unsuitable amusement for Christian people.

Traditionally, the comb of the cock is a symbol of courage rivaled only by the mane of a lion.

COFFEE: If the bubbles formed on the surface of a coffee cup float in your direction, money is supposedly on the way. Should they float away from you, expect trouble ahead.

COFFIN: Tradition holds that a living person should never sleep in a coffin or even place an article of his clothing there. Should an article of one's clothing be placed in a coffin inadvertently (perhaps it was donated to an ill person) one's luck is said to rot in the same manner as the corpse. The best attire for the deceased would be his wedding clothes, for they will wash him of all his sins.

In Brittany, a belief holds that the left arm of the deceased must never be placed under his body in the coffin, or he will come back to haunt. Likewise, it is wise to kiss the deceased before he is put into his coffin, so he will not cross your path after burial.

Tradition holds that a coffin maker or carpenter is always warned in advance, in a mysterious or strange manner, about whom he must make a coffin for next.

Children's coffins should be taken out of a house by a window, rather than by the front door, in order to protect other mothers who may enter by this portal. Likewise, an ordinary object, such as a marble or other toy, that was owned by the child should be placed in the coffin.

Should there be difficulty in placing the coffin in the actual grave, it is said that the soul of the deceased is struggling in its attempt to leave or battling against evil forces. Should the coffin fail to go into the grave at all, it is a bad omen for all assembled.

No animal should approach a coffin as it is being placed in the ground, as it could take hold of the soul of the deceased.

Nails taken from a coffin and stuck into a bedroom door were believed to ward off nightmares. According to a German superstition, should a nail taken from a coffin be driven into the footstep left by a man, he will become lame and will remain so as long as the nail is in the footprint. German hunters hold that nails stuck into the spoor of a game quarry will hinder animals from escaping.

A belief in Somerset is that coffin rings, when dug from a grave, will prevent or cure rheumatism. This tradition is no doubt the basis for the wearing of copper rings or bracelets alleged to cure arthritis. These are sold in many fashionable pharmacies and drugstores throughout Great Britain and the United States.

COIN: Toss a coin into a spring or fountain, make a wish, and it will come true. This is perhaps the most popular belief attached to coins.

Coins themselves date back to the tenth century B.C. Since coins were originally made of silver or iron, it was thought that they were able to combat sorcery or witchcraft. In fact, the old Kentish name for coins that have been cursed is "hegs." This is derived from the word "hag," a name often given to witches.

Coins bearing the date of one's birth or pierced coins, placed in a bride's pocket before the marriage ceremony, were said to be especially fortunate.

Coins found during a storm were said to have fallen from the heavens and to be enchanted.

Should you hear a cuckoo for the first time in the year, or should you try clothing on for the first time while you have coins in your pocket, you will have money all year long.

To dig up an ancient coin while plowing a field is said to be the curse of Satan, unless each side is spit upon at once.

Should you receive change that includes a coin with a hole in it, it will bring good luck. Indeed, the tradition that coins with holes are lucky is evidently ancient and grew perhaps from the practice of wearing shells or stones with sea-worn holes as talismans to keep away evil spirits and especially to prevent drowning.

In many parts of the world, coins were placed on the eyes of a person upon death to prevent the eyes from reopening. In Serbia and Bulgaria, there exists a strange practice of taking coins from a corpse's eyes and washing them in wine. Once the wine is given to a widower, he will henceforth be "blind to any lovers of an unfaithful wife."

Coins given at Holy Communion are said to be especially blessed. Should they immediately be handed to a person suffering from rheumatism, who rubs the affected part, a cure will soon come about.

Other beliefs include these: finding a penny and picking it up will bring good luck. Should you see such a coin and not pick it up, however, bad luck will ensue. Keeping pennies in a jar in the kitchen will bring good fortune. A bridegroom presenting his bride with a coin that she wears in her shoe at the wedding will bring about a happy marriage. Seeing someone with polka-dot clothing will bring you money. Keeping a bent coin in your pocket will bring good luck, as long as you take it out at every new moon and spit on it. Incidentally, on seeing a new moon, turn a piece of silver in your pocket and make a wish. Whatever is wished for will come about.

If you place the first money you receive each day into an empty pocket, it will attract more coins. Such money is called a "hand-sel." Superstitions hold that it should be kissed and spit on before you place it in the pocket.

Other traditions hold that in order to have money in your pocket, you should always place there a small spider, called a "money spider."

Finally, never give new coats, pocketbooks, or wallets as gifts without first placing a coin therein. (I remember my grandmother followed this tradition throughout all her life.)

COLD: An eighteenth-century cure for the common cold was to pare the rind of an orange very thinly and thrust a roll into each nostril. Still another tradition is to catch in one's hands leaves falling from an oak tree under an autumn wind.

COLOR: Generally speaking, only the color green is an object of superstition. For whatever reason, actors will not wear it in theaters, and many actors refuse to wear it or own objects of this color even at home.

Green is the color of the earth and vegetation and has always symbolized hope and immortality. Hence, it is often used to signify health. In the Middle Ages, however, it was ascribed to the Devil and criminals, and was used by sorcerers to evoke forces of evil. In Scotland it is said that rifle bullets have a preference for the green square of the target. From these traditions, no doubt, came the actor's fear of green on the stage.

The significance of the other colors changes according to the object. When it comes to black and white, for example, the former is said indicative of evil and the latter, good. Hence, white is linked with virginity and purity. It is not surprising, therefore, to find lilies and other white flowers at weddings and baptisms.

Black, the opposite of white (in actuality, the absence of color), has traditionally been the sign of respectability. Thus, it is worn at funerals and is prominent in the dress of priests and court magistrates. For the most part, black is associated with the demonic. Hence, black animals are often sacrificed. While one can use touches of black when decorating, too much black (black-painted walls, for example) is said to absorb one's vitality.

The color blue is related to both sea and sky. In this form it is symbolic of that which is sought after, but not often obtained (for example, the bluebird of happiness). In the Orient, blue is used to protect against the evil eye. Blue eyes are considered a mark of magical powers, and blue stones of this color, likewise. The color blue is said to protect children from bad luck up to the age of three. The Virgin Mary is often depicted in blue. Color psychologists suggest using this color for bedrooms and other places of rest.

The color yellow, on the other hand, draws its value from other symbols to which it has been connected—for instance, the color of the sun. It is also said to be symbolic of fear. (Yellow was the color the Nazis chose for the star they made the Jews wear.) Some believe that yellow is the color of the intellectual. It is thought to be an excellent color for use in classrooms, as it supposedly stimulates thinking.

The color red has always been linked to blood, fire, and passion. It is said to be the ruling color of hell itself, and red has also been connected with war. In Japan, especially, red is considered a very positive color. Because of its great power, some say it is best used in small amounts. In the modified form of purple, it is the color worn by monarchs and cardinals.

Tradition also assigns the various colors to planets and signs of the Zodiac, but this again is a subject for greater exploration. Indeed colors have worked their way into our language: green with envy, scarlet sin, red with passion, and white with innocence are popular expressions.

COMB: Before the plastic era, combs were often manufactured from living things, hence, they became a talisman as well as objects of everyday use.

If made from ivory, the qualities of an elephant were brought to mind; if made from an animal's horn, the animal from which it was taken; if made from a shell, the mystique of the sea. Tortoise shell combs were said to calm nervous people and to refine their intelligence. This was no doubt due to the traditions surrounding its original possessor.

Over the years, many superstitions about combs developed. The following are some of them: Combs that were used on a dead person should never be used by the living, since they will surely bring death. If you use the comb of a dead man, you will become bald. A comb or brush containing one's hair should never be thrown away, or else a witch or sorcerer could get hold of it and use it for spell casting.

In the United Kingdom, tradition holds that a mother should never comb a baby's hair until teething has finished; otherwise, for every tooth of the comb that breaks, the child will lose a tooth long before it should.

Should someone accidentally drop a comb, it is said to be a bad omen to pick it up. Actors and singers are said to consider it bad luck to drop a comb before a performance. To counter such an ill omen, they are said to step on it with the right foot when picking it up.

A woman who lets a man carry her comb will later lose his attention, says an old American tradition.

COMET: Throughout time the appearance of comets with their long tails have caused fear and apprehension. To primitive man their appearance marked certain omens of upcoming disaster. In the Middle Ages, those of a religious bent thought for certain that a comet would announce the second coming of Christ.

It is said that every great war occurred soon after the appearance of a comet. Hence, it is considered unlucky to engage in any new business enterprise when a comet has been seen in the sky, and children born during the appearance of a comet are believed subject to sudden death.

Ancients believed that comets have a particular affinity for royalty. Thus, their appearance was said to mark sudden upheavals in government and radical changes of politics. Comet years are reported to be good for wine production, however.

Shooting stars and meteors have similar traditions. Should one wish for money when a shooting star is seen, belief has it that money shall soon appear. Those who are ill are said to soon recover upon seeing a shooting star, and should one see a shooting star while setting out on a journey at night, the trip will be successful.

Lovers seeing shooting stars and wishing for health, wealth, and happiness will certainly have their wishes gratified.

CONSUMPTION: Should one swallow baby frogs before breakfast, his consumption will be cured, according to a Midlands tradition. Yet another belief among the Surrey folk is that the ill person should be carried or led through a flock of sheep as they leave the fold in the morning.

Among the Arabs, a cure was certain to occur if one put a dish of water on the patient's head, dropped melted lead into it, and then buried the lead in a field.

CORK: Pieces of cork are said to cure cramps. The trick is to go to bed wearing garters made from bits of cork. This will prevent the leg muscles from cramping during the night.

CORNS: It is said that one can cure corns by stealing a small piece of beef and burying it in the ground. As the beef rots away, so shall the corn disappear.

CORPSE: Here we find a number of traditions that have persisted, despite the advancement of science and medicine. Here are a few popular beliefs: Should a corpse remain longer than usual, there will be another death in the family shortly.

Should an animal jump over a corpse or a coffin, such promises great ill for the family of the deceased, unless the animal is sought after and itself killed.

According to a Gaelic tradition, should one neglect to cut every string in the shroud of a corpse before placing it in the coffin, the dead will move about.

If a corpse is carried over private ground, that ground is said to become a right-of-way.

Should a corpse remain unburied on a Sunday, another resident shall pass away in the village before the week is gone.

If one visits a house in which a dead body is lying in state, one must touch the corpse as a token of peace. If a corpse is taken across a field, that field will become barren and crops will refuse to grow, no matter how fruitful it may have been before.

Widespread is the belief that guns fired over a corpse thought lying at the bottom of a river will cause the gall bladder to break and the body to float to the top of the water.

It is said that a corpse is especially blessed if rain falls on it.

A Norfolk belief is that removing or exhuming a body will result in a death or calamity for family members of the deceased.

In Cornwall, tradition has it that one should never carry a corpse to church by a new road.

Sailing folk believe it is unlucky to have corpses on board ship. When a dead person is buried at sea, they look away as it disappears into the waves. Should they look at it, tradition holds that they will soon join their mate.

COUGH: It is said that to get rid of a cough that seems to defy medical treatment someone should boil two or three snails in barley water, without the afflicted person knowing it. This is said to have effected great cures. If this doesn't work, a hair should be taken from the person's head and placed between two slices of buttered bread. These should be given to a dog and the following words should be spoken: "Good luck, you have. May you be sick and I be salve." Devonshire residents believed that this transfers the cough from the patient to the dog.

COW: Common among western farms and held sacred in the Orient, it is not surprising that we find a number of traditions surrounding cows.

In Scotland, for instance, milk from a white cow is said to be of inferior quality, while Americans maintain that red cows have the best meat.

Should a cow low three times in your face, it is said to portend death. Should a cow break into an enclosed garden, a death will likely occur in the family to whom the garden belongs. Should three cows break in, it is said there will be three deaths.

Holy water should be poured down the throats of cows on Midsummer Day. At the same time, the Athanasian Creed is sung to them in Latin to protect them from evil.

Should a milkmaid not wash her hands after milking, her cows will go dry.

It is said that cows eat buttercups to help them make butter. Meanwhile, to protect one's cows from wolves, butter must be offered to Saint Herve, say those who live in Breton.

Should a cow refuse to calf, cut the end of its tail in fourths or hit it three times with a hazel stick.

It is said that when a farmer purchases a cow, he must lead it away with a rope around its neck. Should one be selling a calf, however, it must be led out of the barn backwards, or else it will later become sterile.

Should a cow raise its tail, rain is on the way. Should it slap its tail against a tree or fence, expect good weather.

Cow dung is believed to heal wounds, especially ulcers of the legs or arms. The wound should simply be plastered for several days in order to see what dung will do.

While driving cattle to market, if one should see a woman before a man, he will have bad luck in the deal, according to Irish traditions. It is also said that the Irish scatter primroses on the ground and hang a piece of rowan (mountain ash) at the barn door to protect their herd from evil influences.

Hares found in the fields where cattle graze on a May Day are said to be witches who seek to steal the milk. A Scottish belief is that one can thwart witches' efforts to suck milk by tarring cattle behind their ears and at the root of the tail on Beltane Eve (May Day Eve).

According to a Cornish tradition, on Christmas Eve cows will go down on their knees to worship the Christ child.

To ensure good fortune in one's dairy, a bunch of mistletoe should be given to the first cow that calves in the new year.

CRADLE: Rocking an empty cradle means that it will be filled within a year, says one superstition. Yet another holds that this will result in the death of the child who last occupied it.

Should one's possessions be seized due to nonpayment of debt, in Northern England, a custom maintained that the cradle remain the property of its original owner. To seize it was said to bring bad luck upon the seller. (See **baby**.)

CRAMP: Among country folk plagued with cramps, often the result of physical labor, there are numerous and somewhat extraordinary cures.

Mentioned earlier is the practice of curing cramps by making cork garters. (See **cork**.) Here are some more: Place cork between the bed and the mattress or between the sheets. Lay one's shoes across the cramp. (This probably works if the shoes were the cause of the cramp in the first place.) Keep a piece of brimstone in bed, and a cramp will never bother you. Rings made from the screws, nails, or hinges of coffins will prevent cramping. Wearing eel skin garters or going to bed with the skin of a mole wrapped around the left thigh is another cure.

CRICKET: Crickets are said to become the protector of the home; hence, to kill one brings misfortune, and should a cricket be seen leaving a building or house, it is an omen of illness or death soon to occur there. Likewise, a white cricket seen indoors is said to be an omen of death.

Should a cricket in one's house become very quiet when one is leaving for a fair, it is said that bad transactions will be made. Should crickets sing louder than usual, expect rain. To hear a cricket chirp on Christmas Eve is said to be the best luck of all.

In the American South a popular custom is to call crickets "old folks" due to their fireside sitting propensity.

American Indians believe that one can obtain a fine singing voice by drinking a liquid made of crickets that have been crushed and boiled.

In ancient Greece, crickets were believed to live on wind and dew.

In Indonesia, should one hear a sound like a jingling of coins made by a cricket in one's house at night, it was said to indicate the presence of the Selanpandai or "the creator of man." If a pregnant woman is living therein and the sound comes from the verandah, the child will be a boy, for that is where men sit. If the sound comes from the room in which the woman is sleeping, she will give birth to a girl.

Yet another kind of cricket, called "Mengalai," is held to be the spokesman of the dead. He is said to live in the support poles under the log house, at ground level, where it is damp and moist. It is believed that he speaks to relatives of someone who has died recently. Should he ask for food offerings and other attention on behalf of the recently deceased and should he not receive proper attention, severe illness will occur to those living in the house.

CROCODILE: Some Indian tribes believe crocodiles make noises like humans in pain in order to attract their victims. It is also said that they shed tears over the head of a victim, after they have devoured his body.

CROP: Tradition holds that crops should be sown from north to south, rather than from east to west, to ensure a good harvest. Likewise, crops sown with the full moon are said to be ready for harvest earlier than those sown with the waxing moon.

In Wales, tradition holds that one can get a good crop of cereal grains by fetching mold from three adjoining fields, inherited by one person, and mixing it with the seed before sowing.

CROSSED: It is said to be unlucky to meet a cross-eyed woman but lucky to meet a cross-eyed man. Should a cross-eyed man marry a cross-eyed woman, it is said to be an omen for great happiness.

Should a person cross knives at a table, bad luck is nearby. Likewise, to place one's shoes or slippers in a crossed position is said to court ill luck. No doubt the superstitions regarding these things stem from the general belief that such crossings are flaunting the cross of Christ.

However, some objects, when intentionally placed in a cross, are said to have great exorcising force. For instance, the French placed two bouquets of flowers in a cross at the doors and windows of a house on the morning of Saint John in order to prevent evil fairies from entering therein. Straw crosses placed over beehives were said to increase their production. Two straws intentionally set in a cross formation will make the blood from a wound stop flowing, and medicine given to an ill person will be more effective if drunk "in a cross" (that is, from each of the four corners of the glass).

Yet, many warnings persist: One should be careful not to step on a cross formed unintentionally by two sticks of straw. Should a sick person's bed be inadvertently placed perpendicular to ceiling beams, it will prevent his recovery. Four friends who meet and separate must be certain to avoid crossing each other's arms.

If two persons inadvertently say the same thing at the same time, they can make their wish come true, if one says a word and the other responds immediately with an associated word. The little fingers of each hand are linked together and snapped after each has made his wish. This is followed by the saying, "I say chimney, you say smoke. Then our wish will never be broke!" Supposedly, the crossing of the fingers is actually a Trinity symbol, since here it is combined with the speaking, the crossing, and the response.

CROW: There is a great deal of folklore connected with crows and ravens due to their wide distribution throughout much of the world.

The Greek writer Porphyry (third century A.D.) wrote that one might acquire the crow's prophetic powers by eating their hearts. According to Greek myth, when Apollo became the lover of Coronis, he commissioned a snow white crow to keep guard over his already pregnant lover while he went to Delphi. The crow failed to report to Apollo that Coronis had become unfaithful with Ischys. In his anger, Apollo turned the bird black.

In Genesis, Noah sends forth a raven from the ark to search for land, and legend has it that ravens guided Alexander to the Shrine of Jupiter Ammon in the Oasis of Siwah in Egypt and later foretold his death. Elijah was fed by ravens, predisposing Christians to regard the bird favorably (although Saint Ambrose called the bird "impious" for not having returned to the ark).

In Great Britain there is a belief that, if the ravens at the Tower of London are destroyed, disaster to the empire is certain.

In China the three-legged sun crow is held worthy of worship.

Tradition holds that a crow never enters the Acropolis at Athens due to the enmity between Athena (whose symbol is the owl) and the crow.

The poet Ovid in *Metamorphoses* refers to a witch, Medea, who infused into the veins of the elder Jason a concoction of aged deer and the head of a crow that had outlived nine generations of men.

It was said that ravens' eggs could be used to dye the hair black. Unless one's mouth was filled with oil while this was applied, however, teeth would turn black also.

In Czechoslovakia, folklore holds that a man who eats three raven hearts reduced to ashes will become a crack shot.

In Russia a witch's spirit is said to assume the form of a crow.

If a Brahman takes money given to him for sacrifice and uses it for his personal ends, it is said he will be doomed to be a crow or a vulture in his next life and for a hundred years thereafter.

In Cornwall, to shoot a raven is to shoot King Arthur. In Wales, if blind people are kind to ravens, they will learn how to regain their sight. In Scotland those who hunt deer believe it a good omen to hear the call of a crow or raven before setting out.

A number of verses appear in American and European folklore to describe the crow's influence. In North America, "Crow on the fence, rain will go hence" is an often cited expression. In Maryland the following verse is found:

One crow—sorrow
Two crows—mirth
Three crows—wedding
Four crows—birth.

The English version is as follows:

One's bad luck
Two's luck
Three's health
Four's wealth
Five's sickness
And six is death.

Still another version goes like this:

One means anger
Two means mirth
Three a wedding
Four a birth
Five is heaven
Six is hell
But seven is the Devil's ownself.

Popular omens about crows abound. Here are some: Should a crow flutter about a window and caw, it portends death. Should a crow fly three times over a house and croak three times, it is a bad omen. An odd crow perched in the path of an observer is a sign of wrath.

Should crows flock together early in the morning and stare into the sun, the weather will be hot and dry. Should they stalk at nightfall into water and croak, rain is at hand.

A famine is near at hand when crows in a flock forsake a wood.

Foul weather is nearby should a crow croak an odd number of times. Should the croaking be an even number, the weather will be fine.

Last, should crows be seen flying towards each other, it is an omen of war.

CRYING: In some areas of Europe it is believed that a child who will cry long will also live long.

CUCKOO: Since the song of a cuckoo is heard only for a brief period at the beginning of spring, its song has long been held prophetic. Should one hear the call of a cuckoo before April 6, a Welsh tradition says it is unlucky. Should one hear the call of a cuckoo for the first time on April 28, however, an entire year's good fortune is assured. In any case, it is considered unlucky to hear the cuckoo's song for the first time if one has no money in his pocket.

Should the cuckoo's sound come from the right, it is said to bring good luck; should it come from the left, ill luck is omened.

Should the cuckoo be heard after Midsummer Day, it is said to be a sign of evil portent.

Should one make a wish upon hearing the cuckoo's song, if reasonable, the wish is said to come true.

Whatever you are doing when you first hear the call of this bird, you should do it frequently throughout the year to bring good luck. Should one make a wish and turn over the money in his pocket when first hearing the call of the cuckoo, the wish is said to come true.

An unmarried girl can determine how many years she must wait for a husband by counting the number of cuckoo's notes first heard in the spring. Then again, should an unmarried woman run into the fields the first thing in the morning to hear the cuckoo, she must take off her left shoe and look into it. There she will find a hair exactly the same color as that of her future husband.

In Finland and Brittany, the call of a cuckoo is said to mean marriage before the coming winter, if heard by an unmarried girl.

In Scotland, it is said that one can determine the number of years one has left to live by saying, "Cuckoo, cherry tree come down, tell me how many years I have to live," while counting the number of times the cuckoo calls.

Supposedly, the cuckoo is so busy answering questions that it never builds a nest of its own. Rather, it deposits its eggs in other birds' nests.

CURLEW: Curlews, which sailors named "the seven whistlers," are said to fly over a ship and call should a storm be brewing.

CUT: Should you wish to heal a cut or wound made by a knife, scissors, or other instrument, simply clean and polish the instrument and the wound will heal cleanly.

Should you run a nail into your foot, removing the nail and greasing it will cause the wound to heal.

According to Pliny, should one wound another person and feel regret for it, he should simply spit on the hand that caused the wound. The pain to the injured will at once be alleviated.

DADDY LONGLEGS: During harvest, in various parts of England, great caution is taken by reapers not to injure the straddle bug, or daddy longlegs. It is believed that harm will come to the crop or to the harvesters should this occur.

In American folklore, the daddy longlegs will help one find stray cattle. One simply chants "Granddaddy, granddaddy, where did my cows go?" Then the bug is said to point a leg in the direction in which the missing cows may be found.

DAFFODIL: According to a Welsh tradition, finding the first daffodil of spring is an omen that one will earn more gold than silver during the coming year. Farmers also believe it unlucky to bring daffodils into the house before the goslings are hatched.

Last, one is advised never to bring a single daffodil into the house. They must always be in a bunch, or ill luck will certainly occur.

DAISY: One tradition holds that it was Mary Magdalene's tears that originally created this special flower. Others maintain that the spirits of babies who die at birth scatter daisy seeds to help cheer their unhappy parents.

In ancient times, the daisy was called "the smile of God" or "day's eye," since it opened its petals to the sun and closed them at nightfall.

Tradition holds that knights in medieval times wore daisies into battle. Any knight who used the double daisy (a stem with two blossoms) as his sign was declaring his love for a particular lady who loved him back. In sixteenth-century France, an Order of the Daisy existed and furthered these traditions.

Due to their affinity to the sun, daisies are said to possess the ability to predict one's future lover. Should you pick a daisy, turn toward the sun when the noon is tolled, and pluck the petals saying, "He [she] loves me or loves me not." The number of petals will yield the answer.

Some popular beliefs about daisies include these: When daisy petals are seen closed, bad weather is on the way. The first daisy seen in the year should be eaten to ensure good luck throughout the rest of the year.

Should one put daisy roots under his pillow, he will dream of his lover. One was also instructed to step on the first daisy seen, or it would grow on one's grave within a year.

It is said that insanity can be cured by drinking a daisy potion for fifteen days. Daisies were used as an ointment for eye infections. Their juice was thought to cleanse wounds: gout, fevers, ulcers, and migraines; remove warts; and even turn gray hair back to black. Daisy tea is said to prevent fever.

Should you wish to know how many offspring you will have, some say to take the yellow center from a daisy, break it up by rolling it between your fingers, and then toss the pieces on your hand, from the back to the front. Those pieces remaining indicate how many children would be born.

While it was considered lucky to step on the first daisy seen in the spring, if one inadvertently uprooted the plant, it was believed that his children would not thrive.

Last, some Americans believe that daisies fed to a puppy will keep it small.

DANDELION: Should an unmarried girl pick a fresh dandelion and blow the head of fluff, the number of breaths it takes to remove the flying seeds will indicate the number of years she will wait before her wedding. The same device can be used to determine how many children she will have.

During the Middle Ages, the dandelion was known as "piss-abed," and one superstition holds that if you pick a dandelion, you will wet your bed.

If the dandelion does not open in the morning, rain is said to be on the way. If it blooms in April and July, the summer will be hot and rainy.

Tea made from dandelions is said to be good for the liver, rheumatism, and for purification of the blood.

DARTS: Often played in English and Irish pubs, there are two popular superstitions about them. First, one should not play against women; second, a player should put his left foot forward to the line and move it from left to right before throwing.

DAY: In ancient times each day of the week was assigned a planetary ruler.

MONDAY, placed under the influence of the moon, was said to be an indicator of the weather for the days of the week to come, but in reverse! Should the weather be foul on Monday, the rest of the week promised to be good weather.

In the Alsace, weddings celebrated on Monday were said to produce an insane couple. In Paris, if one wore an emerald on a Monday, it was believed that you would not be able to do anything right for the rest of the week.

Certain Mondays during the year were considered particularly unlucky. These were the first Monday in April (the day of Cain's birth), the second Monday in August (which marked the destruction of Sodom and Gomorrah), and the last Monday in December (the day of Judas's birth).

Monday is said to be a day during which one should not enter into any contracts, ask for favors from others, or make promises.

TUESDAY was assigned rulership by Mars, the God of War. In the West, Tuesday is an excellent day for combat, but in the East, Arabs fear fighting on this day.

Tuesday is said to be auspicious for commerce and held as a wonderful day for marriage. However, you must not wear a flower in your buttonhole on Tuesday, and a woman should not undergo an operation, trim her nails, or expose herself to fire or danger.

WEDNESDAY is placed under the planet Mercury. It is said to be a lucky day for Moslems, who believe that God created light on Wednesday. Some magicians take a rest on this day since Mercury rules the mind.

One is advised never to get married nor wear gloves on a Wednesday, nor is it a good day to make large purchases; and, should a new moon fall on this day, expect the worst. It is, however, a good day to start a new course of medical treatment, write letters, or seek favors from mercurial people.

THURSDAY is under the rulership of Jupiter, and is considered lucky by Arabs and Germans. It is held a favorable day for weddings and, in the East, for bringing a new bride into one's home.

Some traditions concerning Thursday are these: Never wear a ruby on Thursday. Never work on Thursday. Never eat chicken on Thursday. Never spin yarn on Thursday.

Thursday is said to be a good day, however, for making important decisions, accepting responsible positions, or seeing your attorney. It is not a good day for starting a new job or sending your children to school for the first time.

FRIDAY falls under the planet Venus. Since tradition holds that Eve offered the apple to Adam on a Friday, it is not considered a favorable day. During the night between Friday and Saturday, devils and witches are said to move about. Criminals were always hanged on Fridays in Europe and in the United States.

Clothing should not be cut out on this day, nor sewn, since it will end up not fitting properly.

There is a British superstition that, if a dead person is buried on Friday, three members of his family will soon follow.

A child born on this day is said to have visions and the gift of curing fevers. In Hungary, should a child be born on Friday, it is considered a bad omen, which can be changed by placing a few drops of blood on a piece of cloth cut from an old article of clothing and burning it.

Should one have a dream on Friday and tell it to someone in his family the next morning, it is said it will come true.

Good sight and hearing are promised should one cut nails and hair on Friday, and widespread is the belief that whatever the weather is on Friday, the same weather will follow on Sunday. Another tradition holds that those who laugh on Friday will cry on Sunday.

Friday is said to be a good day for flirtation, dancing, getting married, and meeting with others.

SATURDAY falls under the influence of Saturn. The Jewish Sabbath lasts from Friday evening to Saturday evening, and, since God created man on Saturday, it is believed that the sun will always shine for at least a few hours on this day.

In Scotland, it is believed that one born on a Saturday will have the ability to see ghosts.

It is said to be a good day for trips and for telling one's dreams, because they might come true. It is said not to be a good day for leaving the hospital or for carrying out any humanitarian activities.

SUNDAY is a favorable day for anything, because it is the day of Christ's resurrection. Children born on this day have a special calling, and medical treatments are said to be most successful when begun on this day.

This is a day for rest, and activities should be limited to those of a humanitarian nature.

An American tradition holds that it is bad luck to put new sheets on a bed on this day, and one who sings a wrong note in a choir on Sunday is said to find a burned meal when he returns home.

The Ashanti and other tribes in West Africa name a child according to the day of the week on which he is born. With slavery, this tradition was brought to the Caribbean and to the American South, where black people were given such names as Quashee (Sunday), Cudjo (Monday), and Cuffee (Friday).

Each planet is said to rule for the first hour after sunrise on its own day. The succeeding hours are ruled by the other planets in the following order: Sun, Venus, Mercury, Moon, Saturn, Jupiter, Mars. At sunset this order is interrupted. The first hour after sunset is ruled by the planet fifth in order from the planet that rules the day. Hence, each planet rules the first and eighth hours after sunrise and the third and tenth hours after sunset on its own day. Knowledge of this rulership sequence is said to be useful to anyone who wishes to perform a particular act successfully since some planets hinder certain actions.

According to French tradition and English sixteenth-century belief, the following days of the various months are held especially lucky or unlucky.

Lucky Days

January 4, 19, 27, 31
February 7, 8, 18
March 3, 9, 12, 14, 16
April 5, 27
May 1, 2, 4, 6, 9, 14
June 3, 5, 7, 9, 12, 23

July 2, 6, 10, 23, 30
August 5, 7, 10, 14, 19
September 6, 10, 15, 18, 30
October 13, 16, 20, 31
November 3, 13, 23, 30
December 10, 20, 29

Unlucky Days

January 1, 2, 4, 5, 10, 13, 15, 17, 23, 29
February 2, 8, 10, 17, 21
March 13, 16, 17, 19, 20, 23, 28
April 10, 16, 20, 21, 29, 30
May 7, 10, 15, 17, 20
June 4, 8, 20
July 5, 13, 15, 21, 27
August 2, 13, 19, 20, 27, 31
September 6, 7, 13, 16, 22, 24
October 3, 6, 9, 27
November 6, 15, 20, 25
December 6, 7, 9, 15, 28, 31

DEAFNESS: According to an Irish tradition, one can cure deafness by anointing the ears continually with the oil of eels.

DEATH: Death, or "transition," as it is called by metaphysicians, is so significant an event that beliefs surrounding this will be found throughout this entire work.

Some of the most common beliefs are as follows: A person cannot die as long as any locks are locked or bolts closed in the house. After death, all windows and doors must be opened in order for the soul to escape.

A hard death will be had by anyone lying on a bed of pigeon's feathers, unless he is lifted in a sheet and laid on the floor. Another tradition holds that no one can die on pigeon's feathers.

Should a white breasted bird appear, according to Devonshire residents, it is a sure omen of death. Should three loud knocks be heard at the head of a sick person's bed or the bed of his relations, death is soon to follow.

Should a pall be placed on a coffin wrong side out, another death in the family is soon to take place. Should the wind blow out a candle on the altar of a church, the minister will soon pass away.

In Wales if a mole is found that has burrowed under the wash house or the dairy, it is said that the woman of the house will die during the next year.

Dogs howling for no apparent reason, especially at an open door, are said to portend death. The same applies to hens laying eggs with double yolks or fish making strange noises when pulled from the water.

An ancient Jewish tradition says that it is possible for a husband and wife to learn who will die first by calculating the numeric value of the letters in each of their names: A = 1, B = 2, et cetera. Should the sum be even, the man is said to die first; if odd, the woman.

Widespread is the belief that animals and insects can sense approaching death and will announce it by cries or other behavior. In fact, some traditions hold that even pieces of furniture will crack or move themselves without reason to announce the passing of a member of the house. Also, trees will blossom out of season to predict a death.

Should one place a cross of willow twigs on a consecrated fountain and should it float, it is a sign of approaching death.

In Brittany, on New Year's Day, fathers toss slices of buttered bread into the air, while naming family members one by one. Those slices that fall on the buttered side indicate those who will die in the year to come.

Also in Brittany, a pitcher of milk is left near a dead body to "white wash" it of its sins before Judgment Day.

Should one write the names of the wise men on his forehead with his own blood on the night of Epiphany and should he then look in the mirror, his own death time and circumstances will be seen.

It is said that, when a dead person keeps his eyes open, he is waiting for another to join him.

A dead person's laundry must be done separately from that of other family members, so that death will not spread. Still another tradition is to maintain a table setting for the deceased, so that his spirit may eat before taking departure.

In general, tradition holds that the souls of those dying violent deaths will wander the earth until released. The soul of a murder victim is said to remain on earth until the guilty person is found or until he himself is buried wearing the shoes that he wore at the time of the crime. Hanged persons were said to remain suspended between heaven and hell indefinitely.

In China, there is a belief that the dead come back once a year on the last night of the year. A bed, food, and water are prepared for them, and a door is left open for them to enter.

Among seamen there is the belief that death mostly occurs at the falling of the tide.

DEW: In the Midland, there is the belief that dew collected from plants on Saint Bride's Day (February 1), if applied to the face, will rejuvenate and improve the features. Some believe that a good complexion can be had throughout the entire year, if you wash your face in May dew at daybreak on the first of May. Dew taken from the hawthorne at daybreak on that day is said to preserve one's beauty forever.

An American saying goes like this:

> When the dew is on the grass, rain will never come to pass.
> When grass is dry at morning light, look for rain before the night.

The Slavs believed that dew protected their milk from witches. Over the years dew has been likened to a pearl, a tear, perspiration from the sky, and the saliva of stars.

In China it is believed that dew gives life to the dying, and the sound of bells is said to make dew disappear.

DICE: Originally used in ancient Greece as instruments of divination, dice were then made from bones. Divining the future by throwing dice or lots was called "Cleromancy" by the Greeks.

Symbolically, with their six sides and six dots, dice are said to indicate the six realms of the universe: mineral, plant, animal, human, psychic, and divine. Originally, these were used to determine the wishes of the gods. In time, whichever player received the best "omen" when the dice were cast was said to be the winner.

Artifacts dating back to 7000 to 5000 B.C. from the cave of "Masd' Azil" in France include pebbles painted in red ocher that are believed to be an early form of dice. Those used in classical times, however, came from small cuboid bones, known as "astragali," found in the joints of many animals, especially sheep. These were discovered on the site of Ephesus in Asia Minor and in Sparta.

The term "crap shooting" comes from the French *crapaud*, a word for toad. The term was used to describe small boys, crouching out-of-sight in the manner of toads, to play dice against their parents' wishes.

Superstitions surrounding dice and gambling include blowing on them and crossing one's fingers before tossing them. Some gamblers prefer to rub them on the head of a redheaded person.

Dice may also be used to divine the future by drawing them one by one. One dot means an important letter is soon to arrive; two dots, that a successful trip will be undertaken; three dots, that one will be taken by surprise; four dots, that problems are on the way; five dots, that there will soon be changes in the family; six dots, that an unexpected sum of money will be obtained.

DIMPLE: In ancient times, people with dimples were thought to have special magical powers, probably because there were so few of them. Legend has it that dimples are made by God's finger or the fingers of angels.

An Irish verse goes as follows:

> Dimple on the chin
> The Devil within.
> Dimple on the cheek, a soul mild and meek.

Another version says:

> A dimple on your cheek
> Many hearts you will seek.
> A dimple on your chin
> Many hearts you will win.

DISH: According to a Scottish belief, should a bride break a dish at her wedding breakfast, it is said to bode ill for the marriage.

DOCTOR: Tradition holds that the first person to be seen by a doctor in a new office is certain to be cured. Calling a doctor to see a sick person on a Friday is considered a bad omen.

DOG: Many are the beliefs with regard to this common household pet. For example, a dog passing between a couple about to be married means ill fortune will come to the couple. A dog digging a large hole in one's garden, say the Gypsies, means there will be a death in the family. Dogs howling are signs of sure death, and being followed by a strange dog indicates good luck.

Measles or a cough can be cured by placing a hair of the patient's head between two pieces of buttered bread and giving it to a dog. What's more, one can determine if an ill person will recover by rubbing his teeth with a piece of food and throwing it to a dog. Should the dog eat it, it is a good sign. Should the dog refuse it, the person will die. Should a dog be given a bone of lamb at Eastertide, it is said he'll go mad.

The Irish hold it unlucky to meet a barking dog first thing in the morning, and according to the Chinese, a dog has seven consecutive lives. The Moslems say a dog must not be killed, since its life equals that of seven men. The Normans said all dogs belong to Satan, except sheep dogs.

Some additional beliefs about dogs include these: If a dog passes between two friends, it will shake up their friendship. If a dog runs between the legs of a woman, say the English, her father or husband will punish her. If a dog is seen eating grass, rolling on the ground, or scratching himself for a long time, it will soon rain. If a dog howls once or three times and then falls completely silent, a death has recently occurred.

Before a bad storm appears, dogs will retreat under a table or into a safe corner. Dogs are believed to see evil spirits and will warn their owners of their presence.

If a dog falls asleep with his paws drawn up around him and his tail outstretched, in some parts of the United States it is said to indicate a death. The direction of the death can be determined by which way the animal's tail is pointing.

It is considered a sacrilege for a dog to enter a church. In many country parishes in Britain a "dog whipper" was employed to expel any dogs that might enter the church during the service.

The idea that dogs are faithful companions or "man's best friend" is as ancient as Homer's *Odyssey*. Ulysses's dog, Argos, waited many years for his master to return. When he did return, even though in disguise, Argos was the first to recognize him. After wagging his tail with joy, he died of happiness.

DOLPHIN: According to the ancients, dolphins loved music and also saved those who had been shipwrecked. It is generally thought among seamen a good omen to encounter a dolphin. Should it approach near the coast, however, it is thought a storm is not far away. Should it go back out towards the north, good weather is indicated; should it turn south, the weather will be rainy and cold.

Dolphins were believed to transport on their backs the souls of sailors who had died at sea.

DONKEY: It is said that Satan can never take the form of a donkey, for since the first Christmas night it has worn a cross drawn on its back. Hence, should a sick child be set on this cross and the donkey make nine circles, the child's recovery is certain. Should a child be covered with a donkey's skin, he will no longer be afraid. Also, a child can be cured of whooping cough by passing it under the belly of a donkey nine times.

The donkey is said to speak on Christmas night, as do other animals. When he is about to die, it is believed the donkey hides. Thus, to see its corpse is a good omen.

Should a man's head be rubbed with donkey's hoof clippings, it is said he will appear to have the head of a donkey.

When a donkey wiggles its ears, it is said that it will rain.

DOOR: Almost universal is the superstition that when a child is being born or a person is dying, household doors and windows should be opened. Tradition also holds that it is bad luck to open a front door unless the back door is closed and that one should never leave a house with all the doors open.

In Germany, pains are taken to avoid slamming a door in a house in which someone has died in case the soul will be so stricken.

In Africa, some will not sweep out a dwelling through a door for one year after a death in case the dust should harm and upset the delicate soul.

When returning from either a baptism or funeral, one should enter the house by another door than the one used in leaving. Should there be only one door, it is said preferable to come through a window.

Some traditions hold that corpses should be removed through the back door or window and never through the front of the house.

Likewise for women who are pregnant or menstruating. It is also considered unlucky to watch a funeral through a door or window.

When a bride has finally left her parents' house for the honeymoon, it is said that the doorstep should be scrubbed with soap and water to wash away any impression left by her feet. Otherwise, her marriage will not be a happy one. Furthermore, a bride should never step over the doorstep of her new home. Rather, she should be carried by the bridegroom. In Yorkshire a kettle of boiling water is poured over the doorstep just after the bride has left her parents' home.

To protect doors, nails can be pounded in the center to represent a cross or one can hang a horseshoe on the door. Saint John's wort hung on the inner side of the front door will suffice for the same purpose. Barn and stable doors may be protected by nailing a screech owl, bat, or wolf's head to the door.

Some additional superstitions about doors: A visitor should leave through the same doorway he entered; otherwise, he will take the luck of the house away with him. Also, a door opening by itself announces an unpleasant visit soon to take place.

In the thirteenth century, Marco Polo reported that each door of Kublai Khan's palace at Peking was guarded by men who made certain that no one stepped on the threshold in entering.

DOUBLE FRUIT: It is considered lucky for one to find any fruit growing attached to another of its own kind. If it is taken and shared with a friend, both will have their wishes answered. In Australia a superstition claims that a pregnant woman eating such a fruit can expect twins.

DOUBT: Jewish traditions hold that, if one is in doubt about any subject, he can simply count the number of buttons on the coat or shirt he is wearing at the time. If an even number, then he is correct; if an odd number, he should admit he is wrong.

DOVE: Tradition holds that the dove is the only creature that the Devil cannot transform himself into. It is also said to be the messenger of Venus and is particularly beneficial to lovers. The dove is often a representation for the "Holy Ghost" of Christianity.

The Greeks associated the dove with Aphrodite, the Goddess of Love. Supposedly, the goddess and her son, Eros were competing in picking flowers. Aphrodite was winning, since she had the help of a nymph named Peristera (dove). So angered was Eros that he turned the nymph into a dove. The dove henceforth was protected by Aphrodite. Tradition holds that Aphrodite herself was born from an egg brooded by a dove and pushed ashore by a fish. Romans, in turn, sacrificed doves to Venus, Goddess of Love, whom Ovid and other poets represented as riding in a dove-drawn chariot.

Tradition held that the oracle at Dodona was founded by a dove, as was the oracle in the Oasis of Siwah, which Alexander the Great sought out.

Doves have also become symbolic of peace, no doubt from the reference in Genesis (Genesis 8:11) to the return of the dove to the ark. On being sent out a second time, the bird reappeared with an olive leaf in its beak.

Tradition also holds that the bird appeared at Christ's baptism (Matthew 3:16 and Mark 1:10). Thus, from the early church to the present day, it has been held as a symbol of the "Holy Spirit."

In the third century, the election of Fabian as Pope was divinely indicated when a dove lit on his head. Some popular beliefs about doves include these: Should a dove hover around the pithead of a mine, it is said there will be disaster. Should a dove fly near the window of a sick person's room or knock on the pane, death is certain. A dove should never be killed, and great misfortune will follow anyone who does kill one. Should twelve doves fly over the head of someone while walking, wealth is soon at hand.

One English folk belief is that a dying person may be kept alive by keeping a live dove in his bedroom, until his family is able to gather together.

Turtledoves nesting near a house keep off rheumatism, according to some American country beliefs, and a dead dove placed on one's chest is also said to cure pneumonia.

Last, in alchemy, a stage of making the "philosopher's stone" is one in which, symbolically, the black raven is said to turn into a white dove. In other words, matter is dissolved and becomes spirit.

DRAGONFLY: Catch one and you are sure to marry within the year. Dragonflies are also said to come to fishermen's aid by hovering over fish.

DREAM: According to a Welsh belief, a sprig of mistletoe gathered on Midsummer's Eve and placed under the pillow will bring one prophetic dreams. Should you wish to dream of your lover, take the blade bone of a rabbit and stick nine pins into it. If you place it under your pillow, you will surely see the object of your affections, says a Yorkshire tradition.

According to some American Indian tribes, dreams occur when the soul leaves the body and travels to different places. A general belief in dreams is that, if you have the same dream three times in a row, its object will be fulfilled.

Nightmares, as opposed to dreams, are said to come from the Prince of Darkness himself. These can be avoided by pinning one's socks to the foot of the bed, by placing a rock crystal under one's pillow, by hanging a diamond or other talisman on your left arm, by folding one's hands on one's chest, and by placing two sticks of straw cut on Saint John's Eve on each of the four corners of the bed.

"Oneiromancy" is the term used to describe the use of dreams for divination practices, a practice followed by almost all the ancients.

DRESS: The left hand and side have always been associated with evil (probably stemming from the fact that it could conceal a weapon while one was outstretching the right hand in a friendly handshake). Therefore, putting clothing on the left arm or foot "first" is generally considered unlucky. This belief stems from an ancient Roman practice of employing a man to wait at the outside door of each house to ensure that no visitor stepped over the threshold with his left foot first. (This is said to be the origin of the modern footman.)

Other general superstitions in regard to dressing include these: If you appear for the first time in a new dress or suit of clothes, you should be pinched by a friend for good luck. You will be ill spoken of should you have any dress or clothing mended while wearing it. Should you place a button in the wrong buttonhole it will bring you bad luck all day. Should you accidentally put on an article of clothing inside out, you will have good luck if you wear it that way throughout the day.

Tradition also calls for the placing of a few coins into the pocket of a dress or coat when worn for the first time.

DRINK: Tradition holds that you should never stir a drink with a knife, or else indigestion is certain.

DROPPING A UTENSIL: Should a young betrothed girl drop a fork when setting the table, her engagement will be broken, according to tradition.

Still another superstition is that dropping a knife while setting the table means a gentleman is soon to call. Should a fork fall, however, a lady visitor will soon appear. Should a spoon fall, expect an uninvited child.

DROPSY: Although fairly uncommon today with the advent of modern medicine, at one time, cures for dropsy were held important.

A sixteenth-century tradition was to take three earthworms, cut off their heads, and immerse them in Holy Water, to which a pinch of sugar and licorice had been added. This mixture was placed in a jar for nine days and then drunk once a day for nine consecutive days. It was said to make the dropsy disappear.

Yet another belief found in Devonshire requires burning fully grown toads and not letting their ashes mix with any other matter. Once reduced to ashes, these are to be ground in a mortar and placed in a wide-mouthed jar that is corked tightly and kept in a dry place. One teaspoonful of the ashes is to be taken for three mornings, as the moon grows in size.

DROWNING: In West Ireland and Scotland, the belief is held that the sea or the river must have a single victim each year. Likewise, a drowning person cannot drown until he has gone under the water for three times.

A tradition held in the Hebrides is that the sea will continually seek for any who have drowned and are not held in its watery grave. Hence, there is a tradition of burying bodies washed ashore as near as possible to the waterline.

Another tradition holds that drowned bodies will float on the ninth day. Yet another superstition is that a body drowned on the bottom of a river can be brought up by firing a gun across the surface of the water.

Should one see a drowned dog or cat while going to a fishing hole, there will be bad luck, unless the fisherman turns around and stays at home.

It is said that the American Indians often took a rooster in a boat over a river in search of a drowned victim. They believed that the bird would crow when it reached the right spot.

Yet another tradition holds that, if you float a loaf of bread that has a quantity of quicksilver in a hole in the middle of it, it will stand still over the spot where a drowned body lies.

Last, a superstition among policemen is that men who have drowned float face down, while women float on their backs, with their faces turned upwards.

DRUNKENNESS: Want to prevent someone from becoming drunk? Want to be able to drink more without becoming drunk yourself? If so, do the following: Take the lungs of a hog and roast them. If eaten after fasting all day, you will never become drunk, no matter how much you consume, says a Welsh tradition.

Someone can be cured of drinking to excess by putting a live eel in his drink. This latter tradition is said to work best if done by an angry wife or husband, without the knowledge of the former!

DUCK: According to traditions in Rutland and other rural areas, duck eggs taken into a house after sunset are said to do no good and will not hatch.

Should a duck lay eggs of a dark brown color, it is considered bad luck for the entire household. The luck can be changed only if the duck itself is destroyed at once.

Should ducks flap their wings while swimming, rain is on the way. Should someone bring less than a handful of violets or primroses to a farmer's wife destruction will come to her broods of young ducks or chickens.

A bolster of duck down is said to guarantee conjugal fidelity.

Last, dead ducks should always be hung with their head down, so that evil spirits can escape from it.

DUNG: Stepping in dog droppings with the left foot is said to bring good luck. Should such droppings be placed around one's house it is said to guarantee happy days ahead.

Dried dog dung is said to cure dysentery, while that of an ox or cow, testicular tumors and sciatica. Goat droppings, if dissolved in vinegar, were believed to cure warts and boils. Mice dung mixed with honey was said to make one's hair grow back.

Since East Indians believe that their cows are sacred, cow dung is believed to drive away evil spirits.

DUST: A general belief is that church dust brought to the bed of a dying person will shorten and ease his transition to the next world.

DWARF: Dwarfs are considered to be special persons and guardians of minerals and precious metals. They are said to be especially gifted as blacksmiths, tailors, bakers, and at predicting the future. They are believed to possess the ability to disappear and become invisible whenever they wish. Hence, it is considered very lucky for a man to meet a female dwarf and for a woman to meet a male.

According to Norse mythology, four dwarfs were given the wits and shape of men by four gods—Austri, Vestri, Svori, and Norori. They were assigned the task of upholding the four corners of the sky.

DYSPEPSIA: Looking for an alternative to bicarbonate of soda? If so, try this Irish formula: Stick a small candle to a penny and place the penny over the stomach, at the spot where it hurts most. Light the candle and place a glass over it. This should cause the skin to be drawn up, as in the European tradition of "cupping." This will lift the evil dyspepsia from the body.

EAGLE: For Christians, an eagle is a symbol of the resurrection, as it is the only bird capable of looking into the sun. Should it be nailed to a barn door, it will keep away evil spirits. Should one eat its brain while it is still warm, it is said to grant fantastic illusions. So great is the power of an eagle that, should its feathers be mixed with those of other birds, it is said to burn and spoil these.

Should one eagle's egg be boiled and eaten by two persons, it is said to keep witches and other evil spirits away. Should an eagle be seen flying about for any length of time or should its screech be heard, it is said to be an omen of death.

One should never steal an egg from an eagle's nest, according to an old Welsh tradition, or he will never find peace again.

One tradition holds that Adam and Eve didn't die, but were turned into eagles who would live forever on an island off the coast of Ireland.

An ancient Egyptian belief was that, every ten years, the eagle soared through the fires of hell and plunged into water in order to acquire a new life.

Among the American Indians, the eagle appears as a major animal character. Its feathers were often used for costumes, head-dresses, and other ceremonial objects. Only the bravest tribesmen were worthy of wearing eagle feathers.

For the Cherokees, obtaining eagle feathers for their "eagle dance" was an arduous task. The eagle killer had to go alone into the mountains for four days, fasting and praying. By using a deer's carcass to draw the eagle and by uttering proper magical songs, it was believed the bird could be killed. Once killed, the eagle would be left at its death place until rites could be performed. The eagle killer would return to his tribe claiming that a Spaniard had done the deed and that "snow bird" had died to protect them. Members of the tribe would then go to collect the feathers they desired.

In ancient times, especially in Mesopotamia, Horus, the Falcon God, was held in great importance. As far back as the third millenium B.C. in Babylonia, the double-headed eagle was associated with Ningursu of Lagash, the Fertility, Storm, and War God.

Among the Mexicans, the conflict between the bird that was believed to soar highest and the reptile or serpent, which creeps into holes in the earth, is graphically depicted.

In Greek mythology, the eagle is an associate of Zeus. In the Old Testament (Daniel 7:4), we read of a lion with eagle's wings. Aristotle, Plato, and Pliny noted that eagles who could survive infancy would indeed live a long time.

Auguries drawn from the eagles were used by both the Greeks and Romans. Tradition holds that, in 331 B.C., a soothsayer, riding close to Alexander the Great, assured him that he had divined by an eagle that Alexander would be victorious over Darius. It is said that an eagle had appeared when Alexander was born.

In the sixth century, the Christian saint, Saint Medard, Bishop of Noyon, was said to be protected during a tempest by the outspread wings of an eagle. Likewise, an eagle has long been the symbol of Saint John.

King Arthur was said to have lived in a cavern guarded by eagles. In bad weather the Welsh would often say, "The eagles are breeding whirlwinds on Snowdon."

Last, one must be reminded of the use of the eagle as a symbol for the United States. However, it is said that Benjamin Franklin wanted a turkey (an American "only" bird) to have this honor!

EAR: Should your right ear itch, it is said that someone is speaking well of you. Should it be the left ear, someone is speaking ill. In Holland, the belief is that an itching in your ear means someone is speaking about you behind your back. If it is the right ear, you are being praised; if the left, one is calling you a scoundrel.

American folklore holds that, if you repeat the name of your acquaintances, one by one, the tingling will stop when the name of the person who is gossiping is spoken. To stop the gossip, it is said you should make the sign of the cross with saliva and then touch the ear so affected.

A tradition exists among some sailors that wearing a gold earring will protect them from drowning, and some people believe that their eyesight will be improved by having their earlobes pierced.

The size and shape of one's ears are said to be indicative of one's character. Small ears are said to indicate benevolence and kindness, but should they be hemmed, beware of insanity. Large ears mean generosity is likely, although such may be accompanied with conceit. Flat ears are said to reveal a coarse nature, while square-shaped ears belong to a noble soul. Long ears are the dominant sign of wisdom and even immortality. A vertical fold or crease in the lobe of an ear is said to indicate possible heart ailments.

Earaches can be cured by obtaining a snail, pricking it, and letting its juice drop into the ear, according to a Gloucestershire belief. (Mumps can be cured by tying a halter around the neck of a child and leading him to a brook in which he is bathed, three times three, in the name of the blessed Trinity. Yet another solution was to wear a rope taken from a black cow around one's neck or a necklace of wool and hot laurel leaves.) Or strip a grass snake of its skin and soak it in brandy. Then pour this into the ears for a sure cure. Likewise, drink water from a bucket that a cat or horse has just taken a drink out of, or place cow urine in the ear cavities.

EASTER: Easter, being the day that commemorates Christ's Resurrection, brings with it a number of traditions. To begin with, it is said that the wind that blows on Easter Eve Day predominates for the entire year. Should it rain heavy on Easter Day, it was an omen of a good grass crop, but very little hay.

On Easter Sunday morning, the sun was said to dance at its rising. Likewise, should one take a smoked glass and look at the center of the sun's disk, one would see a lamb and a flag therein.

Children born on Easter Day were said to be particularly lucky. New clothes for the year should be worn on this day, and holy water taken and saved from Easter Sunday was said to cure all manner of illness.

One tradition stemming from the early days of Christianity was that of "lifting" or "heaving" at Easter. Said to represent the

Savior's Resurrection, men would lift women on Easter Monday and women, the men, on Tuesday. Each leg was taken hold of, and one or more arms, so that the person could be lifted up in a horizontal position three times. It was said to be a rude, indecent, and dangerous diversion practiced chiefly by the lower class of people.

It should also be mentioned that girls were often placed in a chair during the lifting or heaving tradition and moved heavenward by boys who claimed a kiss for their trouble.

Still another English tradition surrounds the distribution of Biddenden cakes. These were small cakes, upon which the figures of two women were impressed. These were given to all who attended Church. Two beliefs exist about the practice. One is that the two women represent twins who were joined together in their bodies and lived together until they were thirty years of age. Another is that the cakes were a gift of two maidens.

The word *Easter,* itself, may be traced to an ancient German Goddess, Ostera, patroness of a cult in which the hare played an important role in spring celebrations. The German word for the celebrations was *Oester* (derived from her name). The goddess Ostera was said to be the personification of the east, of the morning, and of spring. Her worship was brought into England by the Saxons, and, when the early missionaries were unable to abolish it, it was changed into a Christian festival.

Eggs are perhaps the most common tradition associated with Easter. They are retained as a symbol of the Resurrection by Christianity. The origin of sacred eggs may be traced to the Egyptians, Greeks, and Romans. Dyeing eggs in various colors was said to be a token of joy, and red dye, a symbol of Christ's blood.

To win an Easter egg by "picking" was said to bring good luck. To find two yolks in an Easter egg omened a great gain in personal wealth. A popular belief was that one should never refuse to eat an Easter egg offered by a friend, or the friendship would be lost. An old Teutonic belief was that rabbits laid eggs on Easter.

The ancient Romans performed various egg games at the time of our Easter in honor of Castor and Pollux, twins who came forth from an egg deposited by the swan Leda.

Lucky ceremonies included rolling eggs down hills and finding hidden eggs. Planting garden seeds or potatoes on Good Friday was also considered especially lucky. Likewise, should one break pottery on Good Friday, it was said to save the house from damage during the rest of the year.

Still to be mentioned here is the Easter Rabbit, who, strangely enough, is connected with the moon. Among some nations, the rabbit or hare is a type of moon, itself. Hindu and Japanese artists often painted the hare across the moon's disk. The Chinese often represented the moon as a rabbit pounding rice in a mortar. In East Indian mythology, Buddha took on the form of a hare in order to feed a hungry fellow. He was transformed in that form to the moon, where he will live forever.

In Warwick, there was an ancient belief that, if the young men in the town could catch a hare and bring it to the parson before ten o'clock on Easter morning, he was bound to give them a calf's head, a hundred eggs for their breakfast, as well as some money.

Another tradition related to the "lifting" or "heaving" mentioned before was one held on Easter Monday, at which time husbands could beat their wives; on Tuesday, the wives could return the compliment. Still another variation is the custom of men taking off women's shoe buckles, which were redeemed with a present. On Tuesday, the women took the buckles from the men's shoes, which had to be bought back with money or presents.

In the thirteenth century, there was a custom of seizing all clergymen who walked by themselves between Easter and Pentecost, and making them buy their freedom with money. This grew from the belief that the Apostles were seized by the Jews.

Another tradition in England was that of the English King and Queen washing the feet of many poor subjects on Easter Thursday. In 1945, Queen Elizabeth was said to have performed this act. King James II is believed to have been the very last monarch before her to observe this annual rite. The water used for the foot washing was mixed with various sweet herbs, and the sign of the cross was made on each person's feet, after which gifts were presented.

The first Easter hymn of which any record exists is attributed to Saint Ambrose in the fourth century.

Brief mention must be made of the use of the lily as a symbol of the Virgin Mother and the resurrected Christ.

Finally, the expression "Easter before Lent" ("Paques avant Careme") is an expression used by the Creole in Louisiana that really has little to do with Easter. Rather, it indicates that a child has been born too soon after a wedding, suggesting that the mother was pregnant at the time she was married.

EBB TIDE: Generally believed, especially among those persons who live near the sea, is that death will not come until the ebb of the tide. A similar tradition is that the best butter is made when the tide has just turned and is beginning to flow.

The Galelareese hold that, when making oil, it will be in great supply if made when the tide is high.

The ancient historian Pliny observed that nearly all creatures on the coast of France died when the tide was running out.

ECLIPSE: Hardly understood by the ancients, eclipses have always been regarded with awe and reverence. This is especially true of eclipses of the sun, since it was believed to be the energy source of all life.

Among the Romans, it was considered a legal offense to speak words suggesting that the eclipse was due to natural, rather than divine, causes. The ancient Chinese "book of history," *Chou King,* mentions the earliest recorded eclipse as taking place on October 22, in the year 2136 B.C.

During an eclipse, Chinese were required to beat drums and gongs, shoot arrows in the air, and make a great deal of noise, allegedly to frighten away the monster that threatened to devour the sun (which was believed to be a toad).

Historians believe that the Babylonians were the first to discover there was a *Saros,* or cycle, of 223 intervals between new moons, after which eclipses of the sun and moon recur. Hence, if an eclipse is seen on a particular day, it is likely that another will be seen in eighteen years, ten days, and seven and three-quarter hours. It will be visible from the same vantage point, but it will not have exactly the same appearance.

Experts believe that the Saros was also known to the Chinese. The first documented use of the Saros was by Thales of Miletus, the Greek scientist and statesman, who correctly predicted an eclipse for the twenty-eighth of May, in the year 585 B.C.

Tradition also has it that Columbus used the predicted lunar eclipse of April 2, 1493, to obtain provisions he and his crew needed from the inhabitants of Jamaica. When the inhabitants of the island were reticent to help him, he threatened them with divine vengeance, claiming that, on that night, the light of the moon would fail. When the lunar eclipse occurred, the natives approached Columbus and asked for his assistance, which he graciously granted.

Since modern science and astronomy now understand the natural cause of an eclipse, it is well to remember this when looking at other superstitions. Here we find a classic example of ignorance being dispelled by knowledge and truth!

EEL: Eating an eel's heart is said to give one powers of divination. However, eating the entire eel is believed to make one dumb.

In Yorkshire, the belief is held that a horsehair kept in water will turn into an eel.

Tradition also holds that Cherokee ball players rub their bodies with eel skin in the belief that it will make themselves slippery and, therefore, hard to catch.

Cramps in swimming can be prevented by wearing eel skin on the naked leg, and eels placed in white wine are said to be an excellent remedy for intoxication. Mention has already been made (see **drunkenness**) of placing a live eel in one's drink in order to cure him of drunkenness.

EGG: Divination by eggs, or "oomancia," has been practiced throughout time. Though primitive man found it difficult to conceive abstractly of the creation of the world, he was able to watch a similar process in the hatching of an egg. The idea of a "world egg" appears in the mythology of many nations.

To the ancient Egyptians, Ra, the Sun God, was said to have been born from an egg. In Hindu mythology the golden world egg, Hiranyagarbha, was said to have hatched Brahma, the Sun, as well as to have formed the universe from its various parts. To the Chinese the first being, P'an Ku, was said to have emerged from the cosmic egg. Likewise, the egg has throughout time been a popular fertility symbol. Peasants carry eggs into fields as a magical charm to increase crops.

To ward off the evil eye, the Scots placed a nail and an egg in the bottom of a sewing basket and piled seed corn on top. The Slavs and Germans smeared their plows with eggs on Maundy Thursday, thereby hoping to cause a large harvest. In Serbia, pain in the testicles was treated with an application of fried eggs sprinkled with sal ammoniac. This treatment was also said to restore lost virility.

In Morocco, men wishing to increase sexual capacity ate an egg yolk every morning for forty days. An unusual Hungarian custom requires the mixing of a little of one's husband's blood with the white of an egg and the white speck from the yolk. This is combined and stuffed into a dead man's bone. The bone is buried in a spot upon which the husband urinates. This will cause a childless Hungarian woman to conceive. Supporting this belief is the familiar expression that a Hungarian man with a large family has "mixed his blood with eggs."

With the hope of seeing their future love, Scot and Irish girls often removed the yolk from a hard-boiled egg and filled the cavity with salt. To be effective, this charm then had to be eaten, including the shell. This was to be done at the magical hour of midnight, and no water could be drunk before the morning. Should a girl dream that her lover was bringing water, it was said she would soon be jilted.

In 1584, *The Discovery of Witchcraft* claimed that witches can sail in an eggshell. That would explain a primitive American custom of inverting a shell of a boiled egg and smashing the other end.

In Morocco, should someone wish to drive another insane, they simply empty an egg, and then write the name of a magical spirit around the shell with a mixture of saffron, fig juice, and egg white. The contents are then mixed with gunpowder and put back in the egg. Should the egg be buried where the victim habitually walks, this charm is said to drive him out of his mind.

Also in Morocco, should parents of a newborn child neglect a traditional gift of money to the local schoolmaster (so pupils can have a holiday), it is said that the boys will take revenge. They will secretly dig a hole outside the parents' door and steal an egg from their chickens. The egg is buried in the hole, while a chapter of the Koran (normally recited at funerals) is read. Should the mother walk over this, it is said that her child will die, and she herself will be afflicted with a continual menstrual flow. In Japan, if a woman steps on an eggshell, it is believed that she will go insane.

In Java, a bride treads upon an egg, kneels before her husband, and then washes his feet with the yolk. This is said to be a sign of her submission to his will.

In Russia, there is an old custom whereby a mother-in-law offers an omelet to a newly married man. This is said to indicate devotion.

Eggs have also been held as magical talismans against the "evil eye." In North Albania neighborhood women bring eggs to a new mother as a gift. Should the new baby be a boy, they take an even number, should it be a girl, an odd. One of the eggs is smashed and thrown against the baby's face as protection from the evil eye.

In the United States, a folk remedy for erasing a birthmark is to rub it with a fresh egg each morning for seven days and then to bury the eggs under the doorstep.

A belief among southern blacks is that an egg from a guinea hen's nest must be taken with a spoon, or the hen will never return to the nest.

Since the practice of eating eggs is common to the United Kingdom as well, a number of English traditions also surround this complete protein. Following is a sampling of them:

Should you throw an eggshell into a fire after eating a boiled egg, the hen that laid it will cease laying. Should you push your spoon through the bottom of the shell after eating a boiled egg, bad luck is on the way.

It is a bad omen to gather eggs and bring them into the house after dark, and if duck eggs are brought into a house after sunset, they will never hatch into ducklings.

In honor of the Sabbath, never bring eggs into the house on a Sunday; nor should you set eggs under a hen on that day.

Eggs brought over running water will have no chickens in them. Should a hen hatch an entire brood of all hen birds from a setting of eggs, death will occur in the family of the owner.

One method of discovering one's future husband was to pierce an eggshell at Halloween, New Year, or some other special occasion and to catch the white of the egg in a glass of water. The shapes that formed were carefully studied and interpreted.

Similarly, if you wish to know the name of your future wife or husband, simply prick an egg with a pin and let the white drop into a wine glass three-quarters full of water. Place some of this in your mouth and go for a walk. The first name you hear mentioned aloud will be that of your future mate.

If you own horses and eat eggs, say the Irish, you must always eat an even number, or evil will come to the barn.

Should you wish to cure a fever, according to a Devonshire belief, simply go to the nearest crossroads in the dead of night and bury an egg. If you do this five times, the fever will be buried with the eggs.

If you save the first egg laid on Ascension Day, it will protect your house from natural disorder, as well as hasten recovery of one who is ill. Should you break an egg over an ant hill, you will be protected against fever. Should the egg be hard-boiled, this practice will cure jaundice.

If you find an egg without a yolk, unhappiness is the result. Should you find a very small egg, it is an omen of death.

Since Saint Laurent was burned on eggshells, one should never burn them, for fear of making him into a martyr.

In Scotland, the first egg laid by a young hen on Halloween was held as a potent charm. Tradition holds, too, that the egg of an owl placed into a cup of a drunkard will cause his desire for liquor to cease. Likewise, a stork's egg.

In some Catholic countries, the tenth egg laid by a fowl is supposed to be bigger than the rest. It is thus offered to the priest. Other beliefs include these: Breaking eggshells over a child will keep him free from the evil eye or witchcraft. Should a child visit one's house for the first time, it is good luck to give him an egg laid that morning. Should you string up blown eggs and hang them in a home, it is unlucky. If hung in an outhouse, however, it will bring good luck.

Although the Easter egg has already been discussed (see **Easter**), a few additional comments can be added here. One legend suggests that the tradition of giving Easter eggs originated with Mary Magdalene who, when arrested by a centurion in Alexandria, gave him an egg. He let her pass. Yet another legend holds that she presented an egg to the Roman emperor as a token of Christ's resurrection.

In France and other Catholic countries, the silence of church bells from Maundy Thursday until Easter is said to be due to the fact that the bells have gone to the Pope in Rome to bring back Easter eggs.

In Macedonia, children believed that eggs were brought by Paschalia the Easter Spirit. In actuality, parents slipped red eggs under children's pillows after attending midnight Easter mass. In

Germany, an Easter Fox is said to bring the eggs. In Switzerland, the Easter Cuckoo. In other parts of Europe, it is the Easter Hare that lays eggs. In America it is the Easter Bunny.

In the Balkans, residents held that Easter eggs had the ability to drive off evil spirits. They were buried in fields to protect the crops.

In Poland, the shells of such eggs were hung in fruit trees to increase the yield. Even the water in which such eggs were boiled was saved and poured across the entrance to the cow shed. It is said that these practices would prevent a witch from stealing the cow's milk.

Some additional beliefs about eggs include these: Should you open an egg and find two yolks, you will get your wish, if you make it while eating. Others believe that eggs have value in the reduction of fever. After the egg has touched the sufferer, it should be buried to transfer the heat to the earth.

For the early Christians, eggs became a symbol of the resurrection. Just as a chick entombed in an egg will emerge from within, so did Christ emerge from the tomb.

Among the Jews, there is the Passover tradition of placing on the table two unleavened cakes, two pieces of lamb, some small fish, and a hard egg symbolic of a bird called "ziz," about which rabbis have numerous tales.

In Persia, too, another legend is found concerning two jealous brothers and eggs. Each brother made an egg, one containing good spirits and the other, evil demons. The two were broken together, so that good and evil became mixed in the world. In memory of these brothers, up until recent times, Persians would present each other with colored eggs.

The yolk of an egg is said to represent the earth; the white, its atmosphere; and the shell, the firmament.

The traditions and myths about eggs are varied and diverse: For the Abyssinians, the world was portrayed as a great ostrich egg, the ancient Hawaiians believed that their island was produced by the bursting of a huge egg laid on the water by a bird, and the Druids are said to have worn an egg about their neck, encased in gold, as a symbol of priestly authority.

The actual origin of decorating eggs for holidays appears lost in time. A grave excavated at Worms, Germany (dating to about A.D. 320) contains two goose eggs painted with stripes and dots. Decoration of eggs existed in Poland before the eleventh century. In the Ukraine, blue dots are often used, symbolic of the tears of the Virgin Mary. There, tradition holds that she took a basket of colored eggs to Pontius Pilate in order to persuade him to show mercy towards Jesus. As she was preparing them, she wept. Her tears fell upon the shells, forming the blue dots.

Another legend holds that Mary dyed eggs in various colors—red, green, and yellow—to delight her infant child.

Still another tradition is that the Virgin Mary left a basket of plain eggs at the foot of the cross on Good Friday. Hence, eggs should be dyed red, the color of Christ's blood.

A popular myth in many countries is that of a goose who lays a golden egg, and mention should be made of the children's story of Humpty Dumpty, symbolic of a character so fragile, that he could not survive falling.

ELBOW: Often called the "funny bone" when bumped against an object, the elbow has special meanings. Should the pain be very bad from such an accident, some say it can be corrected by hitting the other elbow with equal force.

An itchy elbow is said to announce that its owner will soon be sleeping in the bed of a stranger of the opposite sex.

Should one wish to avenge himself on an enemy, it is said he must bite his own elbow. If he can make this gesture, his enemy will be either drenched in a thunderstorm or struck dead.

ELDER TREE: Tradition holds that an elder is a very special magical tree that protects man and animals. Belief in the magical powers of the elder are said to come from the tradition that the cross upon which Christ was crucified was made of elder wood. Likewise, it was an elder tree from which Judas hanged himself after he betrayed Christ.

The elder is said to ward off moles and snakes. Should one be a victim of a magical spell and beat his clothes with an elder stick, it is said that each whack will reach out and strike the witch or sorcerer.

Burning elder wood in a hearth is said to prevent hens from laying. Beating a domestic animal with an elder stick will cause the animal to perish. Likewise, should boys be beaten with an elder stick, their growth will cease.

In Lincolnshire, an elder tree could never be struck by lightning, according to popular belief. In Sussex, should one wish to cure a wart, he could simply rub it with a green elder stick and bury the stick in muck until it rotted.

Burning elder wood in one's home was said to cause a death in the family. Carrying elder twigs in one's pockets was said to make a horse calmer and more under control. Wounds that have been treated with the leaves of the elder tree, gathered on the last day of April, were believed to heal quickly without infection.

In Bavaria, it was believed that fever could be cured by sticking a twig of elder in the ground, without speaking. Elder wood was also believed to cure epilepsy or at least to prevent it.

Should a twig of elder be cut into nine parts and worn as a necklace, the Irish said that epilepsy would be cured.

ELM: Leaves falling from an elm tree are said to predict disease among one's cattle. Elms are said to be the "tree of justice," since, next to the oak, they are known for their longevity.

In Teutonic mythology, Embla was the first woman. She was believed to have been created from an elm by the three gods—Odin, Hoenir, and Loki—who gave the tree breath, soul, and warmth.

American folk remedies call for infusions of elm bark for prevention of bed sores and for treatment of burns.

In Devonshire, it was said that the right time to plant barley was when the leaves of the elm were as big as a mouse's ear.

ELEPHANT: Because of its size, the elephant is often used as a good luck charm.

Elephants are said to mate at night and in hiding. They rejoin the herd only after purifying themselves in the river water. When they are ready to die, they are said to leave the herd and to go to an unknown place at which their ancestors are buried.

In Africa rings or bracelets made from elephant hair are said to keep away evil spells.

In the United States, the elephant has become a symbol for the Republican party. This was due to publication of a cartoon by Thomas Nast in 1874; it carried the caption "Republican Votes" under a picture of an elephant.

It is said that flies who bother elephants are killed when the elephants fold their skin.

ENEMY: A traditional method for destroying an enemy is to make a clay image of him or her. Stick it full of pins, nails, and broken glass, and then place it in a running stream, with its head to the current. Variations of this same tradition call for placing it in your freezer, in your oven, or in your fireplace. Of course, you could also send it to the person it represents, which is often done in Haiti by those who practice voodoo.

EMERALD: In Ancient Egypt, Uat was the name for water and also meant the color green. Since water was symbolic of the earliest form of the soul, the same word came to signify the hard green stone, the emerald.

According to Pliny, the emerald is the third most precious stone, after diamonds and pearls. It is attributed to Venus and to Friday, the day sacred to that goddess. Emerald is the birthstone for May and is associated with the zodiac sign Gemini.

In American folklore it is said to confer happiness in one's marriage, if worn in a ring or pin.

The thirteen precepts of Hermes were engraved upon emerald. An emerald is also said to be the Pope's stone, and its green color believed to mark both the power of spring and alchemist's light. Biblical tradition holds that an emerald fell from Lucifer's forehead during his downfall.

Popular belief is that it must always be presented on a Wednesday; if offered on a Monday, it will lose its power and can even become unlucky.

According to Russian folklore, the emerald is an enemy of dirt and will prevent its owner from being untidy.

The emerald is said to control sensuality, although some believe it is an aphrodisiac. To maintain its color, it should be dipped in wine and then rubbed, or soaked, in green oil. It is said that whoever places an emerald under his tongue has the power to invoke demons and make them appear. Likewise, a specially consecrated emerald was believed to possess the ability to set prisoners free.

Worn in the form of a ring, it was thought to cure epilepsy, dysentery, and to facilitate childbirth. Likewise, it is said to prevent demons and sorcery and to cure viper bites. If worn upon the left arm, a belief was that it would prevent one from falling under the spell of others, and a simple touch of an emerald was thought to cure a blind man and all vision troubles.

Litigants were advised to wear emeralds, which would cause trials to result in their favor, and sailors engraving the name of the sea god on a light blue emerald were said to be free from tempests.

ENGAGEMENT: In ancient times engagements called for ceremonies as great as that of the wedding itself.

Prior to the exchange of promises, tradition held that a man must let his hat fall on the ground and then touch the young woman's left hand with his right.

It is said that, like marriage, there could only be "one" engagement. Should a man or woman get engaged two times, it was believed they would go to hell; a third time, and the Devil could take their soul.

In Brittany, in the Middle Ages, a man wishing to get engaged hung a hawthorn branch on the door of his wife-to-be on the night of May 1. If the young woman wished to refuse his offer of marriage, she substituted a cauliflower for the hawthorn.

It was said a young man should never ask for a girl's hand in marriage himself, but rather send one or many representatives to the girl's family. Should these people run into difficulties, such as stumbling, sneezing, or should their ears ring during their quest, they were instructed to immediately abandon their pursuit and return back to the sender. The belief was that the marriage would be an unhappy one. Likewise, if they encountered on their way a monk, priest, layman, hunchback, virgin, blindman, pregnant woman, dog, cat, horse, stag, road deer, wild boar, magpie, or lizard.

Should the messengers hear thunder rumbling in the distance, or should one have a ringing sound in his left ear or should his left nostril bleed, it was said to be an excellent omen for success. The marriage would even be happier should they come across a cortisan, she-goat, wolf, pigeon, toad, spider, or cicada.

It is said that the sought-after young woman should hide once the parson or notary arrived, later on, to formalize the engagement, so that her lover would have to seek her out and thereby offer her more gifts.

Should a family wish to refuse a groom-to-be, they would cause embers to rise in the fireplace or place a frying pan upside down therein. Should the girl's mother receive the guests with a flat cake, it was said to be a sign of refusal.

Once sealed, a contract was held valid only when the young people closed their fists, locked their little fingers together, drank from the same glass, and cut bread together with the same knife.

The engaged couple was also expected to bury their past life by breaking plates and glasses.

Should a member of the parish die during the engagement period, it was said to portend an unhappy marriage.

On the very eve of the wedding, the dowry was taken to the fiancé's family, who pretended to refuse it. Before the actual engagement, it was said that lovers could attract each other by rubbing hips together, squeezing each other's hands, tapping each other's knees, or pinching or touching hands through a holed stone. A young man could also announce his desires by offering the young girl a cake in a phallic shape, a ring, or a basket.

American traditions hold that the day on which the engagement ring is purchased also portends the success of the engagement. Should the engagement ring be altered for any reason, should it wear badly or become loose before the wedding, it is said to be an omen that the match will not be a happy one. Should the ring be lost or should it break, it is considered a bad omen.

It is said that a young woman can break off an engagement by presenting a knife to her discarded suitor.

EPILEPSY: This disease, little understood by the ancients, but greatly feared, had a great number of unusual beliefs associated with it.

In ancient times, "the falling sickness" was held divine in origin. Those suffering from it were considered "blessed ones."

In later years epilepsy was thought of as a curse, and cures were sought. Burying a black cock alive, at the last spot where the epileptic fell, especially if a lock of the victim's hair and some nail parings were included, was said to be a cure. Wearing a ring made from a half crown, given in a church collection after celebration of Holy Communion, was said to cause the condition to vanish.

Drinking extract of mistletoe was also believed to cure this illness, according to a Lincolnshire tradition. Driving a nail into the ground where the patient fell also was thought efficacious.

Eating the heart and blood of a crow for nine days was said to relieve the disease, as was burning the patient with a red-hot church key along the head.

The fits could be avoided, but not cured, by tying three hairs of a milk-white greyhound around one's neck as an amulet.

EVIL EYE: The belief in an evil eye or in the Italian "malocchio" at one time dominated the intellect of the United Kingdom in the sixteenth and seventeenth centuries. It was no doubt inspired by the Biblical phrase "Eat thou not the bread of him that hath an evil eye" (Proverbs 23:6).

The belief that some people have the "eye of the Devil," and that, with a single glance, they can cause misfortune, is itself an ancient one. According to the ancient historian Pliny, Libya was once the domain of the basilisk, whose eye was said to possess such a devastating power, that it would destroy itself if it saw its reflection in a mirror. The effect of a zap from the evil eye could allegedly bring misfortunes of every kind, with the sexual organs being particularly liable to attack.

To describe the experience of having been bewitched by the evil eye, country folk coined the expression "overlooked." Anyone whose eyes were of a different color, or were narrow, deep set, or somewhat crossed could be accused of possessing the ability to bewitch.

It was believed that spinsters usually had the evil eye, since they no longer had a menstrual flow. The evil eye was said to especially affect women who had just given birth. Hence, a number of traditions emerged to protect the newborn, many of which have already been mentioned in this work. (See **birth** and **babies**.)

To protect you from the spell, the sign of the horns could be made behind your back, should someone be seen looking at you for too long a time. The wearing of betony leaves and nine grains of salt around your neck in a small sachet was also suggested. A piece of iron, a key, or a horseshoe could also be effective.

Wearing a cross of jet was frequently suggested, in the belief that it would split, if glanced upon by a person having evil intentions. Skin from a hyena's forehead, mugwort hung up in the home, catochites (a special stone) worn in a ring or about one's neck, spitting on the right shoe before putting it on, or wearing a necklace of jacinth were various methods employed to ward off this evil.

The practice of sweeping a child's face with the bough from the pine tree was considered a most potent preventative, as was hanging up the key of the house over an infant's cradle. Giving a child a piece of coral that had been dipped in the baptismal font was also held effective.

In Romania, a child or adult decorated with red ribbons was thought impervious to the influence of the eye.

During the medieval period, any individual held responsible for inflicting the evil eye was tried for witchcraft. The origin for this practice was the infamous *Malleus Maleficarum*, the handbook of the Inquisition, which held, "there are witches who can bewitch their judges by a mere look or glance from their eyes."

It was said that, should one possess the power of the evil eye and find it failing, nine toads strung together and buried alive would rejuvenate it. In Scotland, where the belief in the evil eye was prevalent, a stranger seen examining a farmer's cattle would immediately be offered some of the milk as a guarantee against disaster. During childbirth, a mother's house would be sprinkled with urine to prevent "overlooking."

It is said that plastering a newly born child with mud or soot in order to make it unattractive, or dressing the boys in their sister's clothes were two ways to ward off this efficacious evil.

In Spain and Portugal, sage and rosemary were considered powerful psychic protectors, as was garlic in Greece and the shamrock in Ireland.

Tradition held that the first glance of the evil eye, especially if delivered from an oblique angle, was the most potent. Wearing an amulet with a grotesque design of a toad or hunchback, or of the eye itself, was said to absorb the venom of this attack.

The ancient Greeks wore the amulet of Medusa, as well as the caduceus—the wand or staff of the god Mercury, which protected him from the evil eye of the gods.

For the Romans, wearing phalli made from gold, silver, or bronze was one way to deal with this potent force. Likewise, babies were often given coral phalli for use as teething rings.

The "fleur-de-lis," which often appeared on various coats of arms, was considered another symbolic barrier against the evil eye.

On the Isle of Harris, young children wore necklaces of white nuts, known as "mullaska beans," in the belief that the beans would turn black should the child be "overlooked."

Inserting the thumb between the first and second fingers, with the fist clenched, or making the "Devil's horns," in which the two middle fingers are held down by the thumb, while the first and little fingers are raised, are perhaps the best-known defenses against this particular psychic attack.

While anyone was susceptible to the evil eye, including animals, the most susceptible were said to be young couples during the first year of marriage, cattle and other livestock, pregnant women, girls at the age of puberty, newborn infants, and children under seven.

Long ago, the Turks engaged in the protective practice of suspending magical globes from their ceilings and from the caparisons of their horses.

In England, covered glass spheres, which came to be known as "witch balls" were used similarly, as were blue beads. Similarly, the symbol of an eye was often painted upon the prow of a fisherman's boat or actually tattooed on the back of a child.

American folklore suggests painting a red spot on one's forehead or carrying a heart-shaped locket or brooch as protection. Red ribbons placed over one's front door or tied to the tails of cattle were often employed in England and Scotland.

Among the Southern Slavs, a victim of an evil eye would wash himself in water into which a copper coin had been placed. After muttering an incantation, he would present this coin to a blind beggar, in the belief that it would transfer the affliction with the coin.

According to the ancient Jewish Talmud, "For everyone who dies of natural causes, ninety-nine will die of the evil eye."

Besides the wearing of charms and amulets, saliva is said to be a fine protection, especially if one spits over one's left shoulder.

Last, one must mention the Order of the Garter, established by Edward III in 1349. Its motto is the following: Make sure the evil is not in the eye of the beholder.

EYE: Should one's right eye itch, it was said to denote good luck. Should the left eye itch, however, bad luck would soon be in attendance. In fact, should one's left eye twitch, the person was being betrayed.

Should the eyes of a recently deceased person not close, it is said that they were looking for followers.

Sore eyes were to be cured by bathing with rainwater gathered on Ascension Day, or the water found in the hollow cup formed by the teasel's leaves. Likewise, rain gathered on Holy Thursday, if preserved and bottled, was also said to be an unfailing remedy.

Should one get dust in his eye, it should be rubbed gently with a gold wedding band. At the same time, one should also rub the unaffected eye, while spitting on the ground or touching the corresponding ear to the suffering eye with a knife.

Cataracts were said to be cured by burning a cat's head and then blowing the ashes in front of the sick person's eyes. Swallow droppings on a person's face would cause blindness, but placing two vervain leaves on the fist opposite the suffering eye, and then attaching them with a thread from a spider's web, was said to bring relief.

Yolks from three eggs laid on a Thursday, or the white of an egg, mixed with alum, also was said to form a wonderful eyewash. Bathing one's eyes with one's own urine was also recommended. Rubbing one's eyes with a four-leaf clover or curdled milk was said to yield great results, and wearing onyx or agates was also thought a powerful talisman against vision trouble.

Inflammation of the conjunctiva was said to be cured by vine shoots reduced to powder and applied in a lotion. A slice of cold veal placed on the eye was also supposed to be effective.

Should one suffer from a sty, rubbing the eye with a green garlic cloth was said to be helpful, as was cow's urine. Ringing a person's doorbell and then running off was also said to rid oneself of this curse.

A one-eyed person was thought to have special magical talents, in particular, double vision.

Eyelashes, too, had special significance. If an eyelash on the right eye turned downward, it was a sign of luck for a man; should it be the left eye, he could expect bad luck. These two omens were reversed in the case of women.

Should an eyelash be placed on the back of one's left hand and a blow of the right palm be used to dislodge it, such was accepted as a means of predicting the future. Should the eyelash not move, it was said that one's wish was lost forever. Should it disappear, however, the eyelash "had gone" to bring the wish to fulfillment.

EYEBROW: It is said that, when a woman's eyebrows meet across her nose, it is a positive sign that she will be happy whether married or not. Another tradition holds that persons whose eyebrows meet will be lucky in all their undertakings.

Contrary to this is the belief expressed in the following couplet:

> *Trust not those whose eyebrows meet,*
> *For in their heart they carry deceit.*

Still another couplet suggests the following:

> *If your eyebrows meet across your nose,*
> *You'll never live to wear wedding clothes.*

In some parts of America eyebrows that met were said to be a sign of beauty; in others, it was the mark of a werewolf or witch.

FALLING OBJECT: A falling window blind, shade, or picture is said to presage death.

Falling or shooting stars were believed to be souls coming down from heaven to animate newborn children. The Maoris held the belief that, at death, the soul left the body and went to the other world in the form of a shooting star.

FALSE DEATH: According to a German tradition, if a person's death is unintentionally reported, when, in fact, he is still alive, that person will gain an extra ten years of life.

FEATHER: To the ancient Egyptians, the feather was associated with the delicate balance between truth and fabrication. Maat, Goddess of Truth and Justice, was often depicted in hieroglyphics as a feather. After death, the deceased journeyed to the underworld and entered the "hall of judgment." Presiding over the hall was Osiris, God of the Underworld, clad in a robe of feathers (his emblem of righteousness), and forty-two judges, each one wearing a "feather of truth" on his head. Tradition held that the heart of the deceased was placed in one pan of the scales and the feather (symbolic of Maat) placed on the other to test for truthfulness. Only if the two pans balanced did Osiris grant admission to the underworld.

Among American Indians, a feather was added to one's headgear for each slain enemy. Since birds were held as links and mediators between men and gods, feathers were often used ceremoniously.

In Hungary, during the fifteenth century, only one who had slain a Turk was permitted to sport a feather.

Feathers of a wren were said to preserve one from shipwreck for an entire year, according to an Isle of Man tradition. Required was the fact that the wren be chased, caught, and killed on Christmas Eve, and, afterward, carried aloft on a pole, with its wings outstretched. Those desiring a feather could obtain one in return for a coin. At the end of the day, the bird, usually featherless, was buried on the seashore. After this, the feathers were a potent charm against shipwreck.

FEATHER BED: Turning a feather bed over on Sunday was said to result in fearful dreams for a week. Should one turn a feather bed on a Sunday, according to another tradition, death would be brought into the house. Likewise, should the feathers of the bed come from pigeons or game birds, no one could die happily or painlessly on that bed.

FEET: It is considered unlucky to meet a man with flat feet on a Monday morning, and ill luck is brought by a flatfooted person entering your house on New Year's Day. Contrariwise, good luck is said to occur when a person with a high instep enters one's house on New Year's morning.

In Scotland, those born feet first are said to have power to heal sprains, lumbago, and rheumatism by trampling on the affected parts of others.

In the Punjab of India, a firstborn child who was born feet first could be used to cure backache by kicking the patient in the back at a crossing.

In Britain, if one scraped his right foot on the ground while walking along the street, it was believed that a friend would be met shortly. Should the left foot be scraped, he could expect a disappointment.

Should one's feet itch for no apparent reason, it is said one is about to make an unexpected journey.

Possessing an extra toe is said to indicate one will be lucky in life, and mentioned elsewhere is the belief that one should not enter a place with one's left foot first. (See **door**.)

FERN: In France, the fern is called "Saint John's hand" and in England, "the Devil's brush."

It was believed that cutting or burning ferns would bring rain. It was also said that, if ferns are hung in one's home, they will protect it from thunder and lightning.

Should one tread on a fern, such causes confusion and loss of direction.

Spores of the fern (known as "bracket seed") were long believed to have curative abilities. If carried in one's pocket, they were said to grant invisibility.

Should one cut a fern root slantwise, a picture of an oak tree is said to be seen. The more perfect the picture, the luckier the fern will be.

Should fern be found growing on a tree, it is said to relieve stomach aches. When crushed, fern seed was thought to cure them as well. If one ascends a mountain holding fern seed in his hand on Midsummer's Eve, a vein of gold will be discovered. It is also recommended to gather fern the night of Saint John, or the summer solstice. You should be wearing a shirt, have bare feet, and an empty stomach when you do so.

Should you inadvertently step on a fern plant on the night of Saint John, it was said you will hear a concert of birds. Should this happen to a pregnant woman, however, she is likely to abort her child.

At midnight, a red flower was said to illuminate the darkness and was often sought after by the Devil. Anyone wishing to pick the fern flower must trace a circle around the fern and detach it from the plant, without turning his head sideways. Whoever turns his head will never be able to put it back in its normal position.

So potent a talisman was a fern flower that it would protect anyone against all spells. It was also said to make possible the discovery of hidden treasure. Should it be thrown into the air and seen to spin, then fall perpendicular to the ground, it was an indication that hidden treasure was concealed there.

Fern seeds, if placed in one's coin purse on the night of Saint John, were said to cause the coins to recreate on their own as they are spent.

Rheumatism and rickets were thought to be cured by sleeping on mattresses or pillows made from ferns.

One can protect himself from snakebites by cutting a branch of this plant with his teeth.

FERTILITY: In some rural parts of the United States a belief holds that, if a married couple throws cow peas across the road near their home, the woman will conceive, even if she has been unable to do so for some time.

FIG SIGN: Making a "fig sign" is an ancient way of warding off the evil eye. Make a fist, putting your thumb up between the index finger and the middle finger. (If you live in an Italian neighborhood, however, it is suggested that you *don't* do this. It is considered an insulting sexual gesture and may result in you receiving a black eye!) It is said that this sign should be used when something good has been done, in order to distract the notice of Satan himself. Legend holds that Barbarossa first used this after a battle, as a sign of contempt for the people of Milan.

The fig sign should be pointed in the direction of anyone who wishes you ill or who brings you bad luck, or in the direction of a black cat, or any other ill-omened creature.

FINGER: Here we have an area in which an entire book could be written. Certainly, divination through analysis of the hand and fingers, sometimes called "palmistry," or "chiromancy," is an area about which entire books have been written.

For the time being, however, some general statements about fingers can be made. To begin with, crossing the index and middle fingers as a sign of good luck or to exorcize the evil eye is certainly common. It is said that the best time to make this sign is when passing by a cemetery or behind someone's back while telling a white lie in order to protect the soul.

It is said that one should be very cautious when it comes to pointing the finger. For instance, should one point the finger in the direction of a ship setting sail, the ship will go down. Pointing one's finger at a person was said to bring to him the evil eye. In order to exorcize this influence, one had simply to make the sign of the horns pointed downward. This is made by extending the index and little finger only.

The ancient writer Ovid records a rite in which spirits of the unburied dead can be held away by pointing the joined index finger and thumb in that direction. Likewise, misfortune was said to come to anyone who points at the sun, the moon, and the stars. In some American folklore, pointing at a fruit tree is said to cause the fruit to decay, while pointing at a funeral may bring about the death of the pointer.

One-handed persons are believed to have been given a gift for clairvoyance and psychic divination as compensation for their physical loss.

Mention must also be made of the fact that, during the Second World War, Winston Churchill's use of his index and middle fingers to make the sign of a "V" for victory became legendary.

Traditions regarding the use of the fingers and hand appear in various myths as means to convey spiritual power and to bring about healing. In the New Testament, Jesus speaks of casting out devils with "the finger of God" (Luke 11:20). No doubt this belief underlies the Christian practice of ordination and confirmation, whereby the priest conveys spiritual power through the laying on of hands.

For the early Christians, a belief was held that one could be protected against demons and other spiritual entities by simply inscribing an imaginary cross upon the forehead with the forefinger. Likewise, American folk traditions hold that many cures can be obtained by rubbing an injured part with a finger wet with spit.

The index finger, however, is sometimes called the "poisonous finger," or "finger of the evil eye." For this reason, it should never be used for applying ointment or healing salves.

In other folk traditions, however, the third finger of the left hand, or ring finger, was said to be able to cure a wound through the simple act of stroking. This was due to the fact that this finger was believed to have a direct connection with one's heart.

The index finger, according to an Oxfordshire tradition, is also known as "witch" or "cursing finger." In the lore among blacks of the American South, it was known as "the conjure" finger.

In Turkey, there is a belief that one must eat with three fingers "only," because the Devil ate with the other two.

Should one inadvertently find himself looking through the spaces between his fingers, it is said to be an omen that a wedding will soon be celebrated.

The finger has sometimes been regarded as a symbol of fate as well. Hence, we find in the "Omar Khayyam," the following:

The Moving Finger writes and having writ
Moves on, nor all thy Piety nor Wit
Shall lure it back to cancel half a
Line . . .

Some believe that the shape of one's fingers indicates personality. Short, fat fingers are said to indicate foolishness and intemperance; long, lean fingers, intelligence (some say that long fingers indicate a spendthrift); while those whose fingers that bend upwards are considered to be brutish, ravenous, and unchaste. A crooked little finger, however, is said to make one rich, and should the forefinger or index finger be larger than the second, it is said to indicate dishonesty. Those born with more than five fingers on one hand, however, were thought by the ancients to be cherished by the gods and to be possessors of great abilities. But while many traditions hold that being born with an extra finger is lucky, such was not the case for Anne Boleyn. She possessed six fingers on her left hand, which may have been a factor leading to her condemnation as a witch by the English people.

FINGERNAIL: Here we find a great number of traditions, many of which have to do with babies: For example, should a baby's nails be cut before it is one year old, it is said that the child will grow up to be a thief. Some beliefs hold that the child will stammer. Should the first parings of a child be buried under an ash tree, it is said that the child will turn out to be an excellent singer.

According to a Spanish belief, one can ruin a child's teeth by cutting his nails on a Monday.

While many traditions hold that children's fingernails should not be cut, a mother may bite them off in perfect conscience. According to one source, however children who bite their own fingernails are potential criminals.

There are rules about cutting one's own nails as well, and even more important, what you should do with the parings. For example, one should never cut or pare fingernails on a Friday or Saturday; to do so will bring bad luck. However cutting one's nails on Good Friday was said to cure toothaches. Equally contradictory is the belief that, should an unmarried girl desire to see her future husband in a dream, she should clip her nails nine Fridays in a row. One tradition holds that, should nails be cut on Sunday, "the Devil will have you all week."

Some believe that a woman who is able to cut her right-hand nails with her left hand will always wear the pants in her marriage. In Japan, girls who bite their nails are held to have a difficult time giving birth and are, therefore, avoided as possible wives.

It is said that sailors believe one should not cut nails during a calm, as it will provoke a storm.

Tradition holds that the Romans never clipped their nails while on a boat, during a religious service, or at night. Among the Irish, tradition holds that one should face the north when cutting his nails.

One can prevent nail clippings from being used by witches by spitting on them three times or cutting them one by one into three pieces.

Among Scandinavians there is a practice of burying nails deep in the ground to keep them away from elves.

With regard to parings, it is generally held that fingernail parings should be kept from falling into the hands of witches or evildoers.

In American folklore is found the belief that one's own nail parings, soaked in wine and served to a lover, will restore affection. Also, if you can obtain nails of a dead man and bury them under your enemy's doorstep, he will be struck ill with a fever and flu until they are removed. Likewise, burying one's parings in a place where someone walks will put that person in your power.

One tradition among Jews holds that nail parings should be burned with a piece of wood in order to ensure good luck.

Other traditions hold that pregnant women who walk over nail parings will immediately abort, and nail clippings buried at a crossroads were said to bring down a fever.

Coloration of the nails was a device used by the ancient Egyptians to drive away evil spirits. In Cromwell's England, such a practice was banned. At one time, men and women in Spain and in the United States who were of mixed blood, colored their nails to conceal their ancestry.

White specks on nails were said to presage good fortune, whereas black specks were held an evil omen. To have yellow specks on nails was said to indicate death.

In England, one tradition exists for divination through the use of white spots on the nails. Should the spot appear on the thumbnail, a gift will soon be received; on the first finger, expect a new friendship; on the middle finger, expect a betrayal; on the ring finger, look for success in love or business; on the little finger, a voyage will soon be undertaken.

Among the Germans there is the belief that, by counting the white spots found on a person's nails, one can determine the number of years they have left to live.

A half-moon appearing at the base of a nail is said to be fortunate. Should the half-moon be large and high, it indicates great generosity. Should the half-moon be small or almost absent, expect dishonesty and cruelty. Should the half-moon be pale or white, its owner is lustful. Should the half moon be two-colored, one's health is fragile.

Some traditions hold half-moons as a sign of longevity. The bigger they appear, the longer their owner is said to live.

FIR TREE: Many references to the fir are found in folklore worldwide and include any kind of cone-bearing tree or conifer.

In Phrygia, the pine tree was held sacred to the "mother of the gods," Cybele, who was also the Goddess of Fertility. According to one legend, she loved Attis, a young shepherd, who was charged with the care of her temple. This required his vow of celibacy. Supposedly, Attis fell in love with a nymph, and, when realizing he had neglected his vow, he castrated himself and bled to death beneath a pine tree.

In another Roman version, this same goddess, whose name is now changed to Rhea, prevents his death by transforming him into a pine, after being assured by Jupiter that the tree would remain "ever green."

Among the Greeks, Thesmophoria was an annual ritual in which food and pine branches were cast into caves, sacred to the goddess Demeter, to be brought forth a year later and placed on her altar. Hence, the pine became a symbol of immortality.

In Norway and Russia, in fact, pine or fir boughs are often placed on coffins before interment.

In central Germany, fir trees were placed before houses when a wedding was about to take place. In northern Germany, recently married couples went through a ceremony in which they held fir branches carrying candles.

When cattle were driven to their first spring pastures, the drivers often fixed fir branches on the last cow in order to ensure the fertility and immortality of the herd.

In Japan, the pine is a symbol of competency and marital faith-fulness. In China, the pine was likewise venerated, since it could withstand the adverse winter weather.

For the Romans, the unopened pine cone represented virginity. Hence, virgins would often wear pine garlands during various ceremonies, especially during those in honor of the goddess Diana.

In Russia, an ancient tradition for the shaman or medicine man required the placement of nine (or multiples of nine) fir saplings before or around his house. In order to become possessed and to prophesy, the shaman was required to leap from one tree to the next in a certain order, thereby eventually arriving at the ninth, in order to prove his connection with both the earth and sky gods.

The resin of the fir tree was long believed to have magical properties and was often used in incense. In the seventeenth century, a character called the "Green Man" and his ally, the "Wode-house," were characters in plays and pageants. They were dressed in the leaves of the fir tree and their symbol was a staff tipped with a pine cone.

In England, should a fir tree be touched, withered, or burned with lightning, the master or mistress of the house will die.

In American folklore, the planting of pine or fir trees in a line is said to produce as many deaths in the family as there are trees. In Kentucky, it is advised not to plant pines at all.

One can prevent dreaming of a fir tree (which is said to mean suffering) by laying a branch of the tree at the foot of one's bed. A partly burned branch was said to be protection against lightning.

Placing a fir bough on one's barn door was said to prevent the theft of grain by human or nonhuman means.

FIRE: An old English saying goes "When a fire burns without glowing, you'll have company without knowing." Many of the traditions in regard to fire appear in various entries of this work (mention has already been made of the fact that sparks ascending from fire were often used for divination), but some traditions are included here.

Many civilizations have their own god of fire, among which are found Apollo, Helios, Hestia, Loki, and Lleu. The Mongols' fire deity was called "Mother Ut"; her father was steel and her mother was flint. To the North American Indians, fire was the representa-tive of the sun on earth. In the Great Lakes area, a special cult worshipped "Grandfather Fire." One must also mention the Parsee, the descendants of Zoroaster, who believed fire the outward symbol of their deity.

According to Greek mythology, Prometheus stole fire from the gods and gave it to mankind, after which he was punished by the angry Zeus. Widespread among many Indian tribes are legends that fire was stolen and passed from animal to animal until finally given to the tribe itself.

In Finland, tradition holds that fire was the child of the sun, and in some European folklore, the agent of fire was expressed as a bird.

For the Druids, fire was connected with the oak tree, a hard wood suitable for making it; the mistletoe, which grew on the oak and was held as protection against lightning; and the acorn, a symbol of the oak, which would often be carried as a talisman. It is said that, at various festivals, the Druids made their herds pass between fires to purify them.

Saint John's fires were a Christian form of these same ceremonies. It is said the Saint John's fire can purify a rosary. It is held as good luck to jump over the flames. Among the Celts, immense fires were lit to celebrate the equinoxes and solstices. In fact, Saint John's Feast Day corresponds exactly with the summer solstice.

Among Christians, fire is said to symbolize God in the form of the Holy Ghost. Hence, it is not surprising that the tongues of flame visited the apostles on Pentecost.

Since a fire was held to be of divine origin, should it not ignite or should it burn badly, it was said to indicate the presence of evil spirits or witchcraft. This could be counteracted by placing the poker upright across the bars, which symbolically made the sign of the cross.

Traditions and superstitions about fire abound: One tradition held that, should the embers of a fire break in two, the housemaid currently engaged would soon lose her situation. Likewise, it was believed that dead embers should be taken out of the fire before the family retires or bad luck will attend the household.

An unusual Scotch superstition holds that, if children play with fire before bedtime, they will wet their bed in their sleep.

In China, fire is believed to dispel evil at weddings and on the bridal night. In Swatow when a bride arrives at the bridegroom's home, she steps over a ground fire made by burning a few wisps of grass. This is said to drive away any devils she may have encountered on the journey there. In Canton, the bride is placed on the back of a female servant, who carries her over a charcoal fire. In Peking, in order to drive away evil, the chair that carries the bride to the bridegroom's house is carried over a vessel containing charcoal.

In Cornwall, should branches of seaweed be dried and fastened in turned wooden frames and stood on the mantlepiece, the house would be preserved from burning down.

In addition, it was believed that a fire burning brightly, after being poked, indicated that an absent lover, wife, or husband was in good spirits and humor.

Last, a fire that refuses to catch on Christmas morning was an omen for a bad year ahead.

FISHING: Fishing is a worldwide pursuit, so it is not surprising that there exist a number of traditions in regard to this art.

It is said that, if a fisherman and his wife have a fight right before he goes to sea, a good catch is assured. The fight must develop on its own and not be staged, however. Should the man draw blood from his wife, it is an especially good omen for a large haul.

On the way to his fishing boat, if a fisherman meets a woman wearing a white apron, it is said to be unlucky. The fisherman should turn back and wait for the next tide. The same is true should he meet a minister. Once on board his ship, bad luck is certain to arrive should the fisherman verbally mention a minister, a church, or a pig.

Should the fisherman lose the first fish he is hauling, the entire trip will be unlucky. Should he catch the first fish in the stern, bad fortune is promised. Some fishermen throw the first fish caught back into the water in order to induce other fish to come to the hooks or nets.

Should a fisherman inadvertently take the name of God in vain, ill luck is said to arrive, unless every member of the crew immediately grasps the nearest piece of iron and holds it for a time.

Should one count the number of fish caught, no more will be captured that day. If a fisherman is right-handed, he should never cast with the left hand. Should fish fail to bite at all, one of the fishermen should be thrown into the water and hauled out again, as if he himself were a fish. This is done, according to a Scottish tradition, to cause the fish to nibble.

During oyster dredging, fishermen are claimed to use a monotonous chant to charm the oysters into their nets. Norwegian fishermen often drink a "white lug," a sort of toddy, believing it will ensure a big catch.

In some countries, should a man fall overboard and appear to be drowning, he will not be assisted. It is believed that to do so would offend the water spirits and drive the fish from their nets. Some fishermen believe that spitting on the bait before casting the hook will make certain their catch.

In Yorkshire, when a fishing boat is first launched, a coin must be placed and kept permanently under the mast in order to ensure good luck. A similar practice consists of cutting a slice in one of the pieces of cork attached to the nets and inserting a coin therein. This is said to convince Neptune, God of the Seas, that the fishermen are willing to pay for any fish they may extract. However, should no fish be caught for some time, the first fish caught was often burned as a sacrifice.

Among some fishing men, a tradition holds that rods should never be changed during the course of a day's fishing, unless the rods have broken. Likewise, one should never sit on a lobster pot or an upturned basket; nor should one exchange a float that has worked well for an improved or new one.

One more superstition: Never wear white clothes while fishing.

Since Christ fed the multitudes with five loaves and two fishes and was said to usher in the Piscean Age, a fish became an early symbol for Christianity.

In ancient Egypt a fish was believed to have eaten the phallus of the God Osiris. For the Chinese, a fish is a sign of happiness; in India, it is one of the eight symbols of Buddha.

Five: The number five is said to indicate union and, of course, appears as a five-pointed star. It is said to be the sacred number of the Mayans.

An outstretched hand with five fingers spread was said to keep evil away, according to the Moslems.

For some reason, however, Greeks avoided saying the word *five*.

Perhaps it was their belief that the five-pointed star represented the secrets of life. Rumor has it that Pythagoras invented this symbol.

Five is said to be the number symbolic for fire, love, and marriage. For Christian numerologists five was said to be indicative of the imperfect law of Moses contained in the first five books of the Bible—the Pentateuch. Jesus, too, suffered five wounds in the hands, feet, and in the side.

One must also recall that we each have five senses: sight, hearing, taste, touch, and smell. It is said that five consists of the first male number **3** added to the first female number **2**. It also consists of the first number **1**, symbolic of God, added to the number **4**, symbolic of the Earth and matter. Five, then, is the number of man as a microcosmic being.

In Gothic churches and cathedrals a five-petaled flower is sometimes shown in the center of a cross.

FLEA: Should a flea bite you on the hand, say the Germans, you will either be kissed or receive good news. Fleas were also said to desert the body of someone near death, and it is believed that if fleas are seen on a corpse, there will soon be another death in the region. Others say a flea biting you means it is going to rain.

European traditions hold that fleas will never enter your bed if it is carefully aired on Maundy Thursday before Easter. Fleas will never crawl into a monk's bed, according to one tradition. Windows of the house should be kept shut on the first day of March in order to prevent the entrance of fleas, say some.

Should a walnut branch be laid on one's bed, fleas will quickly exit. According to Pliny, male urine and rue mixed together will accomplish the same thing.

In East Anglia, fleas were said to be caused by witches. Sticking pins into a piece of flannel that had been next to a patient's skin, and burning it at midnight, was said to rid one of fleas. Should you want someone to be eaten by fleas, however, put violets on his chest, says one tradition, and a shirt cut out on Good Friday, a day in which no one should labor, was said to attract fleas to anyone who wears it.

Foxgloves, if strewn around, will cause fleas to leave one's home, according to an Irish tradition. Should a housewife rise early on the first of March and brush around the lintel and hinges of a door, according to an English tradition, fleas will neither enter nor remain.

Another tradition holds that one can rid oneself of fleas by leaping across the Midsummer bonfire. The historian Pliny held that one could banish fleas by scraping up dirt found beneath one's right foot when the sound of a cuckoo was first heard. According to American folklore, if you bring a sheep or goat into the house, it will draw fleas to itself.

A fable exists in which a fox waded deep into a pond carrying moss in its mouth. The fleas were said to enter the moss, which the fox then let float away.

Yet another method to rid oneself of fleas was connected with the sacred palm tree, said to be one of four trees from which the cross used to crucify Christ was made. One had simply to place a palm leaf behind a picture of the Virgin Mary on Easter Sunday at the first stroke of the Resurrection bell. One would then say, "Depart, all animals without bones." This was said to keep away fleas for a year.

FLOWER: Many of the traditions with regard to flowers will be discussed under the specific types. Here we shall consider some general traditions surrounding what the ancient Egyptians considered harbingers of fortune.

To begin with, it is considered unlucky to bring flowers into the house outside of their season. Likewise, should flowers that normally bloom in the summer flower inside one's house during the winter, it is said to be an ill omen.

One should never give an even number of flowers, as this will cause bad luck.

Should one be bringing flowers to a hospital patient, they should never be red and white mixed together in the same bunch. This is said to be an omen for death in the ward, though not necessarily for the person to whom they are given. Rather, one should choose red flowers alone—red symbolizes life. It is said unlucky for a sick person to place flowers on his bed and one should never present flowers taken from a grave.

During the eighteenth century, many specific beliefs with regard to flowers existed in the United Kingdom. If placed in the house, agrimony was said to produce sleep. Lily and antirrhinums were said to produce wakefulness. A rose was believed to cure fertility. Schambrune and verbena, if mixed together, were said to excite love; verbena alone, to create discord.

Each flower is said to have a secret meaning, according to various Greek myths. In the Orient, a language of flowers was often used in place of the written word.

Lady Mary Wortley Montagu (1690–1762), who, upon relocating to Turkey with her husband, sent letters back to England in which she devised various meanings for the flowers she personally collected. Of this she wrote:

There is no color, no flower, no weed, no fruit, herb, pebble or feather that has not a verse belonging to it: and you may quarrel, reproach, or send letters of passion, friendship or civility, or even of news, without even inking your fingers.

By selecting one of various kinds of roses, a would-be lover could indicate some forty different feelings. Lady Montagu's meanings for a few flowers are as follows: anemone—refusal; apricot—timid love or doubt; azalea—ephemeral passion; bramble—envy; foxglove—sincerity; gardenia—secret love; cinnamon—"my fortune is yours"; straw—"suffer me to be your slave"; pear blossom—"give me some hope."

A German tradition holds that if you take a flower to the dining table with you, then wipe your lips with it after drinking wine and present it to your lover, you can be sure of his or her undying love.

Flowers planted during the time of the new moon are said to bloom best, and planting sunflowers is said to bring good luck to your entire garden.

Should you imagine that you can smell flowers, it is said to be an omen of death.

The use of flowers at a wedding is an old tradition. The orange blossom, for one, has been carried by brides from the beginning of time. Since the orange is a tree that blooms and bears concurrently throughout all seasons, it is said symbolic of fruitfulness for the couple. Its use was possibly introduced into Europe by the returning Crusaders. It was a common practice among the Saracens to use sprigs of the orange blossom as a crown on the bridal veil. The English poets Spenser and Milton thought the orange to be the "golden apple" presented to Jupiter by Juno on their wedding day. Roses and lilies of the valley are also favorites among brides.

The rose, by tradition, is dedicated to Venus and is, therefore, a symbol of love, joy, and beauty. Myth holds that Cupid gave a rose to Hippocrates to bribe him on his celebrated oath not to reveal the indiscretions of Venus.

Myrtle is still another flower often used. It symbolizes constancy in duty and affection.

Although modern wedding ceremonies often incorporate a flower girl, the origin of this custom can be traced back to medieval times. One or two young girls carrying garlands of wheat walked before the bride in the marriage procession. This symbolized fruitfulness for the newly married couple, as well as an abundance of happiness.

Tradition has also assigned specific flowers to months.

Month	Flower
January	Carnations and Snowdrops
February	Primroses
March	Daffodils or Violets
April	Daisies
May	Hawthorn or Lilies of the Valley
June	Roses or Honeysuckle
July	Waterlilies
August	Poppies or Gladioli
September	Convolvulus or Asters
October	Goldenrod or Dahlias
November	Chrysanthemums
December	Holly

FLY: Flies that fall into one's glass or food are said to be a sign of prosperity. According to legend, the fly was actually excommunicated by Saint Bernard; to get revenge, it pesters us.

One recipe for chasing flies away for an entire year is to string three eggs together and hang them over the front door on Ash Wednesday. A herring hanged from the ceiling on Good Friday is said to bring similar results.

If flies are not chased from a room in which a woman is about to give birth, it is believed she will have a girl.

Jewish legend relates that Elisha was only recognized as a prophet because flies would not approach his place when he sat at the table.

In Actium, Greece, an annual sacrifice of an ox took place in the

Temple of Zeus to honor him as an averter of flies. Constantinople was totally freed from the annoyance of flies by Apollonius of Tyana, who erected a bronze fly to scare off real ones. In Norse mythology, Loki transforms himself into a fly to torment his enemies, and in an Irish myth, Etain himself is transformed into a fly.

For many Christians flies were regarded as evil, due to their affinity with the Devil. However, in one legend, Saint Colman describes a kindly fly, who would mark his place in a book whenever he went to take part in religious services.

FOOL: Encountering a fool or simple-minded person is held to be a good omen. Should a fisherman meet a fool or a deformed person on route to his boat, it is said that he will have good fortune.

Parsley sown by a fool will grow better than that of his neighbor. As such, a simple-minded person was thought blessed by God. Should he leave one's village or town, it was believed that his weakness would be transferred to others.

Fox: According to a Welsh tradition, seeing several foxes together is unlucky. Should a lone one be seen, however, good luck is said to follow. Should foxes enter one's courtyard, disaster and death is thought nearby. In some parts of Wales, it is also believed witches can transform themselves into foxes. Hence, the tradition arose of burning a fox at the "need fires" to warn any witches against assuming this shape!

An unusual cure for whooping cough is to place milk in front of a fox. When he has drank as much as he wishes, the rest is drunk by the patient and the cough is said to vanish.

In Bohemia, if shy, one would wear a fox's tongue in order to become bolder. A scraped pig skin attached to a hazel stick, wrapped around the chicken coop three times, is said to keep foxes away. Should a woman wish to be free of any female problems, she should carry on her person a testicle taken from a live fox.

In Japan, the Fox Goddess, Koki-Teno, is portrayed as a cunning and dangerous animal skilled in magic, including the ability to take the appearance of a beautiful woman.

FRIDAY: Although Friday was named after Fria, or Freya (also known as Venus), the Teutonic Goddess of Love, it is said to be an unlucky day to do many things. It is generally considered good to be born on this day, however. Children born on a Friday are said to have the gift of curing fevers and will have numerous visions and second sight. (Among the Hungarians, however, one born on Friday was advised to have someone cut a piece from his clothing, rub a few drops of blood on it, and cast it into the flames.) Yet, tradition holds that Adam and Eve fell from grace on Friday, that the great flood was started on Friday, that the Temple of Solomon fell on Friday, and, of course, that this was the day of Christ's crucifixion. What's more, several major financial panics have led to the expression, "Black Friday."

Traditionally, Friday is held an unlucky day on which to get married, to sail, to start a new job, to open a new play, to cut one's nails, and to change one's bed linen. However, it is said one's Friday night dreams, if discussed the next day, will come true.

Weather superstition holds that, should it rain on Friday, it will be clear on Sunday, although, rain or shine, it is still believed to be a bad day for one to court another's favors.

An exception to this Friday tradition of ill omens seems to be the history of the Americas. Columbus set sail for Spain on Friday, August 3, 1492. On Friday, October 12, the New World was sighted for the first time. On Friday, November 10, 1620, the Pilgrims' *Mayflower* arrived in Provincetown. On Friday, December 22, 1620, the Pilgrims landed at Plymouth Rock. Last, George Washington was born on Friday, February 22, 1732.

In Italy, tenants will never enter a new house on Friday.

In both the United States and Great Britain, tradition assigned this day for the hanging of criminals. Hence, it was often called "Hangman's Day."

Another tradition holds that should one commit a theft on a Friday, it will be unsuccessful and will most likely lead to one's arrest. Likewise, one should never go to trial on Friday, for he is likely to lose at law.

One who sings on a Friday is said to weep on Sunday.

Should a Friday fall on the thirteenth of a month, it is said to be a "doubly" bad omen. According to the Romans, the worst possible day of the year for a wedding is Friday, the thirteenth of May.

In the two different versions of the well-known rhyme describing the characteristics of someone born on each of the days, "Friday's Child" is either "loving and giving" or "full of woe."

The exception to the bad omens of Friday is, of course, Good

Friday, which is, among other things, held to be the best day on which to wean children.

John Gibbons, the eminent scientist, held that Friday was an unusually lucky day, since it was the day on which he was born, christened, and married. As he, like Columbus, was fortunate in all of his undertakings, you must judge for yourself the truth of these notions about Friday.

One must note, of course, that the assignment of Friday as a day of ill fortune comes from strongly Christian sources and not from those of other religions. For instance, among the Hindus, Friday is considered lucky for the making of friends and the wearing of new garments.

FROG: In mythology, references to the frog are relatively few, but, when they do appear, they are quite specific.

To the ancient Egyptians their Goddess of Childbirth, Heket, had the head and sometimes the entire form of a frog. In an Egyptian myth, Heket and her ram-headed husband, Khnum, were the first to "build men and make gods."

One has also to recall that frogs were called up by Moses and Aaron as the second plague of Egypt (Exodus 8:6). Likewise, for Christians in the book of Revelation, seven angels "poured out on the earth the seven bowls of the wrath of God." It was said there when the sixth wrath came, "three foul spirits like frogs" appeared (Revelations: 16:13).

In Greek mythology the wandering Leto, after giving birth to Apollo and Artemis, was prevented from quenching her thirst in a pool of water by rude shepherds. Leto changed them into frogs.

In Queensland, Australia, an aboriginal myth holds that a great frog caused drought and suffering by swallowing all the water in the world. In the belief that, if the frog could be made to laugh, he would bring up the water and all would be well, several animals were brought to entertain him. It was not until a squirming eel was found, which made him roar with laughter, that the waters burst out to flood the world and drown mankind.

Among the Huron tribe in North America there exists a similar story. All water was contained in the belly of a huge frog, until Ioskeha stabbed him, thereby returning the waters to the lakes and rivers.

In Japan, the frog is one of the animals of the zodiac.

The frog was held symbolic of fertility due to the fact that it lays a great many eggs at one time. It was also held as a reliable weather predictor, since it croaked whenever rain was on the way. In fact, a Hindu hymn, "Rigveda," suggests that frogs were worshipped for bringing rain.

Traditionally, the Orinoco tribes in Venezuela keep frogs captive and beat them in times of drought. For the Hindus, pouring water over a frog or hanging it up was said to yield the same result. In Malaya, one had simply to swing a frog at the end of a cord to bring rain.

During Roman times, the frog was a popular mascot and was believed to bring good fortune to the home of its possessor. There were all sorts of useful purposes frogs could suit.

Should one wish to get information from a sleeping woman, for example, you need only put a frog's tongue on her heart.

To make yourself popular, you could carry a frog's decayed bones. A green frog, enclosed in a pot of fresh earth and buried in the middle of your field, was said to protect the field against birds. To cure warts, one could simply impale a frog on a stick and rub the warts on the frog. They would disappear as the frog dies, says a Welsh tradition. Already mentioned was the ancient belief that young frogs, if swallowed, would cure cancer.

One should never kill frogs because they are said to be the souls of dead children. It is also said that they possess the power to "sterilize" those who touch them.

Ashes of a pregnant frog, if attached to a woman's belt, were believed to cause her menstrual flow to cease. The same ashes hung around the neck of a hen were thought to cause its bleeding to stop. Yet another tradition holds that hair will not grow on places rubbed with these same ashes, if dissolved in water.

Should a frog come into one's house on its own accord, it is believed to bring good luck.

Hanging the dead body of a frog in orchards and vineyards will protect against fog and storms. If hung in a grainery, the grain itself will be guarded.

One suffering from eye inflammations can be cured by hanging the corresponding eye of a frog around his neck. The physician, Galen, held that a frog boiled in water and vinegar, held in one's mouth for some time, would cure toothache. Spitting in a frog's mouth was believed yet another way to cure toothache, while an Arabic text of the ninth century claims that this same act will prevent a woman from conceiving for an entire year.

In the seventeenth century, epilepsy was believed curable with a powder made from a frog's liver.

The eye of a frog plucked before sunrise and swallowed or worn as an amulet was thought to cure fever.

In American folklore a soup made from nine frogs is said to cure whooping cough, while a wish made upon seeing the first frog in spring was believed to come true, if kept secret. A frog found when neither the sun nor the moon was shining, if one of its hind legs was cut off, was said to cure gout, cancer, and tuberculosis. The tradition that the croaking of frogs indicates rain is also widespread. Likewise, some Indian tribes, in accepting this same belief, capture frogs and tap them regularly in order to ensure a supply of water.

Last, mention must be made of the fact that the Wends, a primitive Slavic tribe, hold newly born children are brought by frogs and not the stork!

FRUIT TREE: Should a fruit tree bloom twice in a season, a member of the family owning the tree will die before the year is out, says a Suffolk tradition. Fruit trees under which a dead animal, such as a dog, cat, or rabbit, is not buried when planted will not bear fruit, according to a Yorkshire belief.

FUNERAL: Although some traditions have already been discussed in another context (see **burial**), yet others still exist for us to explore. Psychologically speaking, funerals are said to be useful for those left behind to accept the reality of the loss of one's loved one.

To begin with, after someone's passing, a house should not be swept or dusted, since in so doing, one might hit or chase away the deceased's soul. A glass of wine or thirteen candles should be set around the bed. If wine, each family member should click glasses with the deceased and wish him a good journey to the next world. One tradition holds that a small pot or jar of honey must be left near the bed of the deceased, should his spirit wish to escape in the form of the fly and need nourishment. Among Christians, it is said taboo to bury one on Friday, as this was the day of Christ's death.

On the other hand, some suggest that a burial should never be postponed over an entire weekend. Otherwise, death, being unsatisfied, will begin to look for another.

Many believe that the coffin should be held head first and that the pallbearers should be in the same occupation, or in the same social position, as the deceased. One tradition claims that at least one door of the house should be left open; otherwise, after returning from the cemetery, a dispute will break out in the family.

Once underway, the funeral procession must never be stopped or in any way interrupted. Otherwise, the soul of the deceased would be able to escape and transform himself into a hostile entity, directing his anger towards those gathered. Those who see a funeral procession pass by should kneel, bow their heads, or remove their hats. In many countries it is considered unlucky to count the number of vehicles in such a procession, since it corresponds to the number of years left in the counter's life!

Should a wedding couple encounter a funeral procession on their way to the wedding, it is said that they will have bad luck. In some processions, a saddled, but unridden, horse belonging to the deceased is taken along in the belief that it may be needed in the other world.

In Scotland, the belief is held that sunlight falling on the face of one of the participants in the procession indicates that he will be the next to die.

A warning: It is said that one should never attend a funeral without being invited. Likewise, children under one year old should never attend a funeral, according to American folklore, and neither should a pregnant woman.

It is believed that, should the coffin not fit into the grave for some reason, misfortune will come to all the mourners. Superstitions about grave site behavior include these: The grave should never be dug on a Sunday, as this day is dedicated to God. Never throw a rose in the grave, unless a stranger from another town is present, or the deceased's soul will never know peace.

Those attending the funeral should wear black to deceive the Devil, for it is believed that this is the one color he cannot see. The Aborigines, however, paint their bodies white in order to make themselves invisible to evil spirits.

Among certain sects of the Jewish faith, no animal is allowed near the coffin or the departing soul will try to enter its body.

Mourners should be given food after a funeral in appreciation of the honor they have given to the deceased. After returning from the burial, everyone should wash his or her hands in front of the deceased's house, after which the towel or cloth used should be thrown over the roof of the house. Yet another tradition holds that the last person to wipe his hands should put the towel on a windowsill, and repeat the Lord's Prayer and one Hail Mary each day until the wind carries off the towel. It is said by some that there should be a tone of happiness, even drunkenness, during the funeral meal. Certainly Irish wakes are known to carry out this tradition!

Among American Indian tribes, especially the Sac and Fox Indians, every person related to the deceased is careful to place something into the grave in the fear the spirit of the deceased will come back and claim any forgotten gift.

Among Southern blacks, the body of the deceased should be placed on a cooling board, A plateful of ashes is left below it to absorb any diseases in the body. The ashes are later thrown into the grave for final disposal.

In some parts of Georgia, everyone present at the funeral wears black. Even household pets are decorated with some bit of black as a means of avoiding the contamination of the ghost. (Likewise, the traditional graveside eulogy is thought to continue the tradition of speaking well of the dead in order to placate its spirit.)

It is said that one should not continue wearing mourning clothes beyond the first year or a second tragedy is certain to occur. Likewise, one should not keep black-bordered paper in a house after the mourning period is completed.

Grave diggers are thought usually to be intoxicated, and those who do rubbings of gravestones in old cemeteries were said to be risking losing their memories.

Last, there is a popular belief that the first body buried in a new cemetery or graveyard will be claimed by the Devil himself. This belief is so strong among some that they have actually refused to have relatives buried in a particular cemetery until some other unknowing soul without kin is found to fill this particular role!

FURNITURE: In the Shetlands, should furniture in a house crack or creak, it is believed to indicate a break in the weather. The ori-

gin of this belief perhaps lies in the fact that, years ago, articles of
furniture in fishermen's homes were generally made of driftwood.

Should a piece of furniture rock or tip over on its own, many say
it indicates a death in the family. This is especially true if a picture
should fall from a wall.

Furniture should be placed parallel to the lines of a room or
house, according to some, so as to avoid the formation of any
unwanted crosses.

At night, it is said that a dead soul can become detached from a
closet mirror in a bedroom; during the day, it remains enclosed and
invisible.

GALLSTONES: If you are seeking an alternative to traditional medical treatment for this, try the following: Boil sheep's dung in new milk until dissolved and drink it each day. This is said to be a sure cure for the removal of gallstones.

GAMBLING: All gambling is a matter of luck, so it is not surprising that a number of superstitions surround this very ancient pastime.

To begin with, playing on certain days is said to be unlucky for some and lucky for others. In general, playing before 6:00 P.M. on Friday was thought a bad omen.

On the way to the game, it was thought good luck to encounter a hunchback. However, seeing a man who squints or a cross-eyed man was said to be a bad omen. One tradition holds that a man should never allow a woman to touch his shoulders before he sits down to play. In fact, he should try to avoid meeting any females on his way to the game. (See **playing cards**.)

GARLIC: An Islamic tradition holds that garlic sprang up where Satan placed his left foot as he was being driven out of paradise.

According to Theophrastus, the Greek philosopher, garlic was placed at crossroads to sustain Hecate, the underworld Goddess of Magic. She was believed to frequent tombs, scenes of crimes, and wherever roads met, bringing along her pack of hell hounds.

The Egyptians held both garlic and onion as divine, according to Pliny.

Throughout Europe, India, China, Japan, and Asia Minor, the garlic plant is regarded as protection against witchcraft and the evil eye. In India, its Sanskrit name means "slayer of monsters."

In the sixteenth century, the Flemish botanist, Clusius, recorded that German miners took cloves of garlic into the mines for protection against evil spirits.

In the Eastern European vampire tradition, garlic was thought to keep them at arm's length. It was suggested that garlic be hung at windows and doors and worn as necklaces to bed. Garlic gathered in May was held to be the most effective.

In Scotland, garlic hung around one's house on All Hallow's Eve was thought to keep away evil spirits. In Sumatra, garlic was used by the Battas in rituals to recover lost souls.

Some Europeans place garlic in a newborn's cradle, together with salt and iron, for the period from birth to baptism. In Sicily, it is placed in the beds of women during childbirth, and making the sign of the cross with garlic was said to drive away various kinds of tumors.

The belief in the curative powers of garlic is quite ancient. The physician Galen, in the second century A.D., called garlic "theriac," meaning an antidote to poison. Chaucer and later writers referred to it as "poor man's treacle" (no doubt a corruption of "theriac"). Other traditions hold that garlic can prevent sunstroke, cure dropsy, drive out intestinal worms, and relieve hysteria. It is believed to be efficacious against smallpox, the plague, and other infectious fevers, as well as leprosy.

English nannies often treated whooping cough by placing garlic in children's socks. Cubans believed that one can cure jaundice by wearing a necklace of thirteen garlic cloves for thirteen days.

If placed in the ground garlic was said to cause moles to "leap forth." In American folklore, garlic poultices were recommended for the cure of rattlesnake and scorpion bites. Country traditions also held that garlic would draw one's disease away. Thus, garlic was often hung in a sick person's house.

Wearing garlic was thought to ensure that one would never become ill. In addition, it was believed that garlic would cure toothaches and bed wetting, and that, if rubbed into the gums of a horse, it could restore its failing appetite. In the Jewish Talmud it is suggested that numerous foods should be seasoned with it.

Roman soldiers supposedly ate garlic to bring them courage. South American bullfighters take garlic cloves into the bullring believing its odor will prevent the bull from charging.

According to the Doctrine of Signatures, garlic is placed under the planetary influence of Mars. From ancient times it was called "a foul-smelling rose."

Should you eat garlic in April, it is said to increase your strength, courage, and success for the day. If cooked the night of Saint John and eaten the next day, it will protect you from evil throughout the entire year. The Italians say garlic will keep poverty away.

In Scandinavia, shepherds were known to rub their hands with garlic before milking animals as well as to hang cloves around their animals' necks to prevent them from being seized by trolls.

In Egypt, garlic was placed in the pessary placed in a woman's womb. Should her breath smell of garlic the next day, it was said that she was expecting a child.

To rid yourself of the odor of garlic, tradition holds that you must eat a raw bean, a mint leaf, an anise seed, a coffee bean, or some parsley.

GARTER: Though little used today, the garter carries with it a number of ancient beliefs. On the eve of her wedding, for example, a woman wishing to conceive should wear a garter of straw or shell. Should the garter be made of wheat, she would conceive a male; if made of oats, a girl. If the bride is not a virgin at the time of the wedding, however, the garter would not work its magic.

A single man who succeeds in stealing a bride's garter at a wedding feast is said to be blessed with happiness and luck; an unmarried girl who places a garter under her pillow will dream about her future husband; and good luck will follow a woman who tries to attach her garter three times and fails. It is also said that a young girl who loses her garter during the procession of the Virgin will conceive a child within the year, whether she is married or not.

Red garters were believed to relieve rheumatism. A garter made from pieces of cork was believed to prevent one from having stomach aches, and should one wear a garter from hair skin and dried artemisia, it is believed he will move faster than a horse. One can obtain similar results by writing a magic formula with one's blood on a wolf skin on a Wednesday in spring.

Still to be mentioned is the association of the garter with modern witchcraft. The garter has always been a badge of office for the high priestess of a coven. A priestess who heads more than one coven may have a buckle on her garter for each of the covens she heads, displaying them with great pride.

In 1348 Edward III founded The Most Noble Order of the Garter, as the highest order of knighthood. The legend goes that the Order was established after Joan, Countess of Salisbury, accidentally dropped a garter while dancing with the king. Edward picked it up and tied it to his own leg saying, "Honi soit qui mal y pense," or "Shame to him who thinks evil of it." As the Order consisted of twenty-five knights plus the monarch, for a total of twenty-six (or two thirteens), which was the basic working unit of a witch's coven, some authorities believe that Edward himself may have been a witch.

GAS: A European tradition holds that a child suffering from respiratory trouble should be carried through a gasworks plant or or through a place where gas is actually manufactured. A cure will then be forthcoming.

GEMS: The use of gemstones for healing and divination could be the subject of an entire work.

The belief that one should receive as a gift a particular stone corresponding to one's sign of the zodiac is well established. Generally accepted is the following listing:

Stone	Birth Month
Garnet	January
Amethyst	February
Bloodstone	March
Diamond	April
Emerald	May
Agate (*Pearl*)	June
Ruby	July
Sardonyx	August
Sapphire	September
Opal	October
Topaz	November
Turquoise	December

In India, however, stones are dispensed according to one's entire horoscope, which must be correctly calculated using the time, place, and date of birth. It is believed that, should one wear a gemstone that is not appropriate to one's horoscope, even though it may correspond to one's birth sign, such can bring ill health and ill luck.

Some of the other beliefs in regard to stones are these: Wearing a ruby will prevent evil and impure thoughts. Jaspar cures madness. Agate is an antidote to the poisonous bite of scorpions and spiders and will bring healing to the eyes. An engagement ring that contains pearls will bring tears to the marriage. Opals are unlucky, except if they correspond to the birth month of the wearer (October).

In the early part of the twentieth century, an American fad was started by a dentist who claimed he was able to discover which stones would impart good luck to women. He set these "lucky stones" in their front teeth. Additional information should be looked up under the names of individual stones throughout the text.

GENDER: To determine the sex of an unborn child, the following traditions are offered: Slip off the wedding ring of the mother-to-be and tie it to a piece of string or thread. Have the mother lay down on a bed while a friend suspends the ring over her stomach. Should the ring begin to move in a clockwise motion, she is carrying a boy. Should the ring move counterclockwise, the child is a girl.

An English tradition holds that, if one obtains a shoulder of mutton and removes all the meat at supper, it can be used to predict gender. The bone must be placed in the fire until it is scorched, and then two thumb holes are pushed through. Through these holes a string is passed and knotted, and the bone is hung on the back door. If the first person (exclusive of family members) to enter by this door is a male, the baby will be a boy. Should it be a female, it will be a girl.

To be mentioned are countless superstitions that allow a child's sex to be determined in advance. For instance, a boy is long associated with the right side and a girl with the left. Should a baby kick on the right side of his mother's stomach, it is thought likely to be a boy. Similarly, should a woman always move her right foot first or have a heavier step on that side, it is said her baby will be a boy.

Another way of determining the sex of a child is to drop a coin between the mother's breasts. Should it fall to the left, the baby will be a girl. Should it fall to the right, it will be a boy. Similarly, should the expectant mother's right breast be larger than her left, it is an indication she will deliver a boy. Should she have more pain on her left side, though, the baby will be a girl.

Tradition also holds that the shape of the mother's belly prior to delivery could also determine the baby's sex. Should her stomach be pointed or round and on the right side, a male child was certain to be delivered. Should it be round and on the left, a girl was believed on the way. Spots and freckles on her face were said to foretell a boy.

Should you obtain a drop of milk or blood from the mother's right side and let it fall into water from a fountain, according to tradition, if it sinks immediately, she is carrying a boy. If salt placed on her nipples does not dissolve, a male child can be anticipated.

Should an expectant mother drop a pair of scissors, it is omened she will have a girl. Should she drop a knife, it is said she would deliver a boy. One can determine the unborn's sex by hiding a knife and a scissor under cushions in a room, and asking the mother to come in. Should she sit on the cushion that conceals the scissors, the newborn will be a girl. Should it be the knife, a boy is due!

Should a mother find a needle during the month preceding delivery, it is said she will deliver a girl. Should it be a pin, however, the child will be a boy.

In Brittany, tradition maintains that an expectant mother place a girl's and a boy's shirt on top of the water in the fountain. Whichever shirt sinks first will indicate the future child's sex.

A Welsh tradition holds that, in order to determine an unborn child's sex, a sheep's shoulderbone should be buried in the fireplace. The expectant father makes a hole in it with his finger and hangs it with a small string over the back door of the house. The sex of the first person to cross this threshold indicates the sex of the child.

It is said that an expectant mother who wishes to have a boy should wear blue clothes and put poppy seeds on her windowsill. Should she prefer a girl instead, she should dress in pink and replace the poppy seeds with sugar.

GEORGE: In the United Kingdom no man with the Christian name of George has ever been hanged. In American folklore a tradition consisted of calling all black conductors and pullmen porters "George."

GHOST: Frederick W. H. Myers, a founder of the Society for Psychical Research, in his classic work, *Human Personality and Its Survival of Bodily Death* (1903), defines a ghost as a "manifestation of persistent personal energy." This simply means that whenever anything connected with anyone who has passed over to the other world is seen, felt or acted upon, a *Ghost* may actually be present.

Hence, should one have a dream about someone deceased, it may be the working of his ghost. Likewise, should one feel the presence of another, who has died, touching them or standing beside them, should the photo or likeness of a deceased person fall from a wall or in some other way be mysteriously altered it is customarily attributed to a ghost. Last to be mentioned are those strange occurrences in which one may actually "see" the form of a deceased personwalking about.

Recently, a Harris Poll indicated that over 60 percent of all widows and widowers believed they had received a message of some kind from their mate who had passed over soon after death took place.

One thing is for sure, the idea of ghosts appears to have remained with us from the dawn of time, despite the advances of science.

To avoid a ghost, two pieces of rowan wood made in the form of a cross by tying them with red thread, if inserted between the lining and the cloth of one's coat, will protect the wearer from ghosts and witches, says a Scottish tradition.

GLASS: Glass, especially in the form of a crystal ball, is believed to reveal the future and to diagnose illness. To be effective, it must be extracted at night by the light of a full moon. If set in silver, it will protect one against angry persons, as well as cure insomnia. Worn as an amulet, it will smother nightmares and cure any illness that comes to one's herd. To do this, one need only soak it in water and then feed the water to the animals.

One tradition holds that a person should never be looked at through a piece of broken glass, or else a sudden quarrel will come about.

Should one break a glass or crystal vase, seven years of happiness will ensue. Should one break a mirror, however, seven years of bad luck are promised.

Among the Russians, a custom exists of breaking a vodka glass at the end of a meal by throwing it over the shoulder. In this way, an offering or sacrifice is made to the gods.

A glass should never be held out to another person. Rather, it should be set down and the person should take hold of it himself.

Whoever drinks from another's glass, especially if taking the last drop, is able to divine that person's thoughts.

In Brittany, if a glass should ring for no apparent reason, it is said to be announcing the death of a sailor.

Recovery from certain illnesses can be had if the bedridden person drinks a glass of water "in a cross"; that is, from the four corners of the glass.

Last, it is thought unlucky to see the new moon for the first time through glass.

GLOVE: Probably the most well-known superstition regarding gloves is that, if you drop a glove, it must be picked up by another, or bad luck will ensue. Likewise, should you lose a glove, it is said to be unfortunate. Finding a pair of gloves, however, especially on a Sunday, is believed to grant you success in business during the coming week. Should you leave gloves behind at a house after a visit, you must return and sit down before picking them up. It is held that you must put them on while standing or you will never again visit the house.

Gloves are said to symbolize nobility, authority, and love. Originally, their use was reserved for the wealthy. To remove them and extend the hand of friendship was an indication of allegiance, whereas to throw them down on the ground indicated defiance.

When used in the wedding ceremony, the bride's white gloves symbolize purity. During the exchange of rings, the bride takes off her gloves as a sign of consent. It is said that a widow who is remarrying must leave her gloves on.

A bride-to-be should never gaze at herself in a looking glass with her bridal gown on, unless she is wearing a glove, according to one tradition. Otherwise, she will become entranced. Two more superstitions: Never wear gloves on a Wednesday. To do so will bring misfortune. Never shake hands without removing your glove.

GLOWWORM: An English superstition holds that one will endanger his love affair, and perhaps even cause the death of his beloved, should he kill a glowworm.

GNAT: Should someone be taken ill, the windows of the sick room should be opened at sunset, so the gnats could fly in. It is held that they will fill themselves with the infection of the ill person, and then fly out and die.

Flying close to the ground, gnats are said to predict rain; flying high in large numbers, however, good weather is said to be on the way.

Tradition holds that Apollonius of Tyana rid Constantinople of its gnats by creating a bronze gnat.

GOAT: The mention of goats in a work such as this is no surprise, since they were associated with the devil in ancient times.

The Greek god Pan was alleged to have been half man and half goat. In ancient Egypt women were said to copulate with a divine goat. Herodotus, writing in the fifth century B.C., recalled that the people of Mendes in the Nile Delta venerated all goats, especially the male ones. Plutarch in A.D. 120 remarked that the most beautiful women were chosen to lie with the divine goat of Mendes.

Tradition in Europe held that the Devil never appeared in human form, but frequently as an animal, and particularly, a goat. Modern anthropologists explain that the head of a coven often donned a goat's head during various ceremonies.

An English and Scottish superstition is that goats are never seen for twenty-four consecutive hours, since they must periodically pay a visit to the Devil to have their beards combed.

Other American traditions hold that goats will eat anything, especially tin cans.

Some other beliefs include these: Goats kept in a stable protect horses from harm. A goat's horn placed under your pillow will cure insomnia. Should you meet a goat while starting a business venture, success was certain. If you hang a male goat on a boat's mast, favorable winds will be assured. Should you find a black goat on a lonely bridle path, there was a hidden treasure there. In American folklore, if a goat could be lured onto one's property, as close as possible to the room of an ill person, the goat could remove sickness from the house.

The expression "to get someone's goat" means simply to frustrate someone, and is based on the ancient belief that goats will destroy another's vineyard if allowed to enter unattended.

Goats were used in coal mines because they were thought to know exactly the minute when it was closing time. They refused to pull a loaded car once the whistle was about to sound.

A popular camp song often sung by boy scouts tells the story of a goat who ate three red shirts off a clothesline. As punishment, he was tied to a railroad track with the hope of doing him in. Just as the train drew near, however, he coughed up the shirts and flagged it down.

GODPARENT: Before the Protestant Reformation, the Church did not allow godparents to marry. If they were married it was considered unlucky for them to stand at the font together during the christening ceremony. Should this happen, it was thought to presage a parting within three months.

GOITER: Before the advent of modern medicine and the use of iodine as a treatment for goiter, it was believed that you could cure yourself of this disease by having the sign of the cross made on your neck with the hand of a corpse. Yet another method was to go to the grave of the last young man buried in a churchyard, on the first of May, before sunrise. There you would pass your hand three times from the head to the foot of the grave, and apply to your own neck the dew collected.

GOLD: It is said that one can cure a sty by rubbing the affected part nine times with a golden wedding ring or with any other piece of gold.

Traditionally, gold ore can be uncovered with the use of a hazel tree stick, the ends of which have been covered with iron. It is said that to wear gold jewelry will prolong childbirth. Women wearing gold were advised to remove it.

GOLF: One should never change a club after taking it from the bag; otherwise, the stroke will be muffed. Never start a game at 1:00 P.M. Never remove the paper from a new ball before reaching the first tee. Never clean a ball once the match is going your way. Never approach a tee from the front.

Some golfers carry in their bags an old club, no longer used, as a lucky talisman.

Some golfers take caution to avoid using the word "shank," since to hit the ball with this part of the club is the worst thing a golfer can do.

When teeing off, the ball should be placed so that the maker's name is visible to the player.

In Scotland, whoever wins the first hole will surely lose the match.

American folklore has it that, commenting about golf, Ulysses S. Grant said, "That looks like good exercise, but what's the little ball for?"

GOOD FRIDAY: Although many of the traditions regarding Good Friday have been mentioned elsewhere (see **Friday**), there yet remain a few to be discussed.

Since it marks the passionate death of Christ, Good Friday is thought to be one of the most inauspicious days of the entire year.

For example, women who wash clothes are advised not to wash clothes on this day or the clothes will never get clean. This is based on a legend that, on the way to Calvary, Christ cursed a washer-woman who waved a wet garment in his face. Also, in re-membrance of Christ, blacksmiths would refuse to drive a nail on this day.

While definite prohibitions for activities on this day abound, the day is said to be especially good for any activities intended to drive away evil. Hence, it is an excellent day to chase flies out of one's house for the entire year (simply hang a herring from the ceiling to do so).

A rooster born on this day will crow more often than any other rooster. An egg laid on this day will never rot and, if kept on the mantle, it will ward off evil. Wine growers shake wine and vinegar vats on this day to ensure the fermentation process. Peas and potatoes should be sown on this day, preferably at noon. Young boys who put on their first pair of long pants on this day are assured of a happy marriage.

In Brighton, fishwives believed buns baked on Good Friday would keep their husbands from shipwreck.

Also, bread or buns baked on this day were believed never to get moldy. They were also held endowed with medicinal properties to cure colds and whooping cough.

Rings, if hallowed on this day, were also said to prevent illness when worn. Likewise, removing bees from their hives on any day other than Good Friday was said to ensure their certain death.

If one can endure thirst on Good Friday, it is thought that he can drink whatever he wants for the rest of the year with impunity. (This is no doubt based on Christ's passion.) One should not climb a tree on Good Friday or an ill end is certain. (Again no doubt based on Christ's being nailed to the cross.)

GOOSE: A Welsh tradition holds that geese leave the farm when a fire is soon to appear. Yet another Welsh tradition holds that should a goose lay one soft egg and one hard one, or two eggs in one day, ill fortune will overtake the household.

Eating goose on Michaelmas Day is thought to bring income for the entire year. In fact, goose is the traditional dinner for Michaelmas Day (September 29). Should the breastbone of the roasted goose be found brown, the coming winter would be mild, should it be white or bluish, it was said that winter would be severe.

In northern Africa, a goose is sacrificed on New Year's Day to ensure a good year.

According to American folklore, goose grease blended with turpentine is excellent for coughs and colds, if rubbed on one's chest. It is also believed helpful for earaches and will sooth rheumatism.

When the goose flies high, it is considered an omen of excellent weather; when low, bad weather would come. American Indians seeing the wild geese fly south in early August predicted a severe winter ahead.

GORSE: Pruning blossoms of gorse, whin, broom, white lilac, or hawthorn is said to invite death for a member of the family.

GOUT: Although modern medical cures exist for this blight, which has been known to affect those who are not rich and famous and otherwise overfed, superstitions such as those following may be found helpful: Catch a spider, remove its legs and apply it to a foot that has been wrapped in deerskin. Pare the toenails and clip some hairs off the stricken leg; then stuff these in a hole in an oak tree, which must then be smeared with cow dung. If, after three months, the gout has not returned, it is held that the tree has taken it. Other remedies: Carry a hematite stone. Call upon Saint Como.

Eat black currant berries from a previously blessed bush. Consume in small quantities of water a red gurnard's head that has been burned and reduced to powder. This is said to be the best cure of all!

GRASS: A British country tradition holds that, when animals are eating grass, rain is on its way.

GRAVEYARD: Although a number of traditions regarding grave-yards have already been discussed (see **funerals**), the following are a few additional ones: Graves on the south side of the church are the holiest. Only those who had committed suicide or stillborn children were buried on the north side. This tradition is thought to be based on the fact that the south wind brings corruption. (Should a stillborn child be placed in the grave of another, it is held a sure "passport to heaven.")

Since tradition maintained that, on the day of judgment, the call would come from the east, graves should always be dug east to west, with the head of the deceased placed in the west.

It is generally considered unlucky to disturb a grave or plow any land in which bodies have been buried.

Pieces of tombstones should never be used to build one's house, for such will build death into the structure. Likewise, broken tomb-stones should never be used for path or road construction, or accidents are certain to occur on that road.

It is generally considered unlucky to walk over a grave, especially if it contains an unbaptized child.

GREEN: When it comes to the color green, superstitions regarding its use are a definite mixed bag. For instance, should a bride include the color green in her wedding ensemble, bad luck is assured.

However, the green bough of a tree, fastened on May Day against the wall of a house, is thought to produce plenty of milk in the summer, according to an Irish belief.

In Idaho there is a superstition that a mild December means those who are ill will die in the spring when the petals begin to fall. This same tradition is echoed in the United Kingdom. There "a green Yule makes a fat churchyard."

In New England, the term "green'un" is used to describe a naive, gullible person who is easily taken advantage of.

GREYHOUND: In Wales, a greyhound with a white spot on its forehead is considered exceptionally lucky.

GULL: Gulls are believed to be the souls of the dead. Hence, to kill a seagull is decidedly unlucky.

Three seagulls flying overhead together are considered by some seamen to be a warning of death.

Yet another tradition holds that whoever kills a gull will go blind. Others believe that a gull tap against the window of a house is a warning that a man at sea is in danger.

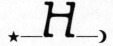

HADDOCK: Christian tradition holds that the haddock was the fish used by Christ to feed the multitudes. The black spots on each side near the gills are impressions of his finger and thumb. In Yorkshire, there is another explanation for those marks. During the building of the Philey Bridge, the Evil Spirit accidently let his hammer fall into the sea. Being somewhat in a hurry to regain it, he caught a haddock instead, and made the marks on the fish which appear to this day.

HAIR: Ever since ancient times, perhaps due to its close association with the head, many have thought that hair possesses magical properties of its own. Hence, a number of beliefs exist about it.

In the Old Testament, the cutting of Samson's hair by Delilah (Judges 16:19), thereby bringing about the loss of his great strength, is an example of this tradition. In the Dutch East Indies, penal authorities threatened hair removal as punishment in order to obtain immediate confessions from suspects. In Mexico, girls tossed their unbound hair in various ritual dances to honor the Maize Goddess or "Long-Haired Mother." Such rituals were thought to encourage growth of the crop.

Cutting the beard of a defeated enemy was held to be one of the greatest humiliations and insults that could be inflicted, and shaving one's hair as an act of mourning has long been held a form of great personal sacrifice. In Fiji, the chief of the Namonsi tribe is reported to have eaten human flesh whenever he had a haircut.

In Ireland, a young man wishing to make his girlfriend "mad with love" would run a hair of hers through the fleshy part of a corpse's leg.

Cutting of the hair was thought to be one of the causes for storms in ancient Rome. In American folklore, traditions hold that one should not cut his hair on a Friday or Sunday, nor should one shave on a Monday. Girls who cut their hair in March were said to end up with lifeless hair, and cutting the hair after dark was said to reduce sexuality.

Another tradition holds that if a woman has a brother at sea she should not cut her hair at night, and, in general, hair should be cut when the moon is on the increase. In fact, women wishing to avail themselves of good luck should cut their hair *only* when the moon is on the increase; if cut when the moon is decreasing, the hair would fall out and lose its luster.

Some believe that hair cut on a Tuesday guarantees a long life. Cutting one's hair on Thursday would bring a great deal of luck. On Friday, one would never be rich. On Monday or Sunday, one would attract bad luck.

One should never cut one's own hair, since it will bring bad luck for those around.

In southern Italy, a coin is placed in the hand of a child whose hair is cut for the first time.

Because of the idea that hair continues to be connected to the body in a magical way, even after it has been separated from it, beliefs exist about discarded hair.

Some believe that whoever cuts his hair during a waning moon, or did not burn the cut hair immediately thereafter, will lose his hair.

In Sussex, a tradition holds that should birds find your hair cuttings and build a nest with them, you will be subject to headaches. It is even worse in Scotland, where, if a magpie uses your hair in its nest, you will die within a year and a day.

Should a person's hair burn brightly when thrown into a fire, it is said to indicate a long life. The brighter the flame, the longer the duration. Should hair smolder and refuse to burn in a fire, however, it is thought to indicate the approach of death.

Should a married woman suddenly develop two curls on her forehead, when normally her hair was straight, she must watch out for her husband. He does not have long to live.

In India, women who are hairy are said to be incapable of faithfulness. However, men without any hair on their chest are thought to become thieves.

People with a great deal of hair on their arms and hands are destined to gain wealth at some future time. Hairy chests are thought to be a sign of strength or great sexuality. Should a man's hair grow down on his forehead and back at both the temples, it is said he will live to a ripe old age. Those who possess a cowlick are held to be lucky.

Tradition holds it useless to pull out a gray or white hair, because ten will grow back in its place.

Should a person's hair catch fire in a fireplace, it is held he or she will die from drowning.

Should one drop their comb while combing hair, it is thought they will be deceived.

One should never comb their hair before a test or they will lose their memory.

Since the loss of one's hair was indicative of the loss of strength or virility, various traditions exist for treating baldness. By tradition, whoever stood in the rain with his head uncovered would never be bald.

Rubbing the skin with onion juice or goose droppings was believed to prevent baldness, and the sudden loss of hair was often thought to indicate a loss of health and fortune as well.

When it comes to hairpins, here again we find an extension of similar beliefs. A hairpin "found" indicates new friendship. A hairpin lost means an enemy is nearby. Should a hairpin fall from your hair and you pick it up, someone is thinking of you. In Germany, however, this is said to portend a love is soon to be lost.

The color of one's hair was also thought to be significant. Blondes were believed to lack blood and earth and, therefore, would allegedly steal from their brunette partners. One possessing blond hair was held to be very malleable and desirous of glory and honor. Black hair was said to indicate a hard-working person. Red hair was said to be indicative of one's possessing the evil eye (Judas was believed to have had red hair), and redheads are stung more often than others. Hence, red hair was held to make one unstable, deceitful, jealous, slanderous and ill-tempered. However, it is considered good luck to run one's hands through the hair of a redhead. Should white hair appear early, it is said to indicate one who is fickle and somewhat of a bragger.

Mention must be made of the belief that gentlemen prefer blondes and a few other myths: According to many, hair and beard grow in the grave. Hair can get curly if you eat bread crusts or pour rum or grapes on your head. If a sailor has his hair cut on board ship before a storm, he will meet with great happiness on his return home.

HALLOWEEN: All Hallow's Eve, or Halloween, held on the evening of October 31, is perhaps the most popular and best-known supernatural celebration.

Before the advent of Christianity, the pagan celts in Northern Europe traditionally enacted two great fire festivals each year. Beltane, on the eve of May 1, and Samhain on the eve of November 1, respectively marked the beginning of summer and winter. These dates are in no way connected with the solstices or equinoxes, or with sowing and reaping, but, rather, seem to date from much earlier times, when cattle were depended upon for subsistence through the winter. In Ireland, the festival is still known as Samhain or La Samon; i.e., the "Feast of the Sun." In ancient times, the festival was celebrated on the twenty-first of February, later the thirteenth of May. In A.D. 837, Pope Gregory IV changed the date to November 1 as well as the name to "All Saints' Day." This was an attempt to christianize a pagan celebration.

The word *hallow* is an old English one meaning "saint" or "holy man," which was used until the fifteenth century. All Hallows' Eve became All Souls' Eve, and, eventually, All Saints' Day.

As celebrated by the ancients, this day was designed to give rest and peace to the souls of the deceased. Bonfires were originally surrounded with a circular trench symbolic of the sun. According to legend, the souls of the departed were supposed to revisit their old homes, warming themselves by the fireside on this eventful night.

In the United Kingdom, many traditions exist based on the recognition that this particular night was dedicated to Satan. All souls in purgatory were said to be released for forty-eight hours during this night.

A Welsh tradition holds that wind blowing over the feet of the deceased brings sighs to the houses of those who will themselves die within the year. Another Welsh tradition is that, if one goes to a crossroads at Halloween and listens to the wind, it will tell you all the important things that will befall you during the next twelve months. Should you take a three-legged footstool and sit at a crossroads while the church clock strikes midnight, you will hear proclaimed aloud the names of the parishioners doomed to die within the next twelve months.

Lighted torches making a circle around fields on this night are held to ensure fertility of crops during the coming year. It is also believed one should drive sheep and lambs through a hoop of rowan wood on this evening to ward off witches and fairies. To see one's shadow cast by the moon was considered distinctly unlucky on this night, and it was believed that one can see fairies moving from one fairy hill to another.

A great many traditions predating the christianization of this holiday are found to divine the future.

One of the most popular was called the "oracle of nuts." A number of nuts were named for lovers and placed upon live coals. If a nut jumped, it was an omen that the lover would prove unfaithful. Should a nut burn and blaze, it indicated that the man represented by the nut loved the girl who named it. Should both nuts named for a maid and her lover burn together, they would soon be married.

According to tradition, Romans used a similar practice in their marriage ceremonies. The bridegroom threw nuts about the room and the boys scrambled for them.

According to Scotch traditions, another method of looking into the future on Halloween was to pull a cabbage blindfolded. A blindfolded young woman groped her way to the cabbage patch and pulled the first plant she stumbled against. The amount of dirt clinging to its roots indicated the amount of her dowry; the shape and size suggested the appearance and height of her future husband; and the flavor of the heart and stem signified his disposition. Tradition required that the stalk be taken home and laid behind the outer door. The first person to enter the next morning was believed to be the future husband.

If a young lady ate an apple while standing before a mirror and combing her hair, her future husband would look into the glass over her shoulder. This would have to be done at midnight.

A young girl would walk backwards out of doors in the moonlight with a mirror (or, if done indoors, with a candle in one hand and the mirror in the other). While doing this, the following rhyme would be repeated:

Round and round, all stars so fair!
Ye travel in search out everywhere.
I pray you, sweet stars, now show to me.
This night who my future husband shall be.

Tradition holds that the face of her future husband will be seen in the looking glass.

Another tradition was to eat a raw herring or a roasted salt herring just before retiring to bed. In one's dreams, the future husband or wife was thought to come and offer a drink of water to quench the thirst.

Going alone to a stream where "three lairds' lands meet" and dipping in the left sleeve of a shirt was another tradition. When done, one would return home, without speaking, and hang the sleeve to dry before the bedroom fire. One should go to bed, being careful to remain awake. It was said that the form of a future helpmate would enter the room and turn the sleeve in order that the other side might dry.

Three plates would be placed in a row on a table. One would be left empty, one would be filled with clean water, and the last with foul water. A blindfolded person who wished to divine the future would be led up to the table. The left hand was put forward. Should it come in contact with the clean water, the future spouse would be young, attractive, and heretofore unmarried. The foul water indicated a widower or widow. The empty dish indicated that single blessedness would follow. To be considered accurate, the ceremony would be repeated three times and the plates arranged differently after each trial.

Should one pare an apple so the peel remained in one long piece, it could be used to predict one's future spouse. Swung around the head three times and thrown on the floor, the letter formed would be the initial of the sweetheart's name.

Still another method consisted of melting some lead and pouring it through a wedding ring into a dish of water. The lead would cool in various shapes, which could be interpreted as suggestive of future events. For instance, bell-shaped drops indicated a wedding; a lead torch suggested fame; a horn of plenty suggested wealth; a trunk, travel.

If one cut letters of the alphabet from a newspaper and sprinkled them on the surface of water, the floating letters would combine to spell the name of a future husband or wife.

Two unmarried maidens would string a raisin in the middle of a thread one yard long. Each person took the end of the string in her mouth. By chewing the string, whoever reached the raisin first would be the first to be married.

If a wedding ring was tied to a silk thread and held suspended within a goblet, while the alphabet was repeated slowly, you could spell out the name of a future partner. Whenever the ring struck the side of the goblet, this letter would be noted and the alphabet begun again.

Should a young girl go directly to her room on Halloween, without speaking to anyone, and should she kneel beside her bed, she could determine the fidelity of her lover by twining together the stems of two roses. While doing this, she would repeat the following lines,

> Twine, twine, and intertwine,
> Let my love be holy mine:
> If his heart be kind and true,
> deeper grow his rose's hue.

If her admirer was faithful, the color of the rose would appear darker.

Should a maiden wish to tempt the fates in general, she would walk downstairs backwards, holding a lighted candle over her head. Upon reaching the bottom step, if she turned around suddenly, the man she wished for would be before her.

In a *Book of Charms* published in Edinburgh in 1690, the following method was given for sighting one's future lady: Place on a table a glass of water in which a small piece of wood is floating. In the night, one will dream of falling from a bridge into a river and of being rescued by one, who you will see as clearly as though you were awake.

Still another method was to go at midnight to a walnut tree, walk three times around it, and look up into the branches. If you did this and asked your true love to bring you some nuts, the true love's face would appear.

A very ancient Halloween divination suggests that you go outdoors at midnight, pluck out a lock of hair, and cast it to the breeze. The direction it blows indicates the direction your future love will come from.

According to the Irish, should you hear footsteps behind you on this night, avoid turning around, for death is following. Finding two kernels in an almond on Halloween is said to be lucky and means marriage within a month. Children born on this night are believed protected until death and endowed with second sight. You should not go hunting on this day or the day following, since you may accidentally wound a soul that is wandering about.

Last, the tradition of "ducking" for apples on Halloween is a very ancient one. Originally done by unmarried girls, it is said that whomever wins the apple and sleeps with it under her pillow is sure to dream of her lover.

HALTER: According to one tradition, a halter with which anyone has been hanged, if placed around the forehead, will cure headaches.

HAMMER: It is believed that, if one places a hammer on a dying person's forehead, he will reach paradise without having to strike a blow (i.e., fight his way there). One tradition holds that the forehead of a dead pope should be tapped with an ivory hammer before burial. Last, it is thought a new husband who wants to be certain he will direct his household should buy a hammer before anything else.

HAND: As hands were the tools of primitive man, they have long been thought to have esoteric or psychic meaning as well. The right hand is said to be the hand of God and is used to take oaths, whereas the left hand was thought connected with the Devil.

Superstitions about hands are numerous. The following is a sampling: An engaged woman should avoid touching her right hand with her left until she marries; otherwise, she will be unhappy. A right hand that itches is believed to announce money or good news; an itchy left hand, an unexpected expenditure. (Should one's left hand itch it is said it should be immediately rubbed on wood.) One should never greet another by extending the left hand, or misfortune will occur. Should two people wash their hands in the same basin of water, it will lead to arguments, unless they spit at once into the basin. Children's hands should never be washed until the age of one year, or else the child will be poor throughout its life. To protect one's self from sorcery, one should wash his hands in urine. Should two couples cross hands while shaking them, there will be an unexpected marriage. Should three people begin to shake hands simultaneously it is a sign of good luck for all. A moist hand is the sign of an amorous disposition. Cold hands indicate a very warm temperament.

A strange tradition takes place at the time of the Jewish New Year. Should one look at his shadow at that time, and not see the outline of his right hand, he will lose a son within a year. Should the left hand remain unseen, the person will lose a daughter. Should one finger be hidden, a friend will die.

HANDKERCHIEF: Should one give a lover a handkerchief, there will be a parting and one will never marry.

Tying a knot in one's handkerchief is held to prevent the Devil from tricking you or making you forget.

In American folklore, young girls hang handkerchiefs on bushes on May Day Eve. At dawn, when they return to claim them, they believe they will find the initials of the man they will marry left in dew on the handkerchief's surface.

HAND OF GLORY: This refers to the hand of a man who has been hanged. Tradition says that it can be used by thieves to enable them to work either "unseen" or in view of the victims without being arrested. It is often shown as a candlestick and, as such, is supposed to have great magical properties.

Candles were to be made with the fat of a hanged man, virgin wax, and Lapland sesame. It is said that the hand should be placed in a container holding saltpeter powder, salt, and pepper. After fifteen days, it should be dried in sunlight, or in an oven fed with vervain and ferns.

Tradition holds that robbers would set fire to the fingers of such a hand before entering a home. Should one of the fingers not burn, it was omened that someone was still awake in the house and that the robbery attempt should be postponed. Yet another tradition holds that the robber should slap the ground with the hand of a woman who had died giving birth to her first child. Doing so would render those within the house unconscious.

HARE: Although the hare, or rabbit, has been discussed elsewhere (see **Easter**), some additional comments can be made herein.

A general belief is that a witch can assume the shape of a hare at will. Hence, witches in the shape of hares were said to ravage farm fields and steal milk from cows. It was believed that they could only be destroyed by a silver bullet, symbolic of the moon.

According to the Algonquin Indians, a great hare formed the

earth, while in Greece and China, the hare was associated with the moon.

Should a hare run along a road, it is said that a house will catch fire during the day. It is also held unlucky to meet a hare, and should a hare cross the path of a bride and groom, even at a great distance from the wedding party, bad luck is thought to attend the couple. Alsacians say one must turn around three times after encountering a hare, in order to counter the bad luck.

It is believed that a hare is so timid, it will never close its eyes, even in its sleep. Since the hare is thought unusually timid, eating one is said to make you fearful.

Carrying bones of a hare's foot was believed to prevent cramping. In France, especially in Orleans, placing a hare's foot under the left armpit is said to protect against toothaches.

A Cornish tradition holds that, should a young maiden die forsaken and brokenhearted, she will return to haunt her deceiver in the shape of a white hare. Should a pregnant woman see a hare, her unborn child will have a harelip.

Should a hare be seen when boarding a ship, or one actually found on board, bad luck is sure to follow, according to a Scotch tradition.

An unusual belief is that hares change their sex once a year.

Hat: It is considered bad luck to put one's hat on the wrong way. In order to get good luck, one should turn his hat front to back. Ball players and jockeys are often seen to do this.

Wearing a hat indoors is said to cause headaches. Should one fail to remove his hat when a funeral is passing, he may find himself in the dead person's place, according to one tradition.

It is believed if one lightly touches the red pom-pom on a sailor's beret with the left index finger, he will become lucky.

A hat should never be set on a table or on a bed. To do so will bring misfortune into one's home.

Should a fiancé forget his hat on his wedding day, he will be an unfaithful husband. A woman who puts on a man's hat is said to want to be kissed.

In the Orient, it is believed that one may draw the evil eye to himself by placing a hat where another person places his!

In America in the 1890s an ingenious hat-removal device used in theaters was the following statement, which was printed on all programs: "The prettiest, wisest, and most charming women take their hats off during a theatrical performance."

HAWTHORN: Since the Roman occupation of Britain, various virtues have been attributed to the hawthorn. In Ireland and Scotland the rowan or mountain ash was thought a natural deterrent against witches and fairies; in England and France, the hawthorn assumed this same role.

To the ancient Greeks, the hawthorn was a symbol of betrothal; hence, its boughs in bloom were often carried by attendants at weddings. In some places, even today, modern Greek brides will wear hawthorn wreaths.

In various May Day festivities, hawthorn trees were often cut down and set before houses. Since May Day was considered one of the best moments for engagements, it is not surprising that the hawthorn is often used on this day. In the south, young girls carry out a tradition in which they bring branches of the hawthorn home and remain silent in the belief that to utter a word will mean that they will not marry during the coming year.

The following is a sampling of the many superstitions and traditions that involve the hawthorn: Anyone who cuts the hawthorn on May Day will be protected only by having a Bible close by, offering a prayer, or by asking permission of the fairies. One should not bring hawthorn flowers into the house, or death will follow. Witches gave hawthorn to their husbands as part of a sleeping potion on those nights when they wished to attend a meeting of the coven.

In Ireland, a single hawthorn is often planted above holy wells at which offerings are left to ensure recovery from illness or fulfillment of wishes.

In France, a sprig of the hawthorn tree is worn in the caps of Norman peasants in remembrance of the crown of thorns worn by Christ.

Yet another tradition surrounding the "crown of thorns" is the "Glastonbury thorn," which flowers in late December, as well as in May. Tradition held that its Christmas flowering occurred because it had been the "crown of thorns." Still another legend held that Joseph of Arimathea thrust his magic hawthorn staff into the ground when he reached Glastonbury.

In Herefordshire, a traditional farmers' custom was to make a hawthorn globe, which was hung on New Year's Day and replaced each year before dawn by a new one. While women made a new one, men took the old globe to the fields, carrying it aflame or burning it as a bonfire. In so doing, they believed it would drive away the Devil, especially in the form of wheat smut disease.

The hawthorn is thought to be a protective plant. It is often offered to newly wed couples and is placed near the cradle of newborns. Witches are said to get caught on it and to be torn by its points.

When in bloom, it is believed that no lightning will strike its growing place, and hawthorn is also believed to cure fevers.

Should one place a hawthorn branch in front of a calvary, good luck in gambling is assured.

According to the Irish, if you cut down a hawthorn tree, you are risking great danger to yourself. Hawthorn boughs fastened on May Day against the walls and windows of houses, and especially the barn, are said to cause cows to produce a great deal of milk during the summer. Generally held is the belief branches of haw-thorns on doors and windows will keep out witches.

HAY: Should you see a load of hay coming towards you, it is good luck. Should you come upon a hay cart from behind, however, the reverse is true.

HAZEL: In Wales, if you make a cap of hazel leaves and twigs and wear it, anything you wish for will come about. From ancient times, hazel was one of the main plants used for the manufacture of wands and royal scepters. References to its use in this way are found in Hebrew, Greek, Roman, and Nordic mythology and in that of other cultures.

To the Scandinavians, it was sacred to the god Thor and held as protection against lightning. According to Roman mythology, Mercury was given a hazel rod by Apollo, which was used to calm human passions and to improve virtues. Christian pilgrims often carried hazel rods throughout their lives and often willed them to be buried alongside their bodies.

The forked hazel twig was often used for dowsing in the belief that it would assist in finding buried treasure. Likewise, it was used for divining water. Another name for the use of hazel in this way was "Moses's rod."

When hazel wood was used to manufacture wands needed for magical practices, requirements were that they be made on holy days—Good Friday, Saint John's Day, Epiphany, or Shrove Tuesday, during the evening hours. They sometimes were made on the first night of a new moon. The cutter had to face east. The wood had to have been cut from the eastern side of the tree and then presented to the rays of the rising sun. The use of a "virgin branch" (a young growth with no side shoots upon it) was said to be most effective.

In Germany, hazel is symbolic of immortality, since it flowers at the end of winter. In Black Forest weddings, the leader of the procession would often carry a hazel wand.

In Medieval England, the hazelnut was said to symbolize fertility. In Sweden, hazelnuts were believed to make one invisible, whereas in Bohemia it was thought that they would cure fevers.

In Scotland, double hazelnuts were often carried in case they had to be thrown at witches.

One tradition holds that carrying a piece of hazel (cut at midnight on Halloween) in one's pocket will prevent its owner from becoming drunk, no matter how much is consumed.

In Ireland, it is believed that Saint Patrick used a hazel rod to drive all the snakes into the sea.

Cutting a hazel rod on Good Friday, or Saint John's Eve, and swishing it through the air while naming one's enemies was said to cause them pain, wherever they might be. In Prussia, a rod cut in spring, during the first summer thunderstorm, was used to make the sign of the cross. This was believed to bless all rain stored for the year ahead.

Some believed that hazel would hatch a golden bough each Christmas night.

The hazelnut was often seen as a symbol of a child in its mother's womb. Those years in which hazelnuts are especially prolific are held favorable for fertile marriages. In some parts of Europe, however, these same years are also said to produce prostitution. Should one find a double hazelnut, it is said that wealth or twins will soon appear.

HEADACHE: Some traditional cures for headaches include these: Grasp tightly with the hand some scraped horseradish. Bind the skin of a snake around your forehead or temple. Place a thumb in the mouth and press it against the roof, say some American folk beliefs.

Should one find moss growing upon a human's skull, if dried, powdered, and taken as snuff, it is also said to cure headache.

An ancient Egyptian tradition for getting rid of a headache was to drive a nail into the great wooden door of the old South Gate of Cairo.

HEARTBURN: This is usually a stomach ailment and has nothing to do with the heart. Some say it may be cured by drinking an infusion of Saint John's wort that was gathered at dawn on Saint John's Day. Other cures include swallowing a powder made from toenail clippings and sucking a piece of coal.

HEDGEHOG: In general it is said that hedgehogs bring bad luck. If you see one, it should be killed immediately. Tradition has it that witches possess the ability to transform themselves into hedgehogs.

According to medieval tradition, the hedgehog could roll itself in apples and carry them away. In Europe, they are believed able to drink the milk of cows, and their presence in a barn was said to keep cows from calving.

Should a woman accidentally place her foot on the head of a hedgehog, it was believed she would give birth to one.

Traditionally, the hedgehog leaves its hibernation on February 2, Candlemas Day. Should he stay outside, spring is said to be coming.

HELLEBORE: Since the Middle Ages, the white hellebore has been credited with the ability to cure incurable illnesses, especially insanity. If eaten in the morning before breakfast, it was said to develop a child's intelligence. The seed of the hellebore was believed to resuscitate scorpions.

The black hellebore, called the "Christmas rose," was said to bring great misfortune to whomever picked it. The white flower, however, was believed to protect against miscarriage and leprosy, and could be used to treat rabies and epilepsy as well.

One tradition holds that hellebore flowers can predict future harvests. Should the plant have four tufts, the crop will be unusually large; three tufts means it will be a mediocre harvest; two tufts, the harvest will be poor.

HEM: Should one's hem become turned up, says American folk-lore, a new and similar garment will be obtained very soon.

HEN: Good luck is said to follow a hen crowing in the house of a newly married couple, but a hen crowing like a rooster is also said to be announcing death. Should it cackle near a house, or not lay as expected, it was believed possessed by the Devil and should be killed.

Rain will come about should hens gather on rising ground and trim their feathers, according to a Derbyshire tradition.

When black, the hen has often been used as a sacrificial animal. Traditionally, too, black hens supposedly have the ability to find money that has been lost.

Hens laying an odd number of eggs were said to be a bad omen. Eggs laid on Good Friday assured strength and fertility to all the other hens on the farm, should one egg be kept intact. (Likewise, cleaning one's hen house on this "special" day was believed to keep away vermin for an entire year.) Eggs hatched on Midsummer's Day, however, were thought to bring misfortune. However, a piece of iron in the shape of a cross, or a ring placed in the nest, was held to protect the brood.

It is said that hens will never lay again if their eggshells are burned. In the United Kingdom, belief has it that when a farmer is about to die, all his chickens will roost at noon and not at their normal time.

HERRING: Fishermen on the Isle of Man believe that, should the first herring caught in season be a female, the season will be a good one. Contrariwise, should the first herring be a male, the season will be unlucky.

Tradition holds that the first herring pulled aboard must be boiled whole, while the others can be put into pots with their heads and tails cut off.

If one eats a salt herring, bones and all, in three bites, without saying a word (even one's prayers), and then goes to bed making sure to drink no water, it is said he will have a dream revealing the future.

Hanging a herring from the ceiling on Good Friday is thought to keep flies away for the entire summer.

HICCUP: In Greece, it is believed that when one gets the hiccups, someone who dislikes him is talking about him to a third party.

Cures for hiccups are numerous and everyone has a favorite. Here is a sampling: Soak a piece of paper that has been cut in the shape of a cross in water and place it on the forehead, according to a German tradition. Breathe into a paper bag, hold your breath, or pass a cold key down the back.

According to a Cornwall tradition, hiccups can be cured by wetting the forefinger of the right hand with spit and crossing the front of the left shoe three times, while saying the Lord's Prayer backwards.

American folklore says that if you frighten a person with a loud noise, the hiccups will most likely disappear.

Hippocrates claimed that sneezing would stop a hiccup. Drinking a glass of water from the far edge of the glass, or through a napkin, was also said to be effective. Likewise, bringing your little fingers as close together as possible without having them touch. Should hiccups occur in Church, it was believed that such indicated the presence of a person possessed by the Devil.

HOLLY: The ancient historian Pliny held that holly was able to keep away lightning spells and evil, if planted near one's house. Should a branch be thrown at any creature, it was said to cause it to lie down and obey the thrower. Holly was also believed to protect one against poison, and it was believed that its flowers would freeze water.

During the ancient Roman saturnalia, holly and ivy were often used as decoration. When the birth of Christ was celebrated at midwinter by early Christians, these same traditions were maintained.

Already mentioned in another context was the tradition of "first footing." The first visitor arriving on New Year's Day brought bread, coal, and salt, and carried an evergreen branch, often a holly, as a token of life. The holly bough carried was required to be a male holly, for female holly would bring bad luck.

Leaves of a "she" holly placed under the pillows of North Country girls and boys were said to bring them dreams of their future partners. Nine leaves had to be collected at midnight on a Friday and tied with nine knots in a three-cornered handkerchief. The charm would work only if no words were spoken until the following dawn.

Yet another tradition held that holly should be used in a "witch's chain" of juniper and mistletoe berries that were tied with acorns and wound around a branch. This was burned by three unmarried girls. As the last acorn went up in flames, each girl was said to see an image of her future husband.

According to one belief, holly was supposedly created by Satan, who wished to mimic the laurel God had just invented. It has long been a symbol of eternity, and some think of its red berries as a symbol of the crucifixion.

A young girl who picked a holly leaf and counted its prickles, saying "girl, wife, widow, nun," did so in the belief that the last prickle, and the corresponding word, would confirm her future.

Holly used in Christmas decorations should be removed on Twelfth Night and burned, according to one tradition.

More superstitions include these: Bad luck will attend anyone who steps on a holly berry. A child can be cured of rickets by passing it through a cleft holly bush. Never take holly into a house before Christmas Eve or quarrels will attend.

When the holly's branches were heavily laden with berries, it was long held to indicate a hard winter with much snow ahead. In the language of flowers, holly stands for foresight.

Last, it must be mentioned that some believe Christ's cross was made of holly wood. Since it was used to crucify Christ, as punishment it was turned into a scrub. Yet another tradition holds that Christ's crown of thorns was made of holly. According to this legend, the berries were yellow, until after the crucifixion, when they were turned red from his blood.

HOLY WATER: Between the hours of eleven and midnight on Christmas Eve, many believe, water changes into wine. Holy water from Palm Sunday was said to possess the power to ward off storms; that from Easter Sunday, to chase away sorcerers and other evildoers.

Should a black cat struggle to escape when placed in a holy water basin, such was said to indicate that the cat was a witch in disguise.

Should holy water be sprinkled in three corners of a bedroom, any rats present will seek to escape by the unsprinkled fourth corner.

To rid oneself of warts one might dip his hands into a basin of holy water. However, the person who takes the holy water next would probably take on the warts.

Children who are held high above a basin of holy water were believed to grow quickly.

HONEYMOON: Before the advent of harvesting sugar cane, honey was the only sweetener known to man and the first means of manufacturing fermented drinks. The ancient Babylonians often swore solemn oaths by the Honey God. In the Indian Rig-Veda, honey and soma are depicted dripping from the fig tree, which represented the universe.

Long held as a symbol of fruitfulness in love and marriage and even as an aphrodisiac, it was once customary for newlyweds to drink a potion containing honey, or mead mixed with honey, on each of the first thirty days of their marriage. During this time, the moon itself went through all of its various phases, so this symbolized the love between the couple. The term "honeymoon," grew from a combination of these two beliefs.

In some parts of India, honey is presented to the bridegroom on the wedding day to propitiate evil spirits. Smearing the threshold with honey as the bride entered the groom's house, or giving her a jar of honey, is a tradition long followed in Croatia. In southern Germany, at one time, beehives themselves were decorated for a wedding.

Mention has already been made (see **bees**) of the tradition of telling one's bees a wedding would take place.

One tradition of the Thonga, a South African tribe, denies a suitor honey on his first visit to the home of his wife-to-be, "because honey slips away like a fish, and the girl might also slip through his hands." Likewise, once married, this same man must refrain from eating honey with his wife until she has given birth, or for one year. He can eat it in the bush, but must return to his home without any trace of it on his hands.

Hippocrates, the founding father of modern medicine, recommended a combination of ass meat and milk, with honey, as an aphrodisiac. Tradition holds that honey was a favorite food for this purpose in the harems of imperial Istanbul.

In some parts of Europe, honey is mixed in cakes given to the boy or girl whose affection one hopes to gain. It is believed that the Magyars actually smeared the sexual organs of young girls and boys with honey, to make certain they would be popular with the opposite sex. In the Balkans, the face of the bride or groom was also smeared with honey.

HORN: Horns were held a symbol of fertility by the ancients. A broken horn (symbolic of its liberated power) was held to be the horn of plenty—the cornucopia.

A Neanderthal burial site (thought to be about 70,000 years old) contains the remains of a nine-year-old boy whose head is surrounded by five pairs of ibex horns turned with their points down into the earth. In the cave of Les Trois Frères in Southern France, thought to be about 15,000 to 25,000 years old, a painting exists of a "horned sorceror," a shaman wearing large stag or reindeer antlers, skins, and a tail.

Some scholars maintain that the concept of depicting the Christian Devil with horns may have been derived from the bull god of Mithraism or from the goat god, sacred to the Teutonic god Thor. Yet another tradition holds that horns were given to Eve by Satan, who then made a gift of them to Adam; hence, the expression, "to wear horns." To the ancient Greeks or Cretans, the horns of the bull were considered to be the seat and focal point of his strength.

In Persian mythology, animal pictures of evil spirits were often horned. The first theological definition of the Devil (Council of Toledo, A.D. 447) says that he is "a large black monstrous apparition with horns on his head, cloven hooves . . . immense phallus, and a sulphurous smell."

Thus, it is not generally advisable to have a horn in one's house. However, in the United States, the horn of an ox (in the United Kingdom and Spain, a stag) is said to protect one from the evil eye.

Making horns with the index and little finger is said to be the best way to drive away the evil eye in Mediterranean countries. Making horns with the index and middle finger is held a sign of mockery.

HORSE: Long held a symbol of earthly power, the horse was projected into the skies by the ancients out of respect for its divinity. In Greek and Roman mythology, Neptune, or Poseidon, created the horse and invented horse racing. Yet another tradition holds that the horse was created from an egg, itself the symbol of creation.

Throughout history, the horse has always symbolized power, pride, and speed. Demeter, the Greek fertility goddess, is sometimes represented with the head of a horse. In many ancient myths, the sun was believed to be drawn across the sky in a chariot by celestial horses. Dag, the Norse god of the day, was believed drawn through the heavens by a white steed, "Shining Mane." Mani, the moon goddess, was held to cross the sky in a car drawn by Alsvidur, the "All-Swift," according to Norse traditions. Diana, Goddess of the Moon, was also believed to travel in a horse-drawn chariot. Lastly, the gods Thor and Helios drove their cosmic chariots across the heavens, while the mighty Odin was believed borne through the clouds on the back of an eight-footed steed.

Since one's most precious possession was often sacrificed to the gods in Imperial Rome, the "October horse" was sacrificed to Mars. In some rites, horses were actually driven over precipices as an offering to the sea deities. Among Germanic tribes, tradition held that one should hang upon trees the heads of horses killed in battle as offerings to the gods.

Funeral rites for a deceased soldier might require killing his horse, so it might continue to serve him in the afterlife—a custom which was said to continue until as late as the fourteenth century. In modern times, this tradition has been perpetuated at military funerals. A riderless horse, carrying its dead master's boots reversed on either side, is led throughout the cortege.

Already mentioned (see **cattle**) in another context is the tradition of burning horses or cattle alive. Practiced as late as the eighteenth century, this was done to remove disease from the remainder of one's herd.

In traditional witchcraft beliefs, it is said that Satan himself could manifest in the guise of a horse. It is believed that, should a witch creep up on a sleeping victim and throw a special magical halter over his head, the sleeper would be transformed into a mount and could be ridden to the witches' sabbath.

To prevent evil spirits and witches from entering stables and riding horses undetected during the night, an amulet, in the form of a stone with a hole in it, was often hung inside the stable door.

As a form of protection against the evil eye, horse brasses were often constructed in various forms, including the sun, crescent moon, heart, swastika, and other symbols.

In some European fertility rites, the horse is featured. A man disguised in a white sheet and horse's head trotted around Kent villages at Christmas on All Soul's Day. Yet another Welsh custom involved a horse's skull—possibly a relic from Roman horse sacrifice times.

In some May Day festivals, the so-called hobby horse played a prominent role.

Among the North American Indians, various horse dances have been utilized.

It is said unlucky to meet a white horse on leaving home, unless one spits on the ground. It is lucky, however, to own a horse whose four legs are equally white-stockinged; but, if one fore and one hind leg are marked, it is held unlucky.

Should horses be lost due to a disease, it is believed one can end the plague by burying one of the dead horses. Should horses stand with their backs to a hedge, bad weather is on its way. Washing a dish towel on New Year's Day and putting it to dry on a hedge is held to make one's horses grow fat and well, if they are then rubbed with it.

Should a horse come out of a stable with its right foot first, it is said that all will be well. Should it come out with its left foot, caution is suggested. Should a horse stop without any reason, it is doing so because it senses a spirit.

Braiding a horse's tail with ribbons keeps away evil spells. Horses will refuse to pass a spot where a funeral will later pass that same day.

The Celts divined the future from the movement of horses behind a chariot.

Tradition holds that horsehairs placed around the neck will cure goiter. If inserted in a sandwich, they will banish worms in children. Should horsehairs be left in water, it is believed that they will be transformed into eels.

Pennsylvania Dutch believe they can free their children from witchcraft by passing them through a horse collar.

A cure for cancer, said to be recommended by John Wesley, instructed one to make an infusion of dried and powdered horse spurs in warm milk and ale.

In some parts of Britain and Europe, a belief exists in a special class of horse handlers known as "whisperers." They are said to have an unusual power over horses, taming any animal through the use of a special word—closely guarded and passed from one generation to another.

To change the name of a horse is to change its luck. When entering a horse in a show or race for the first time, one should mutter "break a leg" as a charm against the jealous gods.

HORSESHOE: Of all the magical symbols and talismans, the horse-shoe is perhaps the most familiar. Why it should have such a time-honored history as a lucky charm is a subject of debate. Perhaps because they were used by blacksmiths (who employed the myste-rious element fire), who worked with an equally magic metal—iron—horseshoes are believed to possess supernatural powers. Perhaps their mystique comes from the fact that the shape resem-bles a crescent moon; or it may be that, when laid on its side, a horseshoe forms the letter *C*, symbolic of Christ.

To the ancients, the horseshoe was considered a powerful pro-tection against witches and evil spirits. Tradition still holds that a horseshoe nailed over the door lintel of a house will bring good luck to all inside. Should a horseshoe be taken from the hind leg of a gray mare, luck will be best of all. In the seventeenth century horseshoes were nailed on the thresholds of many doors in Lon-don. So fashionable was this tradition that a popular greeting of the same period was, "that the horseshoe may never be pulled from your threshold."

Farmers were advised to nail horseshoes over their stable doors to prevent evil spirits from riding their animals at night, tiring them out, and making them useless the next day. (Traditionally, the eve of May Day was said to be the night witches rode animals to their sabbath, a tradition called "hag-riding.")

So widely accepted was the belief that nailing a horseshoe to the mast of a ship could avert storms and shipwrecks, that Lord Nelson fastened a horseshoe to the mast of his ship, *Victory*.

Should the butter refuse to churn, a dairymaid often dropped a heated horseshoe in to break the spell. In Ireland, some country folk actually nailed a horseshoe to the bottom of the churn.

Other traditions held that, if one thinks his horse is bewitched, he should feed it soup containing horseshoes, nails, and iron filings.

Should a man find himself impotent, a Moroccan belief holds that he should write a charm on a horseshoe, preferably an old one, which is heated by a blacksmith and then dipped in water. This water, if drunk every morning for a week on an empty stomach, was said to return one's virility.

To cure whooping cough, German folklore suggests feeding a child from a wooden plate that has been branded with a horseshoe.

Most lucky of all is finding a horseshoe in the road. It must be picked up, spit on while making a wish, and then thrown over one's left shoulder. Another tradition suggests taking it home and nailing it over one's door.

It is said that a horseshoe should have seven holes in order to be lucky. Three should be placed on one side and four on the other side of the center heel. This is supposed to ensure double luck, since seven is a number of good fortune.

The wishbone, or collarbone, of a chicken or turkey is also considered lucky, since it resembles a horseshoe. Two unmarried girls, pulling on each end, can determine which one will marry first by seeing who receives the larger piece.

Pennsylvania custom places the horseshoe with the prongs pointing towards one's house so that good luck will enter.

A relatively new custom is to send floral gifts in the shape of horseshoes to new business ventures in order to ensure success. Likewise, finger rings made from horseshoe nails are believed to convey luck.

Still debated is whether the horseshoe should be hung with the open end upward, so that it will catch and hold good luck or with the open end downward, in order to prevent evil doers from passing underneath.

For some, the shape of the horseshoe is said to be an emblem of sex and productivity. Many believe that the arch formation of the Moorish mosques and temples is an extension of the shape of a horseshoe.

HOSPITAL: Already mentioned in another context (see **flowers**) is the fact that one should never bring red and white flowers, symbolic of death, into a hospital.

Other superstitions include these: Should a nurse inadvertently knock over a chair in the ward, a new patient will soon arrive. Should a nurse twist her apron strings while dressing, she will soon be given new duties. Carelessly placing blankets over a chair, while making up a bed, presages a death in the ward.

If one can choose the day of entry into a hospital, Wednesday is said to be preferable. Likewise, should one leave a hospital on a Saturday, he will soon return. (It was also thought an ill omen to call one's physician on a Friday.)

Sleeping in the bed of someone who has died was thought by the ancients to assure the new patient of the same fate, and the very first patient to see a doctor in a new hospital was believed to be quickly cured.

Hot cross buns: The practice of making crosses on food with a knife or icing was said to keep evil spirits away. Traditionally, cakes were made from wheat as part of the pagan spring festivals. Originally, the buns baked on Good Friday were simply called "cross buns." Buns baked on Good Friday were believed to stay fresh for an entire year. Should they be taken to sea, it was believed that they would prevent shipwrecks.

House: According to a Yorkshire belief, one can bring luck to a new house by going into every room carrying a loaf of bread and a plate of salt.

In ancient times, according to belief, anyone who crossed the threshold of a new home for the first time would die. Hence, ritual sacrifices, of walling a man or a child in "alive," during the construction of a house, were often commonplace. This, in time, gave rise to sprinkling the blood from a male goat or a rooster on the threshold. In Brittany, some would wet the ground with some wine, as a substitute for blood, by pouring it into a small hole that had been previously dug.

In place of ritual sacrifices, the laying of the cornerstone of a house often became significant. For some, the eldest son was instructed to take on this task. After laying the stone, it was tapped three times. In some regions, it is the eldest daughter who gives the taps. This is followed by her kissing the workers.

Still another tradition held that one should take three pieces of paper, upon each of which the name of God has been written, and bury them in iron boxes at three different corners of the cellar. This was so demons and evil spirits would flee by way of the fourth, unprotected, corner.

Burying a pitcher that contained a virgin girl's blouse was said to protect the house against fire.

In the Auvergne region, people throw a bouquet of flowers on the roof of a house as soon as it is completed. A tree decorated with ribbons is often set up on the upper part of the roof during construction. For others, throwing dried fruit or money from the roof to the people gathered below is a way of conveying blessings on the new structure.

In England, belief holds, if a leek is growing on one's roof, the house will be struck by lightning. In Wales, however, this belief is reversed. It is lucky to have the roof of one's house covered with this plant.

The tradition of bringing a housewarming gift to one who has just moved into a new house is a modern remnant of many old beliefs.

HUMMINGBIRD: Should a hummingbird pick at a girl's breakfast, it is said that she will marry during the year. If she is already married, a woman will have a child within the year. In Latin America, hummingbirds are thought to be a refuge of dead souls.

HUNCHBACK: General belief holds that meeting a hunchback is lucky. To touch his hump is considered even more fortunate!

HUNTING: You can increase your luck by firing a shot into the air at midnight on New Year's Eve.

Should a hunter encounter a clergyman or a pregnant woman before firing a single shot, it is believed he must cross his fingers at once or return back home. Should this not be done, he will find himself the victim of an accident or will return without any game.

Most lucky of all is the hunter who has a virgin jump across his gun before setting out.

Missing the first shot is said to omen bad luck for the rest of the day.

HYENA: The shadow of a hyena brushing past a dog will make the dog mute, according to an ancient Egyptian belief. Folklore holds that the hyena changes its sex every year and can imitate a man's voice to attract its prey.

HYMN: Should a clock strike twelve while a hymn is being sung during the morning church service, a death is likely to occur in less than a week, says a Sussex tradition.

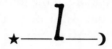

INFLUENZA: An Irish tradition says that to cure the flu one should take some clay scraped off the threshold of one's door, make it into a paste, and apply it to the chest of the patient. Carrying a sachet of camphor or eating fat slugs and dog droppings on an empty stomach were said to do the same thing.

During flu epidemics, a common practice was to place a spoonful of holy water in the evening soup. Wrapping the patient in a warm, bloody lamb, or rabbit skin was also held effective. Placing a pigeon that had been quartered alive on the painful area, or a hot brick rubbed with garlic and moistened with vinegar, was thought equally effective. Cow dung or a dead hen or rooster were also used in the same way.

Oysters, dissolved in milk, or a potion of milk and wine mixed with boiled dog droppings, were said to cure flu, if drunk on a regular basis. Swallowing an egg yolk that contained five or six live lice, urine from a seven-year-old girl, or soot from a chimney, was invaluable. If all else failed, drinking nine drops of "he"-goat blood that were boiled in white wine would work.

Should one gather stones after a funeral procession has passed over them and boil them in water or milk, flu was certain to depart. Spitting into a fire and throwing some eggshells or cabbage cores in it was also said to lessen the illness. Should the patient still remain ill, he was instructed to take four small ferns and chicory root and place them in four pots of boiling water. To this was added a spoonful of honey and licorice. If consumed between meals, this was said to be a certain cure.

INITIALS: In American folklore, if the initials of your name spell a word, no matter what the word is, you will become rich and famous.

INK: Should you make an ink blot while writing a letter, it is considered a good omen. Should the letter be a love letter, the person receiving it will think well of you.

INTOXICATION: While some of the traditions with regard to drinking and getting drunk have already been discussed (see **drunkenness**), a few others remain to be mentioned.

Mixing some of a drunkard's fresh blood in some red wine and giving it back to him is said to dispel the desire for drink. A crushed owl's egg consumed in wine or in an omelet will do the same thing, and powder made from a dead man's bones (stolen from a cemetery by the light of a full moon) is also held effective.

One tradition maintains that the best way to sober up a drunk man is to roll him in manure and make him drink olive oil. This strong treatment is followed by having him smell his own urine and wrapping his genitals in vinegar-soaked linen.

One can drink without becoming drunk if roasted pig's lungs are first eaten, according to a Welsh tradition. Two spoonfuls of betony water and one of olive oil are said to do the same thing.

INVALID: One who has been ill for some time is advised to walk around the house in the direction of the sun the first time he goes outdoors. Should he walk in the opposite direction, according to a Cornish tradition, he will suffer a relapse.

IRON: Iron has long been held to possess the ability to ward off demons and dismiss the evil eye. In Anglo-Saxon countries, touching iron was more popular than touching wood for attracting good luck.

Placing two knives or a sickle in the form of a cross is said to protect a house in which a child has just been born or someone is dying. Wearing a wrought-iron bracelet facilitates conception of a child, and biting a piece of iron on Easter Eve is held to prevent toothaches for an entire year.

One should never bring old iron into the house or it will bring bad luck. Placing a hot iron into the cream, during the churning process, is said to expel the magic of any witch.

The use of iron was forbidden by the Druids when cutting mistletoe. Likewise, the stones in the Temple of Jerusalem were supposedly never in contact with iron.

One tradition holds that, should iron touch a plant used for healing purposes, the plant would lose its power. On the other hand, should a piece of iron touch the part of a body where illness lies and then be nailed to a tree, it would take away the illness.

ITCHING: Itches are said to predict coming events. On the right side of the body, they presage a lover's thoughts; on the left side, however, someone is slandering you. Should your nose itch, you will soon kiss a fool; your feet, you will soon be treading on strange ground. Should the right hand itch, money will be received; the left hand, money will be paid out. Should the knee itch, you will soon kneel in a strange church. Should the elbow itch, you will sleep with a strange bedfellow.

IVORY: Ivory is of animal origin, so it is said to keep away evil spirits. Bracelets, amulets, or jewelry made of ivory are thus said to bring good luck. Ivory is also believed to have the ability to keep away corruption, especially that of cancer.

IVY: Throughout the ages, ivy has a long tradition with many beliefs attached to it.

It is first connected with the god Dionysus. When Zeus's wife, Hera, discovered that Zeus had bedded Semele, the daughter of Cadmus, King of Thebes, Hera suggested to Semele that she should ask Zeus to unveil himself to her. When he did so, his divine flames consumed her and almost killed her unborn child, Dionysus, but for a sudden growth of ivy. To protect the infant, Zeus placed the child in his own thigh, until it was ready for birth.

Still another version of this legend has Semele abandoning Dionysus under an ivy bush. *Kissos,* or *cissos,* the ancient name given to ivy, is believed to have been Dionysus's earliest name. (Another name for Dionysus is Bacchus, God of Wine.)

In still another legend, Kissos is the name given to a nymph who dances so furiously at a Dionysian feast that she collapses and dies of exhaustion. Dionysus, grieving her untimely death, changes her into ivy.

Also believed to be a source of divine inspiration, ivy was used in ancient times for a poet's crown. Ivy was also used by the Greeks to make victory crowns for conquering heroes in the games held at

Corinth. Likewise, at Greek wedding ceremonies, a wreath of ivy is given by the priest to the newly married couple. Presumably, it indicates fidelity, due to its twining propensities.

According to Pliny, ivy is an excellent preventer of intoxication. A drink made of ivy berries before alcoholic beverages is said to prevent drunkenness. Likewise, ivy leaves taken afterwards will prevent a hangover. Taking wine in which ivy leaves have been steeped, especially if drunk from a cup made of ivy wood, was also recommended.

Folklore holds that ivy may be used to treat corns, serve as an eye lotion, cure skin rashes, and cure the common cold.

Ivy growing on a house was said to protect it against witchcraft and other evils. Should it fall off and die, misfortune was said to be on the way. In Wales, such an event was held to predict that the house would pass into another's hands.

In Scotland, wreaths of ivy, sometimes combined with mountain ash and honeysuckle, were placed over the entrance to the byre and under milk containers in the barn to protect the animals. German cowherders often made ivy wreaths, which they placed upon their cattle when leading them out to spring pasture for the first time.

Children with whooping cough would be cured if allowed to drink all they wanted from cups made of ivy wood, it was said.

Should boys gather ten leaves of ivy at Halloween, without speaking, throw away one, and put the remaining nine under their pillows, they will dream of love and marriage, says one tradition. In Oxfordshire, should a girl place an ivy leaf in her pocket, the first man she meets will marry her, even if he is already married!

In Scotland, should an ivy leaf be placed into a girl's bosom while she said the following, her intended would soon be at hand:

> *Ivy, ivy, I love you.*
> *In my bosom I put you.*
> *The first young man who speaks to me*
> *My future husband he shall be.*

Other superstitions include these: should an ivy leaf be placed in water on New Year's Eve and still be fresh on Twelfth Night, the year ahead will be favorable. Should black spots form on the ivy, an illness is certain; should spots fall all over, death will come within the year. The gift of an ivy plant breaks friendship. (Thus it is unlucky to have it around the house.) Should ivy not grow upon a grave, the soul of the person buried there is restless. Should it grow abundantly on the grave of a young woman, she died of a broken heart.

In American folk medicine, ivy was considered useful as an antidote for poisons and as a dressing for wounds, burns, and ulcers. Powdered berries were often used for jaundice. Others claim it effective as a depilatory and for dyeing one's hair.

Last, in the language of flowers, ivy is said to be symbolic of fidelity and marriage. A sprig of ivy with tendrils is said to mean "assiduous to please."

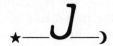

JACKDAW: According to traditions in the United Kingdom, the jackdaw, a Eurasian bird related to and resembling the crow, is considered to be an omen of ill luck if seen singly.

JADE: Throughout the Orient, jade is considered to be lucky and a powerful amulet. Placed in the mouth or on the eyelids of a deceased person, the Chinese say it will help bring back the spirit for another life on earth.

In Africa, it is thought that jade attracts rain, and likewise in Mexico. It is also believed to encourage plant growth.

When Spaniards invaded Mexico in the sixteenth century, Aztecs offered the invaders objects and pebbles of jade.

Sir Walter Raleigh in 1596 wrote that the Amazons would barter gold for jade so that they could treat disorders of the spleen.

Jade is considered effective for warding off ailments of the groin and kidneys; it is sometimes called the "kidney stone." Since jade is harder than all other stones, it was long thought that it could break up gall and kidney stones. In Central America, these ailments were treated by laying jade against the skin near the affected part.

Wearing jade is reported to cure kidney and bladder ailments and to make epileptic attacks cease.

The Maoris of New Zealand use jade amulets or pendants called "hei-tiki," often carved to resemble a little man. Sometimes held symbolic of the human embryo (hence fertility symbols), hei-tiki represent the continuing life force, and are handed down in families or from friend to friend.

A Taoist legend tells how the beautiful Jade Queen lived in a palace in the inaccessible mountains of the west. The Emperor sought her out and reached her in the course of a single night by riding eight bewitched stallions in turn. In Another Chinese tale the moon is the home of Yu-t'u, the Jade Hare, who is said to brew the elixir of life from crushed jade.

Alchemists in the West often confused white jade with the philosopher's stone and said that dew drunk from a jade chalice would prolong life.

JANUARY: British tradition holds that a mild January means winter weather will continue until the end of May. Another tradition says that January is an unlucky month for kings and monarchs. Charles I was beheaded in January; Napoleon III died in January; as did King Victor Emmanuel.

JAPONICA: The large green berries of the japonica flower, which form after seeding, often grow as large as an apple. English tradition holds that these were "the forbidden fruit" in the Garden of Eden. No one, therefore, should pick the fruit. As this particular belief is only prevalent in Kent, in other parts of United Kingdom japonica is often made into jelly or jam.

JAUNDICE: Taking on the yellow color characterized by this illness gave rise to a host of strange and unusual cures! For instance, eating nine lice on a piece of bread and butter (itself yellow in coloration) was said to cure jaundice, according to a Dorset tradition.

Should a person urinate on nettle nine times in a row, at dawn, or wear around the neck or in the armpit a sachet containing a crushed hard-boiled egg (sometimes the yolk only), one could cure the condition. Dried hen droppings in white wine were also recommended. Drinking a young boy's urine every day on an empty stomach was supposed to be helpful. Hanging a clump of mistletoe that grew over a bramble bush from the pot hook on the hearth was also said to work. Once the mistletoe balls dried the jaundice was said to disappear.

When jaundice is first discovered, if one takes an egg and breaks it over an anthill, the ants will bury the illness with the egg.

Tradition also held that one could "exorcise" jaundice by taking a coin in one's right hand and making three circles with it around the patient's face, while saying, "I beseech you and command you, in the name of the living God, Emmanuel, and Abraham to leave this body."

A common recipe required one to hollow out a fat carrot and fill it with the patient's urine. The carrot should be left to rot or hang in a fireplace so that the urine would evaporate. The patient was then required to eat it raw or cooked.

JOCKEY: The very mention of the word *superstition* to a jockey is said to cause him to walk away. This itself is an omen of bad luck to him. It is said that no jockey will have his photograph taken on his mount *before* the race.

Should he drop his whip or crop before or during the race, it is a sign of bad luck. Many jockeys believe their favorite whip is like a mascot.

Another tradition holds that a jockey's boots should never be placed on the floor in his dressing room. If done inadvertently, the jockey should walk around his boots three times before ordering his valet to replace them on the shelf where they belong.

Lastly, no jockey wishes to be called such before riding. Rather, he prefers to be called by his proper name.

JOURNEY: One should not turn back after starting a journey or bad luck will attend the rest of the day, says an English superstition. An antidote to the bad luck is to speak these words: "To ask for meat and drink, eat them and then set out again."

JUNIPER: Legend holds it that the juniper tree came to the assistance of the Holy Family during their flight into Egypt; hence, its presence is said to ward off demons and evil spirits. Juniper fires were held to drive away epidemics.

In the language of flowers, if given as a gift, juniper means protection and asylum from enemies.

To pacify gods of the underworld, juniper berries and branches were burned as incense by the ancient Greeks. Berries were also burned at funerals to drive away evil spirits. Last, its berries are believed to have many therapeutic values, as well as the ability to drive away snakes.

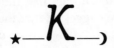

KETTLE: Should an unmarried girl turn a kettle so that the spout faces the chimney or wall, it is said that she will be an old maid and never find a husband.

KEY: In general, keys were long held as symbols of initiation, power, and prosperity. Should a wife's keys continually get rusty, such omens an inheritance. When a person is near death, all keys should be turned and the doors thrown open, so that the soul can leave the body. On Saint Valentine's morning should an unmarried girl look through a keyhole and see a cock and hen together, she will be married before the year is out.

Jingling a ring of keys on a Wednesday (Mercury's Day) will make the person go crazy.

Should a person who loses his way stop at a crossroad, close his eyes, and toss his key ring over his left shoulder, the longest key will indicate the direction in which he should travel.

An excellent talisman can be had by taking a small gold key and wearing it crosswise. Since touching a key is touching iron, one should carry a key and grab hold of it whenever a phantom, sorcerer, witch, or priest is encountered.

It is said that a key will return a werewolf to human form, if beaten with it until blood is drawn.

Placing a key under a child's pillow will protect the child from evildoing.

KEY WEST: In Florida, one of the Key West islands is called Cayo Hueso or Bone Island. It contains a great heap of bones discovered amidst great speculation. Though first thought to be the site of a battle, later examination suggested that the bones were due to the death of an entire village or villages from disease.

Tradition holds that all women living in Key West are beautiful and all men handsome.

Visitors said to arrive when the moon is full and who watch the sunset from the deck of the Pier House have been known to become bewitched and to find themselves unable to leave the island. It is because of this magical enchantment that the cats living in Ernest Hemingway's former mansion have more than five toes!

KINGFISHER: Tradition holds that the kingfisher, or halcyon, serves as a bow and arrow to God. Hence, to see it is thought to be a good omen. If hanged by its bill, it is said that a kingfisher will tell the weather. A sailors' tradition holds that, as long as kingfishers are sitting on their eggs, no storm or tempest will occur.

Hearing the sound of a kingfisher coming from the right omens success in business, while from the left, misfortune is nearby.

Tradition holds that this bird breeds at midwinter in a nest that floats on the sea, during which time the wind and waves remain unusually calm for seven "halcyon days."

KISS: Kissing newly born or young children is said to be unlucky. Children who have not yet learned to talk should not kiss each other or they will become deaf and dumb forever. In Brittany, people once greeted each other by kissing each other's cheeks three times—twice on the left and once on the right.

A young virgin girl who lets herself be kissed on the mouth will become pregnant, held one tradition. Should she kiss a man with a moustache and not let a hair from it stick to her lips, she will become an old maid. Any young woman unexpectedly kissed by a dark-complexioned man will soon receive a marriage proposal.

Kissing a widow after a burial will let her know one shares her sorrow. A person should never kiss another on the nose or discord between the two will come about.

One should never kiss another over his or her shoulder. Such is said to evoke the kiss of Judas. One tradition holds that Romans pressed their lips on their wives' as a test for sobriety.

Visitors to the Pope customarily kiss his ring or foot. Kissing the

Bible is to affirm one's oath. Tradition holds that witches kissed the Devil "under his tail" at the sabbath.

During the colonial period in New Amsterdam (now New York City), a bridge crossed the East River at what is now Second Avenue. Tradition at that time was that, whenever the bridge was crossed, a kiss could be exacted from one's companion!

KNIFE: Knives traditionally used for hunting and sacrifice were long thought of as powerful talismans; hence, two knives accidentally crossed on a table were an omen of misfortune.

Superstitions about knives abound: Should a knife be given to a friend, he should also give a small coin to ward off evil or prevent the dissolution of the friendship. Should one knock a knife off a table, a current love affair will come to an end. Another superstition claims that this portends an unexpected gentleman caller. Should a knife fall during a meal, tradition holds that it should not be picked up until the meal is over.

A knife in one's pocket will prevent fairies from lifting you at night, according to a Scottish tradition. One should never toast bread with a knife or one will toast away their luck. A girl should never receive a gift of a knife or any other pointed instrument from her suitor, or her love affair will soon be broken off.

According to a Welsh tradition, should a girl walk backwards, placing a knife among the leeks on Halloween, she will see her future husband pick up the knife and throw it into the middle of the garden.

According to a Kent tradition, a knife placed under the window will keep away Satan.

Should the blade of one's personal knife stay bright, it indicates safety and well-being; should it become dull, one is in danger of illness; should it rust or break, misfortune will attend one's family.

Leaving a knife on a table overnight invites a robber. Should one spin a knife on top of a table, the person it points to will die before the others. Should someone forget his knife, he must go in person to get it, or misfortune will be his.

One can protect against loss of a new knife by giving a dog the first piece of bread cut with it.

A person with colic will recover quickly should he eat using a white-handled knife.

KNOCKING ON WOOD: To knock on wood or touch wood to maintain one's good luck is perhaps the most common superstition yet retained by the educated sophisticate. Some claim the practice developed from the touching of a wooden crucifix in ancient times. Others hold that the important point is to make a noise loud enough to drive away evil spirits.

Attributed to no less a personage than Winston Churchill are these words: "I rarely like to be any considerable distance from a piece of wood."

Tradition also holds that, while a college student, Sir Walter Scott gained success in his recitations by invariably fingering a wooden button attached to his coat. As the story goes, when one of his fellow students secretly cut it off, he was so flustered on discovering its absence, that he failed hopelessly and was sent to the back of his class.

KNOCK OF DEATH: Three loud and distinct knocks at the head of a sick person's bed are said to be an omen of death.

KNOT: Knots have often been symbolic of various occult forces. Sorcerers tied knots when trying to cast an evil spell. A fiancé's codpiece was knotted to keep the couple from consummating their union ahead of time.

During storms, sailors traditionally tied knots in their clothing. Gamblers seeking to attract luck have been known to tie knots in their shirts. Girls often tie knots in their hair with ribbons or in the form of braids. A lock of a sick person's hair, if knotted, is said to bring about a recovery.

In Russia, a bride's belt contains many knots in order to combat the evil eye. Should one's belt become undone, it is considered a bad omen. Should it belong to the officiating priest of a wedding ceremony, however, it is held to presage that the marriage will be fruitful and the wife will soon conceive. One tradition holds that grooms should go to the altar with one shoe untied in order to prevent evil spells from being cast.

An English tradition holds that, immediately before the marriage, every knot about the bride and bridegroom should be loosened. After the ceremony, the bridegroom should retire with young men and retie his loosened knots; the bride should do likewise with her bridesmaids.

During childbirth, the woman should undo any knots that are part of her clothing. This is said to facilitate delivery. Likewise, in a coffin, the deceased should not have his shoelaces tied. Otherwise, his soul will be prevented from leaving the earth.

One way to cure warts was to tie knots in a length of thread—one for each wart—and then throw the thread away. Whoever picked up the thread would get the warts.

Knots also symbolize marital fidelity. In some Mediterranean countries, a husband required to be away from his home ties two branches together from two trees near his house. When he returns, should he find the knot undone, he knows that his wife has been unfaithful.

Some sailors tie three knots in their handkerchief. When the first is untied, it is said to bring a steady wind; the second, a tempest; the third, a perfect calm.

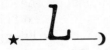

LADDER: The tradition of never walking underneath a ladder is perhaps as common as throwing spilled salt over one's shoulder. Tradition holds that a ladder leaning against anything forms a triangle, which is symbolic of the Trinity. Therefore, to walk under the ladder flaunts the Trinity, enabling one to fall into the hands of Satan himself!

Should you inadvertently pass under a ladder, bad luck can still be avoided, if you cross two fingers and keep them crossed until you see a dog.

The ladder superstition may have evolved from what is called "the head taboo." This is the belief that a spirit lives in one's head, and for this reason, nothing should be placed over it.

In Holland, should you pass under a ladder, you are certain to be hanged, it is said. In American folklore, the belief is that a person should never climb up a ladder if a black cat is passing underneath it. Stepping or passing between the rungs of a ladder, thereby forming a cross, is also said to bring misfortune.

LADYBUG: The ladybug, sometimes called "ladybird," is said to bring you good luck if it lights on your hand. Killing a ladybug, therefore, is said to bring bad luck.

This particular insect has been called by names that have associated it with Our Lady, such as *marienkafer* (merry beetle), in Germany, for instance. It has long been associated with the Virgin Mary and Saint John and it is believed to have been blessed by God himself. Some traditions say that it even understands human language.

223

It is said that, should it light on one's hand and then fly away, there will be nice weather on the next Sunday. Should it light on one's hand on a Sunday, it is held to bring good luck, if it rests long enough for one to count to twenty-two.

A children's game found in many countries is to catch a ladybug and hold it on the palm of the hand while saying:

> *Ladybug, Ladybug, fly away home,*
> *Your house is on fire and your children are gone.*

It is believed that the ladybug will fly off in the direction from which a lover will come.

In Burgundy, the number of little black dots on the ladybug's back indicate the number of children a woman will have. In the United Kingdom, they are said to indicate happy months to come.

According to a Norse legend, the ladybug came to earth via lightning.

In American folklore should a ladybug light on one's hand, new gloves will soon be forthcoming; should it light on one's dress, a new dress; and so on.

LAMB: Symbolically, in Christian tradition, the lamb is said to be a symbol of Christ, who himself is referred to as the "lamb of God." In ancient times, since it was often used for ritual sacrifice, the lamb stood for purity and innocence. Even today, the term "flock" is used to describe members of a church, with Christ often called "the Good Shepherd."

If the first lamb of the season be "tail first," a country tradition says that the year will be hard and nothing beyond milk and vegetables will be had. Should the lamb seen be "head foremost," however, a year of plenty is predicted.

The lambing season begins with the birth of twins; good luck follows the flock throughout the entire year. One tradition holds that the first lamb born to a flock should be rolled in snow to bring luck.

Already mentioned is the tradition of burning a lamb alive in order to cure disease in the sheepfold.

Although an undesirable family member is often called a "black sheep," in some parts of Europe, the birth of a black lamb is an omen of good luck. In some parts of England, though, a black lamb is said to be evil. The birth of black lamb twins predicts a major calamity, unless the throats of the twins are cut before their first "baa."

LAMENESS: Generally speaking, encountering a lame man is held as a bad omen. In Anglo Saxon countries, seeing one from behind is said to predict trouble ahead.

Should a funeral encounter a lame donkey, it is said that the deceased will go to hell.

LAMP: The invention of modern electricity has rendered many of the superstitions concerning oil-burning lamps obsolete. However, there are a few to discuss anyway.

A person who walks at night should always carry a lamp or lantern to drive away evil spirits, it is said. Therefore, lamps should be left lit at the head of a newborn child's or a dying person's bed. On the eve of All Souls' Day, lamps should be left lit in one's house.

A farmer should never place his lantern on a table, according to a Herefordshire tradition, but should put it underneath, or ill will come to his cows. Should you approach the lantern of someone asleep, it will kill him. Likewise, lamps placed at the head of a dying person's bed should never be extinguished, but should go out on their own, after the last breath has been drawn.

In Greece, a fluttering lamp is said to predict misfortune or an upcoming death. One tradition holds that, if three lamps are lit in the same room, a marriage will soon be coming. Another interpretation of this is that it announces an approaching death.

Maids desiring marriage were often instructed to make their lovers stand immobile between three lamps. The lamps had to be lit by themselves and the man could not move for the time it took to recite the rosary.

LAPWING: In Scotland, it is an ill omen to see a lapwing flying overhead while it makes its unusual screeching call. Tradition holds that souls of men, doomed never to find peace, live in the bodies of these birds. Their call is the word "bewitched" chanted over and over.

LARK: This bird, a favorite to lovers worldwide, is said to symbolize sublimation. An ancient belief was that the lark would sing more sweetly if it were blinded with a red-hot needle.

Should you wish to know what the lark is saying, you must lie down on your back in a field and listen, says a Scottish tradition.

Eating three lark's eggs on a Sunday morning, before the ringing of the church bells, will grant you a sweet voice.

A lark's eye wrapped in wolf skin and worn secretly in your right pocket will make you irresistible. Placing the same eye in a glass of wine will cause whoever drinks it to fall in love.

One can determine the seriousness of an ill person's case by bringing a lark to the bedside. The lark will turn its head if the person will die and stare straight ahead if recovery is on the way, it is said.

One will be victorious over enemies and nature by carrying a lark's foot as a talisman.

LAST PIECE: Taking the last piece of food or dessert from a serving plate will make you an old maid!

LAUGH: Excessive laughter is seen by many countryfolk as an evil omen. One tradition holds that, if someone laughs before breakfast, they will cry before nightfall.

LAUNCHING SHIPS: Originally, bows of ships were smeared with human or animal blood to symbolize their being given life. In time, the blood was replaced by red wine and, later, champagne. Should the bottle not break on the first try, it is an ill omen.

LEAD: Lead, traditionally the metal of death, corresponds to the planet Saturn and the astrological sign Capricorn.

Saturn was the outermost planet known to the ancients and was symbolic of limitation and boundary.

Country folk believe lead can be discovered with the help of a forked stick of pinewood used as a dowsing rod. In alchemy, the belief was held that one need only pass through white lead or mercury to arrive at gold.

Religious relics were often encased in lead caskets in the belief that such kept their sacred force held within and unable to dissipate into the air. The medieval Pope Boniface VIII used a lead seal in the form of a lion (symbolic of courage and mastery) to keep pain in check during an operation for stones.

Should a person desire to kill or harm another, one tradition held that their name should be written on a piece of lead which is then buried in the ground and magic would do the rest.

Generally held is the belief that witches and other demons cannot be killed with lead bullets. Silver must be used instead, possibly due to its connection with the moon.

According to a Scottish belief, should one shoot a witch who is in the guise of a hare with a lead bullet, the bullet will rebound and strike the person firing.

Already mentioned was the tradition of young girls melting lead and letting it fall into a tub of cool water in droughts. It was believed that the shapes the lead took on would characterize the future husband's occupation. (See **Halloween**.) For example, a hammer suggested a blacksmith; a needle, a tailor.

LEAF: Catching falling leaves in one's hand in autumn is believed to guarantee freedom from colds all winter.

Leaves of oak and ash trees were used by many countryfolk to predict summer weather. Should the ash leaves appear before the oak, a wet summer was said likely. Should the oak appear before the ash, rainfall would be light. Leaves turning upward, as if to catch the rain, were said to indicate the onset of a storm. Should a number of trees shed heavily before the autumn, a bad winter was likely.

One popular children's game consists of catching leaves between Michaelmas (September 29) and Halloween (October 31). It is believed that, for every one caught, a happy day may be expected in the coming year.

LEAP YEAR: Years in which an extra day is added to the calendar, February 29, are favorable for all new undertakings and changes in one's life or profession. Being born on February 29, however, is not so favorable, since one will not have a birthday every year. Yet, children conceived or born on that date were believed especially blessed.

One tradition says that, during leap year, a girl may propose to her chosen mate, without feeling unusually forward in so doing. In Scotland, during leap year, a girl desiring to propose must wear a scarlet flannel petticoat, which is made partly visible below her dress. If not worn, men are able to reject their proposals, without fear of bad luck.

LEATHER: Wearing leather is said to scare evil spirits away.

LEEK: According to a Welsh tradition, fighters who rub leek or garlic on themselves will overcome any opponent and never be wounded.

Left-handed: Statistically, about seven percent of the population is born left-handed, yet in the Middle Ages being left-handed could cause one to be suspected of being a witch.

Should a left-handed person be forced to use his right hand, he will become a stutterer, according to American folklore. It was once common practice to retrain "southpaws" to write with their right hand.

European belief says it is unlucky to meet a left-handed person on a Tuesday morning. Meeting such a person on any other morning of the week, however, was said to bring good luck.

No doubt the reason left-handed people are discriminated against is due to the association of the Devil with the left. Christ was seated at the right hand of God, not the left.

Another tradition maintains that left-handed persons are clumsy. However, Leonardo da Vinci painted the famous *Mona Lisa* with his left hand! The Moslems keep the left hand for all unclean acts, including petting dogs.

Romans used the word *sinister* to designate the left.

Letter: Letters from two friends crossing in the mail presages a quarrel or misunderstanding between them.

Lettuce: For the Romans, lettuce was an aphrodisiac; hence, it often appeared at weddings. Furthermore, it was believed that lettuce could be used to prevent drunkenness.

A tradition found in Surrey (and, apparently, nowhere else), holds that an abundance of lettuce plants in one's garden will prevent a wife from conceiving.

Lightning: To North American Indians, lightning was believed to be the flashy beak of the great Thunderbird, as she flew through the storm. In ancient times, lightning was said to indicate the gods were angry.

An oft-quoted belief is that lightning never strikes twice in the same place.

The Germans once believed that wood struck by lightning would protect barns on the night of May 1. In American folklore, wood struck by lightning should never be used in the fireplace, because lightning will strike it again.

A harvest is said to be plentiful should lightning strike on the twenty-seventh day of the month; and poor, should this happen on the twenty-ninth.

Generally accepted is the belief that, where lightning has struck, "devil's pebbles" or "lightning stones," having the shape of hatchets or arrowheads, will be found. In the Alsace, should a fragment of one of these hatchets be placed in a wound, it was said to confer invincible power on the wounded person. He could then kill with a single closed fist by exclaiming, "May lightning crush you!"

Various methods exist to protect oneself from lightning. In the United Kingdom, if one carries the rare coal found under the mugwort plant at noon or midnight on Midsummer's Eve, it will protect him from lightning.

Should a piece of hawthorn cut on Holy Thursday be brought into one's house, it supposedly will protect it from being struck by lightning, as this was the thorn tree under which Christ was born.

Placing acorns near windows is said to be sound protection against lightning. Holly used at Christmas is also good protection. You can also protect your house by gathering a snakeskin around your head, feeding a fire in the hearth, throwing salt and laurel leaves into that fire, clothing yourself in natural silk, placing a pot hook from the hearth on the windowsill, or simply sleeping in a feather bed.

Should you be outdoors when lightning appears, take refuge under a tree only if it is a beech, walnut, or hawthorn, some say. (Conventional wisdom says to stay away from any kind of tree during an electrical storm.)

One tradition holds that, when Satan sought to destroy the earth with thunder, the Virgin Mary created lightning "flashes" to warn mankind. These would grant them time to cross themselves. As a sign of respect to the Virgin Mother, one must click his tongue three times when a lightning flash is first seen.

Yet another tradition holds that all mirrors should be veiled and scissors hidden when lightning first appears. Infants exposed to lightning are said likely to catch scabies.

Last, dogs' tails are said to draw lightning to them!

LILAC: It is generally believed unlucky to take lilac into the house.

In the language of flowers, a white lilac offered by a young man symbolizes the purity of his intentions. Lilac should never be given to a sick person, though, or a relapse is likely.

A mauve or blue lilac symbolizes a request of marriage.

LILY: This flower has long been held a symbol of motherhood and fruitfulness. One myth says that the lily was born from a drop of milk that fell to the ground from the breasts of Zeus's wife, Hera. In a fit of jealousy, Aphrodite dressed the lily with a pistil like the penis of a donkey.

References to the lily are found in the mythology of Egypt, Assyria, Babylonia, and Sumeria.

In Crete, the lily was held sacred to Britomartis, the "sweet virgin" who was pursued by the bull Minos. After leaping to her apparent doom, she was saved by the nets of a fisherman. Afterwards, she was given the name Dictynna, meaning "mother of the nets."

To symbolize virginity and fertility, Greeks and Romans often placed wreaths of lily and corn on the heads of brides. For the Greeks, Hera, goddess of marriage and childbirth, was the patron of the lily.

Among the Jews, legend holds that Eve shed tears over a lily when she discovered she was pregnant, after expulsion from the Garden of Eden.

In biblical times, the lily was said to represent power against evil. Hence, when Judith killed the Assyrian General Holofernes she wore a crown or wreath of lilies.

Possibly due to the ancient connection between the flower and virginity, Christianity early on assigned the flower to the Virgin Mary. In various chapels dedicated to the "Lady," the lily will be seen among other carved flowers and leaves. The Cistercian Monks regard the Virgin as their patroness, and the lily as their symbol.

In the early days of its use by the Roman Catholic Church, the lily would often have the stamen and pistils removed, so it would be truly symbolic of the Virgin. It is also held symbolic of the angel Gabriel.

Legend holds that Saint Thomas, doubting the Christ's resurrection, caused his tomb to be opened and found inside a mass of lilies and roses.

Tradition holds that lilies may be used to drive away witches on the Eve and Feast of Saint John.

According to an old English tradition, should a man tread upon a lily, he will destroy the purity of his wife and daughters. Yet another tradition holds that, should lilies spring up on the graves of those executed for crimes, those persons were in fact innocent!

Grown in the garden, lilies are said to be a barrier against evil spirits. As the lily is sometimes associated with death, however, many country folk will not bring the lilies indoors.

If lilies were to be placed in vases containing cow's milk many believed it would dry up all the cows in the neighborhood. Should one mix a lily with the sap of a laurel and place it under manure, it was said to produce worms. Should these worms be placed in someone's pocket, the person would not be able to sleep. If rubbed with them, he would catch a fever. If you reduce a yellow lily to powder, mix it with food, and feed it to a young girl, you know she is still a virgin if she has to urinate immediately after eating this meal.

LILY OF THE VALLEY: According to an Irish tradition, lilies of the valley are fairy ladders on which the "wee folk" run up and down.

Another tradition holds that Saint Leonard was wounded while fighting a dragon. Where his blood fell to the ground, lilies of the valley grew to commemorate his victory for Christ.

In Great Britain and in France, the flower is also known as "Our Lady's tears."

Used medicinally, the flower is thought to improve one's memory, stop the pain of gout, and may also be helpful in heart disease.

It is held unlucky to plant a bed of lilies of the valley. Anyone doing so will die within twelve months, according to a Devonshire belief.

In the language of flowers, the lily of the valley indicates "the return of happiness."

LINDEN TREE: For the Germans, this tree consecrated to Venus is said to guard villages and families. On May Day, dances around its trunk are common.

LION: Tradition holds that the lion fears only the rooster, whose mane is as great as its own.

According to the Romans, only a cock's crow or the grinding sound of empty chariots could frighten a lion. It is said that a lion will erase its tracks by sweeping them with its tail and that it sleeps with its eyes open.

Eating the heart of a lion was believed to bring one courage, according to African tribes. Wearing the eye of a lion under one's armpit was said to keep away other savage beasts; wearing its skin was held to make one invincible.

Being the "king of beasts," it is thought that a lion will never harm another king.

LIPS: Should your lips itch, it is said that they will soon receive a kiss. Smacking one's lips is an invitation to the same delight.

LIZARD: According to those who know about such things, there are some 2,100 species of lizards, varying in size from a few inches to the so-called komodo dragon, which is ten feet in length.

As many species actively warm themselves in the sun and some possess the ability to replace a lost tail, they have long been held an object of awe and curiosity.

In Egypt, they were associated with fecundity, since their activity increased when the Nile flooded. A Dahomey tradition holds that the lizard fetched fire from the sun. In Europe it was long believed that, during hibernation, the lizard becomes blind. The belief was that, in spring, the creature would climb an eastward-facing wall, look to the east, and, when the sun rose, its sight would be restored.

Pliny said that a lizard talisman would restore sight to the blind. In medieval times, Christians regarded the lizard as a symbol of rebirth and resurrection, possibly due to the pagan Roman influence. (The Romans had often depicted the lizard on grave monuments as a symbol of hope and life beyond the grave.)

Generally held is the idea that the lizard is either a god, a kin to the god, or his messenger. For instance, in Samoa, several gods exist in lizard form. For the Maoris, Tangaloa, the Heaven God, is believed to incarnate as a green lizard. Tongaiti, the Night Heaven God of the Hervery Islanders of Polynesia, was believed to be a nocturnal spotted lizard. In Australia, the Aranda believe that the sky will fall if they kill a lizard. (This is probably connected with their sky and earth myths.)

In Italy, some believe fairies can appear as lizards. In Germany, folktales speak of a lizard who was really a bewitched princess.

Among Jewish folklore, the lizard was held unclean and was believed born of sexual intercourse between Satan and a witch. In fact, in some areas of France, lizards were buried alive under the threshold as a protection against witchcraft. In Shakespeare's *Macbeth*, lizard is one of the ingredients of the witches' brew.

For the Slavs and some French and English peasants, the lizard was held as protection against snakes and was often fixed on the roof of a stable to ward them off. For a lizard to cross the path of a bride was believed to produce an unhappy marriage. In some parts of the United Kingdom it is believed that, if a lizard sees a snake approaching a sleeping man, it will awaken him.

Since some lizards have the ability to regenerate their own tail, sometimes an abnormal two-tailed lizard may appear. Italians regard such a two-tailed lizard as being unusually lucky.

In Samoa, the lizard is believed to be the sun and is said to possess the ability to ask the Weather God for good weather.

One Christian tradition in Germany holds that the lizard licked away Christ's drops of blood, and, therefore, should never be killed. In Sicily, small lizards, called "San Giovanni," are never killed, since they are believed to be in the presence of the Lord in Heaven and to light the Lord's lamp.

Finding a lizard's tail is said to be gaining a highly prized talisman. The tail of a green lizard, kept in the right shoe, guarantees wealth and happiness.

Girls desiring to become good seamstresses should allow lizards to run across their hands.

In the Alsace, there is a belief that, should one kill a lizard, rain will come the next day.

A Languedoc tradition holds that, should a lizard bite a woman's breast, she will quickly lose weight. In Provence, it is said that when a lizard bites a cow on the nose, the cow soon dies.

Eating green lizards was thought to cure skin diseases. Other diseases allegedly cured by lizard ingredients include running eyes, syphilis, warts, and various liver complaints. In Arabia, lizard medicine was thought a cure for impotence. In Madagascar, lizards buried alive were said to cure fever. In medieval England, tradition held that, by licking a lizard, one could acquire the ability to heal wounds and sores in the same manner.

One tradition holds that fruit trees can be prevented from bearing bad fruit by smearing them with the bile of a green lizard. Pliny reportedly advocated this procedure and it was practiced into the twentieth century in Silesia.

LOADSTONE: In the Cornwall section of England, tradition holds that sciatica can be cured and kept away by carrying a piece of loadstone in one's pocket.

LOOKING GLASS: Looking glasses, as contrasted with mirrors, were often smaller and hand-held. For this reason, they were more subject to accidents than larger, carefully mounted mirrors.

Should you break a looking glass, it is said that you will lose your best friend. Generally held is the tradition that to break a looking glass means seven years of bad luck.

Yet another belief is that, while a corpse is lying in the house, all looking glasses should be covered over. Also, some believe that the shadow of a prospective bride or bridegroom can be seen in a looking glass on Saint Agnes' Eve.

As mentioned elsewhere (see **bride**), a bride will have bad luck if she gazes at herself in a looking glass after getting fully dressed for the wedding.

LOOKING UNDER THE BED: A country belief is that you should look under your bed before retiring for the night in order to ward off Satan.

LOVE: Although a great many traditions and superstitions regarding love and courtship have already been discussed throughout this work, a few additions still follow.

Should a courting or engaged couple be photographed together, it is believed the engagement will be broken off. Should an unmarried girl sit on a table while talking to her lover, she will never marry. Should a rose be plucked on Midsummer's Day and put away, it will remain fresh until Christmas. If then worn at church, it is said that the intended partner of a girl will come and take it from her breast.

Those who wish to stay in love are advised to pluck a twig from a laurel tree and break it in two; then each one should preserve a piece. It is held that a young girl who fails to look north when leaving her house, before breakfast, will remain unmarried.

A girl desiring to know her prospective husband should go to the churchyard on Valentine's Eve. As the clock strikes twelve, she should run around the church saying:

> *I sow hemp seed,*
> *Hemp seed I sow.*
> *He that loves me*
> *Come after me and mow.*

It is said that her future husband will then make his appearance.

Should yarrow be plucked from a man's grave and placed under one's pillow at night, one's lover will appear in a dream.

A frequently practiced American folklore tradition holds that a girl wishing to meet "the" man of her life must stand by her house and count ten red cars, see a redheaded girl dressed in mauve, and see a man with a green tie. The man who next appears after this will be her betrothed! For menfolk who wish the same information, they have simply to eat the last piece of bread at a meal and wait for the first girl to come along!

It is held unlucky for a man to offer a marriage proposal on a train, bus, or in any other public place. Girls proposed to at a dance, who refuse, are said to become unusually lucky.

LOVE LETTER: Since Venus is the Goddess of Love and has rulership over Friday, this is the day on which love letters should be offered. Tradition requires that they should always be written in ink. Love letters should never be mailed on Sundays, nor should love letters be burned.

Should your hand shake while writing the letter, it is a sign of mutuality. Should the ink blot, it is a sign that the other person is thinking of you.

You should never ask for a postcard by writing a letter. When a letter arrives damaged or improperly stamped, such announces misfortune.

It is ill-advised to post love letters on three days—Christmas Day, February 29, and September 1.

Should you wish to determine whether your lover is true and faithful, set fire to one of his or her letters. If the flame is high and light in color, the love will persist; if weak and blue, the love will soon come to an end.

Tearing up love letters is said to be superior to burning them.

MACKEREL: The next time you are tempted to eat this fish, remember this English tradition, which says mackerel should not be taken until Balaam's ass speaks in church. This refers to a pastor reading the biblical story appearing in Numbers: 23–24.

MADNESS: Should one wish to be cured of madness, an Irish charm has long been held quite effective: Obtain three substances—honey, milk, and salt—not procured by human means, and drink them before sunrise in a sane spell.

A strange belief seldom heard about is that it is considered unusually lucky to live in the same house as an insane person.

An old European cure for the bite of a mad dog requires that the dog be caught, killed, and its liver removed and burned to charcoal. This is powdered and eaten by the victim in a bread and butter sandwich.

MAGNET: (See **loadstone**.)

MAGPIE: Those in the know say that the magpie first appeared in Europe in comparatively recent times. Hence, the folklore surrounding this bird is not of great antiquity.

According to one tradition, the bird itself is a hybrid between the raven and the dove—the two birds released by Noah from the ark. Therefore, it was never baptized in the waters of the flood.

A German tradition holds that witches ride on magpies or even appear as the birds themselves.

One Swedish legend holds that, in August, magpies go away to draw the Devil's wagons of hay. That explains the shedding of their neck feathers, which causes them to appear as though rubbed by a horse's yolk.

In China the bird is thought lucky, but in Scotland and elsewhere, the magpie is said to be the Devil's bird and is believed to have a drop of Satan's blood on its tongue. Tradition holds that it can acquire human speech, if its tongue is scratched and a drop of human blood is inserted therein.

On listening to the chatter of magpies, one often hears an almost humanlike sound. In fact, domesticated magpies in captivity have been able to imitate human words.

In Brittany, it is said that the magpie has seven of the Devil's hairs on its head. Because of a connection of the bird with Satan, it is considered unlucky to kill a magpie, or at least unlucky to do so at certain times during the year.

The black and white plumage is due to the fact that, unlike other birds, it never went into full mourning after Christ's crucifixion. A Christian tradition in France says that magpies actually pricked Christ's feet with thorns while He was on the cross; the swallows tried to pull them out, causing their breasts to become blood red. As a result, magpies were condemned to nest in tall trees while the swallows could find easy shelter under the eaves of houses.

A well-known folk rhyme conveys divination traditions long held regarding this bird. The rhyme is:

> *One for sorrow,*
> *Two for mirth,*
> *Three for a wedding,*
> *Four for a birth.*

Should a single magpie croak near a house, it is said that one of the inhabitants will die. A Somerset tradition holds that one should always take off his hat to a magpie and bow respectfully, or evil ends will come about. Another tradition holds that one should cross oneself once a magpie is seen. If one is going fishing and sees two magpies flying together, a good catch is omened. Should a magpie precede a person going to church it is an indication of death. Likewise, seeing a magpie while starting out on a journey foretells bad luck, unless one returns and postpones their business.

In southern Germany, a magpie calling near a house portended disaster, but, should it merely chatter, a guest was soon to arrive.

English folklore also relates the chattering of magpies to the arrival of strangers.

Shropshire countryfolk often express wishes when a magpie is seen. They also believe that magpies never carry sticks to their nest on Ascension Day, but rather perch quietly without doing any work. Another tradition holds should you fail to wear something new on Easter Day, magpies will let droppings fall on your clothes.

Because of the exceptional nest built by this bird, which has an entrance at the side, magpies are thought to know a magical herb that they apply across the nest entrance to keep other birds away.

In Yorkshire, it is believed magpies congregating on dead branches means rain will come before night. In Devonshire, a magpie returning to the rookery in the middle of the day is said to omen rain. Should the bird be seen to make aerial dives and twists, bad weather is believed on the way.

Should magpies desert their rookery, it is said an omen of ill luck for those on whose land it was built. The birds are said to abandon their nest before the downfall of the family owning the estate.

A Finnish tradition holds rooks always know when a game-keeper has died. It is said that they will form in a line and fly over his coffin as it is carried to the church for the funeral.

Eating the brain of a magpie makes one go crazy, according to some. People of the Vendée say a male magpie is black and white and a female white and black.

MAKEUP: According to American folklore, spilling face powder or makeup is an omen that there will be a quarrel with a friend.

MANDRAKE: The tubercle of the mandrake often takes on a human form, which, no doubt, inspired a number of fictitious attributes about its great powers.

As the root contains an alkaloid similar to atropine, in ancient times it was often used for killing pain or inducing sleep.

Pliny reported that patients undergoing various operations chewed a piece of the mandrake root to anesthetize themselves.

The mandrake has also been used for convulsions, rheumatic aches, toothache, and as a treatment against general melancholy. In large doses, it was said to provoke delirium and eventual madness, however.

A sixteenth-century herbalist, William Turner, said that one should simply smell the "apples of the mandrake" (which in actuality are berries) and they will cause him to sleep. Should too many be smelled, according to Turner, one can actually become dumb.

Josephus, the Jewish chronicler (first century A.D.) held that the mandrake's prime use was to expel demons from those who were ill, since they could not stand its smell.

Quite frequently, when depicted, the plant was shown with roots resembling the trunk and legs of a man or woman.

In the Old Testament (Genesis 30:14), Leah used the mandrake to induce Jacob to sleep with her, after which she bore a fifth son.

Arab folklore regards the mandrake as an aphrodisiac, calling it "apples of Jan," or "devil's apples." According to their belief, it will even help the infertile to conceive.

In England, the mandrake was known as "the love apple," an appellation that was later transferred to the tomato.

Shakespeare paid homage to the mandrake when Falstaff in *Henry IV (Part II)* referred to Justice Shallo as, "lecherous as a monkey, and the whores call'd him Mandrake."

Some said the mandrake was conceived under the gallows, from the semen of a hanged man's last ejaculation.

In addition to its medicinal usages, most folklore surrounding the mandrake concerns specific rituals that must be followed in order to gather it. In general, the belief is held that a person who pulls a mandrake root will fall dead. The root of the mandrake will shriek and groan when pulled from the earth, and whoever hears this sound will die shortly thereafter or become mad. Anyone who looks at a mandrake was believed to go blind.

One tradition for gathering mandrake required the herbalist to stand with his back to the wind, draw three concentric circles around the plant with his sword, pour a libation, and then, turning towards the west, dig up the plant with his sword. If these instructions were not specifically followed, the plant would disappear, it was said.

As the cry of the mandrake was said to be fatal to those who heard it, after loosening the soil around it, herbalists often tied a cord between the plant and their dog, moved out of earshot, and incited the dog to pull up the plant. Tradition held that the animal would perish. It was said that the herbalist should beware of contrary winds, or he, too, might hear the cry of the mandrake as it was drawn from the ground, and would suffer the same fate. Still other traditions hold that should one fail to follow the exact instructions for extracting it, he may become blind or be struck insane by a bolt of lightning.

Once pulled up, tradition required any green leaves to be cut off and the root to be placed in a bed of red soil. A red berry was placed on it for a mouth, and two juniper fruits were placed on its eyes. It was required to be kept this way in a glass jar that should be exposed to the sun, and watered each day with human blood. At the end of three days, it was believed to come to life, and after four days could speak and divine the future. So dried, the mandrake root would be kept in a coffin or secret cupboard, or worn as a talisman in a small sachet around the neck.

The mandrake was also thought to increase one's wealth, open all doors and locks, and to bring fertility to one's wife or husband, even if sterile or impotent before. So great a talisman was the mandrake, that it was willed to its master's youngest son and was said to obey him in the same way as it did his father.

During the medieval period, possessing mandrake often brought charges of witchcraft. In 1630, three women were evidently put to death in Hamburg for this reason alone.

Three additional traditions involving mandrake are these: The leaves of the mandrake shine in the dark; one who tries to pick the leaves will actually fly away; and elephants will mate after eating mandrake.

MAPLE TREE: In American folklore carrying a newborn under the foliage of a maple tree will make him strong and vital.

MARCH: The belief that, if the month of March is a wet one, a bad harvest will follow is widespread. Should it be dry and cold, however, it is said exceedingly good for crops, especially wheat.

In the Alsace, the nights March 20 and 24 are held unlucky for birth, and are called "black nights." On March 10 one should spit on each fruit tree to ensure a good harvest in memory of the Four Martyrs.

MARIGOLD: In the west country of England, another name for the marigold is "drunkards." If you pick them or look at them for a long period of time they are said to cause a desire for drink that is insatiable.

One tradition holds that the marigold derives its name from the fact that it was worn on the breast of the Virgin Mary. The Anglo-

Saxons called the marigold, "husband man's dial"; hence, its use as an active ingredient in love charms and in wedding garlands. Germans hold it unlucky for love, and in other countries, it represents grief, pain, or anger.

Since it blooms all year, following the pattern of the sun, it opens its petals early each day and closes them by midafternoon. Should its petals not open before seven o'clock, rain or a thunderstorm will follow, says a Welsh tradition.

MARRIAGE: Although a number of traditions regarding marriage have already been discussed (see **brides, love**), there are many more generally held traditions.

It is said that one should never marry during a waning moon or during the three days following a new moon. Marrying on either one of the spouse's birthdays is also considered unlucky. June is held the ideal month for a marriage, since it is placed under the aegis of Juno, Jupiter's wife, who was said to rule happiness of married couples.

It is best advised to marry on a Monday or Tuesday, although Saturday marriages are often commonplace. Should one marry on Saint Valentine's Day or another popular holiday, it indicates a happy union. Marriages on the last day of the year are considered lucky.

Marrying during a snowstorm is considered lucky.

According to a Yorkshire tradition, one should be careful not to go in at one door and out at another on one's wedding day or bad luck will result.

To marry a man whose name begins with the same letter as one's own is held unlucky. Should a younger daughter marry before her older sisters, the older girls should dance barefoot at her wedding. For a bride to accidentally break a dish at her wedding banquet is an ill omen. Should an unmarried person at the wedding dinner sit between the bride and groom, another wedding will soon take place.

The tradition of breaking a glass at the wedding, practiced by the Jews, is also held sacred to the Hindus. The sound of the glass is believed to scare evil spirits away. It is also said to symbolize the consummation of the marriage.

Not so well known is the fact that a betrothal was long held to be nearly as binding as the act of marriage itself. In seventeenth-century New England the Puritan settlers practiced "bundling," a custom often followed in England, Scotland, Ireland, Wales, Holland, Norway, and elsewhere. The couple to wed were encouraged to spend the night together in her bedroom. They wore all their clothes and were separated by layers of bedding. In Holland, where bundling was known as "queesten," suitors climbed through the window of the girl's home and met her in bed. The girl laid on the sheet and the boy between sheet and cover. An iron vessel and pair of tongs were set nearby for her to sound an alarm should the young man's overtures become too bold. It was considered a great honor for one's daughter to receive such visits. Should a pregnancy result, however, the child was taken to the parents' wedding and concealed beneath the mother's cloak, though visible for everyone to see.

In the Calvinist village of Staphorst, this is still practiced. However, custom holds that the couple *must* marry only if there is evidence of a pregnancy.

In Scotland, "hand fasting" also provided a similar testing period. Men and women chose a companion at the annual Dumfriesshire Fair. Those participating lived together as husband and wife until the following year. Should the experiment not be successful, they were held free to take another partner. Periodically, a priest, nicknamed "book-in-the-bosom," arrived to solemnize such unions.

The tradition of calling the "banns" or marriage contract terms as a preliminary to marriage is an ancient one. In Lincolnshire it is known as "spurring." If the banns are read once, people will say, "Why thoos gotten one's spur on thee!" It was held unlucky to hear one's own banns called and said to omen that children of the marriage would be deaf and dumb. In Poland, it is held that a girl hearing her first banns would break her pots soon after she was married.

Should the parents of the bride be unable to afford the expense of a wedding, tradition in Manx (Isle of Man) was to place a sieve in the kitchen so that guests could drop in coins to help with the cost of entertainment. This became known as the "penny wedding." Yet another tradition was the selling of ale, known as "bride's ale," to the wedding guests by the impoverished bride.

In the north of England and in Scotland a family finding themselves in a similar position would hold a "bride-wain." Carts and horses were taken to the homes of friends and relatives, who gave cornmeal, wool, and anything else they could spare.

Should the husband-to-be possess wealth, but not wish to inherit any debts from his wife, tradition required her to arrive at her own wedding dressed in nothing but a shift. A bride walking naked from her house to that of her future husband was said to assure the same thing.

Once married, the husband, and not his wife, should lock the front door before the family retired for the night. Should she perform this task, there would be a quarrel that very evening, it was said.

Weather conditions on the day of the wedding were supposed to predict the happiness of the couple. Should it rain, wealth or a sad future was omened to come about. Wind was said to indicate misunderstandings. Cloudy, heavy skies were thought to bring about innuendos, such as the husband being cunning and the wife frivolous. Snowflakes indicated prosperity and future children. Should the sun shine, however, this was the best blessing of all!

MAY: The month has long been dedicated to the Virgin Mary. The month symbolized regeneration. While marriage in May was often taboo, it was said to be an excellent month for engagements.

It is said that cats born in the month of May can never catch mice or rats, but will have a propensity for snakes and slow worms. It is also said that they will suck the breath from young children.

Washing one's face with May dew, gathered at daybreak on May Day, is said to grant one a good complexion throughout the rest of the year. Likewise, May dew sniffed up one's nostrils is held a cure for dizziness.

In some parts of Britain, the belief is that a May-born baby is always sickly and oftentimes unruly.

Many are the traditions surrounding the May flower. Here are a few: Never bring the May flower into the house, or death will follow. Never sleep in a room into which the blooming whitethorn has been placed during the month of May. Commonly cited is the following: "If you sweep the house with blossomed broom in May, you're sure to sweep the head of the house away." You can keep

OMENS, SIGNS & SUPERSTITIONS

freckles away by gathering May flowers before sunrise. One who desires to live a long life should eat sage in May.

MAY DAY: May Day, the first day of May, is a holiday superimposed on the ancient festival of Beltane, an important day in the Celtic calendar. Beltane was a fire festival, during which cattle were driven through ritual fires on their way to their summer grazings. In 1771, a "tore of Scotland" described the remnant of this ceremony as follows:

A square trench was cut in the ground on which was placed a wooden fire. Over this was a large caudle of eggs, butter, oatmeal, and milk. The ritual began with the spilling of the caudle on the ground, and everyone took a cake of oatmeal, on which was placed square knobs, each dedicated to a particular God thought to preserve the flocks and herds. After facing the fire, each person broke off a knob and flung it over his shoulder saying, "This I give to Thee—preserve thou my horses: This to Thee, preserve thou my sheep."

The month of May's name is taken from "Maia Majest," the ancient Italian Goddess of Spring. She was Vulcan's wife. Tradition called for the sacrifice of a pregnant sow to her on the first of May.

In many of the ceremonies practiced on May Day, you find a combination of Roman observances, in honor of the Goddess Flora, and the nature worship of the Druids.

Tradition held that young people should go to the woods and gather garlands of flowers. As a symbol of rebirth, the greenery would be brought back to town, which was a symbolic way of conveying the fertile powers of nature back to the human civilization.

Central to the May Day celebration was the traditional maypole or May tree. In the United Kingdom, this was often a white hawthorn symbolizing the transition from spring to summer. In the Americas, a pine tree took its place.

In continuation of an ancient Scandinavian custom, a mock battle was staged between two persons, representing summer and winter, from which summer always emerged the victor. A "queen of the May" was always elected. The crowning of the May Queen is a surviving rite of this ancient tradition, as is the ceremonial dancing around the decorated tree or maypole.

The object of the various May Day rites, though forgotten in modern times, was to grant fertility, good luck, and to endow crops. As a good omen for the success of the harvest during the coming season, various sports, music, and dancing were all indulged in.

In ancient times, it was customary to have a "lord of May" as well as a May Queen. In the evening, when the bonfires were lit, the queen of May withdrew from her companions, while the king of May was left to conduct the night's activities, which often lasted until the next morning. One tradition associates this lord of May with the fabled Robin Hood.

In eighteenth-century England, a dance performed by the local milkmaids was a general May Day feature. A "garland" was constructed from polished milk pails and other dairy articles, including silver cups, tankards, salvers, and other things begged or borrowed from neighbors. Arranged in the form of a pyramid and decorated with flowers, leaves, and ribbons, the garland was carried from house to house, while the milkmaids danced to the music of a fiddler. As a substitute for the tin garland, a cow decorated with ribbons, leaves, and flowers was sometimes led about.

Central to all the May Day celebrations was the erection of a maypole, decorated with ribbons and flowers, around which various dances took place. Parishes of London often competed with each other in the height and decoration of their maypoles, the cost of which was often recorded in the church warden's accounts. The most famous maypole in London's Strand was 134 feet tall and was later transferred to Wanstead, in Essex, where it was used to support the largest telescope then known. During Cromwell's time, all May sports were prohibited and the poles taken down and burned.

In America, the Puritans became great enemies of the May games. It is recorded that the first maypole was set up in 1627 in New England by Thomas Morton and his "motley crew." The pole itself was a pine tree, 80 feet long, wreathed with ribbons, with the spreading horns of a buck nailed at the top. Tradition holds that there was also present a barrel of strong beer and a liberal supply of bottles of even stronger drink. So outrageous was Morton's celebration, that Governor Bradford quickly intervened, claiming "that they could find nothing so heathenish to compare it with since pagan times."

Be that as it may, a number of traditions have yet survived of which the following are representative: One who gives another (either for love or money) the coal of fire (or the light of any kind) on May Day is said to bring ill luck on his house, according to an Irish tradition. To keep away evil spirits, cattle should be slightly singed with a lighted straw on May Day Eve. Cattle should be bled on this day, and the blood dried and burned. To assure that good butter and that freedom from the influence of witches is present throughout the year, herbs gathered on May Day should be boiled (with some hairs from a cow's tail) and preserved in a covered vessel, according to Irish tradition.

Bringing the branch of a blossoming hawthorn into the house on May Day was reason to grant a dish of cream to a maidservant, according to a Cornish tradition. In Scotland, it is believed that any hares found among the cattle on May Day are actually witches who are seeking to steal the milk, and they should be killed. Another Scottish tradition holds that pieces of rowan should be placed on the doors of the cow houses on May Day. Cows are believed to lose half their milk should it rain on May Day.

On the Isle of Lewis, in the village of Barbas, an ancient superstition exists. Should a woman be the first to cross the Barbas River on May Day, the salmon will not come into it for an entire year. To prevent this from happening, a man was appointed each year to cross the river at sunrise.

Yet another tradition holds that, if one looks through smoked glass into an unused well, he will see his future spouse. To find one's true love, she should throw a ball of yarn into an old cellar or barn, then rewind it, repeating the following:

> I wind, I wind, my true love to find,
> The color of his hair, the clothes he'll wear.
> The day he is married to me.

It is said that, if one is patient, and winds long enough, her "true love" will appear and wind with her!

In Germany, May Eve corresponds to the pagan festival Walpurgis, when all homes are sprinkled with holy water.

Just as May Day was taken over from the pagans by the Christians, so, during the twentieth century, it has taken on another connotation. It is now strongly associated with communist and socialist philosophies; this started in 1889, when the French Socialists declared the day devoted to the "working class."

MEASLES: According to a Cornish tradition, measles can be cured by cutting off a cat's left ear and swallowing three drops of its blood in a wine glass full of water.

Yet another tradition holds that hair, cut from the nape of one's neck and placed between two slices of bread and butter, should be fed to the first strange dog to pass. If the dog eats it without loathing, he will take on the measles and the patient be cured.

MEAT: Should your meat shrink while being cooked, it is held unlucky for the household. Should it swell, however, prosperity is soon to come.

MEDICINE: You should never sell bottles that once contained your medicine, or the prescription will have to be "refilled," says an English tradition.

A medicine that will guard against all illnesses can be manufactured when the sun is at its zenith. Gather four rue branches, nine juniper berries, and a walnut. Toss into this mixture a dried fig and a little salt. If consumed several times on an empty stomach, it will bring about miraculous cures.

MICE: According to one tradition, at the time of the flood, there were no cats. Noah took pairs of rats and mice into the ark as instructed, but soon found himself overrun with vermin. He asked the lion (King of the Beasts) to correct the situation. The lion sneezed, and from his nostrils appeared a pair of cats, which soon reduced the mouse population.

Yet other accounts say that, while God created the cat, the mouse was created by Satan himself. The mouse sought to destroy life by nibbling a hole in Noah's ark. Fortunately for all, the mouse was caught by God's cat and the hole was closed by a frog who crept into it.

Still another tradition holds that mice fell to earth from clouds during a storm.

Mice were also thought to often be used as "familiars" by witches. This was true of other household pets, as well, including cats, owls, and dogs.

In Irish literature there is the belief that poets can banish mice. According to a Middle Irish tale, mice ate an egg that the seventh century poet Senchen had put aside. The angry Senchen satirized mice so completely that ten were said to fall dead after hearing his verses. Senchen got so carried away that he then went on to satirize cats and the lord of all cats. The cat, however, took revenge by carrying him off on his back. He was saved from death through the intervention of Saint Kierian.

The story goes that Saint Colman had a pet mouse that nibbled his ear as a backup alarm clock—if his pet cock's crowing proved insufficient to rouse him. Saint Gertrude is said to have been the patron saint of mouse and rat catchers, and often appears in paintings with mice running up and down her distaff.

Should mice scamper into a house in which they have never been seen before, a member of the household will die, according to one North Country tradition. Likewise, should a mouse run over a person, it indicates approaching death, and should a mouse squeak behind the bed of an invalid, it is certain he will not recover.

Folk remedies include these: A mouse minced and given to a patient cures measles. Whooping cough, likewise, can be cured by roasting a mouse and giving it to the afflicted. A child who wets its bed at night can be cured by imbibing a roasted mouse. According to Pliny, a roasted mouse will cure colds, sore throats, fever, and, if mixed with honey, makes an excellent mouthwash.

It is said that when a building is about to fall, all the mice will desert it.

A Scottish tradition says that one can clear a house of mice by catching one and holding its tail before a fire. As it roasts, all the other mice will leave the premises.

MICHAELMAS: Michaelmas, the feast of Saint Michael (September 29), celebrates the defeat of a dragon, or giant, by this first of the Seven Archangels.

MIDSUMMER'S EVE: As is the case with most Christian holidays, pagans throughout Europe had long celebrated the solstice, June 21, to mark the beginning of summer. At one time, bonfires were lit to strengthen the weakening sun and keep evil spirits at bay. The success of the harvest was believed governed by the distance from which the fires were visible and the height people attained by jumping over them. Called "leaping," this common folk custom had, as its intent, stimulation of the crop growth through sympathetic magic.

In order to prevent the crops from being affected by evil forces, burning torches were carried throughout the fields; fires were lit windward, so their smoke would blow over the grain. A piece of blazing turf was often thrown into the growing corn or carried around cattle, while wheels covered with burning straw were often rolled downhill in imitation of the sun's descending course.

Customs of this kind are traceable back to the Middle Ages, although, by analogy, their origin most likely predates the Christian era.

In Glamorgan, for instance, a cartwheel covered with straw was set afire and rolled down a steep hill. If the fire went out before reaching the bottom of the hill, it was said that the harvest would be poor. Should the wheel remain lit all the way down, the harvest would be good. Should it still be on fire once it reached the level ground, it was held that the harvest would be abundant.

In Ireland, cattle were often driven through smoke (as in the tradition of those English fires) of fires set specifically to drive away disease of the herd, called "need fires."

Since John the Baptist was born on the twenty-fourth of June, Christian intervention attempted to move the day of celebration to this date. Despite this fact, many who held to the old beliefs continued to light bonfires on the twenty-first, which were now called "John Mass Fires."

In Cornwall, it was held that the gathering time of the snakes was Midsummer's Eve.

Since, by tradition, midsummer was the time when the sun's power began to diminish, evil spirits and witches were said to be unusually active on this day. It was believed that witches held their sabbath on Midsummer's Eve, riding on black three-legged horses or brooms. In the seventeenth century, John Aubrey wrote that this was the night witches would break open hen eggs in order to see what their future would be.

Superstitions about Midsummer's Eve are numerous and varied: Should it rain on Midsummer's Eve, the nuts will be spoiled. Should you pluck a rose on Midsummer's Day and put it away, it will be as fresh as ever on Christmas Day. Should you then wear it to church, the person you will marry will come and take it. Should an unmarried woman fast on Midsummer's Eve, and, at midnight, take a clean cloth and place on it bread, cheese, and ale, then sit down as though to eat (leaving her street door open), the person she will marry will come into the room, bow, and drink to her. If you were brave enough to go to church at midnight, you would see a procession of the apparitions of those who would die during the course of the year.

Unmarried girls gathering yarrow from a young man's grave, then laying it under their pillow on Midsummer's Eve, would see the ghost or shade of their husband to be. The maid should collect slips of orpine, a purple flowered crop popularly known as "midsummer men," and stick them together in a crack. If they leaned together, a marriage would soon take place.

Fern seed gathered on Midsummer's Eve was alleged to make men invisible. It also possessed the property of revealing treasure, glowing deep in the earth with bluish flames. So great was this tradition that Shakespeare referred to it in *Henry IV (Part 1)*: "We have the receipt of fern seed. We walk invisible."

Hazel wood cut on this night was said to guide one to hidden treasure. One must attain it by walking backwards and cutting it with both hands between one's legs. To determine whether it would work, one was instructed to hold it near water and it would squeak like a pig.

MILK: Milk was said to symbolize spiritual food, purity, and immortality due to its white color and abundance.

Traditionally, it was held inadvisable to spill a few drops of milk on one's threshold. Fairies would be attracted to this beverage and might then pass through one's door. Likewise, spilling a drop of milk on the ground was thought to bring seven days of misfortune, during which no activities should be undertaken.

As a form of sympathetic magic, the milk taken from a cow milked for the first time was deposited in a bronze basin. This was to ensure its abundance in the future. So that a cow would remain a good milker, a few hairs were pulled from its tail when sold.

When a cow who recently calved was milked for the first time, tradition held that three drops from each udder should be passed through a ring to avoid infection and to purify the milk.

Should you inadvertently put your foot into a milk bucket, or throw this sacred elixir in a fire, the udders of your cows were believed to dry up forever. Tradition held that the same thing would happen if fig wood was thrown into your fireplace. Placing a glowworm in your house, however, was said to guarantee an abundance of milk.

Witches, disguised as snakes and other animals, could suck the udders of one's cows, according to tradition. If you suspected that this had taken place, you were advised to rub the udders with "passion grass."

Milk sold should be laced with a pinch of salt, so no one could bewitch the cow from which it came.

Another tradition held that fires caused by lightning could be extinguished with cow's milk.

As an act of witchcraft, it was believed that one could steal cow's milk from a neighbor by placing a bucket in the fireplace and "milking the pot hook."

Last, in order to make mother's milk disappear after weaning, a husband was advised to urinate in his night bonnet and then place it over his wife's breasts.

MINCE PIE: In England, a south country tradition holds that, for every mince pie eaten in a different house, one will have a month's happiness.

Yet another tradition maintains that eating one mince pie on each of the twelve days of Christmas will bring a month of good luck for each pie.

In Roman times, mince pies containing different ingredients were baked in an oblong shape. At Christmas, it was regarded as a symbol of Christ's cradle.

MINERS: Generally believed is the notion that if you meet or see a woman on the way to the pit, during the night shift, bad luck will follow. Another tradition holds that, should a miner wash his back frequently, it will cause physical weakness.

Once a miner has left for work, bad luck will attend him should he turn back and reenter his house. He can avoid the bad luck by knocking on the window or door three times to retrieve his forgotten article. But under no circumstances should he reenter his house.

In the belief that trolls, who work unseen in the mines, are adverse to Christianity, Cornish miners will never place an "X" mark on a wall or any other place. This mark will irritate the trolls and cause bad luck.

No miner should ever whistle below ground. It is generally thought unlucky for a cat to be seen anywhere near a mine.

An unusual tradition holds that, if miners see a snail on the way to work, they should drop a piece of tallow from their candles by its side. The origin of this tradition is unknown.

In American folklore, rats that get into the mines with the mules' hay will pour out of the mine prior to a disaster.

In Michigan, miners hold it unlucky to work on Wyth Sunday (the seventh Sunday after Easter or Midsummer's Day). They also refuse to work on Boxer Day, December 26. Strangely enough, though, they willingly work January 1 in the belief that working on this day brings work for the rest of the year.

MINT: The mint plant is believed to love dampness and to grow wildly near streams. According to legend, a young nymph named Minthe allowed Pluto, God of the Underworld, to seduce her. Pluto's wife, Persephone, was so outraged and jealous that she transformed the nymph into a mint plant.

MIRROR: Of all the various superstitions today, perhaps best known is the one that says bad luck results from breaking a mirror! In general, it is believed that breaking a mirror results in seven years of bad luck. Should a mirror break of its own accord, however, the person owning it will lose a best friend.

A mortality among family members was thought certain should a mirror fall and break, and seeing one's face in a mirror by candlelight was also thought unlucky. In Scandinavia, a woman will never look at herself in a mirror by candlelight for fear of permanently losing her beauty.

Should a person see his image reflected in the mirror in the same room as a deceased person, it is said he will shortly die himself.

A Durham tradition held that children should not see themselves in a mirror before they were twelve months of age. Otherwise, they would not live a long life.

Never place a newborn child in front of a mirror, or he will become an epileptic, holds one tradition. Hanging a piece of broken mirror on the child's back, or tracing a cross on the mirror, is said to dissipate this evil.

Some believe that mirrors should be covered in a house where someone has died to prevent his soul from being trapped in the glass.

Ancient is the notion that a mirror framed on three sides only can be used by a witch or magician to see over long distances (somewhat similar to a crystal ball).

Among actors and theater-going crowds, the tradition is that a real mirror must never be placed on stage.

One medieval tradition was that, if you write on a convex mirror with blood and then hold it up to a full moon, your destiny written on the mirror would be written on the moon.

In Scotland, if a girl eats an apple in front of a mirror with her eyes closed, and then opens her eyes over her shoulder, she will see her future husband, it is said. In many countries, should a couple first see each other in a mirror, they will be forever happy.

Likewise, a Hungarian tradition holds that, at midnight on New Year's Eve, should a girl dip a mirror in a spring, she will see the image of her husband on the mirror. On the night of Epiphany, should you write the initials of the three wise men on your forehead, with your own blood, you can see in a mirror the hour and circumstances of your death.

It is said that should you break a mirror over a friend's portrait, it betokens the death of the person portrayed.

In the French countryside, mirrors were used to chase hail away. In Africa, mirrors were used by witch doctors to attract rain.

Since mirrors reverse space, making the left right and the right left, they have been held to transform evil forces into friendly ones. Hence, in China, when someone died on an unlucky day, a mirror was placed on the door to reverse the evil influence. In the Caribbean, the finger of one dying is rubbed against a mirror to release his soul.

Thanks to the influence of Hollywood, well known is the fact that the images of vampires are never reflected in mirrors.

In ancient times, the art of catoptromancy, or mirror divination, was practiced by seers or "scryers." A metal mirror was dipped in water and held before an ill person, whose image was either disfigured or clearly defined. If disfigured, it was said the sick person would soon pass; if clearly defined, a recovery was predicted.

Most famous of the so-called mirror diviners was the magician, Dr. John Dee (1527–1608), who was known traditionally as "Queen Elizabeth's Merlin." Tradition holds that he discovered the "Gunpowder Plot" of 1605 through the use of his magic mirror, a black, highly polished stone.

To be recalled is the fact that, for the ancients, pools of water were the first mirrors. With the passage of time, the Egyptians, Greeks, and Romans created man-made mirrors from bronze or silver. Glass mirrors first appeared in Venice at the onset of the thirteenth century.

Lastly, one must recall the famous Louis Carroll creation, *Alice Through the Looking Glass*. In this work, Alice walked "backwards" to meet the Red Queen, while the Queen screamed with pain "before" her finger was pricked.

In case you are caught up in the daily habit of examining yourself in the mirror, mention must also be made of the Greek legend of Narcissus. He became so fascinated by his youthful image reflected in a fountain that his death was brought about through his own self love.

MISTLETOE: Certainly well known is the traditional Yuletide custom of kissing under the mistletoe. According to Norse mythology, the goddess Frigg was so happy when her son Balder came back to life that her tears turned into pearls on the mistletoe. Because of this miracle, mistletoe was placed under her protection, thereby preventing it from ever being used again for evil purposes. As Frigg is the Goddess of Love and Marriage, kissing under her mistletoe symbolizes protection for the love both people express.

Another name for mistletoe is "the golden bough." This particular name comes from the fact that, when the plant becomes dry, its leaves take on a golden tinge.

Mistletoe is itself a parasite that springs from seeds deposited by birds on the barks of trees. The woody "sinkers" are inserted into the host plant, from which it derives its sustenance. It is said the most magical of all mistletoe grows on oak trees. It has also been known to grow on evergreens and conifers.

According to legend, if cut for magical purposes, a knife or sickle made from gold had to be used. Pliny reported that the Druids did exactly this, and took particular care to prevent the mistletoe from touching the ground. (They believed that otherwise it would lose its virtues.) A white-robed priest would cut the mistletoe only on the sixth day of the moon, allowing it to fall into his white cloak.

Two white bulls were then sacrificed, after which it was believed the plant's magic was assured. Placed in water, the water was then distributed as a talisman against evil.

Some authorities hold that the custom of kissing under the mistletoe is derived from the fertility symbolism of the plant. For a woman to be kissed under mistletoe was a magical way to ensure that she would bear children; the plant was long used as an aphrodisiac.

Pliny recalled that the plant's healing properties were able to reduce epileptic seizures and encourage fertility.

Well known was the use of mistletoe as protection against the evil eye, witchcraft, and the Devil. It was often given to sheep and cows, after they had given birth, for that reason.

In Britain, mistletoe has long been associated with Christmas (whereas, in Scandinavia, it is traditionally associated with Midsummer). British folklore requires mistletoe to be hung on Christmas Day or on New Year's Eve, left for twelve months, and then burned.

During the early nineteenth century, renewed romantic interest in the Druids caused commercialization of mistletoe and the erection of imitation "Stonehenges." It was at this time that churchmen branded mistletoe a "pagan" plant and banned it from the church.

One interesting pre-Christian legend surrounding mistletoe holds its bright colorization was the "flame of fire," seen by Moses in the burning bush.

One custom suggests that branches of mistletoe be attached to the door of newlyweds to bring them happiness. Yet another suggests placing it in front of their bedroom to ward off nightmares.

It is said that one must never take all the boughs off a mistletoe plant, or it will bring bad luck. It is believed that, if one hangs mistletoe in a tree with a swallow's wing, all the cuckoos in the area will assemble there.

According to English traditions, Saint Vitus's dance can be cured by drinking water in which mistletoe berries have been boiled.

Should mistletoe not be burned on Twelfth Night, it is said that all the couples who kissed under it will be enemies before the end of the year!

Often cited is the belief that mistletoe was regarded by the Druids as sacred, since its leaves grew in clusters of three. Although three has been held the number of the Trinity, Church decorations often excluded mistletoe, because of its pagan associations.

In American folklore, the belief is that should an unmarried girl stand under mistletoe and not be kissed, she will not be married that year. Similarly, should she refuse to be kissed, she will die an old maid.

Among Southern blacks belief holds that a preparation of mistletoe will dry up mother's milk. Potions of berries are often administered to produce fertility, as an antidote to poison, and to ward off epilepsy and convulsions.

Mole: Moles, who often frequent the night, after emerging from their tunnels in earth, are said to come out into the open to hear the angels.

A molehill built near one's house indicates that one of the inhabitants will soon be ill. Should the mole dig near a kitchen or bathroom, the woman of the house will die, according to an English tradition.

Wearing a mole's foot in a sack around your neck is believed a fine talisman against cramps, toothache, and other illnesses. Should you wrap a mole's foot in laurel leaf and place it in a horse's mouth, it is thought that the horse will instantly become fearful and take flight. Should this same foot be placed in a bird's nest, the eggs will be valueless and nothing will be found inside the shells. Should a black horse be rubbed with water in which a mole has been boiled, it will become white.

Moles: It is held that moles on the face or body are its stars and can reveal the future according to their placement.

Generally speaking, those on the left side were considered unlucky; whereas those on the right were said fortunate. Round moles bring luck, while those oblong in shape, misfortune. A mole in the middle of one's forehead brings wealth. A mole on the back of the neck was said to indicate a danger of hanging. A mole on the left breast of a girl was thought to enable her to choose any man she wished. Should the mole appear on the right breast, however, poverty was foretold.

In some countries, black pepper is thrown on an expectant mother in the belief that her child will be born with moles or other birthmarks. Birthmarks are called both the "mark of God" and the "mark of the Devil."

Hairs that grow out of moles are omened to be tokens of great luck.

In American folklore, a mole on one's nose indicates success in business. Should the mole be on one's shoulder, it indicates great fortitude; on one's hands, self-sufficiency; on one's legs, self-will; and on the chin, loyalty to one's friends!

The following old English rhyme provides additional insight:

> *A mole on the arm*
> *can do you no harm.*
> *A mole on your lip*
> *you're witty and flip.*
> *A mole on your neck*
> *brings money by the peck.*
> *A mole on your back*
> *brings money by the sack.*
> *A mole on your ear*
> *brings money year by year.*

MONEY: According to a general tradition, you will always have money in your pocket if you place in the pocket a small spider called the "money spider." Similarly, should you place in your pocket a bent coin, or a coin with a hole in it, and take it out and spit on it during every new moon, a continuous cash flow is assured. (It is interesting to note that ancient Chinese money often had a hole in its center.) Likewise, one should place the "first" money received each day into an empty pocket, so it may attract more coins. (This first money is called *handsel.*)

Some believe that money is on the way if someone with polka-dot clothing is seen.

Never keep money in more than one pocket or the entire lot will be lost.

Money or the lack of it has been a concern of mankind's since the earliest of times. It is no wonder that superstitions concerning prosperity versus poverty abound.

MOON: The earliest calendars known to mankind marked the passage of time not by the sun and seasons, but by "moons." The moon, therefore, has long been regarded as a divine personage.

According to a Rumanian myth, Sun had an incestial desire for his sister, Moon. To avoid meeting her brother, Moon went about only at night when she could not be seen. To discourage him, she made ugly marks on her face.

According to an Eskimo legend, the Sun is a woman. The moon is her lover, who visits by night and smears the sun with ashes so that he may be seen more clearly. While doing this, he leaves shadows on his own face which now appear to us as craters on the moon.

Yet another Scandinavian story tells about a boy named Hjuki and a girl named Belia. As they are drawing water from a well, the moon, who wishes them to serve her, carries them off to heaven in a bucket. The moon waxes, as they ascend up a hill, and wanes, as they descend downward. The names of the two children—Hjuki and Belia—mean "increasing" and "decreasing."

Among the Uaupe Indians of the Upper Amazon Valley, the first menstruation of a young girl is said to be "defloration by the moon."

In many folk legends, girls are warned not to stare at the moon or lay in moonlight, or they will be impregnated by the moon and will give birth to some kind of a monster.

In mythologies worldwide, rulers of the moon are female deities. For the Canaanites, the name of the moon goddess was Jerah (for whom the city of Jericho was named). For Egyptians, Isis and Hathor were associated with the moon. Hathor was often represented as a cow and milk-giving mother. Her head was surmounted by golden horns, on whose cusp lay the moon.

For the Babylonians, the goddess Ishtar was given similar honors. For the Greeks, Artemis and Diana, hunting goddesses, were both connected with the moon as well. Hence, it was not surprising that, in medieval Europe, Diana became the patroness of witches, since she already ruled 'horned' animals such as the stag and goat.

Common is the belief that a woman's physiological functions are linked with the moon. The very term *menstruation*, meaning "monthly," refers to an occurrence that takes place each and every lunar month.

It is unlucky to look at the new moon for the first time through the branches of a tree or through glass. (This does not include spectacles, of course.) It is also held unlucky to point at the moon and one should always bow to the new moon, indicating respect, especially the first new moon of the year.

Yet another tradition holds that, at first sight of a new moon, one should turn a silver coin in his purse or pocket and make a wish.

It is said that all crops that grow above ground should be sown when the moon is waxing; all crops that grow below the ground, when it is waning. Likewise, one should never marry or give birth when the moon is waning.

It is said that if a young girl holds a silk handkerchief at the face of a full moon, desiring to know when she will marry, the number of moons appearing will indicate the number of years she has yet to wait.

One tradition holds it favorable to spit in one's hands and rub one's face at the first appearance of the new moon. At the waning of a moon, one should neither cut one's nails or hair.

Should two moons occur in a single calendar month (especially May), it is believed there will be floods and other calamities. A ring around the moon omens an upcoming storm or rain. Likewise, it is said that dew falls heaviest on moonlit nights. A poor harvest in the coming year is omened by a full moon at Christmas. Likewise, a full moon on Sunday is believed to bring bad luck.

It is said to be unlucky to see the new moon on your left, rather than on your right or straight ahead.

Those living near the ocean generally hold a belief that the number of births will be high at the time of high tide, since the moon is said to affect uterine contractions.

Generally believed is the idea that the best time to pick flowers for herbs, or to fell trees, is when the moon is on the decline. It is believed that trees will bear good fruit if pruned during the moon's increase.

Commonly held among some country folks is the belief that pigs killed when the moon is waxing will yield bacon richer and fatter. Similarly, sheep's wool was said to grow thick with the waxing moon.

The connection between lunatics and the moon is age-old, and anyone who deals with the general population will acknowledge an increase in eccentric behavior or violence during the time of the full moon. The word *lunatic* itself is derived from the Latin word *luna,* meaning "moon." In England, The Lunacy Act of 1842 actually defined a lunatic as a demented person who enjoyed lucidity during the first two phases of the moon and was afflicted following the full phase.

An English tradition holds that a housewife seeing the new moon for the first time should run quickly into her bedroom and turn a bed.

Although it is traditionally held that nights of the full moon often give rise to antisocial behavior, a Finnish tradition holds that public dinners always be held at the full moon, or disaster will follow. One authority suggests this is due to the bad state of repair of the roads in Finland, which are generally unlit!

According to a Welsh tradition, should one move to a new house or change one's residence, the time of the new moon is the most favorable. Should a member of the family pass away at the time of the new moon, three additional deaths are likely to follow.

A commonplace belief among many peoples is that one should never sleep with the moon shining on his face. Either the face will become distorted or the sleeper will become insane.

For those who have not yet been filled with moon magic, here are some additional beliefs: A robbery attempted on the third day of a new moon will fail. If one becomes ill on the eighth day of the new moon, he will die. The best marriages take place on the full moon or a few days before. When traveling, should one see a crescent moon on the increase, good luck is nearby. One should never undergo surgery, except in an emergency, when the moon is full. Likewise, a new moon is said to increase the risk of infection.

A feather bed will only be comfortable if it was filled with feathers after the moon has passed the full.

Mention must be made of an unusual moon tradition found in American folklore. "Moon cussing" was the practice in Cape Cod of walking along the shoreline swinging lanterns on a moonless night. Incoming ships, thinking the lights were lights of anchored vessels, would run aground or be wrecked, thereby affording salvage operators an unusual opportunity.

MOP: Among sailors, it is an ill omen for a mop or bucket to fall overboard.

MOSQUITO: Mosquitos are sometimes held as omens of good luck.

One tradition maintains that a mosquito entering a sick person's room at sunset will take away the illness when it leaves.

Rain is said to be on the way when mosquitos fly close to the ground. When flying high in the air, however, good weather will come.

You can cure mosquito bites by rubbing them with vinegar, oil, butter, onion, garlic, or lemon peel and then blowing on them, it is said.

MOTH: In Yorkshire, white moths flying at night are believed to be souls of the departed; hence, it is unlucky to kill them. Contrariwise, should a black moth fly into your house, it is said someone in the house will die. Some traditions hold that death will occur within one month, while others extend it to a year. Among some country folk, a moth entering a house indicates an important letter will arrive the next day.

MOTHER-IN-LAW: American Indians believe a man will go blind if he looks into the eyes of his wife's mother. A Scottish proverb (1721) holds that a woman is assured of happiness if she marries the son of a dead mother.

MURDER: It is generally held unlucky to see a murder or pass a dead body lying on the ground. One tradition holds that souls of those who have been murdered are earthbound for as long as their natural lives would have been. Yet another tradition is that such souls are earthbound until their killer is discovered and his or her own life taken!

The image of a murderer is permanently imprinted on the eyes of the victim, say some.

MUSHROOM: In some cultures, mushrooms are called "sons of God." According to an Essex tradition, mushrooms may be pulled safely when the moon is full. Most traditions surrounding mushrooms are connected with how to determine which are edible and which poisonous. Since these beliefs are often complicated and best left to experts, Zolar suggests following an age-old adage, "When in doubt, leave them out!"

It should be mentioned, however, that mushrooms were sometimes used as love potions in the belief that they contained an aphrodisiac.

In recent years, the ancient, religious use of psychedelic mushrooms has become a common phenomenon among students.

MUSKRAT: In American Indian folklore, the muskrat was the animal that formed land after the Great Flood by piling up dirt taken from the muddy waters. Muskrats are able to predict weather by how they build their homes, it is said. Should the homes be built higher out of the water than normal, it will be a wet spring and a possible flood will come about. Should it build a shallow or flimsy burrow, the winter will be mild. Should the walls be built very thick, a cold winter is certain.

It is believed that laying the furry side of the muskrat's pelt against one's chest will heal asthma.

MYRTLE: According to a Somerset belief, myrtle is the luckiest plant to have in one's window box. Tradition also holds that myrtle will not grow unless planted by a woman, and that, while planting it, she must spread her skirt and look unusually proud.

A Welsh belief is that myrtle planted on each side of one's doorway will bring love and peace to the homestead.

Myrtle was long connected with death and resurrection; hence, it was carried by Greek settlers, when a new colony was founded, to symbolize the end of one life and the beginning of another. Tradition holds that myrtle was the principal scented tree in the Garden of Eden.

In Germany, an engaged girl is advised never to plant myrtle, or it will cause the betrothal to be broken off.

For the Greeks, the myrtle tree was dedicated to Aphrodite, Goddess of Love. After the rape of the Sabine women, Roman soldiers crowned themselves with myrtle in honor of the goddess Venus.

Myrtle symbolized the eyes for those of the Jewish faith, signifying one's atonement for lustful thoughts.

Last, in Germany, brides wear myrtle to prevent themselves from becoming pregnant on the wedding night.

NAIL: Since they were constructed from metal, it was believed that nails were able to ward off evil forces. They are also a symbol of the crucifixion, since they were used to nail Christ to the cross.

Finding a rusty nail in your path brings good luck. It should be carried or driven into your kitchen door. Driving nails into your door in the form of a cross is said to bring good luck and to protect anyone in the house against evil. One tradition holds that small boxes full of nails should actually be buried under the house.

According to an English tradition, you can cure the flu by nailing a lock of the patient's hair to an oak tree. This must be done in person, however, and requires that the patient wrench the lock from his head by a sudden pull.

Yet another tradition for the same malady holds that one should go to a crossroads at midnight and, upon hearing the clock strike, turn himself around three times and then drive a ten-penny nail into the ground. One must then walk backwards, away from the spot, before the clock has finished the twelfth note.

Generally believed is the fact that a nail has curative powers. Should you drive a nail into a tree, it guarantees the tree its proper growth.

Should you wish to cure yourself of a toothache, a nail must be driven into a tree, or a wall of a house, with all of your strength. In the Alsace, a person's gum would be struck with a nail until covered with blood. The nail would then be hidden away from sunlight or moonlight. In a few days, it was said, the toothache would be gone.

Anyone cutting himself with a nail should drive the nail, once found, into an oak tree to prevent infection.

It is held that a nail from a crucifix placed on an epileptic's arm will calm him. Likewise, coffin nails were said to ward off nightmares and to protect a newborn against evil.

A number of unusual traditions exist in American folklore. For instance, those lacking ammunition often shot squirrels with nails. After recovering their game, a claw hammer or similar device was used to remove the nails.

In Colonial times (and especially during the war), when nails were rare and costly, they were sometimes actually "willed" by one householder to his descendants. Tradition held that the number of nails in the house had to be returned to the owner when he left as debt repayment, in order to prevent him from burning it down to recover his "original investment."

NAME: A generally accepted tradition is that a child should never be named after a brother or sister that has already died in the family; otherwise, he will be called in a similar manner.

A somewhat strange belief is that a woman who has had two successive (though unrelated) husbands with the same surname can cure whooping cough and other illnesses simply by cutting bread and butter and giving it to the patient.

Having seven letters in one's name is very lucky, while people with thirteen-letter names should add one more letter for better luck.

One should never tell anyone outside the immediate family what a new child's name will be, before it has actually been christened. In England, any person named Agnes will go mad and any boy named George will never be hanged. Likewise, a betrothed woman should never use her married name before she is actually wed or the marriage will be called off!

Among seamen, certain names are considered unlucky and never mentioned at sea. It is thought unlucky to change the name of one's ship, and ships whose names end in the letter *a* are said to be ill omened.

Long held is the tradition that a person should have a "real name" and a "secret name." According to Plutarch, no one in Rome knew the real name of the guardian deity, and to inquire anything about it (even whether it was male or female) was forbidden.

Among North American Indians, the "real" name was considered sacred and concealed.

In the Book of Revelation (Revelation 19:11), the rider on a white horse is called "faithful and true," but it is said of him, "he has a name inscribed which no one knows but himself."

In primitive initiation rituals, when a boy becomes a man, he is often given a new name. This tradition was also followed by witches who were said to have a "witch" name used only at the coven.

While American women often use their maiden name, especially if they have independent careers and established reputations, this practice would not be considered a good omen for marital success, according to European folk belief.

Long accepted is the Christian tradition of naming one's children after various saints or martyrs, thus securing their protection and angelic care.

NAPKIN: A generally held belief in the United Kingdom is that a guest folding his napkin after the first meal in any house will never return. Guests who have stayed a longer period, however, are able to fold their napkins without any repercussions.

NARCISSUS: Greek legend holds that Narcissus was so enamored of his own reflection in a pond, that he fell into the water and drowned. When his body was washed upon the shore, it had been changed into the flower now known as narcissus. The word is said to come from a Greek word meaning "numbness." Psychologically, the word is often used to describe anyone who is so in love with himself that he is unable to share love with another.

According to the ancient Greeks, the narcissus flower's scent was so strong that it could cause headaches, madness, and even death.

In folk medicine, narcissus root was advocated as an antiseptic and for healing wounds. When mixed with honey, it was used as a pain killer.

NECK: According to the Dutch, a pain in the neck or a stiff neck portends that a person will be hanged.

One can cure a stiff neck by wrapping it in a wool stocking or sock, already worn, but not washed.

Yet another cure is to rub it with cotton that has been saturated with olive-oil, in which the top of a poppy has soaked. One is also able to bring about a cure by wrapping a towel containing warm laurel leaves around one's neck.

It is said that the tradition of wearing necklaces, or neckties, comes from circular objects that were originally worn as talismans.

NEEDLE: It is said that you should stick yourself with a needle before offering it or loaning it to a friend, or it will break up the friendship.

Simply uttering the word *needle* upon arising in the morning is said to bring ill luck. It is likewise a bad omen to find a needle in the street, especially if it is stuck in a spool of black thread.

It is a bad omen for a seamstress to break a needle while sewing a bridal gown. The unhappiness of the future couple is indicated. However, should she stick herself and bleed, her blood should be left on the gown for good luck.

Needles used to sew burial shrouds were said useful for casting evil spells. Should one place such a needle under a place setting, it will kill the appetite of the diner.

One tradition holds that a pregnant woman finding a needle on the ground will have a girl. Should she find a pin, however, she will deliver a boy.

A young woman seeking a husband should stick seven needles into a lighted candle while praying to the Virgin Mother, until the wick is consumed. By doing this she can obtain the love of the man of her dreams, while rendering him impotent with other women.

NEST: Should a bird use someone's hair in making its nest, says one tradition, a person will suffer headaches. In Australia, it is said this same situation will cause pimples.

NET: Traditionally, a betrothed girl who mends her future husband's net in public offends him, since her act announces her desire to manage the household after marriage.

Should one fish with nets on All Saints' Day, he will draw in only corpses. A Yorkshire tradition holds that small coins should be placed in one of the knots in a net or its cork to thank Neptune for his generous gifts.

NETTLE: According to folklore, a person who carries nettle on him will be safe from lightning. Likewise, should a person take hold of a nettle plant and pull it up by its roots, he will be cured of fever.

NEW YEAR'S DAY: No matter where it is placed in the calendar, the first day of the year has traditionally been celebrated in anticipation of the twelve months yet to come. It should be noted that the celebration of the new year on January 1 is a relatively modern device. For the Jews, the new year was always a moveable feast. In ancient Babylon, it was celebrated in what would now be March and April. In ancient Egypt, it was linked with the annual flooding of the Nile River. Until the introduction of the Gregorian calendar in 1752, the new year in the British Isles began in March.

Superstitions and customs concerning New Year's Eve and New Year's Day are numerous. The following is a sampling: Empty pockets or an empty cupboard on New Year's Eve is an omen of a year of poverty. It is held an ill omen, too, if one lets the fire die out on New Year's Eve. Other traditions hold that one should open the window a few minutes before midnight to let any bad luck out and any good luck in.

The custom of using noise makers originates from the belief that evil spirits gathering about will be driven away by the raucous behavior; likewise, the tradition of ringing out the old year and ringing in the new with church bells.

Should the wind blow from the west on this night, there will be a great abundance of milk and fish, but a great or famous person will disappear during the year. Should the wind blow from the east, there is danger of a famine, or some other calamity. Should it blow from the north, cold weather and storms will surely follow. Should it blow from the south, warm weather and prosperity is certain. If the night is clear, however, and no wind is found, an abundance of all things is held to come about.

It has long been held that neither iron, nor light, nor anything else should be taken out of your house on New Year's Day. Doing so was believed by the ancients to take away your luck.

The first man to cross the threshold of your house, after midnight has struck, should be dark haired and should carry a shovel full of coal, says one tradition. Should a woman or fair-haired man be the first to enter, ill luck is expected.

In Scotland and England, there is a general belief that, if a new suit or dress has money in its pockets on this first day of the year, the pockets will never be empty.

In the Alsace, should the first person encountered by a young woman be a man, she will marry within the year. Should it be a woman, however, she will remain single. Should she find herself in front of two men, she will take a lover.

It is said that the last drink drained from a bottle on New Year's Eve brings good fortune to whomever swallows it.

Babies born on New Year's Day have lucky lives. Should a clergyman be the first to enter your home on New Year's Day, it is a fortunate omen.

Cleaning chimneys on New Year's Day was an old English tradition; it was believed that luck would descend and remain throughout the entire year. Bringing a cake or loaf of bread as a gift to one's home on New Year's Day was said to bring prosperity for the rest of the year. In some rural country areas, special New Year cakes were baked and thought to bring special luck.

Lending something to a friend on this day was believed to bring good fortune, and money earned on New Year's Day will return a hundredfold.

Symbolically speaking, the new year is often represented as an old man with a scythe and a young male child. January itself is named after the Roman god, Janus, who faced backwards and forwards simultaneously.

At one time it was customary to toll muffled bells just before midnight, and, as the clock struck twelve, to remove the wrappings in order to emit a louder, clearer chime. Such symbolized the weak and feeble old year, giving way to the new powerful one.

One ancient tradition in Babylonia, symbolizing the end of the old year, was the severing of heads from various statues. In England, a remnant of this tradition maintained that, should one's shadow when sitting by a yule fire appear without a head, he or she would die before the year was out.

In Japan, New Year's Day is celebrated with eight cakes offered to the sun and moon goddess. North American Indians extinguished tribal fires, scattered the ashes, and then ceremoniously relit the fires. In France, pancakes were often tossed on a griddle to bring good fortune. In Northern Europe, boar-shaped cakes were baked.

One tradition holds that water drawn from a well on New Year's Eve turns into wine.

In ancient Roman days, it is said that tradesmen would perform a small amount of work on the first day of the year to ensure sufficient work throughout.

The Druids often distributed mistletoe on this day, giving rise to a gift-giving custom that has persisted. In England, the royal family often received various presents on this day. It is said that Queen

Elizabeth I received a pair of silk stockings from a Mrs. Montague, her silk-woman, on New Year's Day. This was the first pair worn in England.

Yet another interesting tradition is the prohibition against washing clothes on this day. It was said to wash away a life.

New Year's Day was thought unusually favorable for divinations, such as picking a Bible verse at random with one's eyes closed.

NIGHTMARE: The word *nightmare* indicates an evil spirit, often in the form of a horse, who would visit during the night and sit on the chest of those sleeping. It was alleged to cause breathing to cease and brought with it unusually bad dreams.

To cure such an affliction, one should hang stockings crosswise at the foot of the bed with a pin stuck in them.

Placing one's shoes under the bed, with the toes pointing outwards, was also believed to prevent nightmares. Laying a knife or some other steel article (or just a piece of iron) under the foot of the bed was yet another method.

NIGHTSHADE: Plants in the nightshade family have long been held to have special magical powers. The bittersweet or woody nightshade (*Solanum dulcamara*) was thought to render protection against the evil eye or a witch's influence, if worn as a garland around one's neck. So common was the use of this particular herb for this purpose that the famous herbalist Nicolas Culpeper (1616–54) wrote that it was "excellent good to remove witchcrafts both in men and beasts: as also all sudden diseases whatsoever . . ."

The so-called deadly nightshade (*Atropa belladonna*) was taken internally by many Europeans who wished to foretell the future or otherwise converse with spirits. It was said to possess the ability to drive people mad and, in large doses, even to kill them. It was also believed to be one of the ingredients witches rubbed themselves with when they wanted to fly. Its name *Atropa* is derived from Atropos, a fate in classical mythology who was said to cut the thread of life. The name *belladonna,* which means beautiful lady, was given to this herb because it dilated the pupils, thus enhancing one's looks.

NOSE: The nose is essential in the breathing process and was seen by some ancient people as a symbol of life itself. Among some primitives, it was often guarded by an amulet or ring to prevent evil spirits from entering the body. Many superstitions have arisen regarding this useful extension.

To begin with, it is said that nostrils correspond directly to one's sexual organs. In the case of a man, if they are thick and vibrant, they indicate large testicles. A straight, long, thin nose on a woman was said to indicate that her sexual organs were large as well.

In France, if one has a short nose, it is said he tends towards laziness. Should the nose be pointed, it indicates a somewhat cranky personality, but, nonetheless, one endowed with a good memory. Turned-up noses indicate lust and boldness; long noses, courage and pride. Should the tip be somewhat fat, it indicates prudence, honesty, and fidelity.

Traditionally, a mother who pulls hairs out of her child's nose each day will assure him of a happy life.

An itchy nose can indicate a dispute, the receipt of a letter, or an unknown lover, depending on the culture. It is generally believed that you should make a wish when your nose itches!

Bloody noses are held, in general, to be bad omens, unless only a single drop falls from the left nostril. In this instance, it is said to announce receipt of a great deal of money. Should the blood flow from the right nostril, however, a family member will fall seriously ill. Should your nose bleed in the presence of one of the opposite sex, it is an admission of love.

An eighteenth-century cure for nose bleeding was to apply moss (taken from a dead man's skull) in such a way that it just touches the skin. Another method was to transfix a dead toad with a sharp, pointed instrument, enclose it in a little bag, and suspend it around one's neck. A cold key pushed down the back was also believed to stop nose bleeds, and the tip of a cat's tail or a small piece of the daily newspaper placed in the afflicted nostril is held to work. Eating pigeon droppings, or placing a coin in a white handkerchief on the middle of one's forehead, is said efficacious. Writing the initials *INRI* (Greek for Jesus the King of the Jews) on your forehead, with your own blood, was also believed effective.

NUMBER: In ancient times, each number had a life and meaning of its own. **One** was said indicative of God, the universe, and the life-giving power of the sun. **Two** indicated duality, balance, and coupling. **Three** was said to be a special magical number, and, in Christianity, stood for the Holy Ghost. It symbolizes perfection, as in a triangle. It is also said connected with divination, as it was from a three-legged stand that Pythia delivered her oracles. The number **four** is held indicative of materiality, a cross, a square, and the foundation of all things, including the seasons and the points of the compass. **Five** stood for the five senses and was the sacred number of the Mayans. **Six** is said to be two triangles, interposed, and is, therefore, symbolic of the "Star of David." It symbolizes three couples, or two triangles, and is, therefore, both odd and even. Six is also a perfect number, since it equals the sum of one plus two plus three; thus, it represents creation. **Seven** is the number of perfection and spirituality—God created the world in seven days; the ancients knew of seven planets; and seven colors are seen in a rainbow. It is said that every seven years one's body is entirely regenerated. **Eight** is indicative of materiality, since it represents the combining of two fours. Last, **nine** represents the end of a cycle and fertility (since human gestation takes nine months). It is a number much used in healing and spells.

General beliefs include these: If the date of your birth can be divisible by seven, you will have an exceedingly lucky life. The seventh son of a seventh son was thought to possess clairvoyance, second sight, and could foretell the future. Generally, it was held that odd numbers were lucky while **thirteen** was perhaps the most unlucky of all.

NURSING: Before the advent of glass and plastic baby bottles, nursing was commonplace, so it is not surprising to find a number of superstitions regarding this practice.

Women who found milk in short supply were advised to drink beer, eat a combination of fennel and honey, or make themselves a poultice of parsley.

Should one be engaged as a wet nurse, it was said she must take special care, so her milk would not dry up. She should never burn wood in the fireplace, hold a needle by its point, or respond to any call from outside her house. She was required to spit on those who stared at her when she was walking with her suckling.

Should milk trickle from the chest of a child, it was thought the Devil had come to suckle him during the night.

Children who refused to nurse were often judged bewitched.

Commonplace was the belief that, once a child has been weaned, it should never again be put to his mother's breast or he will become a liar. Also, children weaned in the spring were believed to turn gray earlier than others. Children weaned on a Good Friday would never eat again.

NUT: In ancient Roman times, nuts were presented to newly married couples to guarantee fruitfulness. In France, nuts were often used to pelt the bride and groom in much the same way that rice is used today.

The expression, "going a-nutting" indicated lovemaking in a somewhat genteel way.

A Devonshire belief holds that a bride who receives a bag of hazelnuts when leaving the church will be fruitful. For this to work, however, the nuts would have to be presented by an old woman, preferably a married one, who herself had a large family of children.

Should children go nutting on a Sunday, the Devil would hold down branches for them, and bad luck would follow them throughout their life.

A good crop of nuts in a particular district presaged a large number of births.

Finding a nut with two kernels in a single shell was held a good omen. One should eat one of the nuts and toss the other over the left shoulder, while making a wish. The wish would be granted.

Last, a love divination ritual required ladies to place nuts in pairs on the top bar of a fireplace grate. Should the nuts remain together and be consumed by the fire, all was well. Should any of the pairs fly apart, it was predicted that the marriage or relationship would not take place.

NUTMEG: According to American folklore, carrying nutmeg in your back pocket will cure rheumatism. Should an unmarried woman carry nutmeg in her pocketbook, she will marry an old man. Nutmeg was also used to improve one's eyesight, prevent boils and cold sores, and also remove freckles.

OAK TREE: Since ancient times, the oak, due to its strength, durability, and longevity, was the most sacred tree in Europe and Scandinavia. In Scandinavia, it was sacred because mistletoe, worshipped by the Druids, grew on its branches.

According to the ancient Jews, Jacob buried the "foreign gods" and the earrings of his household under the Oak of Shechem. It was also said the followers of Baal conducted their sacrifices below an oak tree or in an oak grove.

The Oracle of Zeus at Dodona was in an oak wood. The temple of the priestess dedicated to Zeus was placed so that the rustling of oak leaves would bring her answers to her questions. It is legendary that the ship *Argo* of the Argonauts was constructed from oaks from this grove. Hence, one timber could speak and advise the voyagers in a magical way.

For the Romans, Jupiter was reputedly sheltered by an oak at his birth. In yet another Roman legend, acorns were man's first food until replaced with corn by Ceres, the Roman Goddess of Agriculture.

So sacred was the oak to the Druids and Gauls, that the Christian missionary, Saint Boniface, was ordered to actually destroy a sacred oak at Hesse in Germany.

In Ireland, oaks were considered one of the "seven noble trees" that could not be cut down without payment of a fine.

In general, so great was the fear of damaging or cutting an oak tree, that, when one was felled, it was said to give a shriek or groan that could be heard a mile away.

In Scandinavia, the tree was held sacred to Thor and was known as the "thunder tree." In actuality, though, the oak tree is so prone to being struck by lightning that, in Sussex, a rhyme says: "Beware of the oak, it draws the stroke." Oak branches were often kept in homes as a protection against lightning, however. In time, these were replaced by acorns, which eventually gave rise to the acorn shape on the shade pulls often found on modern window shades.

Oak leaves were commonly believed to protect one from witchcraft. So strong was the belief in its efficacy against spells that the heathen king, Ethelbert (A.D. 522–616), required Saint Augustine to preach to him under an oak tree, which would protect him from any spell the christian might attempt to cast on him.

The Romans often made crowns of oak leaves that were held to symbolize bravery. The oak leaf crown was their highest award for winning a battle, destroying an enemy, or saving the life of another soldier. Contemporary military honors reflect this tradition in awarding "oak clusters."

Newly married couples would often dance around an oak tree for good fortune. A single oak tree planted at a point on the parish boundary, called the "gospel oak," is another relic of past beliefs. On Rogation Day (one of three days preceding Ascension Day, the fortieth day after Easter), processions went around "beating the bounds" of each parish, stopping to read various gospel verses under each boundary oak tree.

Oaks were often planted at crossroads and were believed to cure certain illnesses.

Charles II was reputed to have been saved at the Battle of Worcester by hiding in the branches of the Boscobel oak. Once restored to the throne, Charles declared May 22 Shick-Shack Day, Royal Oak Day, or Oak Apple Day. (A shick-shack was an oak twig, possibly bearing an oak apple.) It was required that everyone had to wear one on this holiday, and anyone not doing so would be beaten with nettles. In the afternoon the shick-shack was replaced by a bunch of ash leaves.

It is said Saint Louis held his Court of Justice under an oak. Henceforth, all oaths taken under that tree, especially one with twin trunks, could not be broken without danger. Likewise, an ancient method of litigation required placing both litigants under an oak. Whoever was touched by the first leaf to fall was presumed innocent and the victor in the trial.

According to a Cornish belief, a nail driven into an oak tree cures toothaches. According to a Welsh tradition, all one's sores will be healed by rubbing a piece of oak on the left hand in silence on Midsummer's Day. One can cure hernias by embracing an oak tree, and the same act is believed to assure women that their husband will be virile and they will mother many children.

Last, mention must be made of the gall fly, a small parasitic insect, which frequents oak leaves often found on the ground. Should one find a small gall fly, tradition requires that it must be opened and examined. Should it contain larva inside, wealth was on the way. Should it be a small fly instead, bad news was expected. Should one find a spider instead, famine in the area was more than likely!

OIL: In Greek and Roman legends, oil was offered in sacrifice to the gods.

One who spilled oil was thought to bring bad luck into his life.

Olive oil was believed able to magically double or triple itself. A spoonful of olive oil, taken every morning for nine days, was believed to cure sterility. Placing a drop of oil in a cup of water was held to indicate whether a man or animal was under the influence of evil. Should the drop remain compact, no spirits were present; should it break up, however, spirits were thought nearby.

OLIVE TREE: According to legend, the olive tree produces a magical oil that will protect one against drunkenness and increase virility when drunk for nine days in a row.

Exactly when and where the olive was first cultivated remains a great mystery, but it is highly likely that it was known to the ancient Egyptians. The first biblical reference to it is in the story of the Great Flood. When Noah released a dove from the ark, it came back with a freshly plucked olive leaf in its mouth (Genesis 8:11). Noah then knew it was safe to come out of the ship, so both the tree and the bird have become symbols of peace.

The Garden of Gethsemane in which Christ pondered his fate was an olive grove (Matthew 26:36). (In fact, whenever a garden is mentioned in the Bible, it is highly likely that an olive orchard is meant.) Olive trees are traditionally long-lived. Even when cut down or burnt away, the root will sprout again.

According to the Greeks, Athena (Minerva was the Roman equivalent) made the olive tree bear fruit. She and Poseidon fought over the possession of Attica. Poseidon either caused a saltwater spring to gush by striking it with his trident or he created a horse. (The legend varies.) Athena caused an olive tree to appear. Since this was considered the more valuable gift, Attica was given to Athena. Thus, the city of Athens was itself named after her and forever held her as their particular goddess. On early Attic coins an olive branch was often portrayed. Likewise, goats were sacrificed to Athena, since they often harmed olives.

According to Herodotus, Xerxes dreamed he was crowned with an olive wreath, which vanished instantly, symbolizing a hollow victory before his Greek expedition.

In the Greek Harvest Festival, the olive was a primary symbol. In more recent times, a tree branch known as the "harvest may" was often used. This, or laurel, was often decorated with fruits of the earth and ribbons, and was then carried in procession until finally fixed over a farm door. Left for a year in this same spot, it was believed to guarantee growth of further crops.

In Christian folklore, when Adam died, the angel guarding Eden gave Seth seeds of olive, cedar, and cypress. These were placed in Adam's mouth. They later sprouted from his grave, forming a single triple-trunked tree. Legend has it that this tree held the symbolic leaf plucked by Noah's dove. Likewise, beneath this same tree David wept, and it was this same tree that Solomon cut down. Another tradition holds that this same tree became one of the crosspieces of the cross upon which Christ was crucified.

In medieval times, olive was a protection against lightning, witchcraft, and evil spells.

ONION: Onions, like garlic, have been the subject of many superstitions. If cut in half and placed under the bed of an ill person, they are said to remove fever. If hung in a sick room, they would draw illness away from the patient.

In India, the onion is said to make one tranquil. (This is to be contrasted with the legend that Alexander the Great fed onions to his troops to increase their desire for war.) The Egyptians held the onion as a symbol of eternity and often took oaths with their right hand placed on it.

One English tradition is to buy onions from a shop that has two doors and to enter by one door and exit by the other.

Onions placed under a pillow by an unwed maiden on Saint Thomas's Eve are said to bring visions of her future husband.

English schoolboys rubbed onion on whatever part of their body was about to be caned, in the belief that it would prevent feeling the strokes. Young girls scratched the name of their lovers on onions and left them in some warm place. Whichever onion sprouted first was said to indicate the more passionate love.

The skin of the onion, if grown locally, was used to forecast weather. If the skin was thin, a mild winter was expected; if thick and tough, a cold and hard winter was certain.

In American folklore, should you place an onion under your bed, it will attract a lover to the house. It was said to keep away, by its strong odor, any person who might be jealous of your happiness. Before the onion can work this way, however, it must first be especially treated by a "witch."

Carrying a red onion in your left hand or left pocket was said to ward off disease, according to Southern blacks. Residents of the Okefenokee Swamp said that onion juice rubbed on the head would make the hair grow.

ONYX: This stone, usually black, brings gloom to one's heart, because its color reminds one of mourning and the darkness of night. It is traditionally ruled by Saturn, oldest of the gods. Often used by sorcerers, it appears in works connected with death and malediction.

At night, onyx is said to promote frightening dreams and clairvoyant visions. During the day, it produces anxiety.

Tradition holds that it should never be worn by a pregnant woman. Contrariwise, some believe the onyx increases a couple's fidelity and will dissipate melancholy, once it has taken hold of a soul.

In India, this stone is reputed to be especially effective for increasing one's immune system.

OPAL: The opal falls under the planetary rulership of Mercury and is believed to contain the power to lure its possessor into strange and unknown realms. Tradition holds that opals were set in the crown of Roman emperors to guard their honor.

Known in particular for its ability to change colors, it was thought of as a living "being" by the Orientals.

During the fourteenth century, the opal was held as an evil omen, and was said to lose its luster when its owner died of an illness. It is sometimes called the "tear stone" and was recommended to be worn only in combination with diamonds to avoid ill luck. It is said that an opal should be offered only in October. When this is done, it will allow all difficulties to be overcome.

Black opals were believed to be especially fortunate as good luck charms.

Opals are reputed to strengthen sight, cure eye diseases, and to make the wearer invisible. They are said to turn pale in the presence of poison and will protect their wearers from contagion. One tradition holds that blondes will stay blonde longer by wearing opal necklaces.

ORANGE: When given as a gift between lovers, oranges encourage their affections. Brides who wear orange blossoms are held to have good luck. Since the orange is a prolific "fruiting" plant, however, the bride may not wish this kind of luck!

ORCHID: The name of this flower comes from the Greek word *orchis,* meaning testicle. Each plant has a pair of tubers, one for this year's growth and one for next.

In Europe and Asia, orchids were gathered for the preparation of salep, a flourlike substance mixed with water that was once carried on long sea voyages as an emergency food.

Dioscorides recorded that women in Thessaly would make salep with goat's milk. They would use the full, new tuber of the orchid should they want to excite sexual desire in their partner. Should they wish to discourage the same, the emptying, old tuber would be used.

Tradition also held that the sex of unborn children could be determined by a similar means. Male children would be born if the man ate the large, new tuber while girls would be born if the small, old tuber was consumed. Hence, in time, orchids became known as aphrodisiacs and a decoction of this plant was said to revive amorous zeal.

OWL: Generally accepted is the association of owls with evil and misfortune. In a Sumerian tablet (dated 2300–2000 B.C.), a nude goddess is shown surrounded on each side by an owl. Scholars believe her to be the Goddess of Death.

Greek and Roman writers often refer to the owl as a bird of ill luck. Ovid and Pliny relate the bird to death and hold that owl calls are sinister. Tradition held that, when an owl appeared in the capitol at Rome, the place had to be cleaned with water and sulphur to drive away any evil the owl may have brought. Romans used pictures of owls to combat the evil eye.

In ancient China, where owl sacrifices were often held, ornaments called "owl corners" were placed on buildings to protect them from fire. In Persia, the owl is spoken of as "the angel of death." In Israel, however, little gray owls are considered good omens when they appear near crops. In Athens, the little owl was associated with the goddess Athena, who ruled the night. Due to its commonality and friendliness, it became an emblem of the city. A common Athenian saying indicating victory: "There goes an owl."

The tradition of hanging up owls in order to deflect storms is an ancient one. Likewise, owls hung up with wings outspread were said to avert hail and lightning.

An owl placed over a child's cot was used to frighten away evil spirits by tribesmen in northern Asia, and sleep can be induced by placing owl feathers under the pillow of a restless child, says an East Indian tradition.

In Great Britain, the owl was held ominous. Chaucer speaks of it as a bringer of death. Shakespeare, in *Julius Caesar* (Act I, Scene 3), lists it among other evil omens.

Owls were commonly associated with sorcery among African tribes. In Madagascar, the souls of sorcerers were called "owls." In Nigeria the Yoruba tribe believe wizards send owls to kill people as their emissaries.

In American folklore, various traditions exist. The Pawnee Indians believed owls were protective; the Ojibwas thought evil spirits often appeared as owls. If a Seminole Indian heard an owl hoot, he would whistle back. Should no further response be heard, he would conclude that "death" was nearby. On the other hand, should the owl hoot back, such was considered a sign of good luck.

Although the owl is often regarded as a symbol of wisdom, it is not unusually intelligent, nor is it blind during the day, and common among American folklore is the belief that an owl can wring its own neck.

In the Alsace, the owl is thought to be a messenger of death.

Should its cry be heard near the room of an ill person, it is said that the person will not recover. Also, an owl was believed to keep rats away if nailed to a barn door, and, in Normandy, an omelette made of owls' eggs is believed to keep a drunk person sober!

If owls' eggs are given to a child, it will ensure lifelong temperance and, if made in soup, they will cure epilepsy and darken gray hair. Owl broth given to a child is reputed to cure whooping cough, according to a Yorkshire belief.

In Scotland, tradition says that seeing an owl in the daylight means ill fortune will come to the beholder. Should one look into the nest of an owl, it is said he will become melancholy and morose for the rest of his life. Should an owl hoot among houses, says a Welsh tradition, a maiden will lose her virginity.

Still to be mentioned is Pliny's belief that an owl's heart placed on a woman's breast will cause her to yield all her secrets.

OYSTER: Oysters have long been held an aphrodisiac. One suggestion is that the oyster resembles the female reproductive organs and, therefore, stimulates sexual interest.

Oysters open during the full moon. A crab tosses it a pearl or other debris to keep it open, thereby enabling it to be eaten.

Long reputed is the belief that one should never eat an oyster, unless the month has a letter *R* in its name.

The Romans anticipated lovemaking by feasting on cuttlefish, octopus, red mullet, electric ray, *and* oysters!

In England, if one eats oysters on the fifth of August, according to belief, one will never die of hunger.

Oysters are thought to be female during the spawning season, and then to change and become male.

Some American sailors wear pieces of oyster shell as protective talismans.

Generally held is the belief that, if you carry a piece of oyster shell in your handbag or pocket, you will always be lucky.

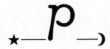

PALM: The word Phoenicia means "land of palms," which was how the ancient Greeks and Romans described this part of the world.

A traditional Arab saying is that the palm has as many uses as there are days in the year. In North Africa, the fruits of the palm are eaten; oil is produced from its kernels (which themselves provide food for livestock); an intoxicating beverage is made from its sap; the leaves are used for thatching, walling, and fencing, and for making matting and baskets; rope is made from the stringlike material found at the head; and should the tree die, its trunk is used to provide timber.

In the Old Testament is found the following, "And he carved all the walls of the house round about with carved figures of cherubims and palm trees . . ." (I Kings 6:29.)

A number of coins of ancient civilizations, including those of Tyre and Sidon, exemplify this tree. In A.D. 70, for example, the Emperor Vespasian struck a coin showing a woman weeping beneath a palm.

In biblical times, branches of palm trees were often carried on special occasions, eventually becoming symbolic of martyrdom. It first became customary to carry palm fronds in procession during the time of Judas Maccabeus. The fronds themselves were mixed with myrtle on the right side and citron on the left. After being carried at the Feast of the Tabernacles, they were kept at home and were said to bring luck and protection during the coming year.

For Christianity, palms are carried on Palm Sunday in remembrance of the day Jesus entered Jerusalem, with people waving palms and strewing His path with them. In actuality, however, Romans cut olive and laurel branches in ancient times to celebrate the return of spring.

As early Christians believed the angels brought palm fronds to carry their souls up to heaven, a custom arose of burning these on All Souls' Day. The arising smoke was said to assist souls released from purgatory to reach heaven.

Christian pilgrims were often known to carry staffs of palms, giving rise to their becoming known as "palmers."

Another Christian legend is about a man named Offero, who, wishing to see Christ child, was told he should assist the disabled. To bring this about, Offero carried people over a dangerous river, using as a support a palm staff. On one stormy night, a child asked to be carried over. In so doing, Offero found the small burden becoming heavier and heavier; nonetheless, he managed to stagger across. The child bid him thrust his staff into the ground. Once he did so, it put out leaves and fruits. When this happened, Offero realized he had carried the Christ child. So converted, he later changed his name to "Christ Offero," Christopher, meaning "Christ bearer."

Yet another legend holds that the palm was one of the four trees from which the cross that crucified Christ was made. Hence, in those countries where palms were not normally grown, a piece of palm was held invaluable as a talisman to drive off evil spirits. A cross made of its leaves was believed to keep away lightning, and should one chew some of the leaves, fever would be driven away.

In American folklore, the tradition of making palm leaf hats remains of unknown origin. In Connecticut, before the Civil War, bales of palm leaves were shipped so that village women and girls could braid it into hats. It is told that enterprising townsmen would pick up the hats and parcel them out to peddlers, who sold them throughout the United States.

According to one tradition, whatever the nature of the wind that blows on Palm Sunday will be the predominant force for the rest of the year. Some say this is only true for "that" special wind that blows during the reading of the gospel accompanying the Palm

Sunday church service. Another weather superstition holds that, on Palm Sunday, should the sun shine clear, fine weather (and a good harvest of corn and other fruits of the earth) will surely follow.

PANCAKE: Generally speaking, pancakes are said to bring good luck and fortune. Should you eat pancakes on Shrove Tuesday and gray peas on Ash Wednesday, it is said you will have money in your pocket year round.

The word *shrove* is derived from *shrive,* meaning "to confess." It is believed that the origin of eating pancakes on this day is due to it being the last festivity before Lent arrives, which is for fasting!

Should you throw a pancake to a cock, and should he eat it himself, bad luck is omened to follow the household. Should he peck at it and leave it for his hens to finish, however, it is a sign of good luck.

Pancakes can be made as large as one wishes. In Estonia, when a peasant woman plants her cabbages, she makes a large pancake. This is done in order to magically encourage her cabbages to have big, broad leaves.

PANSY: It is believed that picking pansies when the weather is good will cause rain before long.

PARSLEY: Though often thought of as nothing more than a decoration on a festive dinner plate, parsley was judged of noble character by the ancient Greeks. Dried parsley was made into wreaths at the Isthmian Games or used fresh at the Nemean. The Romans, on the other hand, strew it on graves and believed it was able to cause epilepsy or sterility. Those persons who were near death were said "to be in need of parsley."

Should one grow parsley in their garden, tradition is that a death will arise in the family before the year is out. Should parsley be sown on any day other than Good Friday, it will not grow double. The person planting parsley must be pure, and it should be sown by a child or an idiot.

Common, too, is the belief that giving away parsley will give away your luck!

Possibly because of the connection of parsley to gravesites, it is said that, if you transplant parsley, your entire garden is placed in the hands of the Devil, and the crops will likely fail. The reason parsley takes so long to grow is because it must see the Devil seven times before flourishing.

A mother who eats parsley while breast feeding was thought to cause her milk to dry up. In Sicily, should a child start to choke when drinking his milk, custom requires sticking a sprig of parsley and tobacco in his anus while spitting three times.

Should a woman plant parsley herself, she can soon expect a child, however, another tradition says that a girl with an undesirable pregnancy can get rid of it by eating large quantities of parsley.

Carrying a small amount of dried parsley is said to guard one against nausea.

Last, during the Middle Ages, a magician wishing to kill an enemy was thought able to do so simply by pulling up a parsley plant and uttering his enemy's name.

PARTING THE HAIR: One European superstition says that, if a young girl finds a part in her hair, where it normally doesn't exist, she will be a widow some day.

PASSING BELL: Sounding a bell as part of a funeral is an ancient tradition. The origin of this practice lies in the belief that the bell will drive away evil spirits, who are ready to seize the soul of the deceased.

Should a clock strike while the passing bell is being rung, there will be a second death within a week, says a Buckinghamshire belief.

PEA: Generally held is the belief that, should you find a pod containing nine peas, you must throw it over your shoulder and make a wish. Whatever you wish for will come true. Another tradition holds that, should you find a pea pod with only one pea, it is an omen of good fortune.

Should an unmarried maiden find nine peas and place the pod on the lintel of the kitchen door, the first man to enter would be her future husband. Yet another tradition in Cumberland required a girl whose lover had been faithless to her to be rubbed over by the neighboring lads with a pea straw.

In American folklore there is the tradition of eating one's peas with honey. This was a creative way to eat peas, balanced on a knife, before forks had been introduced in the Colonies. A popular rhyme said to be often quoted in Puritan Boston was:

I eat my peas with honey.
I've done it all my life.
It makes the peas taste funny,
but it keeps them on my knife.

PEACH: For the Chinese, peaches are considered symbolic of longevity and immortality. Peaches in the celestial orchard were believed to ripen only once every three thousand years. Placing sprigs of peach blossoms over one's front door will keep evil spirits away, say the Chinese.

In the north country of the United Kingdom tradition holds that when leaves of a peach tree fall before autumn, a murrain or cattle disease is expected.

PEACOCK: According to a Hindu legend, Hindra, the God of Thunder, Rains, and War, became a peacock in order to escape the demon Ravana. As compensation, he was endowed with a thousand eyes in his feathers, the ability to rejoice when the rains come, and the power to kill snakes.

Legend holds that the peacock dances happily when he sees clouds or hears thunder. One of the 108 postures of classical Hindu dance signifies being "sportive like the peacock."

Aristotle refers to the peacock as "the Persian bird." Alexander the Great imposed severe penalties on anyone killing Indian peacocks.

Sacred to Hera, one legend relates how the goddess sent Argus, the hundred-eyed giant, to guard her husband's mistress, Il. When Zeus sent Hermes to charm and kill Argus, Hera was said to use the giant's eyes to decorate the peacock's tail.

For Christians, the peacock was adopted early as a symbol of the Resurrection, as, after molting, it once again becomes clothed in splendor. Saint Augustine believed its flesh was incorruptible. Possibly from this arose the belief that peacock feathers placed with objects preserves them from decay. In many medieval paintings, angels' wings are portrayed as peacock's plumes.

A fifteenth-century manuscript "Hortus Sanitatis" states it is a sign of rain when the peacock "mounts on high." At the same time in England, the belief that peacock calls frightened away serpents and other poisonous insects was commonplace.

During the sixteenth century, peacock feathers were often given to those caught cheating or lying.

In India, since the peacock killed snakes, a belief arose that its bile and blood acted as antidotes against poison.

In the Punjab, persons bitten by snakes were often smoked in peacock feathers. Similarly, travelers were advised to carry a peacock to ward off snakes.

In Ireland, calls of the peacock are believed to forecast rain.

Other folklore relates that body parts of the bird can effectively cure disabilities, including tuberculosis, paralysis, asthma, catarrh, headaches, and infertility. Hindus and Moslems often wear peacock feathers to ward off evil spirits. On special occasions umbrellas of peacock plumes are often carried by royal personages. In India, the mere sight of the bird is said to be an omen of good luck and peace.

In China, tradition holds that a general of the Chin Dynasty, taking refuge from his enemies, was so grateful for not being betrayed by the peacocks, he thereafter presented peacock feathers to those who had shown bravery in battle.

Although generally held auspicious, in Java the bird is associated with the Devil. In Northern Iraq, the Yezidis hold that the Devil is not evil. They refer to him as the "Peacock Angel."

Yet another explanation as to why displaying peacock feathers is said to bring bad luck is that Greeks and Romans used the feathers to decorate the holy temples. Such was done with the injunction that no one but the priest could touch them. Should one break this taboo, death was the punishment dispensed.

Tradition holds it unlucky to display peacock feathers and that bad luck will follow anyone who does so. Some believe the eye appearing at the end of each feather may itself be an evil eye, causing things to happen that one does not desire. No doubt this tradition comes from the Greek legend of Argus.

The North American Indians say the peacock "has an angel's feathers, a Devil's voice, and a thief's walk. Indians also believed wearing the bird's feathers made a person vain, arrogant, and greedy.

Commonplace among actors is the belief that bringing a peacock's feather on stage, or even into the theater, will mean disaster for the play.

An interesting Islamic belief is that a peacock opened the wicker gate of Paradise to admit the Devil.

For a woman to see a peacock in a park is an omen that she will soon marry. For an unmarried woman, keeping peacock feathers in her house will drive her suitors away!

PEARL: A pearl is symbolic of the mating of sea and sky. One tradition holds that a drop of morning dew fell into a shell and it was fertilized by the moon. Yet another holds that a white bird, fertilized by the sun, dove into the sea and yielded a pearl eight months later.

Pearls are thought to have aphrodisiac qualities if worn as a talisman. The pearl is said to cure feminine depression. Should it be mounted on a pin, it is supposedly able to heal insanity and jaundice, and to immunize against snake and insect bites. Some say it will even ease heart pain, and giving a pearl to a newborn child ensures him a long life.

PENNY: According to Welsh sailors, one should throw a penny over the ship's bow when going out of dock to ensure a successful voyage. Likewise, you should always carry at least one penny for good luck.

PEPPER: Tradition holds that, if you want an unwelcome guest to leave, simply place a pinch of pepper under his chair.

It is said that one should never eat pepper when he has a fever or the fever will increase.

According to a Texas tradition, earaches are cured by filling a piece of cotton with black pepper and placing it in the ear. Also, swallowing whole chili peppers will cure a cold.

Many believe that pepper in any form is an aphrodisiac.

PERIWINKLE: A Welsh tradition is that, should you dig up a periwinkle plant from a gravesite, the dead person buried there will appear in your dreams for twelve months.

PHOTOGRAPH: Among primitive persons, it is considered an ill omen or taboo to be photographed. Belief holds that a person's soul is captured in the picture; hence, to take the picture away would be to take away the soul, making it available to the Devil.

A popular superstition is that, if a betrothed couple is photographed together, they will never marry. It is also thought bad luck to be photographed with a cat or another animal, since the animal can actually be a witch in disguise.

When three people are photographed together, some say that the middle person will die. Should you wish to place a curse upon another person, simply turn his picture to the wall or upside down. If it is turned both upside down *and* backwards, it is said the magic is even stronger!

PICTURE: Generally held is the belief that a picture falling in the house means someone in the house will die within a month. Should the picture contain a portrait of a person, whether in the house or not, his death will follow in the same manner.

PIE: According to an Irish tradition, it is lucky to see two pies, but unlucky to see just one.

PIG: Domestication of the pig was reportedly first done by the Chinese. For the Buddhists, the pig is a symbol of indolence; for the Europeans, the pig is a symbol of license; for most of us, it represents gluttony and obstinacy.

For the ancient Egyptians, pigs represented Osiris at sowing time and Seth at the time of harvest. Generally held as unclean, swine herdsmen attending pigs were not allowed temple entrance nor permitted marriage outside their own class. Egyptians ate pig meat only at the Midwinter Festival, and the animal could only be sacrificed at the time of the full moon. A remnant of this ancient belief is the tradition that pigs should be slaughtered only when the moon is waxing, or the meat will shrink in the pot!

Ancient Greeks sacrificed pigs to their gods at the time of sowing corn.

Neither Jews nor Arabs eat pork; nor is it consumed in Scotland and in parts of Northern Ireland.

Philip II of Spain, a staunch Catholic, consumed large quantities of pork during the time he lived in England. Hence, in sixteenth-century Spain, anyone with a distaste for the meat was thought to be a secret follower of Judaism and, therefore, placed themselves in danger of arrest by the Inquisition.

For the Celts and other Teutonic peoples, pork suggested hospitality and other world feasts. The Anglo-Saxons and the conquering Normans enjoyed pork. No doubt this led to the common English custom of serving it at Christmastime. A boar's head with an orange in its mouth was traditionally brought to the table at Queen's College, Oxford, during the Christmas season. In Scandinavia at Yule, a loaf baked in the shape of a boar is made from the last wheat of the harvest.

For devout Christians, pigs are symbolic of both good and evil. The patron saint of swine herds, Saint Anthony, was said to look after even the smallest pig of a litter, which came to be called a "pantony pig."

In the New Testament, demons expelled by Christ from afflicted humans were said to have immediately entered the bodies of swine (Matthew 8:31).

In the folklore of New England and Ireland, the black boar was long held one of the possible expressions of the Devil himself.

In 1457, a sow and her young pigs were condemned to death, and only a last minute pardon, "due to their extreme youth," saved the piglets.

At one time, among the English agricultural class, pig racing was held an acceptable passtime. Involved youths chased after a pig whose tail had been coated with soap.

A Scottish tradition says it is unlucky for a pig to cross one's path.

In Ireland, pigs running around the farm with straws in their mouths indicate a storm approaching. A pig is also held to give a peculiar whining sound when its master is approaching death. In Ireland, too, it is lucky to drive a pig into one's house on May Day morning. Should a pig enter at any other time, however, great poverty is likely.

An unusual Irish tradition is that pigs have the ability to "see" the wind and are, therefore, a very useful weather prophet. In some parts of the United States, people believe hogs can actually predict a coming tornado.

According to a Welsh tradition, pigs bathed in the same water that scalded previous pigs to death will grow better.

A general country belief is that a woman touching a pig during the curing process will cause the bacon to turn bad.

Pigs should be killed during the increase of the moon, or the bacon will shrink and waste away in the pot, say many rural traditions. When one is preparing for a fishing trip, it is unlucky to mention the word *pig*.

Should a pig be struck with an elder branch, legend holds it will die immediately, and one is said sure of coming success should he find himself in front of a sow and her litter.

PIGEON: Although some traditions regarding pigeons have already been discussed (see **dove**), there remain a few others to be mentioned.

To begin with, a pigeon sitting on a table indicates sickness; yet, no one sleeping on pigeon's feathers can die. Should a white pigeon alight on your chimney, it is a sign of death in the house. If one who has a fever applies living pigeons cut in half to his feet, the fever will be cured.

Should pigeons congregate on a house roof, a rain storm is near. While you are out walking, if a flight of twelve pigeons passes over your head, you will be coming into wealth.

In American folklore, persons who are pigeon-toed are believed to be greedy, since the pigeons are greedy birds.

Feeding strange pigeons brings you new friends. Pigeons making their home on your roof will attract good luck to you. Should their home be pulled down, however, the woman of the house is likely to die. Rain is on the way when pigeons fly in a circle over any body of water.

Young pigeons are said to kill their father in order to marry their mother.

PIN: Finding a pin and picking it up is said to bring good luck for the entire day, as long as the point of the pin is pointing away from you. Should the point be pointing toward you, however, it will bring you bad luck, but only if you pick it up.

It is said lucky for a bridesmaid to throw away pins, and one tradition holds that whoever steals pins from a bridal gown is assured of her own marriage within the year. Meanwhile, it is bad luck for a bride to have even a single pin stuck in her dress during the wedding ceremony. It is said that her family will feel the consequences. After marriage, however, finding a bent pin is thought an excellent talisman for a new bride.

Should a woman be pregnant, she must not pick up a pin by its point or her milk will dry up after the birth of her child.

Already mentioned in another context (see **gender**) is the tradition that a pregnant woman finding a needle will have a girl. But should she find a *pin,* she will have a boy.

A pin should never be given to another, unless one has first stuck himself with it. Should you be forced to loan a pin, you must turn your back and let the other person find it and pick it up himself.

Pins should never be used to remove splinters or bad luck will ensue.

A Yorkshire belief is that one should never have a pin with them while on board ship.

Pins used for making shrouds are excellent amulets against fear. They should be worn on the inside of one's jacket collar. Should they be used for any other sewing, however, they will cause death.

An unusual practice was for a gamekeeper to stick a pin into a fence or style over which the victim of a shooting accident was lifted. Similar in content was the tradition of, after a funeral, sticking a pin into the churchyard gate through which a body has passed.

PINE CONE: Pine cones are said to be excellent weather prophets. They will remain open when the weather is fine, but close when rain is on the way.

PIPE SMOKERS: A French tradition is that pipe smokers should never light their pipes from a lamp or candle of any kind, or their wives will become unfaithful. It is said that, during the early period of travel in the United States, it was common practice to calculate the distance by the number of pipes one's guide had smoked. Three pipefuls were said to indicate twelve miles journeyed, after which a short rest period was often allowed.

Should a pipe smoker make a ring with the smoke he exhales, it is said to be a good omen for himself and those around him.

PLATE: Generally held is the tradition that, should one break a plate, two more breakages are soon to follow.

If a bride breaks a plate at her own wedding reception it is an omen of an unhappy marriage.

Eating off a cracked plate is held to be a good omen, but turning the plate on the table in front of you is said to bring bad luck.

Should a plate be set on a table upside down, it is said to mean that the person to use it is destined to soon die.

On the evening of a funeral, family members of the deceased should add an extra plate to their dinner table, so he can gain strength before his long journey.

PLAYING CARDS: It is considered unlucky to take your pack of cards with you if you are engaged in a dangerous occupation (pilot, seaman, or miner, for example). Likewise, if you are a burglar, you should never steal a pack of cards or you will certainly be caught.

Warnings include: Never travel with playing cards, unless you wrap them first in a violet-colored silk. Never throw cards away. (To do so is to throw away luck.)

The only way to destroy cards is by fire, but not before buying a replacement pack. While the old pack is burning, take the new one from its box and wave it three times in the smoke. Never use cards that you used for telling fortunes for games, and never use cards used for games for telling fortunes.

Belief has it that there is never a good hand at cards that contains the four of clubs. It is said that this particular card belongs to the Devil and is symbolic of his four-poster bedstead.

One should never pick up the cards before the dealer has finished shuffling them or allow one's chips to lie scattered about the table.

Under no circumstances should a player pick up the cards with his left hand or sit cross-legged. Should he have a favorite card, he is advised to try to touch it with his index finger before sitting down to play. If he is playing with a partner, better luck can be assured if he sticks a pin in his partner's lapel.

One should never whistle or sing while playing, as this will definitely bring bad luck. However, should a card player walk around his chair three times before sitting down, he will be granted good fortune, according to some traditions.

Cards should never be played on a polished surface or in the company of a dog. Cards should be played on a table that is covered in green. To play without such a cover is considered unlucky.

One should never lend money to an adversary to play with. To play oneself on borrowed money, however, is considered fortunate. (A general belief among gamblers is that borrowed money cannot lose. Likewise, the old adage of "beginner's luck.")

Should an unlucky player commit suicide, all those playing against the bank are certain to win.

One should never allow another person to look over his shoulder while playing or to put his foot on the rung of his chair. Likewise, one should never play at the same table with a cross-eyed man.

Should a player lose his temper, it is a sign that he will lose the game.

Winning the first game is said to indicate that one will win the third, as well.

Should one's luck go sour, it is said that it can be reversed by turning his chair around three times or by playing with a fresh deck of cards.

Certain cards are said to be inauspicious if drawn early in the game. Drawing the four of clubs, nicknamed "the Devil's four-poster bed," is one example. It is also considered a bad omen if a black card falls on the floor during the game. A run of black spades is regarded as an exceptionally bad omen.

Two pairs, consisting of aces over eights, are also held unlucky and are known as the "dead man's hand." Wild Bill Hickok was holding this when he was shot.

In Scotland, the nine of diamonds is called "curse of Scotland," because it was used by the Earl of Stair to give coded instructions for the infamous Glencoe Massacre in 1692.

A tradition in Britain holds that should a player inadvertently place a matchstick across another previously placed in an ashtray, bad luck is certain.

Last, it is said that, for success at card playing, one must have a host of personal mascots or talismans, such as locks of hair, small animal charms, holy relics, tiny horseshoes, and coins with holes through the middle.

PLOVER: Superstition has it that plovers, or shore birds, embody the souls of those who assisted in the crucifixion of Christ. Hence to see seven plovers together is said an ill omen.

PLOW: Tradition is a plow should never be stepped over; otherwise, whatever ground it plows on thereafter will become infertile.

Farmers who leave their plows in the fields for the winter will see their lands infested with wolves.

Should a baby's navel refuse to heal, a plowshare buried while five Lord's Prayers are recited over it will bring about a healing.

PLUM: According to a Welsh tradition, plum trees blossoming in December mean a death will occur in the house of the owner of the trees.

POINTING: It is generally held bad luck to point at anything, and pointing at a ship about to disembark is said to cause it to sink during its journey. Likewise, pointing at anything in the sky is thought to offend the gods!

POKER: Placing the poker and the fire tongs on the same side of the fireplace indicates a quarrel in the house. Another general belief is that one wishing to make a fire draw should simply place a poker standing upright against the bars of the grate. (This forms "the sign of the cross.")

POODLE: According to a German tradition, black poodles put on the graves of priests or clergymen indicated that they had failed in their calling, or that they had broken their vows.

POPPY: To the ancients, since they grew in wheat fields, poppies were ruled by the goddess Ceres, the Roman Corn Goddess. Poppies and wheat growing together symbolized life and death.

Since antiquity, poppies have been thought to possess prophetic qualities; hence, they were often used by those seeking to divine the future.

The white poppy, a hallucinogenic plant, is used to make opium, morphine, and heroin.

The corn poppy is reputed to be evil, with tradition holding that whoever stares at its center will go blind. The flower was said to have been punished by God for its vanity and pride. He then authorized Satan to touch it with "his" flowers, leaving black marks on the base of its corolla.

Corn poppies can also be used to determine whether you are loved or not. Simply snap the petal between your fingers. The louder and drier the noise, the greater one's love for you.

It is generally held unlucky to bring a poppy indoors, since it can cause illness. The juice of the yellow celandine was believed to remove warts, corns, and calluses. Tradition held that this same flower could be useful for treating the plague, dropsy, and jaundice, if worn in one's shoe without socks or stockings.

Carrying some celandine together with a mole's heart was said to render one invincible and able to win trials. Should celandine be placed in a sick person's room, the plant was reputed to cry out when the sick person was going to get well, and to laugh, or make the sick person laugh, when the illness would not improve.

In Derbyshire, England, poppies were called "earaches." If gathered and placed in the ear of the person picking them, they were said to cause severe earache. In Yorkshire, they were called "blind buff." Here tradition holds a poppy placed on one's eye will blind it!

It is believed that swallows place a celandine leaf over the eyes of their young to cure blindness.

Last, belief is that poppies spring from the blood of slaughtered warriors. Since the First World War, they have been used as a symbol of remembrance for those killed in battle. On Memorial Day artificial poppies are sold to raise money for veterans groups.

POT: Being a common household item, a number of traditions surround the use of pots. A woman who breaks an earthen pot, while thinking of her lover, will be happy with him for as many years as there are broken pieces. Similarly, a young girl who submerges a pitcher in a fountain will marry in as many years as there are bubbles that rise to the surface.

In the border counties of England, a tradition exists that, if the meat shrinks in the pot when cooking, one will have a downfall in life. If it swells to a large size, however, the master of the house will be prosperous.

Burying a jar containing a frog and a magic formula in the fields is said to protect sown seeds from hungry birds, and one can protect fields from unexpected late frosts by burying a jar containing twelve crayfish in river water.

Should a pot be taken off the hook hanging from a chimney, tradition holds that the vibration of the chain must be stopped at once. While it is in motion, the Blessed Virgin is said to be crying. Similarly, when a pot hook is hung for the first time, a fire should be lit, into which seven grains of salt are thrown. This is to keep away evil spirits. Another tradition requires that any new animals brought to a farm be brought before the pothook before being accepted into the family. Also, pot hooks should be thrown out of a window, during storms, to prevent them from attracting lightning.

POTATO: Generally held is the belief that carrying a potato in your pants pocket cures rheumatism.

One should never plant potatoes on Good Friday or a bad crop will follow.

When new potatoes are first dug up, every family member must taste them; otherwise, the spirits in the potatoes will take offense and the crop will not keep. Yet another tradition is that one should make a wish when eating new potatoes for the first time.

In American folklore, should a pan of potatoes boil dry, rain is thought on the way.

In a small town in upper New York State, an overcrop of potatoes beginning to sprout gave rise to the idea of cutting them into thin slices, deep-frying them, and marketing them in transparent bags. Earl W. Wise soon became known as the creator of "potato chips."

In Vermont, when coffee became unavailable, potatoes were cut, stored away, dried, roasted, and then ground into "coffee."

PREGNANCY: As it is, perhaps, the most commonly shared female experience, it is no wonder that numerous traditions and superstitions surround pregnancy. Commonly held is the belief that a pregnant woman should never sew, knit, or spin yarn, for such will cause her child to be strangled by its umbilical cord. Similarly, she must never pass under a table or clothesline, wash windows, cross her legs, or bow down two times in a row. Nor should she approach death, or walk on a grave; otherwise, her child will die at once.

She should never look at herself in a mirror or weigh herself. To prevent a premature birth, one German tradition holds she should carry one of her husband's previously worn socks.

Should she wish to have a boy baby, she should wear blue clothing. Should she wish a girl, pink is advised.

Common is the belief that everything a woman does or comes into contact with during this time will affect the baby's body and mind. Should she wish for a scholarly child, she should read scholarly books. If she looks at anything ugly, such as a monster, the child will be born with an image of what she saw. Should she touch a rabbit, for instance, her child will have a harelip. Should she touch a cat, the child will have the head of a cat. Should she touch an albino animal of any kind, her child will be born with red eyes. Should she touch her face, after being frightened by an animal or an insect, her baby will have a facial mark. In France it was recommended that mothers-to-be should look at handsome engravings on French coins to ensure that their children have similar countenances.

If a pregnant woman often feels nauseated, it is said that the cause is an abundant head of hair on her baby, which is tickling her stomach!

One should never mention anything to a pregnant woman that she does not have. Her unfulfilled desires are held to be detrimental to her child. For instance, should a craving for strawberries be unfulfilled, her child will be born with a strawberry mark on its body. One tradition held that pregnant women had the right to steal at least three fruits or vegetables for this reason. Two were said to be for herself and one for the child. Should a mother-to-be find a twinned hazelnut or almond, she will give birth to twins.

According to American folklore, a mother nursing her child cannot become pregnant.

Mothers are said to lose a tooth for each child they bear.

Commonly held is the idea that pregnant women have extraordinary and unusual dietary desires, which should always be satisfied to ensure the health of their newborn.

Last is the absurd tradition that a woman swallowing an octopus egg while swimming will give birth to an octopus!

PRIDE: An English tradition says that you can judge the pride of another person by taking one of their hairs and pulling it through the nails of the thumb and another finger. The degree of pride is said to correspond to the curled appearance of the hair once this is done.

PRIMROSE: You should never bring primroses into a house where there are hens laying, or the chickens will not hatch.

According to a Welsh tradition, should the primrose bloom in June, such is an omen of bad luck.

Some countryfolk believe that this flower will cure insomnia.

PROVERBS (BOOK OF): You can determine the character of a prospective wife, assuming she is no more than thirty-one years of age, by consulting the first chapter of Proverbs. The verse corresponding to the young woman's age is said to describe her character.

PUMPKIN: Like gourds and cucumbers, pumpkins are symbolic of fertility. For the Chinese, the pumpkin is the supreme ruler in the plant kingdom.

Tradition holds that you should never point your finger at a pumpkin or it will rot immediately.

Pumpkins will grow unusually hardy, if planted on Good Friday.

Pumpkin seeds are said to repress one's amorous desires, and crushing and mixing pumpkin seeds with oil enables them to be used to remove freckles.

On Halloween, of course, a face is carved on a pumpkin and a candle is placed inside. Such magical pumpkins drive away evil spirits that abound on this very special evening. (See **Halloween**.)

PUPPY: A Devonshire tradition says that a sacrifice of three puppies buried brandwise will rid a field of weeds.

Rabbit: Although some of these traditions have already been discussed (see **hare**), a few remain to be mentioned.

Rabbits in general are symbolic of prosperity, success, and fertility, since they are unusually prolific. However, seeing a white rabbit on the way to a mine omens disaster.

Seamen avoid saying the word *rabbit* before going on board or sailing. Should this animal have to be referred to, it is strongly advised that they use another word.

Repeating the words *white rabbit,* three times very fast on the first day of the month is said to ensure prosperity, according to one tradition.

You can see the object of your affections in a dream by taking the blade bone of a rabbit, sticking nine pins into it, and putting it under your pillow, says a Yorkshire tradition. Also, baby rabbits, since they are born with their eyes open, have the ability to keep the Devil away.

In American folklore, carrying a rabbit's foot to bring luck is a traditionally accepted belief. To be effective, however, the foot should be taken from the left foot of an animal that has been killed by a cross-eyed person during a full moon. Women desiring a large family are often advised to carry a rabbit's foot, and suspending a rabbit's foot over a cradle or placing it on a newborn's skin is said to protect the child from evil.

A custom among English actors was to present a new actor or actress with a rabbit's foot to be placed in his or her first makeup box. Using this to apply stage makeup was believed to ensure one's success. Should it be lost, however, ill luck was said to follow. Some countryfolk also use wet rabbit skins to reduce sprains and swelling.

For those who may be confused as to the difference between hares and rabbits, the former are said to have longer ears, large hind feet and long legs suitable for jumping. While traditions in regard to hares and rabbits vary geographically, they are essentially one and the same.

RAIN: As rain is essential to a good harvest, it is no wonder numerous traditions exist regarding it.

Burning ferns is believed to be one way to cause rain. Dipping a cross in holy water was said to have the same effect. In Navarre, France, where custom held that prayers to Saint Peter brought rain, on one occasion, when nothing happened, village inhabitants carried the image of the saint to the river, where it was completely submerged.

Many believe that your rheumatism or corns can indicate that rain is on the way. Likewise, wheat and barley are said to wilt, salt to clump up, and bread to get soft. When a cat rubs a paw behind its ear as it cleans itself, rain is thought nearby, and should a slice of buttered bread fall to the floor on the wrong side, you can count on rain.

Rain falling on a wedding party, as it emerges from the church, is held as a good omen. Rain falling during a burial means that the soul has reached heaven.

It is said that rainwater cures eye illnesses, and money washed in rainwater will never be stolen.

In Welsh folklore, a child placed in rainwater will speak earlier than others.

Should it rain on July 15, according to an Anglo-Saxon belief, it will rain for forty days.

Two saints, Medard and Barnabas, are said to be enemy brothers who bring rain or good weather. Saint Medard causes rains that seem never to stop, whereas Saint Barnabas ensures good weather.

Last, mention should be made of the ancient Roman tradition of dropping small images into the Tiber River to bring rain to Rome.

RAINBOW: According to legend, God created the rainbow as a symbol of his promise that he would never again send a flood to destroy the world. (Genesis 9:11–17.) This statement in the Old Testament is the origin of many of the traditions about rainbows held by Christians and Jews throughout the world.

In mythologies, too, the rainbow assumes a similar role, as a living spirit, demon, god, or goddess. In ancient Greece, Iris—the wife of Zephyrus, the West Wind, and sister of the dreaded Harpies—was the Rainbow Goddess.

Among the Kaitish tribe in Central Australia, the rainbow is believed to be the son of the rain. As such, he often causes droughts, since he desires to protect his father from falling down. Hence, should a rainbow appear when rain was needed instead, magic was thought necessary to drive it away.

In Burma, the Karens believed the rainbow is an evil demon that can destroy humans by devouring their "ka-la," or spirit. Should anyone die through drowning, a fall, or by wild beasts, it is said that he was one of the rainbow's victims. Thus, whenever a rainbow was seen in the sky, it was believed to portend another violent death. Children at play were immediately called home.

Among the Zulus in Africa, the rainbow is associated with snakes. It was thought that a snake always appears whenever the rainbow is visible. When seen with its end touching the earth, it was believed to be drinking water from a pool. Should it meet any man on dry land, he would be afflicted with disease.

For Polynesian peoples, the rainbow is believed to be a ladder by which heroes climbed to heaven. The great God Indra, in Hindu mythology, hurls thunderbolts and uses the rainbow to shoot his lightning arrows. A similar belief was held in Finnish mythology concerning Ukko, who was believed to control thunder and bring rain. Of him it was said that he shot fiery copper arrows of lightning by using the rainbow.

In Scandinavian mythology, Bifrost was a rainbow bridge linking heaven and earth. Belief held that the gods rolled along it when they visited Midgard, the World of Men. Souls of slain warriors, who had been chosen by the Valkyries, were carried over this same bridge to Valhalla. Tradition held that the god Heindall lived beside this rainbow bridge to defend it against the frost giants.

According to Irish traditions, a rainbow seen on a Saturday is certain to be followed by a week of rainy weather.

A German tradition holds that a rainbow seen in the morning promises rain the next day. Seen in the evening, however, a fine day will follow.

Common is the belief that, should one dig at the end of a rainbow where it touches the ground, a pot of gold will be found.

In the north country of England, when a person saw a rainbow, he would make a cross on the ground with two pieces of stick to "cross the rainbow out."

Many believe that one of the rainbow's ends actually pumps water from rivers or ponds to nourish the clouds. In Languedoc, the belief is that water crossed by the colors of the rainbow is poisoned. Some sailors believe a rainbow can inhale a vessel that crosses its rays.

A Czech belief is that pointing at a rainbow with one's finger will cause thunder. The finger will be struck and will fall from the hand. In Yugoslavia, whoever crosses the end of a rainbow will change sex, and should one succeed in throwing an object across its rays, it is believed the object will be transformed into gold.

In North Carolina, it is said that a rainbow spanning one's house means there will be a death inside. Likewise, should any person walk through the end of a rainbow, a member of his family will die within the year.

Wishes made when the rainbow first appears in the sky are generally thought to be granted.

RAKE: Should a rake accidentally fall over with its prongs pointing upwards, tradition in the United Kingdom says that there will be heavy rain the next day.

RAT: Perhaps the superstition most quoted of all is the one that says rats desert a sinking ship. Whether they are the first to know that the ship is sinking, or whether they are the cause, they will, nonetheless, leave before the sailors do. While rats leaving a ship are a bad omen, rats boarding a new ship are said to be a very good sign.

Rats leaving a house or building are said to presage its collapse. Should they suddenly enter into one's home, however, it is omened that a family member will soon die. Should rats chew one's bedroom furniture, such is a sure sign of death.

Dried rats' tails are said to be a cure for a cold, and, should a child lose a tooth, he should toss it at a rat and ask it to bring a sound replacement.

Rats are said to be governed by a "king rat."

In order to rid your barn or loft of rats, it is said you should sprinkle three corners of the room with holy water. The rats will leave by the unsprinkled fourth corner. Remember, however, that if all the rats leave the barn, the barn is likely to collapse.

RAVEN: A Cornish tradition holds that shooting a raven is like shooting King Arthur. A Welsh tradition is that blind people can regain their sight by being kind to ravens, who will teach them how to do so.

It is said that one can determine his future by counting the number of ravens he sees. One raven is said to indicate sadness; two ravens, happiness; three ravens, marriage; four ravens, birth. Should a raven croak when there is an illness in the house, it is an ill omen.

To the ancient Greeks, the raven was sacred to Apollo and was believed to attend the god.

In Norse mythology, the raven is dedicated to Odin. Tradition holds that he let loose two ravens each morning in order to gather information about what was happening in the world. In the evening, the ravens would perch upon Odin's shoulder and whisper to him about whatever they had witnessed.

Tradition held that the raven was initially white, but was changed into black for babbling too much.

RAZOR: While numerous traditions think it unlucky to give a friend or relative a razor as a gift, since it might "cut" the friendship, electric shavers and safety razors have no doubt made this tradition doubtful.

RED: Red has long been held a color that frightens the Devil and his witches, and generally drives away evil, so it is not surprising that a number of traditions surround its use. (See **colors**.) Already noted was the practice of tying red thread around the tails of cows, when first turning them out to pasture in the spring. Likewise, one should tie a red ribbon in a daughter's hair to protect her against evil until she reaches puberty.

According to weather superstitions, red skies bring good weather, if seen at night, but bad weather if seen in the morning.

In American folklore, the use of red carpets as a symbol of luxury began in the 1890s. Such were often laid out from the front door to the curb when a particularly festive occasion was planned.

Another tradition requires a mother to tie red ribbons to her baby's carriage, adding another ribbon whenever anyone praises or compliments the baby. Tying a red ribbon for luck somewhere inside a new car is an extension of this same belief.

RHEUMATISM: Although a number of formulas for curing rheumatism have already been mentioned, there are others to be mentioned here.

In general, if you carry in your pocket a potato that has been begged or stolen, you will never have rheumatism; likewise, carrying the right front foot of a hare. Carrying a piece of mountain ash is said to do the same thing, according to a Cornish tradition.

A woman who has delivered a child feet first is rumored to be able to cure rheumatism.

In Africa, tradition requires a mother to make small cuts on various parts of her child's body. She then inserts green pepper or spice to drive away the demon who causes this illness. In Java, rubbing Spanish pepper under the nails of the fingers and toes of a rheumatic was said to bring a long-lasting cure.

Strangest of all is this Welsh tradition: The patient was stripped and buried up to the neck for two hours in a churchyard, in standing position. Should the pain not disappear, the burying was repeated at the same time and place the next day. It was continued this way for nine days. Should the pain still remain after this, a three-day rest was ordered, after which the whole procedure was begun again.

RIBBON: Ribbons are talismans, since they form a ring when tied. Hence, a headband, like a turban or crown, is a symbol of distinction and wisdom. In the Moslem tradition, a turban that is green is prohibited; however, red or white can be worn.

A silk ribbon or scarf worn around one's neck is said to prevent sore throats. Should the ribbon be worn around the head, it brings happiness, especially if it is a red one.

Tradition holds that migraines can be cured by wearing a ribbon, previously worn by a lover, around your head.

RICE: In the West, rice is considered an ancient symbol of fertility.

It is still thrown over newly married couples for good luck and prosperity.

In the Orient, rice is equivalent to wheat and bread and is the mainstay food product. In Japan, plays are performed and prayers said to propitiate the rice spirits, thereby ensuring a good harvest. The chinese often burn a handful of rice to assure that their crops are abundant. A Southeast Asian tradition says that rice has a soul to which sacrifices must be offered.

In Arab countries, a grain of rice is thought to be a drop of Mohammed's perspiration.

In American folklore, an unusual utensil, about fifteen inches long, called a "rice spoon," was always laid on a table before a meal. This was said to be particularly popular in Charleston, South Carolina, although its origin remains unknown.

RIGHT TURN: Turning to the right, or moving "sunwise," is widespread in many superstitions and traditions. No doubt, the origin of this lies in the belief that the left side is evil and the right good.

Commonplace is the expression "getting off on the right foot." To step forward on the right foot when starting a journey or a marriage was said to omen good luck.

RING FINGER: A Somerset tradition is that stroking the ring finger along any sore or wound will heal it.

RINGING: A general belief among sailors is that, if a glass tumbler is hit and emits a ringing sound, such is the cry of a drowning sailor. Placing one's finger on the rim of the glass and stopping the ring absolves one from having the sailor's death on his conscience.

ROBIN: According to a Breton tradition, when Christ was hanging on the cross, a robin plucked a thorn from His crown and pierced its own breast; hence, the red-breast color long associated with this bird.

According to a Welsh legend, the robin flew with a drop of water to a land of woe and fire in an attempt to quench the flames. In so doing, its feathers were scorched; hence, the "scorched breast."

In France, it is believed that the robin singed its breast fetching fire from heaven.

In the Inner Hebrides, it is said that, when the Christ child was born, the fire in the stable almost went out. The robin fanned the embers back into flame, but, in so doing, burned its breast feathers.

In Western France, on Candlemas Day, a robin's body was spitted on a hazel twig and set before the fire. Since hazel was a magical tree for the Celts, the origin of this ceremony is no doubt pre-Christian.

In Germany it was believed that a robin could avert lightning.

In the sixteenth century, robins were believed to cover dead bodies with moss.

Commonly accepted is the tradition that various ills will befall anyone who injures or disturbs a robin's nest. Should one rob a nest in Suffolk or Bohemia, belief holds that a broken limb may be the penalty.

Cows belonging to a man who kills a robin were said to yield bloody milk. An Irish tradition holds, should one kill a robin, a large lump will form on the right hand and prevent the murderer from working.

In fact, so strong is the belief that one should never injure a robin or disturb its nest that the following proverb is often quoted,

> If a robin you should dare to kill,
> Your right hand will lose all its skill.

Generally held is the belief that a robin tapping three times on a window with its feet means a member of the household will soon die. Likewise, a robin flying into a room through an open window omens death in the house.

In American folklore, a robin is thought a good luck sign if seen in the spring and if flying upward. It is held bad luck, however, should it be flying downward. Similarly, it is very bad luck for anyone to take a robin's egg from its nest.

In yet another rhyme, this time from Suffulk, the robin is given the ability to predict the weather:

> If the robin sings in the bush,
> Then the weather will be coarse;
> But if the robin sings on the barn,
> Then the weather will be warm.

In Germany it is seen as a good omen if a newly married couple see a robin on their way from the church.

ROPE: It is believed one should never mention the word *rope* on board ship or in the theater.

A hangman's rope brings happiness and luck to whoever possesses it, however. Should it be placed in contact with a sore tooth, it promotes recovery. Replacing one's pants belt with a rope made from hemp is said to cure lumbago, if worn daily.

ROSE: Traditions about the origins of the red rose vary. Some say it grew from blood from Venus's foot as she pursued Adonis or from the dead Adonis himself; others say that it came from the blood of Christ. (They obviously accept the belief that the crown of thorns was made of rose briars.) Another legend: On Olympus, Cupid spilled the nectar of the gods. Where it touched the ground, roses grew. In any case, generally accepted is the legend that all roses were originally white, and became red only after blood was spilled on them. A Persian tale maintains that this was brought about by a bird pressing its breast on a thorn.

In the Islamic tradition, roses arose from drippings of sweat from Mohammed's brow. In India, Vishnu's consort, Lakshmi, was born from a rose.

In Scandinavia, they believed that the rose was protected by fairies and dwarfs and their king, Laurin.

Long held and generally accepted is the belief that the rose is the special flower of Venus. So common is this belief that portraits of the goddess often illustrate her crowned with roses or carrying a rose-edged scepter. Likewise, Cupid and Hymen are often represented with rose wreaths. Even Bacchus is sometimes crowned with the flower.

The Romans cultivated the rose primarily for its petals, which were used for decoration and to make wine. Shrines of various gods and monuments for the rich and famous were often garlanded with roses. Couples at weddings often wore chaplets of roses, while those of the brides included the flower myrtle.

For Christianity, the rose, with its five petals, was soon associated with the five wounds of Christ. Similarly, red roses were held symbolic of various martyrs' blood. In the Middle Ages, a festival called "Rose Sunday" perpetuated the tradition that, after her ascent to heaven, the Virgin Mary's tomb was found filled with roses and lilies.

During the twelfth century, it was a papal custom to bestow golden roses on foreign visitors to whom the pope wished to convey a special blessing. This special golden rose was blessed on the fourth Sunday of Lent. In time, being somewhat ostentatious, the custom died out.

The expression *sub rosa* (from the Latin for "under roses"), stems from the fact that amorous couples would often meet in silence and secrecy. In the sixteenth and seventeenth centuries it was customary to paint or carve a rose on the ceilings of council chambers in which secret meetings were held.

From Roman times to the present, roses were often strewn on graves. In Turkey, the flower is sometimes carved on tombstones of women. As the white rose was long held a symbol of virginity, bushes of this kind were often planted on the graves of virgins.

One Saxon tradition is that, on the death of a child, Death may be seen to leave the house and pick a rose outside; hence, the general superstition that dropping rose petals on the ground portends death.

Some of the many superstitions about roses follow: Roses flourishing in the autumn are a sign that an epidemic or disease will come the following year.

Whoever eats rose petals may acquire some of the rose's beauty. Should you snap petals between your fingers, the louder the noise, the more you are loved.

A woman desiring to conceive should wear a red rose around her neck in a small sachet, and a young woman wishing to marry can do the following: She can pick a rose, wrap it in white paper on Midsummer's Eve, and keep it until Christmas Day. Then, if it is still found intact, she can place it in a buttonhole, and the first young man who admires it will be her future husband.

Last, in the Victorian language of flowers, over forty different sentiments can be expressed simply by choosing different colors and varieties of roses. (See **flowers**.)

ROSEMARY: Rosemary, said to be symbolic of remembrance, is often used by mourners at a funeral and dropped on the coffin to indicate that the deceased will not be forgotten.

As a token of faithfulness and love, sprigs of rosemary were once dropped in wine before the bride and groom drank at wedding feasts.

Generally held is the belief that rosemary protects one against

evil spirits, the evil eye, and witchcraft. Should rosemary be placed
on one's door, it will keep witches away from the house.

In Northern England tradition holds that rosemary worn on
one's body will strengthen the memory and guarantee success to
the wearer in anything he might undertake.

An unusual tradition regarding this plant holds that it will only
grow where a woman is head of the household.

Crushed rosemary dropped into a barrel of beer is said to prevent
all those who drink it from becoming drunk.

The Welsh believed that any food picked with spoons made from
rosemary wood becomes nutritious.

RUE: Generally held is the belief that rue protects one against
witches and the evil eye. It is said symbolic of sadness or repen-
tence and is, therefore, traditionally thrown into the face of a
betrayer as an insult.

Legend holds that it grows best when the plant is damaged or
hidden away in some secluded space. The ideal placement of such
a plant is supposedly under a fig tree.

Placing sprigs of rue in one's socks or in the house attracts
happiness. You must never offer them to others, however, it is said,
or you will give your luck away. Most beneficial of all are rue
leaves on which butterflies have laid their eggs.

Rue is said to cure vertigo and various eye ailments, and eating
four sprigs of rue at breakfast, accompanied by a fig, a nut, a little
salt, and nine juniper berries, will immunize against pain for
that day.

RUST: Should articles made of iron or steel, such as keys, knives, et
cetera, become rusty, a Welsh tradition holds that someone is
laying up money for you!

SAGE: Sage was held sacred by the Romans. According to tradition, it must be gathered with one's right hand after a proper sacrifice of bread and wine. It is said to be useful for treating eye ailments, calming various emotional disturbances, and assuring pregnant women of an easy pregnancy.

It is believed that, if sterile women go to bed for four days, drink its juice, and then have relations with their husbands, a child will be born from this union.

Should sage be placed in a glass flask under some manure, it was held to beget a worm or magical bird that had the tail of a blackbird. Its blood rubbed on someone's stomach was supposed to cause a loss of consciousness for more than fifteen days. Should the bird be burned and its ashes thrown into a fire, a clap of thunder would be provoked. If thrown into a lamp, the walls would be covered with imaginary snakes.

In order to gain good health, some say you should eat sage in May. Tradition holds that the plant should never bloom, for the flower itself brings misfortune.

A young girl who picks twelve sage leaves as the clock strikes midday on Saint Mark's Day—one leaf for each stroke of the clock—will see her husband (that is, if she is to have one).

Wherever sage grows profusely in a garden, it is said that a woman of strength will live there; hence male gardeners attempt to restrict its growth in English country gardens!

In Great Britain, sage is used medicinally to gargle with.

Tradition holds that, as the plant flourishes or dies, so will the affairs of its owner.

SAIL: It is said by the Welsh to be bad luck to stitch or mend sails on the quarter deck.

SAILING: As sailing is one of the world's oldest professions, it is not surprising to find a host of superstitions and traditions regarding it.

In general, many seamen believe that a ship with a dead body on board will move more slowly than normal. Similarly, a belief is held that a sailing vessel will move faster when running from an enemy. Some old sailors actually believe that greater speed can be obtained if they speak to their vessel as they would to a horse.

Ill luck is held to follow any ship that sails on a Friday or whose name has been changed, for whatever reason.

Certain practices have been considered taboo on board a vessel ever since ancient times. Here is a sampling: To lose a mop or bucket overboard is an ill omen. Whistling on board ship is also thought unlucky, since it can bring about a storm. Such whistling would be permitted, however, when a sailing ship is becalmed. The use of certain words at sea (such as *pig*) presage disaster. Women on board are an evil omen. A child born on a ship, however, is considered good luck, as is the presence of any children.

New ships should be launched by breaking a bottle of champagne over the bow. The original tradition was to smear human blood over the prow, so that, when it dipped into the water, it offered a sacrifice to the god Neptune. In time, this tradition was altered and red wine was used instead. Today the use of champagne seems commonplace.

A dead kingfisher nailed to the mast will indicate the direction of the wind. Should three magpies be seen, a successful voyage is indicated. One magpie, however, is an ill omen. Seeing a seal or albatross indicates good luck and favorable winds. Killing either of these creatures, however, was thought very bad luck.

Dolphins and porpoises seen playing about a ship presage a storm. Eight-armed cuttlefish are held by sailors as an ill omen. Similarly, a shark following the ship is a sign of death for one of the passengers or crew.

Sailors have specific beliefs attached to wearing tattoos. Among United States Navy men, a pig and cockerel tattooed on one's left instep is said to protect a sailor from drowning. Some sailors even believe that tattoos will prevent them from catching venereal disease. Equally unusual is the tradition that a seagoing man can guarantee his safety before leaving land by touching his girlfriend's or wife's pudenda. This act, known as "touching the bun," is said to bring great luck.

Last, it is said that good luck will come to anyone who touches a sailor's collar.

SAINING: *Saining,* from the old English *segnian,* or the Norse *signia,* meaning "to sign with the cross," is a tradition that still exists in some rural areas.

In the highlands of Scotland it is believed that a newborn baby should be "sained" shortly after birth. Candles are lit and whirled around the bed on which the mother and infant are placed. The whirling must be done in the direction in which the sun moves around the house.

One tradition holds that saining should be performed by placing the bed in the middle of the room and having the midwife or nurse circle it with an open Bible three-times-three times—each three for the persons of the Trinity.

On the occasion of death, after the body has been washed and laid out, one of the oldest women present lights a candle and waves it three times around the corpse. Three handfuls of salt are placed in an earthenware plate and laid on the breast of the deceased. Three empty dishes are arranged on the hearth, as close to the fire as possible, and all attendants going out of the room return to it backwards, repeating a rhyme: "Thrice the torchee thrice the saltee."

SAINT MARK'S EVE: Should one watch at midnight on Saint Mark's Eve (April 24), he will see the ghosts of those who will die during the year pass into the church.

SAINT MARTIN'S DAY: An Irish tradition holds that no woman should spin on Saint Martin's Day (November 11), nor a miller grind his corn. Yet another tradition requires the spilling of blood on this day. Should a black cock or a goose be unavailable, custom requires cutting one's finger and letting the blood drop on the earth. Blood was also sometimes sprinkled over the floor of one's house especially the threshold.

SAINT SWITHUN'S DAY: Legend holds that, on his death bed in A.D. 862, Saint Swithun, the Bishop of Winchester, expressed the desire to be buried outside in the churchyard, rather than inside the church, so "that the sweet rain of heaven might fall upon my grave." This was done according to his wishes. However, when he was canonized at a later date, the monks felt that a saint really should be buried inside the church. On the fifteenth of July, arrangements were made to move his body. Legend says it poured with rain on that day, and continued to rain for forty days. The monks concluded that the saint was adverse to their plan and abandoned it. Having done this, the rain was said to cease. From this grew the tradition that, if it rains on Saint Swithun's Day, it will continue to do so for forty days.

SALIVA: In the New Testament Jesus cured a blind man with saliva (John 9:6). Numerous traditions have evolved: Spitting while taking an oath, for example, makes the oath as valid as if it had been sworn on a Bible or a cross. Also, it is said that you can make a difficult task easy by first spitting on your hands.

Superstition holds that a man who has accidentally wounded another can keep his victim from suffering by spitting on the guilty hand. Spitting on the bites of insects is believed to soothe them, and in Sicily wet nurses often place saliva on their breasts before nursing.

Should a person find himself in the presence of the evil eye, he should spit on the ground three times to protect himself. As soon as someone passes who is suspected of possessing the evil eye, one must spit on the ground. Hair or nail clippings should also be spat upon to prevent them from being used in magical spells.

When a child is first born, the midwife should spit on him or her to protect them. Likewise, whenever a compliment is paid to the infant, his mother must spit.

Farmers spit on their fields wherever they are going to start reaping, and all new garments should be wet with a little saliva before being worn.

In Scandinavia, one can bring luck to a hunter by spitting on a broom and tossing it after him.

Anyone journeying by foot should spit on his right shoe before setting out.

Gamblers can bring down luck by spitting on the ceiling.

When one does not know the purity of water about to be drunk, it is said they should spit into it. Should the saliva dissolve or break up, the water is potable. Should the saliva remain intact, one should abstain from drinking the water.

Last, a seamen's tradition holds that one should always spit with the wind or a tempest will be unleashed, and to ensure a good catch, fishermen are advised to place saliva on their worms after placing them on the hook.

SALT: One of the best known superstitions of all is the practice of throwing a small amount of salt over one's left shoulder after it is spilled. One tradition holds that salt thrown over the left shoulder blinds the eyes of the Devil. Salt was so important that it was often used as money. In fact, the modern word *salary* is derived from the Latin *salarium,* meaning "salt allowance."

As salt preserves food, it symbolizes life, incorruptibility, and the absence of decay. Since salt is itself sterile, it also symbolizes barrenness. After the destruction of Carthage, the Romans sold salt upon the site to symbolize its sterility and to announce their victory.

The Sky God, Ukko, casts a spark of fire which turns into salt, from the heavens into the sea, according to a Finnish myth. In the Old Testament, the eternal bond between God and Israel is depicted as a covenant of salt. (II Chronicles 13:5.) For Christianity salt was an element of the holy water used in exorcism and in baptism. The Aztecs worshipped the Goddess of Salt.

It was said that black magicians and necromancers were thought to never eat salt with their bread before raising the dead, as it would cancel out their spells. Similarly, alchemists held salt as symbolic of the body, the female, and earth. In their attempts to create gold, white salt was one of the ingredients often employed.

A pinch of salt is often left in a baby's cradle to guard it against evil until baptized. Another tradition holds that a child's first tooth to come out should be placed in salt before it is cast into a fire.

To many psychologists, salt is often synonymous with sexuality since it resembles semen. At one time, it was used to indicate licentiousness and sexual copulation. In Shakespeare's *Othello,* for example, Iago refers to passion as "hot as monkeys, salt as wolves in pride."

Plates of oatmeal and salt were often presented to the bridal couple at Irish weddings to ward off the evil eye.

In American folklore, salt was left in a room in which someone had died to purge the sins of the deceased. To symbolize the soul's survival, salt was left in the coffin as well.

In the New Year's Day custom of "first footing" (see **New Year's Day**), a dark man representing "luck" often brought salt to the householder.

Abstention from salt is obligatory among certain South American Indian tribes during the planting of the corn crop. Likewise, some primitive hunters also avoided eating salt before setting out.

Among some seafaring men it is taboo to mention the word *salt*, since it is symbolic of the sea itself. Meanwhile, ship's carpenters often placed salt between the planks of the ship to ensure the safety of the craft and crew.

Wearing a small sachet of salt around your neck is said to protect you against the evil eye, and those who fear the evil eye should only go out after dark if they have salt in their hands. Other beliefs include these: Throw a small amount of salt on the threshold of a new house and place a salt shaker on the dining table before bringing other furniture in. Place salt on the four corners of your fields on April 1.

It is held unlucky to salt your own food, since salt symbolizes friendship. Your fellow diner should do this for you. Too much salt in the food is generally held to mean the cook is in love. Also, should a salt shaker be knocked over, it is said a friendship will soon come to an end. Furthermore, a host should never offer salt to his guests, says an Italian tradition.

Salt can be used to predict recovery of a patient. The person takes three grains of salt in the right hand. If they dissolve at once, it is thought he will die. If they don't, a recovery is expected.

In Scandinavia, spilling the salt does not bring bad luck, unless the salt gets wet.

When a baby is first born and goes out of the house, it should carry with itself an egg, some salt, a piece of bread, and a small amount of money. Doing this will mean the child will never want for life's necessities, says an English tradition.

Last, according to German tradition, should a young girl forget to place the salt shaker on the table while setting it, she has lost her virginity.

SATURDAY: A Highlands tradition holds that anyone born on a Saturday can see spirits. It is also considered bad luck to work all day on Saturday.

God created man on Saturday, so it is believed the sun will always shine for at least a few hours on this day. A superstition in Saint Kilda, Scotland, holds that children should always be baptised on Saturday or they will die. When it comes to marriage, however, Saturday is said to have "no luck at all," and should one tell "Friday's dream" on a Saturday, it will come true.

In Ireland they say, should a rainbow be seen on Saturday, it will be followed by an entire week of rain. (See **day**.)

SAUCEPAN: Should you wish to know the destiny of a dead man's soul, simply place a black cat in a copper saucepan for one day. If the cat is found alive next morning, the soul is in heaven or purgatory. Should the cat be dead, however, the soul is thought to have been damned.

It is said that an unmarried girl who wipes the bottom of a saucepan with a piece of bread will never find a husband.

SCALE: Tradition holds that scales allow one's sins to be weighed. Hence, a virgin can sit on one side of a scale without unbalancing it, but anyone who weighs more than the Bible is likely to be a witch. Sometimes an ill person would be placed on one side of a scale and his weight in rye or wheat on the other. If the scale tipped toward the side of the grain, it was believed the illness had changed sides and the patient would recover.

Tradition holds that a newborn must never be weighed, for it is not right to measure one of God's gifts.

SCARLET FEVER: One can cure scarlet fever by cutting some of the hair of the patient and placing it in the throat of an ass, says an Irish tradition.

SCHOOL: Schoolchildren who drop their books on the way to school make errors in their lessons.

Since teachers have eyes behind their heads, one who stares at them will be asked to recite.

SCIATICA: Carrying the knucklebone of a leg of mutton is said by the Cornish to bring about a cure. Already noted is the tradition of carrying a raw potato or a piece of loadstone to do the same thing. (See **potato** and **loadstone**.)

Scissors: An African belief is that a pair of scissors opening and closing during a wedding ceremony indicates the groom will become impotent.

Should a dressmaker drop a pair of scissors, it is said she will receive an order for mourning clothes.

Other superstitions about scissors include these: Never give a pair of scissors to a friend without first sticking yourself; otherwise, the friendship will be cut apart. Never accept a pair of scissors without giving a coin in exchange, or bad luck will result. Never pick up scissors you have dropped by yourself. Rather, a friend should be called upon to do this.

Never cut children's nails with scissors; rather, the mother should bite them off, or the child will become a thief.

Last, should a pair of scissors fall and stick into the ground, such presages a coming death.

Scythe: A skeleton carrying the scythe is a well-known symbol of death. Likewise, "Father Time" is often depicted as an old man with a scythe—no doubt derived from the sickle of the Roman god Saturn, who was said to rule death. Hence, any scythe found in a field indicates death. Tradition holds one should make the sign of the cross and then quickly depart from its presence.

The Druids were rumored to use a gold scythe to cut mistletoe from the sacred oak tree.

The first time you use a scythe, it is said you must draw a drop of blood with it, or it will not be effective in the future and may wound you again.

The first tuft of grass cut with a scythe should be given to a cow or ox. A scythe stuck in a roof protects the house from lightning. If two scythes are crossed and placed at the foot of a cradle, the newborn will be protected from evil.

Last, a scythe placed on top of a haystack and left to rust is believed to keep the stack from overheating and thereby possibly catching fire.

Sea: Although a number of traditions regarding the sea have already been discussed, a few general statements can yet be offered. (See **ships, sailing,** and **ocean.**)

According to a Welsh tradition, a spoonful of seawater each morning helps you get to old age. While still on land, should you hear the sound of the ocean coming from the west, it is said that good weather will soon come about and will continue for some time.

A Scottish tradition says that you should never go to sea after seeing a pig first thing in the morning. Likewise, you should never set out to sea in the morning after finding an earthenware basin turned upside down.

When going to the ship, a sailor should never place his sea boots on his shoulder. Rather, he should carry them under his arm or ill luck will come.

A Welsh tradition holds that one ship should never lend anything to another or good luck will be given away as well.

SEAGULL: Generally held is the belief that it is unlucky to kill a seagull. Three seagulls flying together overhead is said to portend death.

SEAWEED: Dried seaweed kept in one's house is believed to drive away evil spirits and to prevent fires. Hung in the porch of one's house, seaweed will shrivel up when the weather is going to be dry and sunny, and swell up and feel damp when rain is nearby.

SELLING: A country belief is that it is unlucky to make an offer for a farm animal when it is not for sale. Should this be done, it is said the animal will surely die.

The coins first received by a tradesman in the morning should be returned to ensure an entire day's success. Similarly, spitting on the money first received each day is said to bring good luck.

SEVEN: Held worldwide is the notion that the number seven is a sacred number. Examples of the special nature of this number abound: There are seven colors in a rainbow, seven deadly sins, seven ancient planets, and God created the world in seven days.

The body is said to change itself every seven years. Doctor Faust's pact with the Devil was for seven years, too. Breaking a mirror will result in bad luck for a similar period.

A woman who can wear seven petticoats at one time is believed to be unusually happy, according to a Portuguese tradition. A woman who leaves her belt wrapped around a tree seven times, for seven days, can protect herself from sterility, according to a Moroccan belief.

A seventh son is said to be especially favored by the gods. In

Scotland, the seventh son of a seventh son is held to have second sight. This special child is able to cure all manner of diseases and is a born doctor.

To speak with wisdom, according to an ancient Greek tradition, you must simply roll your tongue over seven times before speaking.

Should your birthdate be divisible by seven, tradition holds that you will be unusually lucky. (See **numbers**.)

SEX: Sex plays a vital role in religion, magic, superstition, psychology, and the entire gambut of human involvements with the supernatural. Widespread are myths that explain everything in the world, including the world itself, as a product of sexual activity of the gods.

For instance, the words *venerate* and *venereal* are both derived from the Roman Love Goddess, Venus.

An ancient Egyptian myth holds that the god Atum created the world by masturbating (or, in another version, spitting), which generated a god and goddess, who then coupled together. It is from their union that the earth and the sky were born, which are forever held together in a tight embrace.

In almost all ancient mythologies Father Sky and Mother Earth copulate annually so that she can bear children in the form of crops and spring plants.

In ancient phallic symbolism, the male "dies" after achieving orgasm and "rises again" with a determined and somewhat predictable potency.

In China, the two great male/female principles, Yang and Yin, are thought to extend throughout the entire universe, with everything therein depending on their exchanges and countless combinations with each other. In Hindu mythology, a similar belief is held and is personified by Shakti and Sheva, male and female deities.

For this reason, it is possible to conceive of the soul's union with God as a type of sexual union paralleled in the acts of human partners. Hence, one who attains an orgasm may be said to have been "possessed" by an agency decidedly nonhuman and hence divine. Various beliefs exist regarding sexual ability. Most widely believed is the idea that men who have large hands and big feet have oversized sexual organs. Likewise, women with large mouths are believed to have large organs. Widely quoted is the belief that

Latin men have greater sexual ability because of the hot climates from which they originate. Common is the belief that men whose bodies are covered with a great deal of hair are more sexual than those who are not. Added to these beliefs is the idea that too much sex weakens the heart and that masturbation will cause blindness.

SHADOW: Among some primitive tribes a man's shadow is believed to be his soul. In Africa, the Zulus use the same word, *tunzi*, for both a man's spirit and his shadow. In English, the word *shade* is often applied both to a ghost or to a spirit dwelling in the under-world.

According to Sir J. G. Frazer in his classic work, *The Golden Bough*, magicians on the island of Wetar in Indonesia believed they could cause their victims to fall ill by simply stabbing their shadows with pikes or cutting them with swords.

In ancient Greece, it was believed a man's shadow could be stolen from him without his knowledge.

In China, it was held that those attending a funeral should not stand close to the coffin when the lid was being fastened on it, or his shadow might fall across it and be enclosed with the corpse. For bearers and grave diggers who, by necessity, had to remain in close proximity to the coffin, the belief was that they could ensure the fastness of their shadow by tying pieces of cloth tightly around their waists.

Generally held is the belief that a person's shadow should never be tread upon, or it will be hurt. Similarly, a stone that falls on a man's shadow indicates imminent death.

Tradition holds that whoever makes a pact with the Devil must give him his shadow as security. From this came the tradition that such a person will see no reflection when looking in the mirror.

One Italian tradition required a man's or child's shadow to be buried in the foundation of a new house. One should pay respect to this tradition by crossing himself when passing near building sites.

Should the shadow of a hyena fall on a dog, it will render him mute, according to an African belief.

SHAKING HANDS: Should you accidentally shake hands with a person twice, you must do so once more, or ill luck will be forth-coming, according to tradition.

SHARK: Long before *Jaws*, legend held that three sharks continuing to follow a ship meant a death would soon take place on board.

SHEEP: Although a number of traditions regarding sheep have already been discussed (see **lambs**), there remain yet a few general comments that can be offered.

It is generally considered lucky to meet a flock of sheep when making a journey.

Many English country folk believe that carrying a small bone taken from the head of a sheep will bring good luck.

Widely held by shepherds is the idea that a lambing season starting out with a pair of white twins will be a good year.

In Scotland, on All Saints' Day (November 1) and Beltane (May 1), sheep should be driven under hoops of the rowan tree to protect them from evil.

It is considered bad luck for a shepherd to count his animals, as this is also being done by a wolf.

In American folklore, the expression "sheep stealing" arose to describe a common New England practice whereby one minister tried to win over members of another minister's congregation.

SHIP: Although a number of traditions in regard to ships have already been discussed, a few remain to be discussed. To begin with, eyes painted on the bows of ships, or other female fig- ureheads placed on the prow of a ship, were thought to frighten away evil spirits.

Much like an infant, a ship has no existence until it is baptised or named. Should a pregnant woman perform this function, it is said the vessel will never return to its port. Furthermore, the bottle of champagne hitting the hull should break on the first blow. It is considered a bad omen for this not to happen.

Nailing a toad to the hull of a new ship was a tradition long followed in the south of France.

No ship should contain a name ending in the letter *a*. However, once named, the name of the ship should never be changed. To do so is said to anger the sea gods, which will cause its destruction.

Should a curse be placed on a ship, one can remove it by spitting, stealing objects from another ship and burning them once they are on board, or making the hull pass through a ring of ropes placed end to end.

Ships should never transport eggs, rabbits, or a dead body. A priest or a woman among the passengers was also thought to be an evil omen. The presence of a child, however, was said to be favorable.

Last, tradition holds that passengers should give presents to each other whenever the equator is crossed.

SHIRT: Generally accepted is the belief that one wearing another person's shirt will assume that person's sins, as well as his power. Hence, a father's shirt placed on a child will protect it from evil.

A godfather should always wear a clean, if not new, shirt to church on the day of his godchild's baptism.

One can determine the prospective health of a newborn by throwing his or her shirt into a fountain. Should the shirt float, it is believed the child will enjoy good health; should it sink, however, ill health may be expected.

Accidentally placing a shirt on backwards is considered good luck. Buttoning a shirt wrong or putting it on inside out, however, is held a bad omen.

Last, tradition says that clothing sewn on a Friday will attract lice.

SHIVERING: If you shiver involuntarily, some say this means someone is walking over the spot where you will eventually be buried. Yet another explanation is that you have been contacted by a spirit who has recently passed over.

Should you suffer a long shiver, upon rising in the morning or when stepping over your threshold, it is said a bad day will come about. Should this happen in the evening before going to bed, however, an excellent night with rewarding dreams is promised.

SHOE: Almost everyone is aware of the tradition of tying a pair of old shoes to the back of a newlywed couple's car. In ancient times, the father of the bride threw an old shoe to the couple. This signified that his daughter had now become the property of the groom. The groom, in order to affirm himself as the new possessor of his bride, placed one of her shoes at the foot of their bed on the wedding night. Should a young bride wish to wear the pants in the family, it was suggested she should take off her husband's shoes on this same night.

An unmarried person can divine his or her chances for marriage by tossing a shoe into the air on New Year's Day. Should it fall to the floor right side up, an engagement during the year is promised. Should it fall and point towards the thrower, a marriage is expected. Should it point towards the door, expect more of a wait.

One tradition holds that whoever has not given a gift of shoes at least once in his life will wander in purgatory barefooted.

It was believed that a child's first pair of shoes should be made of wolf skin in order to protect the child against evil spells.

In the United Kingdom, if a new pair of shoes squeak, it is said that the owner never paid for them.

Additional superstitions include these: When rising in the morning, always put the right shoe on first in order to ensure a happy day; placing a shoe on the wrong foot is thought an ill omen.

According to a Jewish superstition, should you hobble around with only one shoe, death will be brought to a relative.

Should you leave shoes turned upside down, a quarrel will break out in the household. Similarly, it is thought a bad omen to leave shoes crossed on top of each other.

Should you sneeze while putting shoes on for the first time in the morning, you must immediately spit to chase away the evil spirits.

You can keep death away from a house by turning a shoe upside down and placing it on the threshold of the front door, some say.

Burning an old shoe in your fireplace is believed to guard the house against epidemics.

Lovers should never give each other shoes as a gift, or it will bring them unhappiness.

The most unfortunate omen of all is placing a pair of shoes on a table. This promises a death or family dispute.

Long before tossing a bouquet became commonplace, the bride threw one of her shoes in the air for her bridesmaids to catch. It was said that whoever caught it would marry during the year.

In olden times, in Russia, a groom's wedding dinner napkin was folded into the shape of a shoe; that of the bride's was folded into the shape of a swan.

In the Alsace region, priests tossed their shoes into the air to drive away hail.

Forgetting to tie your shoelaces omens a good day. Not fastening the left shoe, however, is said to bring misfortune. Should you find a knot in your shoelaces, it is said to be fortunate. Should you find the left shoelace undone, someone is speaking ill of you. Should the right shoelace become undone, however, someone is speaking well.

Your wishes are easily granted if made while lacing another's shoes.

Never wear one shoe with a brown shoelace and one with black. (Black is said to be the color of death and brown that of the earth in the cemetery.)

Last, it is said that only crooks, swindlers, and other cheats wear showy and expensive shoes. Beware of people whose shoes are also said to stay "miraculously" clean and to never show signs of wear!

SHOOTING STARS: According to a Welsh tradition, you must wish upon a shooting star, when you first see it, or you will be unlucky for the entire year.

Shooting stars are souls coming from heaven to animate new-born children, according to a Yorkshire belief.

In American folklore, one is advised to repeat the word *money*, until the shooting star is no longer seen. Others say you must make your wish before the star falls completely, or the wish will not be fulfilled.

SILVER: Silver is considered feminine in nature and magically connected with the moon.

Because of its connection with the gods, it is legendary that silver can never be enchanted. Therefore, when used as a talisman, it can only increase the power of its object, but it has no power of its own.

Should a piece of silver jewelry begin to tarnish, it is said an omen of death.

In American folklore, especially in New England, it was believed that the only way to get rid of a witch was to shoot her with a bullet made of silver.

SINGING: Often quoted is the verse, "If you sing before seven, you'll cry before eleven."

Generally, it is considered unlucky to sing while making bread, to sing while playing cards or to sing before breakfast, which certainly rules out singing in the shower.

This idea may have come from the Greeks, who believed that one must "earn" his happiness each day. Therefore, to sing first

thing in the morning was to express something which one had not
yet earned.

SISTER: A German tradition says that sisters who marry within a
year of each other, or on the same day, will end up with one or
both marriages unhappy.

SKIN: Commonly held is the idea that skin disorders indicate the
end of an illness, since such is trying to escape the body.

If you wish to have attractive skin, says one tradition, you should
never wear furs on a Friday.

Eating a lizard or rolling in the grass on the morning of Saint
John's Day will cure many skin disorders. Rolling while completely nude in a field of oats is also said to do the same.

One can cure various itches by putting a frog on them every
night or by using saliva.

Drinking an infusion of walnut leaves gathered before dawn on
June 24 is believed to purify an ill person's blood.

Children who have bad skin should never have their nails
clipped, or their condition will grow worse. Coating their nails
with lard, or fixing their hair in a bonnet of cabbage leaves, is said
to bring great improvement to their condition. Similarly, holding a
child up before a gray donkey eight days in a row is thought to do
the same.

In Germany, should you drink cold coffee, it is said to make the
skin unusually smooth.

Should a woman rub her skin with a baby's first wet diaper, her
face will remain youthful.

SKULL: Often regarded as the center of soul power, the skull is
found in a number of traditions and superstitions.

Excavations of a number of ancient burial sites have uncovered
numerous skulls sometimes turned in various directions, no doubt
towards the mythical land of the dead.

In ancient Norse mythology, the heavens were believed to be
constructed from the skull of the giant Ymir.

Skulls were often used to decorate the facades of buildings and
were often placed in the cornerstones of old churches. For example, in 1895 it was found that the west wall of Darrington Church
near Pontefract was set upon a skull of an individual apparently
buried some 600 years earlier.

On Easter Island, sacred caverns were placed under the guardianship of various skulls. In some of these, heads of warriors were found, facing the direction from which invasion was anticipated.

In the seventeenth century, Sir Thomas Browne referred to the practice of using the skulls of one's enemies as drinking cups.

Another tradition, popular among the Scandinavians and Germans, was the drinking of human blood from the skulls of those they conquered in order to acquire the dead warrior's strength.

The skulls of saints were once commonly displayed in churches throughout Europe. In Cologne, the skulls of eleven thousand holy virgins were placed for many to see.

In long houses in New Guinea, enemy skulls were often displayed on racks, together with shields. This represented the spirits of the warriors held responsible for the murders. Accepted was the fact that the conqueror could command the services of the spirits of those he had killed, even though they had passed into the afterlife.

In Borneo, headhunters often use the skulls of enemies as pillows.

In the seventeenth century the skull and crossbones were often carved on gravestones to symbolize mortality.

The ancient Egyptians, among others, practiced artificial cranial deformation by tightly bandaging the soft skulls of young children.

During the Middle Ages, a special elixir, known as "spirit of the human skull," was prepared from the unburied skull of a criminal. It was used as a treatment for epilepsy. According to Irish tradition, headaches can be cured by an inhalation of snuff made from skull scrapings. King Charles II was said to favor a distillation made from filings of skull bones, spirits of wine, and sage.

Should a man swear on a skull and tell a lie, he will be struck dead, according to an Irish tradition.

In American folklore, moss taken from the skull of a murdered man possesses special properties, especially as a love potion.

SLEEP: Generally held is the belief that a horseshoe, leaf, or key placed under a sleeping person's pillow will cause him to dream of the future.

According to one tradition, a sleeper's head should face the church. If this is not possible, then the head should face southward. Another tradition holds that the person's head should always be pointed north, so the earth's magnetic waves will flow properly.

Should a woman fall asleep while working, it is said she will marry a widower. In order to break the spell, a German tradition holds that she must take off her shoes and place them in front of her face.

Already mentioned is the tradition that the first person of a newlywed couple to fall asleep on the wedding night will be the first to die.

A blackbird's right wing hung from a red string in the middle of the main room of a house is believed to keep the inhabitants from sleeping. Smoking a mixture of red tobacco, toad powder, and honey is held to bring sleep to an insomniac.

Those who sleepwalk are said to have been badly baptized, which means the ceremony should be done again.

In American folklore, there is a belief that, when two persons sleep together, the stronger will lose some of his energies to the weaker. Yet another belief is that one should never sleep in a bedroom in which plants are placed, as they will absorb oxygen needed by the sleepers.

SLIPPER: Generally held is the tradition that crossing a pair of slippers will cause bad luck to follow.

SMALLPOX: Although virtually eradicated due to vaccinations, the following cure remains as a remnant of the power inherent in one's belief.

According to a Cheshire tradition, smallpox may be cured by taking a bun from the shop of a person who, when she was married, did not change her name. This must not be paid for, nor must the clerk be thanked for it. If given to a patient to eat, it is said it will cure smallpox.

Another belief: If the windows of a smallpox patient's room are opened at sunset, so that the gnats can enter therein, they will load themselves with the infection, fly out from the room, and die.

SMOKING: In American folklore, it is held unlucky to be offered a broken cigar; likewise, should one's cigar burn unevenly on one side, or should one's cigarette keep from burning out. It is unusually lucky, however, to catch a smoke ring and put it in one's pocket.

Among most American Indians, smoking was held an important

ceremonial act. Among the Sioux, should one speak during a peace pipe ceremony, the pipe was immediately dropped, with no one daring to smoke it again. Similarly, it was believed that disaster would befall anyone refusing to smoke the pipe when it was passed to him.

SNAIL: Generally held is the tradition that, when going in search of snails, it is best to place one's jacket on inside out.

Should a child cough in the evening, two or three snails boiled in barley or tea water was believed to cure the illness.

SNAKE: Headaches can be cured by wearing a snakeskin around one's head, according to a North Lincolnshire belief.

To cure a snakebite, one must simply bind a dead snake on the wound it has caused, says a Cornwall tradition.

A German tradition says a snake falling down your chimney is an ill omen. Never compare a snake to the size of your arm, or the arm will immediately be covered with scales, holds another belief.

Other superstitions include these: Snakes never bite pregnant women. Snakeskins placed on a woman about to give birth will facilitate the event. Should a pregnant woman be frightened by a snake, her child will have a snakelike constricted throat. Snake teeth will cure fevers, if hung around a sick person's neck. The head and teeth of a snake will bring luck to a gambler.

Snakes never die until the sun goes down, no matter how many pieces they may be cut into. A snake crossing the path of a bridal party on its way to the church omens an unhappy union.

Elder trees planted on Saint Peter's Day, February 22, are said to drive off snakes.

Grass snakes were believed able to suck cows' udders. By killing the first grass snake seen in the spring, one was sure to triumph over his enemies. The dead snake's skin was to be hung in the chimney.

Spitting on a viper before eating will cause the viper to die instantly. Wearing emeralds will protect you against viper bites.

In American folklore, the belief is that a rattler always rattles before it strikes and that a snake hypnotizes its victim before attacking. American superstition also includes the belief that the "hoop snake" will take its tail in its mouth and roll with great speed at its enemies.

In Britain, a live adder found on one's doorstep was believed an omen of death.

Wrapping a rattlesnake skin around the affected part is believed to cure rheumatism, according to a tradition in Kentucky.

In some parts of Europe, families were advised to have their own "house snake," which would serve both as a rat catcher and a guardian house spirit.

SNEEZE: The common practice of saying "God bless you" when another person sneezes stems from the ancient belief that the soul leaves the body when the person sneezes, and only a blessing can bring it back.

According to Aristotle, a sneeze was divine, but a cough vulgar.

Sneezing from noon till midnight was considered a good omen; but from midnight until the next noon, a sign of ill fortune.

According to one myth, Prometheus made an artificial man. The first sign of life it showed was a sneeze. It was through the nostril that life entered into his body.

To sneeze three times in rapid succession is considered a good omen, and should you sneeze after making a statement, it places the seal of truth upon it.

When a Hindu sneezes, those nearby say "live," to which he replies "with you."

According to one tradition held by the Zulus, when one sneezes, an angry spirit has entered the body; a sneeze is one's effort to expel it.

Some say a sneeze before breakfast announces receipt of a present during the week.

The day of the week upon which you sneeze is thought to forecast the future. Should you sneeze on Monday, danger will be kept away; on Tuesday, you will kiss a stranger; on Wednesday, you will receive mail. Sneezing on a Thursday was thought best of all. Sneezing on Friday was said to court misfortune. Sneezing on a Saturday would announce a lover. Sneezing on Sunday was held worst of all and was believed to predict a "Devil for the week."

According to a Jewish tradition, sneezing when speaking of a dead person is an ill omen. To break this spell, you must touch your earlobes and say, "They are in their world, we are in ours."

Should you sneeze on New Year's Day, a disastrous year is ahead, according to a Chinese belief.

Should you sneeze from the right nostril, good luck is forthcoming; but from the left, expect bad luck.

The Japanese say a single sneeze portends that someone is saying something good about you. Two sneezes, however, means you are being insulted.

Should two people sneeze at the same time, good fortune is said to come to both, according to a popular belief.

Should you feel like sneezing, but don't, you can be assured that someone loves you, but is not admitting it.

Generally held is the belief that a newborn is possessed by fairies until he or she sneezes, and, according to a Scottish tradition, no idiot child has ever sneezed, or can.

Should a sailor sneeze on the right side of a ship when embarking, the vessel will have a fortunate voyage. Should the sneeze occur on the left side, however, foul weather is ahead.

One tradition holds that Adam sneezed after Eve took a bite of the apple.

SNOWDROP: This does not refer to a drop of snow, but rather to the little flower that symbolizes purity. English tradition holds that a snowdrop should never be taken into a house; otherwise, some member of the household will die before the flower blooms again.

SOAP: According to a Highlands tradition, it is unlucky for the soap to slip out of your hands while using it.

SOCCER: A British tradition holds that it will be an unlucky match for one's team if, before dressing, the ball is not bounced between the oldest and youngest player, and caught on the bounce by the youngest.

As a game, football is not mentioned by name until the fourteenth century. Edward III instructed his sheriffs to suppress football, as the game was said to interfere with training men in the art of archery. Originally, no rules or grounds were specified for the game. Traditionally, it was played on Shrove Tuesday, when it symbolized the victory of spring over winter. As a contest between those married and unmarried, the game appears as a relic of a fertility rite.

In Chester, the game was believed to commemorate kicking the head of a captured Dane. In Derby, the game was said to celebrate a victory over the Romans. In Cornwall, at Saint Ives, the mayor once threw a ball coated with silver, possibly a relic of sun worship, and crowds fought for it without limitations and rules.

Soot: Should a clot of soot fall down from the chimney during a wedding breakfast, bad luck will attend those married, say the Scots.

Soot hanging from a fire grate omens a stranger shortly visiting your house, according to the English.

Should a large piece of soot suddenly fall down the chimney, money is said to be on the way to one member of the household. A variation of this particular belief holds that bad weather is on the way.

Spade: Generally held is the belief that you should never bring a spade into a house over your shoulder, since this omens that a grave is being dug for one of the residents of the house.

A grave digger's spade should never be used in your own garden.

Waving at anyone with a spade is said to result in their death, unless a handful of earth is thrown at the person doing the waving.

Sparrow: Tradition holds that a sparrow present at the crucifixion of Christ repeated, "He lives, he lives," thus encouraging the Romans to make Christ suffer. As punishment, God tied its feet together with an invisible string, which caused it to hop and no longer walk.

Should one catch a sparrow and keep it, this omens death in the house, according to a Kent tradition.

In Brittany, belief is common that a sparrow spreads news from one tree to another, and that, when killed, someone will be denied news of a loved one. Another tradition holds that, when the bird dies, its tree dies as well.

Sparrows are said to predict rain by chirping.

In Britain it is said that a sparrow is symbolic of one's household gods and, therefore, deserves special attention.

Spider: Perhaps best descriptive of the traditions regarding spiders is the popular English saying "If you would live and thrive, let a spider run alive."

Traditionally, a spider spun its web to hide the infant Christ Child in the manger when Herod's messengers came to look for him. Because of this, it is thought unlucky to kill a spider or disturb its web.

Spiders are also said to have saved the lives of Mohammed and Frederick the Great.

One tradition holds that whooping cough can be cured by wrapping a spider in raisin or butter, or closing one up in a walnut shell. The malady is said to fade away as the spider dies.

Spiderwebs have also been used for bandaging wounds and curing warts. In the United Kingdom it is believed that killing a spider will bring unwanted rain.

In Scotland and the West Indies, should you kill a spider, your dinnerware or wine glasses will break before the day is out.

Superstitions about the spider abound: Should you run into a spiderweb, it is said you will meet a friend. Should you see a spider running down its web in the afternoon, a journey comes soon. Should a plow kill a daddy longlegs, the cows will go dry. Should you find a spider in your clothes, a return of money loaned is forthcoming.

Never clear spiderwebs away from stables or barns, since they protect the animals. Should you catch the golden money spider and put it in your pocket, you will always have ready cash. (In Norfolk, tradition holds that a money spider suspended over one's head is a charm for winning football pools.)

In American folklore, finding a spider is said to indicate good fortune, and swallowing a spider with syrup was believed to reduce fevers.

The Pawnee Indians regarded a Spider Goddess as the giver of fertility. They used a webbed hoop, resembling a spider's web, to catch buffalo.

In the Alsace, however, it is held a good omen to kill a spider (except in the morning), and to do so, one must crush it with the right foot!

SPITTING: (See **saliva**.)

SPLASHING: Common is the belief that if an unmarried girl continually splashes herself while washing clothes, her husband-to-be will be an alcoholic.

SPLINTER: Some gamblers leave a splinter in the left foot untouched for seven days in order to win at gambling seven Sundays in a row.

Applying rabbit fat to a splinter is said to make it come out on its own. A compress with urine is said to do the same.

When removing a splinter from one's foot, it is believed one must suck the drop of blood that forms, make the sign of the cross, and offer the suffering to Christ, who wore the crown of thorns.

SPOON: It is generally considered unlucky to stir anything with a spoon in the left hand.

In Scotland, a baby grabbing a spoon for the first time with its left hand will be unlucky throughout his life.

According to a Cornwall tradition, pouring gravy out of a spoon backhanded is said to lead to quarrels in the house.

Two spoons inadvertently placed in the same pot or on one's saucer are said to omen a wedding in the family.

Should a spoon fall inadvertently to the floor, this indicates a visit from a young child. Similarly, a spoon falling from a cup and landing upside down says that a surprise should be expected. Should it land right side up, however, such omens disappointments.

SPRAIN: Tying an eel skin, three strings soaked in holy water, or a string from a flour sack around a sprained limb is said to cure the sprain. Applying a herring, split in two, to the injured area was a practice often employed by those living near the North Sea.

Bathing a twisted ankle in water flowing under a mill wheel was also recommended.

Applying a salve with bran, olive oil, juniper oil, and vinegar was also held to stimulate healing.

In the north of England, tradition required the injured person to lay his sprained limb on the ground, so that a "stamp-strainer" could stamp on it with his bare feet. The limb was then bound up in the skin of an eel.

SPRING CLEANING: A general tradition holds that it is unlucky to spring-clean one's house after the month of May.

SQUIRREL: Generally held is the belief that shooting a squirrel will bring bad luck to the hunter.

Legend holds that the squirrel was the only animal to witness Adam's eating of the apple in the Garden of Eden. As the story goes, the squirrel at that time had the tail of a rat. So horror-struck was he by seeing this sight, that he drew his tail across his eyes to shut it out. As a reward, all squirrels were henceforth given the thick brush of a tail they now possess.

STAG: As the stag possesses the ability to regenerate its horns each year, it is symbolic of fertility and rebirth. Should one encounter a stag, however, it is considered a bad omen.

The horns of a stag ground into powder are reputed to be an aphrodisiac that will promote fertility.

STAIR: Tripping while going upstairs is said to be a good omen. Some believe it predicts a wedding soon to come in the household.

It is not considered wise to pass another person on the stairs. Rather, you should cross your fingers and wait on the landing until the other person has gone by.

To avoid falling up or down stairs, some advise that you cross yourself before using the stairs.

STAR: Generally held is the belief that seeing the first star of the evening is lucky and that a wish made will be granted, if kept a secret.

Never point your finger directly at a star as this is said to insult the gods. Never count stars or, according to one belief, white spots will appear on your fingernails. A variation of this tradition is followed in Charent, where young men who wish to marry count ninety-nine stars for nine days in a row. It is believed they will marry the first girl they encounter on the morning of the tenth day.

Shooting stars are thought to be matches falling from the Devil's pipe. It is said they can announce a baby's birth or someone's death. One can make a wish on the first viewing of a shooting star, but it must be concluded before the star disappears.

One tradition says that holding a piece of gold in the left hand and making wishes on the night of Saint John, directing them towards the third star, will be most effective.

STEALING: An interesting Herefordshire belief is that wearing a toad's heart hidden on your person enables you to steal without being discovered.

STEEPLEJACK: Members of this profession believe they can guard themselves from accidents by tying a knot in their suspenders.

STILE: According to a British seamen's belief, you should never set a stile in a footpath that leads to the sea. To do so is said to bring bad luck to all who pass that way.

STOCKING: Anyone who places the left stocking on first will have good luck throughout the day, according to a popular superstition.

Should a woman put her stocking on inside out first thing in the morning, it is said she will have a quarrel during the day. Should she put on both stockings inside out, it is thought she will quarrel with her lover three days in a row.

If a person wears two old socks or stockings of two different colors, he will be protected against the evil eye.

While putting on your sock or stocking, should the toes accidentally go into the heel, a letter awaits you.

Some actually say that, when your socks or stockings fall down for no reason, someone is thinking of you.

STONE: Finding a stone with a hole in the center is said to be a good omen, especially if worn on a chain around your neck.

Tradition holds that you can stop an epidemic from spreading in a flock or herd by rubbing the head of the contagious animal with three pebbles. Having the animal drink from a bucket in which three stones have been placed in well water is said to do the same.

One desiring help should throw a stone into a church or cemetery.

Rubbing, praying to, and making offerings to upright stones are believed to aid one in obtaining marriage, greater fertility, and conception.

STORK: The early Christians believed that a stork flew around Christ's cross and showed him sympathy.

Tradition holds that Aristotle made killing storks a crime in Greece in 330 B.C.

In Roman mythology, the stork was sacred to the goddess Venus. Hence, when storks built their nests on house rooftops, it was considered a blessing from the goddess and a promise of love.

A stork flying over a house is said to omen an upcoming birth, and a pair of storks resting on the rooftop promises good luck. Yet another tradition is that a stork's nest on one's house protects the house from fire, since its bill is red.

When the stork reaches its old age, some say its young look after it and nourish it, until death.

An ancient Roman law compelled children to care for their

needy parents in their old age. The law was called the "Stork's Law" (*Lex Circonaria*).

Traditionally, the stork returns to build its nest on the same spot each year. To notice its return is said to be a good omen. Greek and Arab legends maintain that, when the birds disappear in the fall of the year, they live as men.

Countless legends hold that storks can be transformed into humans. A German version says that, when a stork is wounded, it weeps human tears.

During the Middle Ages, writers often quoted Aristotle's belief that the male stork kills his mate if she is unfaithful, and Chaucer refers to the stork as the "avenger of adultery." One tradition exists concerning a stork who blinds a human adulterer, out of thanks to the husband who had allowed it to nest on his house.

In Bavaria, good baby boys are reputed to ride on the stork's back, while naughty ones are carried in its bill.

Should a Christmas mummer, disguised as a stork, nudge a woman or girl, it is believed she will become pregnant.

Children's songs are sung to the stork in Holland and Germany, asking it to bring a brother or sister.

Weather prognosticators hold that a stork arriving late in the spring indicates favorable weather. A white stork foretells a dry year, while a black one indicates coming months of rain.

Should storks circle over a group of people, one will die soon.

Certain types of storks are believed to kill small snakes. For this reason, anyone killing a stork in ancient Thessaly was held as a murderer.

A stork's stomach was long thought a remedy against cattle disease. Feet afflicted with gout were often bound up by the stork's sinews, no doubt following the principle that a bird with legs as long and healthy as a stork must be able to alleviate human pain.

The gall of the stork can be used to cure scorpion stings, according to Jewish folklore.

STORM: If one cuts nails and hair during a calm sea, it will provoke a storm, say many seamen.

Should a storm break out just as a coffin is lowered into a grave, some Scots would say the deceased has most likely sold his soul to the Devil!

An English countryside tradition says that a marigold flower not opening before seven in the morning means there will be a storm that day.

Raging storms can be calmed by opening a window and hurling a handful of meal outside, while commanding, "There, that's for you, now cease!" So says a superstition in Austria.

Ringing church bells to ward off storm damage is a tradition still followed in some parts of Europe.

STRING: Almost everyone is familiar with the tradition of tying a piece of string around a finger to aid one in remembering something that has to be done. This is said most efficacious if the string is tied to a finger on the left hand, since the left side is where memory lives.

In ancient times, thread or string was held to link life with destiny. Clotho was said to spin man's destiny, while Lachesis was held to weave the web of luck. When death came, Atropos was thought to sever the thread of life.

Thread was thought the means by which the deceased ascended to the other world; it was at one time placed in coffins for this purpose.

A bizarre ritual in which mourners played a lottery of death, each one picking a single thread, has come down to us. Traditionally, the one drawing the shortest thread was held to die next.

Among actors, it is considered lucky to pick up a long thread or a piece of string from the floor of a theater. Such ensures a long and successful play production.

As a medical amulet, string protects against sterility and death.

In the Far East, ghost traps are made from string. These are set on the outskirts of villages to catch demons that move about.

Tying knots in strings as symbols of sealed bargains is a magical practice around which many traditions exist.

Wrapping a red string around one's finger three times and then throwing the string on the ground is said to transfer warts to whoever picks up the string. Another tradition holds that the finger should be wrapped with black string, which is then thrown into a grave during a burial. As the string rots, the belief was the wart would disappear.

Tying a red string around one's little finger, on the hand corresponding to a bleeding nostril, is a traditional cure for a bloody nose.

Should you cut a string for no reason, it is said you have endangered yourself with a year of poverty.

It is considered unlucky to burn string.

STUMBLE: Generally held is the thought that, should one stumble at a graveside, they will soon join the deceased.

Stumbling downstairs is also said to be a sign of bad luck, as is stumbling in the morning when you first leave your house.

Should a horse stumble on a road, it is also thought an ill omen.

Similarly, stumbling is said to indicate a wedding. Should you dream of a wedding, however, on the same night, such omens death.

STY: Curing sties in your eye can be accomplished by procuring the tail of a black cat, from which one hair is pulled out, and rubbing the tip nine times over the sty. This must be done on the first night of the new moon, however, it is said.

Rubbing a sty nine times with a gold wedding ring or the finger ring of an unmarried woman is said to be equally efficacious.

Should neither of these two methods work, take a copper penny, press it on the sty, and then throw the penny away. Whoever picks up the penny will pick up your sty!

SUICIDE: The spirit of anyone who has committed suicide is said to remain earthbound. Similarly held is the belief that a pregnant woman walking over a suicide's grave will miscarry.

SUN: Commonly held is the belief that, should the sun's face be hidden, such as during an eclipse, a national disaster will take place.

Children born at sunrise are said to be clever, while those born in the afternoon or at sunset are held to be lazy, according to the Welsh.

One can keep freckles away by applying May flowers gathered right before sunrise.

A Cornish tradition holds that the sun will never shine on one who commits perjury.

It is believed by many that only an eagle can look directly into the sun.

SUNDAY: Although a number of beliefs surrounding Sunday have been discussed in other contexts (see **days**), the following represent a few others.

Many say it is unlucky to turn a feather bed on a Sunday. In American folklore, it is considered bad luck to change the bed sheets on this day.

If a child with whooping cough is carried into three parishes on Sunday morning after fasting, he will quickly recover, according to a Devonshire belief.

Never cut your nails on a Sunday. When you are ill, your fever will most likely be highest on Sunday. Should it be lowest on Sunday, however, a relapse is thought certain.

Should you sneeze on a Sunday morning, after fasting, you will enjoy your true love for evermore.

All medical treatments should begin on this seventh day.

SWALLOW: Well known and oft quoted is the statement of Aristotle, "One swallow does not make a summer." Long held as the harbinger of springtime, swallows have a long tradition as birds of omen.

The Greek myth was that the swallow's song was like the chattering of a foreign tongue. The swallow came about when Tereus cut out the tongue of his wife's sister Philomela, so she would not tell that he had sexually violated her. When discovered, the gods transformed all three into birds. Tereus was turned into a hoopoe, Philomela into a nightingale, and his wife Procne into a swallow.

Legend holds that a fluttering swallow seen near the head of Alexander the Great portended tragedy. Dionysus, however, had his safe return predicted by swallows.

Both Greeks and Romans often forecast weather by the swallow's flight, and generally held in Europe is the belief that swallows flying low mean bad weather will soon appear. The Chinese believed that one could induce rain by throwing swallows into water.

A Swedish legend says that a swallow was said to hover over the cross, crying "Cheer up, cheer up."

French tradition holds that the swallow picked off the crown of thorns, and, in so doing, ignored the wounds made in her own breast by the spines. Ever since, the swallow has had stains of blood on its breast. Another belief among the French holds that magpies pricked Christ's feet and head with thorns while he was resting in a wood, but that swallows came and extracted them. For this reason, says the legend, the magpie is forced to build its nest in tall trees, while the swallow nests in man's dwellings.

An English folk rhyme clearly illustrates the swallow's position in popular hierarchy:

> The robin and the wren,
> Are God Almighty's cock and hen:
> The martin and the swallow,
> Are the two next birds that follow.

Long held is the belief that white or red swallow stones, believed to be secreted in the bellies of the nestlings, have medicinal value. A legend from the Middle Ages says that a swallow can fetch a pebble from the seashore to restore the sight of its fledgling birds.

Body parts of the bird were said to cure snakebite, epilepsy, and rabies. Droppings from a swallow were used to treat diphtheria, and mud from its nest, erysipelas, a skin inflammation accompanied by fever.

In France and Hungary it is said that a swallow flying under a cow's belly means the milk will be bloody.

In Yorkshire, a swallow coming down a chimney was held as an omen of death. In Czechoslovakia, should a girl see a solitary swallow, it is said she will be married within the year. Contrariwise, should she catch sight of a pair of swallows, she will remain unmarried.

Those who treat swallows badly are assured of ill luck. For example, your house will be burned down if you have destroyed a swallow's nest, says a Tyrolean belief.

Should a swallow's nest be disturbed, the crops will go bad. In Britain, it is believed that should one kill a swallow, rain will commence and last for four weeks. Some say destroying a swallow's nest will cause you to fall from a tree. Robbing a swallow's nest can cause one's horse to go lame, say the French.

Up until the nineteenth century, the belief was held generally that swallows disappeared in autumn and reappeared in spring by hibernating under the water or in crevices in the earth.

Generally held as a sign of luck is a swallow building a nest on

ZOLAR'S ENCYCLOPEDIA OF

your house. Should the swallow start to build and then abandon the nest, however, it is considered unlucky.

Generally held is the tradition that a swallow lighting on your shoulder is a certain sign of death.

Should a swallow build a nest in your house, the house will be protected from both fire and storm.

It is said that if one eats swallows when they are in heat, one will be inclined towards love. According to another tradition, one can gain love by offering a ring that has stayed in a swallow's nest for nine days.

Should a woman step on a swallow's egg, she will become sterile, according to a German tradition.

Last, according to Irish belief, every swallow has in itself three drops of the Devil's blood!

Swan: Because of their size and rather conspicuous white plumage, swans have always occupied a prominent place in mythology and folklore.

Engravings and designs that date back to the Stone Age depict the swan and other long-necked birds in designs that include the sun disc, suggesting that these birds were linked with solar mythology from a very early period.

Since swans appeared every year at the time when the days were lengthening and the power of the sun was increasing, it is said they helped usher spring in. To this day, some inhabitants in Northern Asia erect poles featuring effigies of flying swans, under which they place wooden models of fish—symbolizing the powers of sky, earth, and water.

The belief that people can be transformed into swans is ancient and widespread. Aeschylus, the Greek playwright, was perhaps first to mention the swan maidens. Aphrodite is represented in art riding on a swan or goose. According to Ovid, Cycnus was turned into a swan by his father, Apollo. It was said that both Apollo and Aphrodite rode in chariots drawn by swans. Zeus was said to have turned himself into a swan in order to have sexual relations with Leda.

Traditions in Siberia and Ireland said that killing a swan would bring misfortune or death. In County Mayo in Ireland it is said that souls of virtuous maidens actually dwell in swans.

Generally accepted is the legend that the swan sings while dying.

Although Pliny is said to have contradicted this belief, it was, nonetheless, endorsed by poets throughout time.

Shakespeare writes, in *Othello*, "I will play the swan, and die in music." In *The Merchant Of Venice* he writes, "He makes a swanlike end, fading in music."

According to a Hampshire belief, swans are hatched during a thunderstorm. Generally held is the idea that a swan can hatch its eggs only during a storm.

In Scotland, it is believed that three swans flying together means disaster is coming.

SWASTIKA: The word *swastika* is derived from the Sanskrit *svastika,* meaning "well-being, good fortune, luck." This symbol appears on a pot found in Argos in Greece dating back to the eighth century B.C. It has also been found in the Indies and is known to have been used by the Navajo Indians.

Long before Hitler's rise to power in 1933, various archaeologists and historians studied swastika symbolism. Guido von List proclaimed the runic equivalent of the letter *G* was itself a disguised swastika. According to List, it had a cosmic meaning as a "sun wheel," symbolizing eternal rebirth and movement. One German investigator believed it was a Christian symbol, later to be replaced by the crucifix in the sixth century.

SWEATER: It is said that garlic merchants in Paris marketplaces wore this woolen garment in ancient times.

Generally held is the belief that, if you put your arms into the sleeves of a sweater before putting in your head, you will never die from drowning. Similarly, it is a good omen to inadvertently put a sweater on backwards.

Last, never mend a light-colored sweater with a dark thread, or evil will be attracted!

SWEEPING: Natives of the African Congo are said to refrain from sweeping the floor of one's house for an entire year after death, so that the dust will not injure the delicate departed soul.

Generally held is the belief that when you sweep dust out of your front door you will sweep away your good luck. If a broom is used, you will sweep your friends away. (For those who are struggling with this particular superstition, the way to save your luck is to sweep all the dust inside and carry it out of the house in a dustpan!)

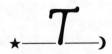

TABLE: Widely held is the belief that a young girl seated at the corner of a table will never marry. Similarly, should she sit down at the table while talking to her fiancé, she will be prevented from marrying him. Also, it is said that a young girl should never sit on a table. It will prevent her from marrying.

One should never place a pair of shoes or boots on the table, nor a pair of bellows, and no one should change their place at the table once it has been assigned.

Children should never crawl under a table, for such portends their death. Should they do this, they must be made to crawl under it again, in the reverse direction.

One should never invite thirteen people to dinner. Either twelve or fourteen must be gathered, or one of the diners will soon die.

Should someone upset their chair when rising from a table after a meal, this indicates that they have been telling lies during their conversation.

Should a tablecloth, when unfolded, have a diamond-shaped crease in the middle, it is said to portend death.

TEA: Two people should never pour tea from the same pot or bad luck will ensue, says a Kent tradition.

Should a young girl let a male friend pour her a second cup of tea, she will succumb to his desires, leading to her own misfortune.

Bubbles in the tea presage the receipt of kisses by the drinker, and a tea leaf floating on the surface of the tea indicates a visitor is soon to arrive.

One should never place milk or cream into tea before the sugar or one runs the risk of losing a lover.

Should a man and a woman pour tea together, it is said they will have a baby.

Inadvertently leaving the top off a teapot is also a bad omen.

TEAR: An unusual superstition holds that, should one deceased be wept over, and tears allowed to fall on him, he will be hindered from resting peacefully in the grave.

TEETH: Generally accepted is the tradition of placing a child's lost tooth under his pillow for the "tooth fairy," who will replace it with money. A child's first lost molar should be thrown on a fire to burn any evil that may be hiding out in his body. Should a baby be born with teeth, it is said to be an ill omen. Should the first tooth be in the upper jaw, such portends death in childhood.

Should one's front teeth be set wide apart, it is said he will be lucky and will travel a lot.

In American folklore, should a person dream of teeth falling out, it is said to presage the death of a close relative. Yet another tradition holds that one will get a toothache from eating anything while a funeral bell is tolling.

TELEPHONE: It is thought an ill omen for the phone to ring and no one to answer.

Widespread is the experience of "knowing in advance" when the phone will ring, or who may actually be calling, before picking up the receiver. This, of course, is an example of clairvoyance.

TEMPEST: A tempest, or severe storm, usually affecting seafaring people, was held by the ancients to have been caused by the anger of Neptune. Hence, carvings on a ship's bow of nude women or sirens were used to calm the seas.

Seeing a white hare on the wharf, or the bare feet of a woman with long toes, is said to be an omen of such a storm, according to a Cornwall tradition.

Generally held is the belief that a tempest will occur should a sinner be married, a hanging take place, or a great criminal be put to death.

Wives of seamen were said to be warned of such storms by invisible knocks at the door or gulls hitting their windowpanes.

A cat who turns its back to a fire was also said to omen the same disaster.

TENNIS: Generally accepted is the belief that holding three tennis balls in one hand, while serving, will bring bad luck.

Tennis players never like to play with a ball for which a fault was called. A fresh one is said to break the bad luck streak.

THIEF: An ancient Devonshire belief is that, if a robbery is committed, you should pluck six leaves of grass from the spot and take them to a "white witch." Tradition holds that for each scratch she makes with a pin on the grass blades, a scratch will appear on the face of the thief!

According to another belief, if you wear a toad's heart hidden on your person, you can steal anything you wish without being caught. Furthermore, if you steal something on Christmas Day and escape detection, you can steal for the rest of the year without being apprehended.

THIRTEEN: Almost everyone knows about the alleged bad luck on Friday the thirteenth! (See **numbers**.)

Generally held is the belief that thirteen people sitting at a table or meeting in a room means one of them will die before the year is out.

For the ancient Egyptians, the number thirteen represented the final step of a ladder of twelve that lead to eternal life.

For the ancient Romans, thirteen was associated with death and misfortune.

For Christians, thirteen represents the Last Supper, at which Christ and the twelve disciples sat. Judas, the betrayer of Christ, was said to be the first person to rise from the table. Hence, tradition holds that there should never be thirteen people at a table; the thirteenth will die within the year.

Some say that the Hindus created the idea of thirteen people at a table being unlucky. In Norse mythology, however, a story is found of an unlucky dinner to which twelve gods were invited. After everyone arrived, Loki, the Norse God of Mischief, crashed the party as an uninvited guest. During this dinner, one of the gods was killed.

A possible explanation for the common belief that thirteen is unlucky is this: when one counts up their fingers and their two feet, the number twelve is arrived at. The "unknown," or thirteen, is then the next number.

Hotel managements and architects usually avoid a thirteenth floor in their buildings. Even if there is an actual thirteenth floor, it is often numbered fourteen.

As recently as 1965, when Queen Elizabeth visited West Germany, her platform number at the Duisburg Railway Station was changed from 13 to 12-A.

In Great Britain, should one's bus ticket add up to the number thirteen, it is thought to bring bad luck. Similarly, the thirteenth day of the month is held unpropitious for starting any new undertakings.

For the early Christians, thirteen was sometimes called the number of sin, since it went beyond the original twelve disciples. In European traditions, thirteen was said to be the number of necromancy, or bringing the dead back to life.

In fact, an early text of Greco-Egyptian origin instructs the necromancer to make a doll representing a woman, and to pierce it with thirteen needles. By placing this on the grave of someone who died in youth or by violence, and reciting a number of incantations, it was said the deceased would actually rise from the dead.

Thirteen is also the traditional number of a coven of witches, consisting of twelve individuals and the Devil, or local leader. Modern witches continue to hold thirteen as the proper number for a coven, and, in some instances, link thirteen covens to form a larger group.

Yet another tradition holds that, in ancient Babylon, thirteen people incarnated as gods. The thirteenth was placed on a throne to one side and was put to death after the ceremony.

A baker's dozen, which consists of thirteen, is held by some to be the "Devil's dozen."

It must be noted that, in the United States, thirteen is considered a lucky, rather than unlucky number. The Masonic symbol of the Great Seal of the United States, which appears on the back of a dollar bill, contains a pyramid of thirteen steps. There are thirteen leaves and berries on the olive branch. The eagle, too, holds thirteen arrows. The thirteen here is thought by many to represent the thirteen original colonies, although, since the seal was designed by members of Congress, especially Benjamin Franklin (who was a

Freemason), those who are knowledgeable in such things suggest this symbolism has even greater meaning.

THORN: A tradition in Somerset holds that, should one pick a thorn on Christmas Eve, while hearing the cracking of the buds, he will be cursed. (The Christmas Eve referred to in this tradition is the old Christmas Eve, January 5.)

A German tradition holds that a young girl accidentally getting a thorn in her dress or clothes will marry a widower.

A Cornish tradition suggests that you can cure a wound caused by a thorn prick by saying:

> *Christ was of a virgin born*
> *And he was pricked by a thorn*
> *And it never did bell [fester] or swell.*
> *As I trust in Jesus, this one never will.*

Generally accepted is the belief that a thorn can be used to drive away witches. Hence, it is often hung over doors or barns on Beltane and Halloween nights.

THREE: Three is said to represent the Holy Ghost in Christianity, the universe for the Celts, and, in general, a family consisting of the father, mother and child.

Universally accepted is the fact that various things happen in threes. Should a person have two accidents, a third is omened.

Gamblers who wish extra luck are advised to walk around the gambling table or their chair three times before beginning to play. In an actor's dressing room, three light bulbs are never turned on at the same time. To avoid being attacked by evil spirits, one should always go out in threesomes.

Already mentioned is the belief that you should never light three cigarettes on the same match.

THUMB: Almost everyone is familiar with the Roman tradition of spectators deciding a gladiator's fate by indicating life or death with their thumbs. "Thumbs up" meant he was to live; "thumbs down" meant he was to die. Symbolically, the thumb up suggests success, while the thumb down means failure.

In American folklore, should one's thumb itch, it is said to predict an unexpected visitor.

Possessing a long thumb suggests stubbornness and will-power. Should the thumb be unusually broad, wealth is said to follow.

A thumb that naturally slants backwards is said to indicate the inability to save money.

Should you inadvertently prick your thumb with a pin or needle, bad luck is held to be on the way.

THUNDER: Curious is the tradition that, when thunder is heard, a bar of iron should be put in barrels of fermenting beer to keep them from going sour.

A Welsh tradition holds that thunder and lightning heard and seen between November and January 31 presage that the most important person in a village will die.

Ringing church bells are believed to keep thunder and lightning away.

Generally held among countryfolk is the belief that, if windows and doors are left open during a thunderstorm, the thunderbolt will go right through the house without doing damage.

When someone is going on a trip, thunder heard in a distance is a good omen.

Depending upon which day of the week thunder is heard, various prognostications can be made. Should it be heard on a Monday, it is said to announce a woman's death. If heard on a Sunday, a rich, noble person or priest will die. If heard on a Tuesday, it announces a good harvest; on a Wednesday, the death of a dishonorable person. Heard on a Thursday, it means an abundance of all things; on a Friday, war is coming. Heard on a Saturday, drought and epidemics are expected.

One tradition holds that thunder heard on the first Sunday of the year means a member of the royal family will die.

A tradition in the Alsace region is that thunder in September means the snow will be high at Christmastime. A popular British rhyme runs as follows:

> *Thunder in the morning,*
> *All the day storming;*
> *Thunder at night*
> *Is the sailors' delight.*

TICKLING: An English tradition holds that tickling a baby's feet will cause the baby to stammer in later years.

TOAD: Some authorities assert that the reason toads play an important role in folklore throughout the world is due to their resemblance to miniature human beings. Often commented upon are their humanlike faces, postures, and movements.

In general they are regarded as venomous, since they are known to exude a poison from glands on their skin when excited. Tradition holds that, during the Middle Ages, bandits were known to force toads into the mouths of their victims.

In the United Kingdom, toads were often believed to be witches' familiars. It was said that a witch could make a magic lotion consisting of toad spittle and the sap of the sow thistle. Crossing herself with this concoction was thought to make her invisible. Hence, in many parts of Europe, toads were killed for this reason. In Romania, however, killing toads was believed to indicate that one was capable of murdering his own mother. Therefore, the toads remained essentially unharmed.

In Cambridgeshire, certain men were held to be in league with the Devil. They were said to have special powers over horses and to be able to make them halt, despite all efforts to make them move. Such persons were called "toadmen." To acquire this "special" power, one simply had to skin a toad, peg it to an anthill, wait until its bones were clean, and then carry the remnants in his pocket until dry. At midnight, during a full moon, these were floated in a stream. They were held to screech, and one bone would set off on its own upstream. If this bone was captured, one gained the powers of a toadman.

Toads, like frogs, were often credited with the ability to predict storms. Country tradition holds that they can actually hear distant thunder that is inaudible to humans.

In an English book on gardening published in 1593, the author advises the reader that, before sowing seed, a toad should be drawn around the garden, placed in an earthenware pot, and then buried in the center of a flower bed. After the seeds have been sown, the toad should be dug up. Otherwise, the vegetables growing nearby were said to acquire a bitter taste.

The Roman historian, Pliny, advocated placing toads in an earthenware pot in fields to avert storms.

Any stone that resembled the toad in shape or color was believed able to cure bites and stings when pressed on the sore part. Such a stone was called a "toad stone." If such a stone was genuine and was held in front of a living toad, the toad would jump forward and seize it from its possessor, according to legend.

During the Middle Ages, many believed that the toad had hidden in its head a precious jewel. Should this jewel be placed in a ring, it was said to forewarn against poisonings of any kind.

Milton, in *Paradise Lost*, gives credence to various toad mythologies by having Satan transform himself into a toad in order to inject poison into Eve's blood.

Should a toad cross the path of a bride on her way to church, many say the couple's well-being and happiness is certain.

Nailing a toad to a boat's framework while it is being built was said to protect it from evil. Placing a toad's heart in the left sleeve of a sleeping woman was believed to make her confess all her secrets.

Eating an egg on Good Friday or Easter Eve means that you are certain to find a toad in it, according to a Lorraine belief.

In American folklore, a toad in one's cellar is said to bring bad luck.

TOAST: Originally, custom required one to pour a bit of a guest's wine into one's own glass (and vice versa) to guarantee that neither would be poisoned; hence the reason for saying something like "long life" or "good health."

The word *toast* itself stems from Elizabethan times, when a small piece of toasted bread was placed at the very bottom of a tankard before ale or wine was added. The toast was thought to improve the taste of the beverage.

Tradition holds that it is lucky to spill a small amount of beverage while making a toast.

Generally held is the belief that, should the glass break in one's hand while toasting, death is certain to come to one of those assembled.

The often celebrated habit of clinking glasses together before toasting is believed to prevent evil forces from opposing the toast.

TOMATO: Not generally known is the fact that the tomato has another name—"love apple."

Tradition holds that it was the tomato, and not the apple, that was offered to Adam by Eve in the Garden of Eden.

Originally, the tomato was exported from South America, where, according to anthropologists, it was found about 500 B.C. The French called it "pomme d'amour" when they first exported it to England.

Once considered an aphrodisiac, unmarried girls feared eating the tomato until they were assured of wedlock. At one time, the tomato was even believed to be poisonous.

A large red tomato in a window is said to drive away evil spirits. If placed on the mantlepiece, it brings prosperity. Pin cushions in the shape of tomatoes are popular talismans for this reason.

TONGUE: If you bite your tongue while eating, it is said you have recently told a lie.

Carrying a piece of a cat's tongue in his pocket is said to save a man from his wife's chattering, and should one find himself able to carry the tip of a human tongue in his pocket, it is omened the pocket will never go empty.

TOOTHACHE: Driving a nail into an oak tree is perhaps the best known cure. Extracting a tooth from the mouth of a corpse, and carrying it in a small bag around your neck, is said to keep you from ever having a toothache. Finding and carrying a double nut in your pocket is also held an excellent preventative.

A Cornish tradition says you can easily cure a toothache by biting the first fern that appears in the spring.

Most curious of all is this Welsh superstition: If you put your right sock and right trouser leg on first, you will never have a toothache.

TORTOISE: Throughout the ages, the tortoise has been held a symbol of longevity, stability, and immortality. To kill a tortoise is said an ill omen.

Tortoise-shell bracelets are thought to protect one against evil.

Among the North American Indians, the turtle is believed to hold the earth in place. Legend has it that a muskrat brought up mud that led to the creation of the world, and a turtle holds it steady on his back.

A turtle causes thunder, according to the Pueblo Indians. Rattles of turtle shells are used to retain some of its mystical qualities.

Turtle oil has long been advocated for its pain-reducing qualities and for producing longevity.

One is said able to relieve gout by hanging a tortoise's foot on the foot of the ill person—right for right, and left for left.

TOWEL: An old English tradition says that, if two people dry their hands on a towel simultaneously, they will quarrel and encounter misfortune. Likewise, lovers should never share the same towel after a bath or swim, or they will soon part.

Dropping a towel or dishcloth omens an unexpected visitor. According to a Scottish tradition, however, one can prevent this by stepping over the cloth backwards.

TREE: As various superstitions regarding particular trees have already been discussed throughout this work, it suffices here to make some general comments.

Well known is the fact that cutting down trees was once held a crime punishable by death.

Knocking on wood or touching wood for good luck is a universal belief. Since trees were once held as home for powerful spirits, by paying reverence to them one was said to gain their protection.

Symbolically, a tree may be said to connect earth, heaven, and water together. Should the tree be struck by lightning, fire is added, and the four elements are together.

In the Garden of Eden was the Tree of Life. The Tree of Life in the Kabbala is said to be a diagram of God, man, and the universe.

Various representations of sacred trees are found engraved on cylinders in Chaldea and Assyria. For the Chaldeans, the tree was an essential symbol. In its later development, it was stylized and represented as a palm, pomegranate, or cypress.

For the ancient Egyptians, various deities were thought to inhabit trees, especially the sycamores. This particular tree was believed to exist on the border of the great desert between this world and the next. Souls of the departed were said to receive supplies of food and water from various deities when these trees were reached. Numerous paintings in the *Book of the Dead* and in various tombs depict such meetings on the soul's travel to the next world.

Throughout the Old Testament, many references are found to sacred groves and to the practice of setting up altars under trees, particularly oaks.

The tree as a god's dwelling place is a concept that appears in

Persian mythology. In this case the cypress was considered sacred, a symbol of Ahura Mazda—Chief of the Pantheon.

In India, tree worship was commonplace, for Gautama, the Buddha, was said to have incarnated as a tree spirit some forty-three times. Widely known is the fact that he received spiritual illumination while meditating under the bo tree.

Mention must also be made of the use of trees as oracles. Of note are Zeus's oaks at Dodona and the laurel at Delphi. Legendary is the withering of the laurels foretelling Nero's death, and the fall of a cypress, which did the same for Domitian.

In modern times, many of us have joined the custom of planting trees to celebrate the birth of a child. Tradition holds that the progress and growth of the tree matches that of the child.

A curious Dorset tradition says that, if you look at the trees in front of your house in the morning on an empty stomach, the trees will not thrive!

TURTLEDOVE: The turtledove or "wild pigeon" brings sterility to anyone it touches. This may seem unusual, since it has long been held as a symbol of fidelity in relationships.

Should its heart be worn in a wolf skin, it will drive away the fire of lust and amorous desire. Should its feet be hung on a fruit tree, the tree will never bear any fruit.

Last, should a hen hatch a turtledove's egg in addition to her own, it is said that only roosters will be born.

TWIN: In ancient times, the phenomenon of twins was little understood. In some cases, both infants were put to death, together with their mother. In other instances, one child would be destroyed and the other saved.

For some primitives, the saying, "May you become the mother of twins" was tantamount to a curse.

Commonplace is the belief that, since a man could only father one child at a time, the second twin must have been the result of the mother's infidelity, or the intervention of God or spirits.

In Togoland, should twins be of different sexes, the boy was kept and the girl done away with. If both were of the same sex, only the stronger, more active child was kept. To prevent the surviving child from grieving for his deceased "other half," he might be given a carved piece of wood or some other memento.

For the ancient Romans, as well as for the Egyptians, twins were held a good sign. The Romans believed that twin gods, Romulus and Remus, founded the city of Rome. The Egyptians, likewise, worshiped Osiris and Set.

In the Judeo-Christian tradition, the disciple Thomas, who is also called Didymus (which means "the twin"), is believed to have been the first missionary to go to India. According to one legend, Thomas was the twin brother of Jesus, born to Mary shortly after Jesus's birth. Tradition held that the three magi were given the swaddling band of Thomas, instead of that of Jesus, when they brought their gifts, and that Jesus and Thomas grew up together working in Joseph's carpentry shop. The two were said to be outwardly alike, but in reality, Jesus was divine and Thomas human.

Mani, the founder of Manichaeism (the Gnostic sect prevalent in the third century A.D.) claimed to have a "twin self" in the heavens, who came to earth and united with him, bringing revelations from God. For many, this "twin" was believed none other than the Holy Spirit.

Popularly held is the tradition that twins are the fruit of relations between a mortal and a god. For this reason, they are said to have been endowed with special power. This would include second sight (clairvoyance) and healing. Popularly held is the belief that, when one twin dies, the other is in some strange way forewarned; or, when one is injured, the other can feel the pain.

Generally held, too, is the belief that women who eat twin fruit while pregnant will give birth to twins. In the south of Africa, for instance, should a man eat a double banana, it is said that his wife will give birth to twins.

Should a husband with a pregnant wife spill pepper, it is said he must throw some over his right shoulder, or she will deliver twins.

Should a pregnant woman have a red streak down the middle of her stomach, it is said she will deliver twins.

Twins are said to protect those nearby from illnesses and navigators from storms at sea. They are believed to possess the power to restore youth and to give men back lost virility.

It is said that twins who marry on the same day should always use different churches.

According to a Roman belief, the first-born twin is a love child; the second, an offspring of lightning. The second child therefore was thought more favored by the gods.

Commonplace is the belief that twins are never as strong as a single child, and twins are said to possess only one soul. Furthermore, should one twin die and the limbs not stiffen, it was believed the dead one was waiting for the other.

Tradition holds that after having twins, a woman becomes sterile.

TWO-DOLLAR BILL: Two-dollar bills, not found anywhere but in the United States, seem never to have gained public favor. Since the "deuce" is associated with the lowest card in the pack and equated with the Devil, fear of possessing the two-dollar bill may have commenced with professional gamblers.

One tradition holds that, should the corner of the bill be torn off as a small triangle, such will counteract any bad luck. The person next receiving the bill is advised to tear off another corner. When all four corners have been torn off, the next person receiving the bill should tear it up altogether.

UMBILICAL CORD: For the ancients, the umbilical cord was thought connected with the life and destiny of each newborn child. Said to be the seat of the "free soul," which was believed to appear in dreams and depart from the body when death came, it was considered very important never to let it fall into the hands of anyone who might use it magically against the child.

The belief was that it must never be burned, or the child would die in a fire; nor should it be thrown into water, or the child would drown. Rather, it should be buried under a rosebush so that the child would have a similar complexion!

Another tradition holds that, if one wishes his son to have a fondness for good living, the cord should be buried at the feet of a grapevine.

Already mentioned is the belief that a pregnant woman should never spin or sew or her baby may be strangled by the umbilical cord.

Similarly, she must always tuck her necklace, and any pendants, inside her dress.

It is said that, if dried and placed in a small white sachet and hung around the child's neck, the umbilical cord will protect it from evil spirits and will improve its growth.

A piece of this cord soaked in water, plus a few of the child's first cut hairs, was believed able to cure him of any illness.

Women who were barren were advised to seek out this magical talisman.

UMBRELLA: A common superstition is never to open an umbrella indoors. To do so is said to bring bad luck for any who live in the house.

Since the umbrella was originally used as a sunshade, opening it anywhere that the sun was not shining may have given rise to this particular tradition.

Another superstition is that opening an umbrella outside when the weather is clear will cause rain to come about.

Other superstitions include these: Whoever drops an umbrella by accident should never pick it up, and if a young woman does this, she will never marry. Never lay an umbrella (or a hat) on the bed. Never give a person an umbrella as a gift.

UNDERWEAR: Generally held is the belief that an unmarried girl who obtains a piece of underwear from a recently married woman will herself be married within the year.

Placing a few valerian leaves in her bra or panties is thought to attract men to a woman, according to one tradition.

Women should wear seven petticoats in order to keep away the evil eye, says a Portuguese tradition.

A girl will dream of her future husband if she places one of her petticoats under her pillow.

Should a woman's undergarment creep up for no apparent reason, it is said she is dreaming about her lover. Should this happen to a married woman, however, such is held to indicate problems in her marriage.

Curious is a Midlands tradition that says, if a girl marries while wearing no underwear, she will be lucky in later life.

A bride who loses one of her garters during the honeymoon is said to have been "advised" that her marriage will not endure.

UNICORN: Writing in about 398 B.C., Ctesias of Cnidos, a Greek historian and doctor, first mentioned unicorns in a fragment of his book on India. Of these, he writes ". . . that their bodies are white, their heads are dark red, and their eyes dark blue. They have a horn on the forehead, which is about a foot and a half in length. The dust filed from this horn is administered in a potion as a protection against deadly drugs."

Even Aristotle mentioned two kinds of unicorns, the Indian ass and the oryx, a kind of antelope that is single-horned in profile.

The Roman writers Pliny (A.D. 23–79) and Aelian (A.D. 170–235) described seven different kinds of beasts. According to Pliny, unicorns can never be captured by men. According to Aelian, they love solitude and are indomitable.

Biblical legend holds that the unicorn is extinct, because it was thrown out of the Ark.

There is a legend that only a virgin can capture a unicorn. She must be seated alone under a tree, since the unicorn is attracted to odors or virtue. Some legends hold that the virgin must be a boy in disguise. Though somewhat ill-fitting, Christian symbolism attempted to identify the virgin as Mary, Christ's mother, and the unicorn as Christ himself. The single horn of the beast symbolized the union of Father and Son. Those hunting for the unicorn were said symbolic of the Holy Spirit, who acted through the angel Gabriel. The king's palace to which the captured unicorn was taken in many legends was held to be symbolic of heaven.

Commonly accepted is the belief that only a virgin holding a mirror can tame a unicorn. Should the girl sent to tame it not be a virgin, it was thought the unicorn would kill her.

Yet another tradition concerns the alicorn, or the beast's horn, as a sure antidote to poison. According to legend, animals gathering at sunset find their water poisoned with venom discharged by a snake. Unable to drink, they wait for the unicorn, who, with its horn, makes the sign of the cross over the water and instantly cleanses it. The horn, therefore, is believed to symbolize the cross; the serpent who poisoned the water, Satan; and the poisoned water itself, the sins of the world.

Possibly as a result of this legend, drinking cups made from horns were used profusely during the Middle Ages and the Renaissance.

In China, a special unicorn called Ki-Lin was reputed to appear at the beginning of a beneficent rain or at the birth of a new emperor. According to one legend, it appeared to announce both the birth and death of the sage Confucius. The Chinese name *Ki* means male, while the Chinese name *Lin* means female. Hence, the beast is a union of male and female elements.

Last, ground unicorn horn has long been held to be very effective as an aphrodisiac. Also generally accepted is the belief that a unicorn's horn will protect man against all forms of poison.

URINE: Tradition holds that urine contains some of the vital life force of the body from which it came and, therefore, provides an unbroken magical link forever with that body. Should one bottle a person's urine before he travels, it will reveal his condition while away from home.

Washing one's hands in urine is said to protect one against the evil eye and witchcraft. Should one rub a newborn's first wet diaper on their face, they are assured of a ruddy, clear complexion.

Urine is said to heal snakebites, tinea, or ear ulcerations.

One can divine the prognosis of a person struck seriously ill with a high fever. His urine should be saved and nettle leaves placed in it. If the leaves remain green, he will survive, but should they dry out rapidly, there is no hope for his recovery.

Most curious is the belief that, to prevent a child from having urinary problems, his godfather should urinate facing the sun on the morning of his baptism.

Children who cannot retain their water, or who continually wet their bed, can be cured by eating three roasted mice. Wearing a pendant containing a crushed may bug, rat, or mole droppings, or slugs roasted in one's oven, is said to be equally effective.

A belief held by seafaring men is that they should never urinate against the wind or it will provoke Satan into sending a tempest.

A German superstition holds that a girl urinating in a man's shoe will cause him to fall madly in love with her.

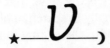

"V" sign: Making the "V" sign with the first and second fingers, symbolizing victory, is something that many of us are familiar with thanks to Winston Churchill. In actuality, however, this sign was first used to signify Satan's horns. Used in this manner, it was pointed downwards, though, indicating that Satan was being contained in the infernal regions below, and, therefore, could not cause any ill. Pointed upwards, however, as in the "V" sign, it is said that this places Satan in a position of triumphing over good. No doubt Mr. Churchill was not aware of the origin of this sign.

Among Spanish Roman Catholics there is a tradition of pointing these two fingers downwards upon first rising in the morning.

Valentine: Legend holds that February 14 is the day on which birds choose their mates. Therefore, should an unmarried girl see a bird on this day, she can divine her future love. Should it be a blackbird, she will marry a clergyman; a redbreast means a sailor; a goldfinch, a millionaire. A yellow bird means she will be reasonably well off. Should she see a sparrow, she will find love in a cottage. Should it be a bluebird, poverty be her lot. If it is a crossbill, she should expect quarrels. Should it be a wryneck, she should expect to remain an old maid. Seeing flocks of doves is thought to generate good luck in all ways.

Whoever of the opposite sex meets and kisses you on Valentine's Day will be your valentine throughout the entire year, it is said.

Valerian: Should an unmarried girl wear valerian in her underclothes, she will attract the opposite sex, according to a Welsh tradition.

VAMPIRE: Generally held is the belief that vampires never rest and are doomed to live eternally in search of blood, which keeps them from truly dying. They must be resting in their coffin, which contains dirt from where they were born, before the first rays of dawn appear.

Anyone bitten by a vampire becomes a vampire himself. Only garlic, iron, bells, and especially the cross assure protection against vampires.

Like any other evil spirit, it is thought that a vampire casts no shadow, nor is one's reflection seen in a mirror.

In actuality, the Hollywood Dracula was based on Vlad the Great, a somewhat ruthless and bloody Hungarian ruler, who lived during the Middle Ages.

VEIN: Commonly believed is that to have a blue vein over the bridge of one's nose means one will never live long enough to wear wedding clothes.

VERVAIN: What is generally called vervain today in Classical times was identified with a plant called "sacra herba" by Pliny. Other names for this herb were cerelias, demetria, perse phonion, Mercury's blood, tears of Juno, or tears of Isis. All these suggest a close link between the herb and ancient fertility rites.

For the ancient Romans, the belief that vervain kept evil spirits from entering their homes made it a popular talisman. Commonplace was the practice of heralds and other court royalty wearing a crown of it. According to Virgil, even Roman witches used it.

For the ancient Persians, vervain branches were associated with solar worship. Its juice was employed by magicians, who rubbed it on their bodies in the belief that this would cause them to gain the affection of their enemies.

Tradition held that one could cut vervain only when neither the sun nor the moon was visible. In exchange for taking vervain, honey was poured on the ground.

Similar traditions are recorded to have been followed by the Druids.

During the medieval period, various charms and potions, especially love potions, were made with vervain. The herb was held a general cure-all and was considered especially effective against snakebites and accidents.

One tradition held that even tumors could be cured by cutting a vervain root in two and hanging one part of it around the sufferer's neck, while smoking the other over a fire. As the smoked branch shriveled up, the tumor was said to follow suit.

Many believed that vervain kept witches and evil spirits away. However, witches themselves often used vervain and called it the "enchanter's plant." It was believed that vervain was a herb that could open locks magically, and should a would-be thief place a fragment of a leaf in a cut made in his hand, he would only have to touch locks or bolted doors in order to open them.

On Saint John's Eve (June 23), vervain was another garland burned in bonfires.

In Germany, wreaths or hats made from vervain were often placed on a bride's head. This tradition originated in ancient times, when the plant was sacred to Venus, the Goddess of Love, and the bridal wreath flowers were said to be picked by Venus herself.

In Rome, vervain was often sprinkled on altars and the steps of temples.

Long held is the belief that, should enemies drink an infusion of vervain, they will reconcile their differences. Should vervain be reduced to a powder, however, and be exposed to the sun, it was said to provoke quarrels. Curious is the belief that, when planted for seven weeks, vervain will yield worms that will be fatal to man.

Should one place vervain in his pigeon house, one will attract all the pigeons in the vicinity.

Curing epilepsy with vervain is an ancient tradition that has been authenticated in modern times through the practice of homeopathy.

It is reputed that one wishing to increase his sexual ability should wear a vervain plant on his chest. Since the sap from vervain trees is often thick and somewhat similar to human sperm, it is held to increase love.

Children who wish to grow up intelligent and agreeable should carry a small amount of this herb in their pocket, and if kept in one's house, it is said to assure prosperity. If worn around one's neck, it is useful in the cure of ulcers and urinary ailments.

If mixed with honey and warm water, it is believed unusually powerful for curing respiratory ailments.

Most curious of all is the belief that, if a hunter continually misses his mark, he should rub the barrel of his gun with vervain.

VIOLET: A popular belief is that one should never take less than a handful of violets into one's house, or bad luck will be the result.

Farmers especially believe that one or two violets will bring death to their chickens and ducks. Like other flowers, should violets bloom out of season, especially in the autumn, it is said that this omens death for the owner of the land.

Violets were symbolic of the ancient city of Athens. One legend holds that Venus, jealous of Cupid's love for white violets, turned them into purple. Yet another tradition holds that Orpheus's lyre was resting on the grass one day. When he picked it up, he discovered that violets had grown underneath it.

The ancient Greeks used violets for treating headaches and insomnia. The Persians used them for wine, while the followers of Mohammed actually worshipped them.

During his exile, Napoleon used the flower as his badge of honor. Hence, violets were banned in parts of France for many years after his defeat.

In the Victorian language of flowers, violets mean modesty. (See **flower**.)

VIRGINITY: In ancient days, virginity was a woman's only possession of great worth. Hence, it was thought that virginity brought supernatural powers to women.

Dragons, unicorns, and serpents were believed able to be fed by the hand of a virgin only. Should a woman attempt to fool them, it is said they would kill her.

Tradition held that only a virgin could pass through a swarm of wasps or bees without being stung. In the United Kingdom, the belief was once held that only a virgin could stare into the sun. In Poland, commonly held was the belief that she alone had the ability to make balls of water.

Should a girl forget to place salt on the table when setting it, it was said she had lost her virginity.

Many were the ways of testing a woman's virginity without her knowing it. According to one belief, if a potion of coal powder is administered to her, she will immediately have the need to urinate.

Most curious of all is the tradition in Central Europe that a woman who has given birth to seven illegitimate children regains her virginity!

VISITOR: Generally held is the idea that one should not watch a departing visitor pass completely out of sight. Such is said to bring bad luck to both and they will never see each other again!

VULTURE: Vultures have long been thought of as birds of divination. They never kill their prey, but, rather, devour abandoned corpses. Because of this practice, they are held an omen of coming death.

In legends surrounding the founding of Rome, the god Jupiter caused six vultures to appear to Remus and twelve to Romulus to indicate the future site of Rome.

According to Pliny, a vulture has the ability to "smell" death as much as three days in advance. Hence, should it hover over a house, such is said to be an omen of coming death.

In the Old Testament, vultures are often confused with eagles. In Exodus one can read, "I bore you on vulture's wings rather than "on eagle's wings." (Exodus 19:4.) Likewise, in Deuteronomy: "like a vulture ... that flutters over its young, spreading out its wings." (Deuteronomy 32:11.)

Since the Hebrew word for "vulture" and "compassion" are similar, an association was made between these large birds and parental care. Some experts believe that the traditional myth that a pelican feeds its young on its own blood may indeed be traced to vultures, who were seen to return to the nest with bloody morsels for their chicks.

Waiter: It is generally considered bad luck for a waiter to have a customer who sits in a seat or at a table other than the one to which he has been taken.

Also unlucky is to get a rather large tip early in the shift. For some, a one-armed or one-eyed customer may also be held bad luck.

Walking: A common tradition is that you will encounter bad luck should you walk under a ladder. A ladder is said to form a triangle, symbolic of the Trinity. To walk under it, therefore, is to defy something sacred. Hence, it will certainly bring ill luck.

While walking with a friend, should you and he have to separate and walk on opposite sides of an obstruction, you will later quarrel or have bad luck, unless one or both of you say the words "bread and butter."

Falling or stumbling over a curb or a stone is also said to bring bad luck, unless you go back and step over the same place correctly.

Walking stick: One tradition held that one's walking stick should be cut from an elder branch on All Souls' Day. It should be hollowed out, and a powder of wolf's eye, a dog's tongue and heart, three green lizards, and three swallows' hearts placed into it. Similarly placing seven vervain leaves, collected on Saint John's Eve, and a stone from a hoopoe's nest, will also enhance its effectiveness. If prepared in this special way, it is held that the stick, corked with a box tree cone, will support anyone's weight while walking. If hung on the door of one's house, it is said to assure its owner of good luck.

WALNUT TREE: Tradition holds that a walnut tree will serve as a refuge for witches during their sabbath.

Sleeping under a walnut tree will cause you to see in your dreams events of the coming year. You should take care, however, for according to some traditions, you may not wake up!

A curious tradition says that whipping a walnut tree will improve the quality of the fruit it bears.

The ancient Greeks and Romans said that eating stewed walnuts would increase one's fertility. In Romania, however, brides who did not wish to conceive were advised to place a roasted walnut into their bodice—one for each year they did not wish to have children. After the wedding ceremony, they should bury the walnuts.

One legend maintains that, if a walnut is placed under a witch's chair, she will become rooted to the spot.

Walnut branches are also believed to protect against lightning.

In American folklore, walnuts are held to cure sore throats and to thicken one's hair. Some American Indian tribes use the bark of walnuts, especially the black walnut, as strong laxatives.

WART: Generally held and often quoted is the belief that, if you put a hand into water that was used to hard-boil eggs, it will soon become covered with warts.

Also common is the belief that touching a toad will cause a wart to appear.

Spitting on a wart every morning will cause it to disappear, according to some American folk traditions. Burying something at a crossroads at midnight, or stealing a dish rag, with which one has wiped the wart, is also said effective.

Methods for the removal of warts are numerous. Here are a few: Tie a red or black string around the wart, and then throw it into the grave of someone about to be buried. Cut an apple in two and rub the wart with it, place the two halves back together and bury it. Rub your wart with a red slug and then stick the slug through with a pin, or throw it into a shaft. Dip your hands into a basin of holy water five times, while reciting the Lord's Prayer or Hail Mary. (In this case, though, the next person to take some of the holy water will take on the warts.) Touch each wart with a green pea and then throw it into a well. Rub a dead mole on the warts and then throw it into water. Stand at a crossroads near a stream and wash your hands when a funeral passes.

In some parts of the United Kingdom, tradition holds that the best way of all to get rid of warts is to steal a piece of meat, rub it over the warts, and then bury it. As the meat decays, it is said the warts will vanish.

WASHING: A Welsh tradition holds that, should you splash water from your hands first thing in the morning, you scatter your good luck for the day.

Should two people inadvertently wash in the same water at the same time, it is said to bring bad luck, unless one of them immediately spits into the water.

Never wash clothing on New Year's Day or you will wash a member of your family away, says a Scottish tradition. Washing a new garment for the first time during the new moon indicates it will never wear well.

A woman who gets her apron unusually wet while washing was thought to be cursed with a drunken husband, according to a Welsh tradition.

Generally held is the belief that a child's right hand should never be washed for the first twelve months of its life, so that he may gather riches easier in later life.

Already mentioned is the tradition that Good Friday is the most ill-omened day on which to wash, since a washerwoman insulted Christ while on his way to Calvary.

WASP: It is considered good luck to kill the first wasp seen in any season.

A curious tradition holds that only a virgin can walk through a swarm of bees or wasps without being stung.

WATER: A Welsh tradition holds that spring water, drawn between eleven and midnight on Christmas and Easter Eve, will turn into wine.

Boiled water should never be left in one's bedroom, as it will bring bad luck to the inhabitant.

Should one draw running water from any important spring on Saint John's Eve, at midnight, it will contain healing properties and will remain fresh for an entire year.

A curious tradition among Scottish brewers is to never mention the word *water,* in fear that its calling will spoil the brewing process.

A Scottish belief says that one person each year must be drowned in a river.

Last, a most unusual water tradition is celebrated in Yorkshire. It requires that hot water be poured over the doorstep, as the bride and bridegroom make their departure. This practice is said to "keep the threshold warm for another bride." Tradition holds that, before the hot water dries up, another wedding will take place from among those who gathered to send off the bride.

WATER LILY: A decoction made from water lilies is said by some African tribes to cause milk to return to a new mother, or to a wet nurse whose milk has dried up.

In Asia, the water lily, known as a lotus, symbolizes wisdom and consciousness of time. The very form of the lotus is believed to symbolize Brahma, while Buddha is thought the center of an eight-petaled lotus.

WAVE: Tradition among seafaring men holds that the ninth wave of any group is always the greatest.

A Scottish tradition is that one can cure consumption by catching the tops of nine waves in a dish, throwing the water on the head of a patient, and afterwards passing him through a fissured rock formation in the direction of the sun.

A most unusual belief is that the souls of all who have been drowned at sea come up to ride the waves on white horses at Christmas, Easter, and All Hallows' Eve.

WAVING GOOD-BYE: According to an English tradition, bad luck follows anyone who keeps waving good-bye at a friend until he is out of sight.

WEASEL: To see weasels has long been held an ill omen, based on the belief that witches can transform themselves into weasels in order to do evil. Hence, the tradition in Wales that a white weasel crossing one's path presages ill luck or even death. Should the weasel in front of you run to the left, it is said one has enemies within one's own house.

So ominous is encountering a weasel that one must stand still, pick up three small stones, throw them in front, and cross one's self seven times should it happen.

One can quiet a dog that barks continually by giving it a weasel tongue to eat. It will then be quiet until the death of its master.

If one has the courage to eat a weasel's heart, while it is still beating, it is thought he will obtain the ability to predict the future for one year.

Last, widespread in Europe is the belief that no one can ever find a weasel sleeping!

WEATHER: Already presented in various contexts have been a number of weather omens and superstitions.

Since the ability to predict storms in advance was something the ancients were desirous of, the various techniques used are themselves legion.

Generally held is the belief that spiders leaving their webs for sheltered crevices are a sign that rain is soon to appear. Likewise, if swallows are flying low, the weather is certain to take a change for the worse. Similarly, should soot fall down one's high chimney, the weather will definitely be bad.

In almost all weather omens or superstitions changes in humidity or barometric pressure are really the cause of the phenomena seen. Of course, these facts were not recognized by the ancients.

Perhaps most curious of all is a German tradition which maintains that a couple having sexual intercourse when it is raining are likely to conceive a female child.

WEDDING: A number of wedding traditions have already been detailed (see **marriage**), so we will mention only a few here.

Generally held is the belief that, if a marriage takes place while there is an open grave in the churchyard, it is an ill omen for the couple.

A cat sneezing in the home of the bride-to-be on her wedding eve is thought to bring good luck.

Commonly accepted is the idea that a bride should never look at herself in a mirror, after she is completely dressed, before she goes to church.

An unusually persistent superstition is the idea that it is unlucky for the bride not to weep heavily on her wedding day.

WEDNESDAY: Those of the Moslem faith believe that God created light on this third day of the week.

According to the Romans, Wednesday was placed under the planetary rulership of Mercury. He, as ruler of communications and short journeys, favors such activities on this day.

Tradition holds that one should never get married, nor wear gloves, on a Wednesday. (See **days**.)

New moons falling on this day are said an especially ill omen.

WELL: An unusual tradition is that one can keep his well from drying up by making it an offering of a piece of bread every New Year's Day.

Water drawn from a very deep well at dawn is said to soothe toothaches.

In ancient days, when hangings were commonplace in England, tradition held that a child baptized with water from the well of Saint Ludgvan would never be hanged.

WEREWOLF: Just like vampires, the werewolf has been glorified by Hollywood and the motion pictures. For the ancients, a werewolf was a person transformed into a wolf through magical means. It is said that werewolves roamed the country at night and would attack babies and other humans.

Werewolves are said to be recognizable by their flat fingers and hair covering their hands.

The poet Ovid first wrote of werewolves at the beginning of the first century A.D.

Tradition holds that bastards more than anyone else are subject to this illness.

In England, Scotland, and parts of France, the werewolf is believed immune to ordinary bullets, and can be killed only by a silver one, especially if first blessed by a priest. Another cure for those so afflicted is to call them by their Christian human name three times.

WHIPPORWILL: In American folklore, the cry of a whipporwill near a house is held an omen of death.

Should a person make a wish upon hearing the first call of this bird in spring, however, and keep the wish to himself, it is said to come true.

Last, should two whipporwills be seen flying side by side, which is rare, such indicates a disappointment on the way.

WHISTLING: Christian superstition holds that a woman whistled while nails were forged for the cross. So, each time a woman whistles now, the heart of the Virgin Mary bleeds.

In general, whistling is frowned upon in mines, ships, and especially in the theater. Should a miner whistle in a mine, it is said an explosion will follow. Whistling on board a ship, tradition holds, will bring about a gale. Last, whistling in a theater or in one of the dressing rooms is thought to omen the play's failure.

Perhaps in ancient times the sound of the whistling wind (thought to be made by spirits) was just too close to that of man.

WHOOPING COUGH: Whooping cough has already been discussed in various other listings. Due to the advent of inoculations and other modern medical treatments, this illness, once commonplace, is today seldom seen.

According to the Gypsies, one can cure whooping cough by letting a snail crawl over sugar until the sugar gets slimy. The sugar is then fed to the ill child.

Tying a hairy caterpillar in a bag around the child's neck is also said to cure the cough. As the insect dies, the cough will vanish.

WIDOW: Should a woman's hair grow in a low point in the center of her forehead, she will be a widow, says an English tradition.

Those who are marrying a widowed person are often advised to make as much noise as possible, in order to drive away the spirit of the deceased, who may be around seeking revenge.

Tradition requires that a widow always wear a glove when receiving her new wedding ring.

Those who have been widowed and who wish to see a new spouse in their dreams should mix coral and magnate dust with the blood of a dove. They should wear this around the neck in a small piece of blue cloth. Similarly, one can tie a branch from the poplar tree to one's stockings or socks and put it under the pillow. Last, one desiring similar information is advised to rub his temples with a few drops of blood.

Many of the homes near Cape Cod and elsewhere along the Massachusetts seacoast were constructed with a narrow space on which a person could stand, or take a step or two, while looking out to sea. Though first called the "captain's walk," they became known as "widows' walks," since many sailor husbands failed to return from their journeys.

WILLOW: Willows are held symbolic of melancholy and forsaken love. Once popular was the custom of wearing a willow garland when one had been jilted.

Pausanias, the Greek historian (second century A.D.), writes of a grove sacred to Persephone, where willows and poplars grew. Orpheus, in the underworld, is also described as holding a willow branch. On Circe's island, there was said to be a grove of willows from which corpses hung.

Willows are often planted in cemeteries to suggest immortality, and in China, coffins were once covered with willow boughs.

In Ireland, the so-called pussy willow was held one of the seven noble trees of the land and was believed effective against magical charms.

Tradition holds it unlucky to take the catkins or pussies indoors. Yet others hold it *good* luck, if they are brought into the house on May Day.

In northern England, an unmarried girl was advised to take a willow wand in her left hand, leave her house secretly, and run three times around it saying,

> *He that's to be my good man,*
> *come and grip the end of it.*

On the third time around her house, she would perceive a likeness of her future husband, who would come and grasp the end of the wand.

In folklore, the willow was reputed to be a cure for rheumatism, since it often grew in wet places, and whoever carries a piece of willow bark is held to be protected from suffering.

The willow tree is also thought to gossip. No one should reveal a secret in front of it, or they will soon hear it repeated by the wind.

In the Far East, tradition holds that, should a girl sleep in the shade of a willow tree, she will find herself pregnant. A Russian belief holds that whoever plants a willow tree digs his own grave.

Last, in the Victorian language of flowers, the weeping willow was symbolic of mourning. The water willow, however, was said to represent freedom. (See **flowers**.)

WILL-O'-THE-WISPS: Strange glowing lights that are sometimes seen in the marshes are called "jack-o-lanterns" or "will-o'-the-wisps." Legend maintains that these are souls of the damned who desire to attract the living to themselves.

Traditionally, one should avoid whistling at them. To drive them away, you had simply to place a needle in the ground and run. It is said they would escape through the eye of the needle.

WINDOW: Since the wood dividing windowpanes makes the sign of the cross, closed windows will prevent evil spirits from entering.

Already mentioned is the tradition of opening the windows in a dying person's room, so that the soul may exit. Also, should a robin tap at the window of a sick person's room, it is an omen that the person will die.

Funerals should never be watched through windows, or one will take the place of the deceased.

Stillborn children's coffins were traditionally taken out of the house through a window, so they would not adversely affect the next pregnant woman to pass through the doorway.

Last, many country folk believe that shutters slamming shut for no reason is an ill omen.

WINDOW BLIND: Should one's window blind fall down on its own, it is said to indicate a death in the family.

Often, bobbins at the end of the window sash are acorn-shaped. This is derived from the belief that an oak tree can never be struck by lightning.

WINE: Wine is said to be symbolic of blood.

Tradition holds that one can make an infant stout by having him drink wine in which his mother's wedding ring has been soaked.

Should nail clippings be mixed with wine, whoever drinks it will become intoxicated immediately.

Wine is said to cure migraines, colds, and fevers, and to aid digestion.

Rabies can be cured by drinking a glass of wine, into which is placed a few hairs from the rabid dog that bit.

Spilling wine on one's shoe is said to be an ill omen, but pouring a glass of wine into the sea is held to calm a storm.

A sickly child can be cured, if given a drop of wine used for the sacraments.

In order to prevent wine from turning sour, one must always pass the bottle around a table in a clockwise direction.

WISH: While there are countless occasions for making a wish that will come true, the following are often cited: Seeing the first star of evening; seeing a chimney sweep; seeing a loaded hay cart coming toward you; seeing a white horse; finding a horseshoe in the road (provided you spit first); while putting on new clothes for the first time; seeing a rabbit; seeing a new moon (provided you turn your apron back to front). Dropping a coin, a pin, or a pebble into a well as an offering is yet another way.

Last, holding the forked bone between a chicken or turkey's neck and breast (the wishbone), and making a wish as it is broken, is yet another tradition. This should be done with two people gripping the bone and pulling. Whoever breaks off the larger piece is believed to have the wish granted, provided he does not laugh, speak, or reveal his wish while the match is going on.

Finally, those who seek to have their wishes granted should perhaps best remember the words of Benjamin Franklin: "If a man could have half his wishes, he would double his troubles."

WITCHCRAFT: Needless to say, fear of the Devil and witches has its origin in ancient times. Much of the misunderstanding regarding witchcraft is no doubt due to Christianity's persecution of those who refused to abandon their pagan beliefs. The word *pagan* simply means "country dweller." The word *heathen* has similar connotations and originally meant "one who dwells or lives on the heaths." In both instances, these derogatory terms were used to describe those who refused to abandon their old, traditional beliefs in worshipping the Earth Mother for Christianity. Anthropologists who have studied witchcraft, such as Margaret Murray, have discredited the belief that witches actually worshipped Satan. Here, as in other instances, what is needed is the freedom to worship according to the dictates of "the god of one's heart." This is true even if the god of one's heart is a goddess, instead!

In fact, in recent years, many seminars have been held and books written to explain and restore to prominence the old religions, which placed women, instead of men, in paramount positions.

Readers who want to learn more about the genuine beliefs of witches are referred to an excellent work written by Margo Adler, entitled, *Drawing Down the Moon.*

WOLF: Here we find an animal that has few equals in regard to its folklore.

In ancient times, Greek gods and goddesses were often associated with wolves. Tradition held that a priest of Zeus could transform himself into a wolf. Leto, Apollo's and Artemis's mother, was said to often appear as a wolf and so was engraved as huntress on the shield of Artemis.

In Athens, any citizen who killed a wolf was required to bury it by public subscription, since the god Apollo was held to have driven wolves away from the city.

Not to be forgotten is the story of Romulus and Remus, the cofounders of Rome, who were tended by a she-wolf as children.

In Germany, tradition is strong that the Devil can assume the appearance of a black wolf. As wolves were often seen on battle-fields feeding on corpses, they were often thought demons.

In Latin, the term *lupula* (little wolf) also carried the meaning "witch." Hence, in Germany, witches were thought to ride wolves to their sabbaths.

Even in the New Testament, reference is made to false prophets as wolves "dressed in sheep's clothing." (Matthew 7:15.)

It is said that a wolf's eye protects children, while the tail of a wolf hung over a barn was held to keep other wolves away.

Wearing a wolf skin shoe was held to protect one against chilblains.

Curious is an English tradition that, should a wolf see a man before the man sees him, the man will become mute!

One should never say the word *wolf*, especially in December, or one is thought likely to risk an actual confrontation.

Generally held among country folk is the belief that, when a wolf is spoken of, its tail is soon seen!

WOODPECKER: To the ancients, the distinctive tapping of a woodpecker was thought synonymous with miniature thunder. Certainly, the bird was calling for and bringing down rain, they thought. Hence, the belief, in the English countryside, that the calling of a green woodpecker foretells rain.

In Scandinavia, too, the woodpecker is held as a sort of weather prophet. Among the French, he is often called "the miller's advocate." In times of drought, he is thought to plead for water in order to turn the mill wheel.

In ancient Babylonia, the word for woodpecker meant "the ax of Ishtar." Ishtar was a fertility goddess. Among the ancient Greeks, the bird was believed to once occupy the throne of Zeus. An oracle, connected with Mars, in the Apennine Mountains contains an image of a woodpecker placed on a wooden pillar. Engraved gems reveal a warrior consulting such an oracle.

According to yet another Greek myth, Celeus, whose name means "green woodpecker," attempted to steal honey that had nourished Zeus while he was a baby. As punishment, the angry god transforms Celeus into the woodpecker. Celeus, in turn, fathered Triptolemus, who was credited with the invention of the plough.

This connection between the woodpecker and ploughing is further supported by a French legend which holds that, during creation, once God made the earth, he called on various birds to help by digging out places that could be filled with water. Tradition says that only the woodpecker refused to cooperate. According to a German version of this same story, the woodpecker refused, not wishing to dirty her plumage. For this reason, the bird was condemned to peck wood and drink nothing but rain.

WREN: In the British Isles, the wren is the only bird associated with a rather elaborate ritual. Held on Saint Stephens' Day (December 26), a number of young men visit neighboring houses, carrying the corpse of a wren or a toy bird representing it. The "wren boys" dress up in odds and ends, such as pajama jackets and unusual headgear. Calling at each cottage, they sing a wren's song in English or Irish and request a contribution from the householder. When they have finished their calls, they hold a party paid for by collections made during the day.

In France, young boys go into the countryside beating the bushes. The first to kill a wren is proclaimed "king" and has the duty of carrying the bird back to town on a pole. The "king" proceeds through the streets on the last day of the year, accompanied by a fife and drum band, and others carrying torches. On Twelfth Day, he is arrayed in a blue robe and goes to high mass at a parish church, preceded by a man carrying the wren fastened to the top of the pole. The pole itself is decorated with olive leaves, oak, and mistletoe. After the church service, the wren king, together with his retinue, pays visits to other local dignitaries. Money is given to participants, and a banquet held in the evening, often concluding with a dance. In some places, the wren is then solemnly buried in a churchyard. It is related that this ceremony, in all its splendor, was finally suppressed in 1830.

To kill a wren is held to bring misfortune. In England, one who kills a wren will break a bone, it is said. In France, unless the murderer is a child, it is said he will go directly to hell. A child, however, will be immediately covered with pimples, even if he merely touches a wren's nest.

Wren's feathers are said to be good luck charms, often sought by gamblers. It is also believed that such will protect one against drowning. Hence, they are often sought by fishermen and sailors.

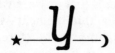

YARROW: Tradition holds that, if you pick yarrow on May Day and place it in your right stocking, which is then set under your pillow, you will dream of your husband-to-be.

Another name for yarrow is "Venus's eyebrow." It is believed to heal wounds and possess the ability to cause women who have ceased menstruation to start menstruating again.

YAWNING: Legend is that, during the Middle Ages, people believed Satan entered one's mouth through a yawn. Hence, the sign of the cross should be made over one's mouth whenever yawning.

Hindus believe one should snap fingers three times when yawning.

Yawning horses omen rain, according to a Finnish belief.

One who yawns with vigor is said to be announcing the onset of a fever, according to Hippocrates.

In American folklore, some Indian tribes believe a yawn indicates that death is calling you. To prevent being carried off by death, you need only snap your middle finger and thumb.

One authority on superstitions with a good sense of humor refers to yawning as a "silent shout for help."

YELLOW: In the United Kingdom, a yellow leaf appearing on a bean or pea plant indicates a death in the household. Yellow is said to be symbolic of fear (see **colors**), and for that reason was chosen by the Nazis for the infamous star Jews were forced to wear.

Yellow is said to be the color of cowards, and, in Spain, was worn by executioners.

385

YEW TREE: Tradition holds that anyone who dares pull a branch from a yew tree will die within the next twelve months. Yews are said symbolic of immortality and, therefore, were often used in the construction of churches for their ability to resist rotting.

Since yews often were planted in churchyards and were associated with the dead, it is generally held unlucky to bring their branches indoors.

Curious is the tradition that one falling asleep under a yew is likely to awake without a memory.

A N
I N V I T A T I O N
★————)

I hope all of you who have read this work had as much fun as I did writing it.

In closing, I invite you to write to me at the following address and share signs, omens, and superstitions that may not have been included in this work.

Shouldn't this be what life is all about . . . having fun and enjoying ourselves? Until next time, my personal blessings go out to each of you.

—Zolar
P.O. Box 6326
Key West, FL 33041